Employment Covenants
and Confidential Information:
Law, Practice and Technique

Employment Covenants and Confidential Information: Law, Practice and Technique

Second edition

Kate Brearley
Solicitor and Partner, Stephenson Harwood

Selwyn Bloch
Barrister

Butterworths
London, Dublin and Edinburgh
1999

United Kingdom	Butterworths, a Division of Reed Elsevier (UK) Ltd, Halsbury House, 35 Chancery Lane, LONDON WC2A 1EL and 4 Hill Street, EDINBURGH EH2 3JZ
Australia	Butterworths, a Division of Reed International Books Australia Pty Ltd, CHATSWOOD, New South Wales
Canada	Butterworths Canada Ltd, MARKHAM, Ontario
Hong Kong	Butterworths Asia (Hong Kong), HONG KONG
India	Butterworths India, NEW DELHI
Ireland	Butterworth (Ireland) Ltd, DUBLIN
Malaysia	Malayan Law Journal Sdn Bhd, KUALA LUMPUR
New Zealand	Butterworths of New Zealand Ltd, WELLINGTON
Singapore	Butterworths Asia, SINGAPORE
South Africa	Butterworths Publishers (Pty) Ltd, DURBAN
USA	Lexis Law Publishing, CHARLOTTESVILLE, Virginia

© Reed Elsevier (UK) Ltd 1999

A CIP Catalogue record for this book is available from the British Library.

ISBN 0 406 00220 7

Typeset by Connell Publishing Services, Thame
Printed by Butler & Tanner Ltd, Frome and London

Visit us at our website: http://www.butterworths.co.uk

To Brenda and Christopher

Preface

Much water has passed under the bridge since the first edition of this book was completed in 1993, in terms of statute law, case law and major changes in practice. Employment law has over this period undergone rapid evolution and of course there have been the radical changes in practice and procedure brought about since 26 April 1999 by the Woolf reforms. All this has necessitated substantial re-writing. In this rapidly changing scene we have tried to stick to our initial plan of adopting a practical approach while entering into the fray on thornier issues and in the latter context trying to avoid too much 'sitting on the fence'.

We have been fortunate once again to have had the benefit of the invaluable advice and assistance of many colleagues. Particular thanks to Andrew Clarke QC, Howard Daley, Rachel Heenan, John-Paul Waite, Tibor Gold, Rufus Waddington, Claire Lee and Chris Bloor, and all those practitioners who have been kind enough to send us transcripts of unreported cases. Thanks must also go to Diane Biggadike, Natalie Banthorp and members of the support team at Stephenson Harwood, too numerous to mention individually for their hard work undertaken with patience and unfailing good humour in assisting us in our task. Recognition is also due to those at Butterworths without whose encouragement this edition would not have been completed and to Kate's parents for their support and efforts in marshalling Kate's research materials into an accessible form.

I (Selwyn Bloch) record a particular debt to my former pupil masters, now The Honourable Mr Justice Burton and HH Judge Serota QC, both of whom have recently been elevated to the ranks of the judiciary, from whom I learned much of what I have contributed to this book, by on-the-job learning, as pupil and then junior counsel to them and by discussion and debate over the years. We both acknowledge the contribution made by our clients, without whom we would not have had the opportunity to hone our skills in the field of employee competition.

The law is as stated at 31 August 1999. We have, however, in some limited instances, referred to certain cases and other material published since that date. Since 31 August 1999 the cap on the compensatory award for unfair dismissal has been raised to £50,000. The Government has also announced that new tax rules regarding personal services companies will take effect from April 2000.

Lastly, our heartfelt thanks to our respective spouses and children who have had much to put up with while we have devoted our attention to this book.

Selwyn Bloch and Kate Brearley
London
November 1999

Contents

Contents

Chapter 3   The implied duty of fidelity   22

Chapter 4   Express terms of the contract of employment   43

Table of Statutes

References in this Table to *Statutes* are to Halsbury's Statutes of England (Fourth Edition) showing the volume and page at which the annotated text of the Act may be found.

All references in the right-hand column are to paragraph numbers. Para references printed in **bold** type indicate where the section of the Act is set out in part or in full.

Table of Statutory Instruments

All references in the right-hand column are to paragraph numbers. Paragraph numbers printed in **bold** type indicate where an Instrument is set out in part or in full.

Table of cases

PARA

PARA

K

L

X

Y

Chapter 1

Aim and synopsis of the book

Introduction

1.1   Normally the interests of an employer and those of his employees are the same. It is to the advantage of both that the business prosper. However, conflicts of interest may and frequently do arise, most commonly where the employee seeks to compete with the employer.

1.2   The aim of this book is to examine this area of conflict primarily from the perspective of the employer and to provide a practical guide as to how to deal with the problems presented by the conflict. We will look at the interests which the employer may legitimately protect and the means of obtaining such protection. By defining the interests which the employer may protect we shall, to an extent, be covering the reverse side of the coin, namely the freedom which the employee has to exploit his general skill and knowledge. However, where appropriate, we shall deal specifically with the position viewed from the employee's perspective.

The employee as a source of competition

1.3   Competition for any business may take a number of forms. One of the principal sources of potential competition to virtually any business, however, is the individuals who work for it. It is they who operate the business, generate and have access to the business' closest secrets and are the link between the business and its customers/clients. In effect they are the lifeblood of the business and it is therefore surprising that so few businesses recognise this potential for competition until they have their first experience of it. In some businesses, for example, highly automated manufacturing businesses, the potential for competition from the workforce generally may be limited. In others, the degree of risk may vary dramatically between different types of individual who work for them, for example, contrast the filing clerk in an advertising agency with a senior executive of the same agency who has a client following amounting to a significant percentage of the agency's turnover. However, any employer who underestimates the potential for competition from those who work for him does so at his peril. To a manufacturing business, the loss of a single skilled manual worker will be insignificant but the defection to a competitor of its entire unskilled manual workforce who were used to working together as a team could be devastating. Similarly, the assumption that because an individual is a member of the 'support staff' he or she is unimportant could prove a costly error. There are many secretaries/personal assistants who are the key to the effective working of their 'boss' and without whom that individual would be of limited danger as a competitor or working for a competitor.

The employer as an obstacle to the employee

1.4 Employers alive to the potential for competition from their employees seek protection by imposing restrictions on employees making it difficult, and sometimes impossible, for them to compete. Such obstacles can be legitimate and enforceable but that is not always so. The law encourages the development by employees of their skills and talent. It recognises that usually there is an inequality of bargaining power between employer and employee and zealously guards the employee against the employer who seeks, in the interest of his business, to stifle the exploitation by the employee of his general skill and knowledge, particularly after the employment has ended.

Types of competitive activity

1.5 Competition by the employee or ex-employee may occur in a number of different forms:

- Actual competitive activity during employment, such as soliciting customers of the employer to place business with a competing business which the employee conducts in his spare time;
- Preparatory activity by an employee who is planning to leave employment and set up in competition with the employer, eg purchasing an off-the-shelf company and office equipment, and copying customer lists and other confidential information;
- Competitive activity after employment, such as soliciting customers of the ex-employer.

Restraint of trade doctrine

1.6 This doctrine was expressed by Lord Macnaghten in *Nordenfelt v Maxim Nordenfelt Guns and Ammunition Co* [1894] AC 535, 565 as follows:

> 'The public have an interest in every person's carrying on his trade freely: so has the individual. Interference with individual liberty of action in trading, and all restraints of trade of themselves, if there is nothing more, are contrary to public policy, and therefore void.'

(See also *Esso Petroleum Co Ltd v Harper's Garage (Stourport) Ltd* [1968] AC 269 and *Petrofina (Great Britain) Ltd v Martin* [1966] Ch 146.) However, if a covenant is designed to protect a legitimate interest of an employer and goes no further than is reasonably necessary to protect that interest, the courts will uphold it. In these circumstances the purpose is not merely to stifle competition.

In this book we do not consider in detail the general ambit of the restraint of trade doctrine, since in the context of the employment contract there is normally no difficulty in identifying what is a restrictive covenant. That is certainly true in relation to covenants which apply after termination of employment. Occasionally there are certain problems in identifying as restrictive covenants terms which apply during employment.

1. General structure of this book

1.7   In considering competitive or potentially competitive activity between employee and employer, the law draws a sharp distinction between competition during the existence of the employment relationship and after its termination. In *J A Mont (UK) Ltd v Mills* [1993] IRLR 172 the Court of Appeal rejected a submission that the distinction between these two stages has now become blurred.

1.8   This book is accordingly divided (broadly) into two major parts in which we consider conflict or potential conflict first, between employer and employee; and secondly, between ex-employer and ex-employee.

- In the first seven chapters we consider the position between employer and employee:
  - the employment relationship (Ch 2);
  - the implied duty of fidelity (Ch 3) and express terms of the employment contract, in particular those whereby the employer seeks to obtain protection for his interests additional to that provided by the implied duty of fidelity (Ch 4);
  - the duty of confidence (Chs 5 and 6). Here we shall look at the position between (1) employer and employee as well as between (2) ex-employer and ex-employee (since it is difficult to look at the one in isolation from the other);
  - in Ch 7 we consider the day-to-day practical steps which an employer can take to deter competitive activity by his employee.
- Chapter 8 (Termination of Employment) marks the dividing line between the two major parts of the book.
- In Chs 9 to 12 we deal with the position between ex-employer and ex-employee. In particular we consider what interests of the ex-employer are capable of protection and the covenants whereby the ex-employer may seek to protect those interests, namely area covenants, customer non-solicitation/dealing covenants, non-enticement (of employees) covenants and confidentiality covenants.
- In Chs 13 to 15 we consider the remedies available to the employer to protect his legitimate interests.
- Finally in Ch 16 we consider the practical issues which arise from the discovery by the ex-employer of competitive activities by the ex-employee. We consider the formulation and implementation of suitable strategies in response to this discovery.

2. Balancing the interests of employer and employee: an introduction

1.9   The interests of employer and employee are governed by the express and implied terms of the contract of employment. By way of overview of this book, there follows a summary of the main aspects of the duties of employment which relate to competition or potential competition between (ex-)employee and (ex-)employer.

2(a) Implied duty of fidelity

1.10   While the employment relationship lasts the employer is protected against most forms of competition by the employee by virtue of the employee's duty of fidelity which is implied into the employment contract. The implied duty of fidelity protects the employer for example against the employee:

- Who uses his normal working hours to work for others in competition with the employer: *Thomas Marshall (Exports) Ltd v Guinle* [1979] 1 Ch 227;
- Who exceeds the limits of preparations permitted by law to an employee who intends, once his employment had ended, to set up a competing business: *Balston Ltd v Headline Filters Ltd* [1987] FSR 330;
- Who competes in his spare time: *Hivac Limited v Park Royal Scientific Instruments Ltd* [1946] 1 Ch 166;
- Who diverts business opportunities away from his employer: *Industrial Development Consultants v Cooley* [1972] 2 All ER 162; or
- Who poaches other employees: *Sanders v Parry* [1967] 2 All ER 803 and *Marshall v Industrial Systems & Controls Ltd* [1992] IRLR 294.

1.11 The duty of fidelity also imposes on the employee a duty to keep confidential and not to use or disclose otherwise than for his employer's purposes his employer's trade secrets and other confidential information: *Faccenda Chicken Ltd v Fowler* [1986] 1 All ER 617.

1.12 The duty of fidelity can in some circumstances require the employee to make disclosure to the employer of wrongdoing on the part of other employees towards the employer: *Sybron Corporation v Rochem Ltd* [1983] 3 WLR 713.

2(b) Express terms applying during employment

1.13 The employer will normally (and is advised to) seek further protection than that which is automatically granted to him by the implied duty of fidelity. This he will do by negotiating express terms with the employee. By these terms he will seek to protect (or expand the automatic protection afforded by the duty of fidelity) in particular his goodwill or business connections and trade secrets or confidential information. Such terms may include restrictions during the employment relationship on the employee:

- Undertaking other work (whether competitive or not) and requiring him to devote his whole time and attention to the employer's business;
- Holding shares in competing companies;
- Using or disclosing for his own purposes the employer's confidential information (defining and thereby putting the employee on notice as to what the employer regards as confidential).

1.14 Within the broad bounds of public policy and statute, the parties are free to define the employment relationship as they see fit. The employer is entitled during the employment relationship to the fullest protection for his goodwill, (including probably the stability of the workforce) and his confidential information. While the restraint of trade doctrine applies to terms applying during employment as much as it does to those applying after employment has ended, it is only rarely that terms applying during employment will be struck down as being contrary to public policy. However, the courts will not grant specific performance of a contract of employment (see para 14.3).

3. Balancing the interests of ex-employer and ex-employee: introduction

3(a) End of implied duty of fidelity

1.15 The implied duty of fidelity comes to an end upon termination of employment: *J A Mont (UK) v Mills* [1993] IRLR 172 and *Stenhouse Australia Ltd v Phillips* [1974] 1 All ER 117 (PC).

3(b) Terms applying after employment

3(b)(i) LEGITIMATE BUSINESS INTERESTS

1.16 The ex-employer is not permitted to prevent or inhibit mere competition by the ex-employee. The starting point is that covenants restricting the freedom of the ex-employee to compete with his ex-employer after the end of employment are void for illegality. However, there are two principal types of business interest which the employer is entitled to seek to protect:

- Customer connection or goodwill (and also connection with suppliers); and
- Trade secrets or confidential information:

Stenhouse Australia Ltd v Phillips [1974] 1 All ER 117 (PC) and *Herbert Morris Ltd v Saxelby* [1916] AC 688.

1.17 These are not the only interests capable of protection. Other legitimate interests include an employment agent's connection with its pool of temporary workers: *Office Angels Ltd v Rainer-Thomas and O'Connor* [1991] IRLR 214 (CA). An employer also has a legitimate interest in protecting the stability of his workforce (which he may seek to protect by a covenant preventing the enticement by the employee of his former colleagues) *Dawnay Day & Co Ltd v de Braconler d'Alphen* [1997] IRLR 442 (CA).

3(b)(ii) ONLY REASONABLE PROTECTION OF LEGITIMATE INTERESTS

1.18 The second hurdle which the ex-employer must surmount is that he must show that the covenants extend no further than is reasonably necessary to protect his legitimate interests: *Herbert Morris Ltd v Saxelby* [1916] AC 688 (HL) and *Mason v Provident Clothing & Supply Co Ltd* [1913] AC 724, 733, 741 (HL).

3(b)(iii) MEANS OF PROTECTING LEGITIMATE INTERESTS

1.19 The employer will seek to protect these interests by covenants preventing the ex-employee from:

- Competing with the ex-employer within a certain area of the ex-employer's business (area covenants);
- Soliciting or dealing with customers (or suppliers) of the employer (non-solicitation or non-dealing covenants);
- Enticing away from the ex-employer's employment former colleagues of the ex-employee (non-enticement covenants);
- Using or disclosing trade secrets and confidential information of the ex-employer.

Chapter 2

The employment relationship

Introduction

2.1　In this book we look principally at issues which arise as a result of there being or having been a contract of employment. In some cases the (ex-) employee may have or have had another role, for example as a Companies Act director, and we will consider how that additional role affects the position. We will only do so, however, where the role is additional to the individual's status as an employee and not where, for example, the individual is a director but not an employee.

2.2　This book is concerned with contracts of employment (and not other kinds of contracts). The law in relation to contracts of employment is (in broad terms) well settled. In contrast, it is unclear how far (if at all) many of the principles discussed in this book would apply to contracts for services (referred to in para 2.4). This is particularly true in relation to implied terms. In *Euro RSCG SA v Conran* [1992] Times, 2 November, Vinelott J did not accept that a consultant owed a duty of fidelity beyond the express terms of the agreement. The first step must accordingly be to establish whether a contract is one of employment. It is convenient at the same time to discuss related questions concerning the creation and form of the contract of employment.

1. Who is an employee?

2.3　An employee is an individual who works under a contract of employment or contract of service: the two phrases are synonymous.

2.4　Broadly speaking, and subject to certain exceptions such as office holders, the law recognises two categories of contract under which an individual may work for another: the contract of employment or service and the contract for services. An individual working under a contract for services is often described as an independent contractor or self-employed. It is important to recognise the existence of these two categories of contract at the outset. In the majority of cases, the courts start from the premise that a contract must be either a contract of employment or a contract for services and then decide which of the two the contract they are considering most closely resembles. A detailed exposition of how the courts draw the distinction between the two categories is beyond the scope of this book. However, the following is a summary which should be sufficient to answer the question in the majority of cases.

1(a) Contract of employment or contract for services?

2.5   Over the years the courts have devised a variety of tests to determine whether a contract is one of employment or for services. However, no single test has emerged as the decisive one: *Lee Ting Sang v Chung Chi-Keung and Another* [1990] ICR 409 (PC) at page 412.

2.6   The approach adopted by the courts today is to look at all the factors, weigh up those in favour of a contract of employment and those in favour of a contract for services and see where the balance falls. In *Market Investigations Ltd v Minister of Social Security* [1968] 3 All ER 732 at pages 737 and 738 Cooke J, (approved by the Privy Council in *Lee Ting Sang v Chung Chi-Keung and Another)*, in considering the application of the organisational/integration test (see paragraph 2.9) doubted the viability of drawing up an exhaustive list of relevant factors and rejected the laying down of strict rules on the weight to be given to various factors in particular cases, a view endorsed more recently by the Court of Appeal in *Hall (Inspector of Taxes) v Lorimer* [1994] 1 WLR 209 in which the following passage from the judgment of Mummery J at first instance (reported at [1992] 1 WLR 939, with the relevant passage at page 944) was approved:

> 'In order to decide whether a person carries on business on his own account it is necessary to consider many different aspects of the person's work activity. This is not a mechanical exercise of running through items on a check list to see whether they are present in, or absent from, a given situation. The object of the exercise is to paint a picture from the accumulation of detail. The overall effect can only be appreciated by standing back from the detailed picture which has been painted, by viewing it from a distance and by making an informed, considered, qualitative appreciation of the whole. It is a matter of evaluation of the overall effect of the detail, which is not necessarily the same as the sum total of the individual details. Not all details are of equal weight or importance in any given situation. The details may also vary in importance from one situation to another. The process involves painting a picture in each individual case.'

Notwithstanding this approach it is important to look at the various tests devised by the courts and the factors that have been regarded as relevant in previous cases. While these will not provide a conclusive answer in future cases, they are the best guidance that can be given and are likely to be of assistance in determining the true nature of any particular contract.

1(b) The tests

2.7   There are four main tests:

1   The control test;
2   The organisational/integration test;
3   The economic reality test; and
4   The multiple test.

1(b)(i) THE CONTROL TEST

2.8   Under this test, if the worker could be told not only what to do but how and when to do it, the contract was one of service, the degree of control being sufficient to make the worker the servant of the master. Control is no longer a conclusive test but it remains an important factor and something which always has to be considered: *Market Investigations Ltd v Minister of Social Security* at page 738.

1(b)(ii)   THE ORGANISATIONAL/INTEGRATION TEST

2.9 This test derives from the judgment of Denning LJ in *Stevenson Jordan and Harrison Ltd v MacDonald and Evans* [1952] 1 TLR 101. The test is whether the worker is 'part of the business' as distinct from doing work for the business which is not integrated into that business but is only an accessory to it.

1(b)(iii)   THE ECONOMIC REALITY TEST

2.10 Often described as the converse of the organisational/integration test, instead of asking whether the individual is part of the organisation, the question here is whether he is separate from it to the extent that he is performing the services as a 'person in business on his own account': *Market Investigations Ltd v Minister of Social Security* at page 738.

1(b)(iv)   THE MULTIPLE TEST

2.11 This test was propounded by McKenna J in *Ready Mixed Concrete (South East) Ltd v Minister of Pensions and National Insurance* [1968] 1 All ER 433 at page 439 where he said that for a contract of employment to exist three conditions had to be satisfied:

- The servant agrees that in consideration of a wage or other remuneration he will provide his own work and skill in the performance of some service for his master;
- He agrees expressly or impliedly, that in the performance of that service he will be subject to that other's control in a sufficient degree to make that other master; and
- The other provisions of the contract are consistent with its being a contract of service.

This test forms the basis of the approach currently adopted by the tribunals/ courts in determining whether a contract is one of employment or for services. See for example: *Express and Echo Publications Ltd v Tanton* [1999] IRLR 367 (CA).

1(c) Relevant factors

2.12 Various factors have been found to be relevant in previous cases. Broadly speaking those factors fall into three categories:

- Those which suggest the contract is one of employment;
- Those which suggest the contract is one for services; and
- What can be described as the 'either way' category. Factors in this category can be evidence of either of the two types of contract depending on the facts.

2.13 In considering the following factors it is essential to remember that only very rarely will one factor be conclusive in determining the nature of a contract. Furthermore, the weight to be given to any particular factor may vary from case to case depending on the circumstances – see most recently the passage from the judgment of Mummery J in *Hall (Inspector of Taxes) v Lorimer*, see paragraph 2.6.

1(c)(i) FACTORS IN FAVOUR OF A CONTRACT OF EMPLOYMENT

2.14 The following are factors which will normally be evidence of a contract of employment:

- **Exclusive service** – an individual who agrees to work exclusively for one business is likely to be an employee: *Bauman v Hulton Press Ltd* [1952] 2 All ER 1121.
- **Mutuality of obligation** – for there to be a contract of employment there must be an irreducible minimum obligation on each party: *Ready Mixed Concrete (South East) Ltd v Minister of Pensions and National Insurance* [1968] 1 All ER 433. In recent cases concerning casual workers and home workers this has been interpreted as an obligation on the employer to provide work and on the employee to accept the work provided: *O'Kelly v Trusthouse Forte plc* [1983] IRLR 369 and *Nethermere (St Neots) Ltd v Taverna and Gardiner* [1984] ICR 612 and most recently as an obligation on the employer to provide a reasonable share of the available type of work the individual was engaged to do and on the employee, subject to a qualification of reasonableness, to accept the work offered: *Carmichael v National Power plc* [1998] IRLR 301 (CA) although note *Carmichael* is subject to an appeal to the House of Lords.
- **Payment of wages/salary** – where the parties to the contract agree that payment to the worker will be by annual wage/salary payable either weekly or monthly, possibly with agreed review dates, that is evidence of an employment relationship. Note, attempts to avoid an employment relationship by mis-describing wages/salary will not be effective, see *Migrant Advisory Service v Chaudri* (unreported EAT 140097) 1999 IRLB 615 where payments described as 'voluntary expenses' were found by the EAT to be wages.
- **Deduction of tax and employees' national insurance contributions** – deduction of tax on a Schedule E/PAYE basis and deduction of employees' national insurance contributions from a worker's wages/salary before he receives it is evidence of an employment contract. Contrast the independent contractor who pays tax in arrears under Schedule D, pays his own national insurance contributions and receives his fee gross.
- **Miscellaneous terms** – inclusion of any of the following terms in a contract will be evidence that the relationship is one of employment. The right to holiday and holiday pay; the right to sick pay, particularly where there is a reference to statutory sick pay; provision of a car/other vehicle; eligibility to join an occupational pension scheme; provision of death in service benefit; provision of permanent health insurance; eligibility to participate in a share option scheme; a right of a business to suspend; the existence of disciplinary procedures and a waiver under Section 197 Employment Rights Act 1996 (as amended by Section 18 Employment Relations Act 1999 when that Section is brought into force).

1(c)(ii) FACTORS IN FAVOUR OF A CONTRACT FOR SERVICES

2.15 The following are factors which will normally be evidence of a contract for services.

- **Ability to send a substitute** – personal service is the essence of a contract of service. Consequently, where an individual is able to send a substitute to perform the agreed duties that alone will normally result in the contract being found to be for services: *Ready Mixed Concrete (South East) Ltd v Minister of Pensions and National Insurance* [1968] 1 All ER 433 and more recently, *Express And Echo Publications Ltd v Tanton* [1999] IRLR 367 (CA).

● **Ability to work for other businesses** – an ability to work for other businesses without restriction, express or implied, is evidence of a contract for services. A restriction against working for rival businesses can be consistent with a contract for services; whether or not it is depends on all the facts of the case. For example, if the effect of the restriction is to prevent the individual working for any other businesses, the contract is more likely to be one of employment.

● **Payment by fees** – where payment is to be by an agreed fee payable in one lump sum or in quarterly instalments, in either case on submission of an invoice or invoices, that is evidence of a contract for services.

● **Payment by commission** – normally workers paid solely by commission are independent contractors. However, payment by commission only has been found to be consistent with a contract of employment: *Hobbs v Royal Arsenal Co-operative Society Ltd* (1930) 23 BWCC 254. In practice, contracts of employment providing for payment by commission only, rather than salary and commission, are rare and are potentially much more problematic following the implementation of the National Minimum Wage Act 1998.

● **Tax status** – payment by a worker of tax on a Schedule D basis is evidence of a contract for services. However, the mere fact that the Inland Revenue have accepted tax on this basis is not conclusive evidence that the individual is an independent contractor. It is persuasive only and the Inland Revenue are at liberty, subject to certain conditions, to change their minds.

● **VAT registration** – where the worker is registered for Value Added Tax and submits VAT invoices for work done, this suggests the contract is one for services. VAT is payable, inter alia, on sums paid for the provision of services; wages and salaries are specifically excluded. (For individuals/businesses providing services on which VAT is payable, registration is compulsory where the value of the anticipated taxable supplies exceeds the statutory registration threshold which is currently £57,000. Voluntary registration is available where anticipated taxable supplies will not exceed the statutory registration threshold. The obligation to register applies if at the end of any month the value of taxable supplies in the previous 12 months exceeds the statutory threshold *or* if at any time there are reasonable grounds to believe that the value of taxable supplies in the next 30 days will exceed the statutory threshold: VAT Act 1983 Sch 1.) For a worker below the statutory threshold wishing to establish that he is an independent contractor, it may be advantageous for him to consider voluntary registration.

● **Provision of tools and equipment** – an independent contractor will normally be responsible for supplying and maintaining his own tools and equipment. Exceptionally, specialist tools or equipment belonging to the business may be used by the independent contractor, see for example *Hall (Inspector of Taxes) v Lorimer* above where Lorimer, who was found to be an independent contractor, performed his role as a vision mixer using premises and very expensive specialist equipment provided by the production companies that engaged him.

● **Financial risk** – an independent contractor bears the risk of his enterprise; he benefits directly from the profits but suffers directly from the losses. Contrast the employee, who generally benefits only indirectly from the profits, with the exception of those whose pay is partly directly linked to profits, for example through a bonus scheme or long-term incentive plan, and is protected from the losses, at least until matters become so severe that pay cuts or redundancies are necessary.

1(c)(iii) THE 'EITHER WAY' FACTORS

2.16 The following are factors which may, depending on the surrounding circumstances, be evidence of either a contract of employment or a contract for services:

- **Personal service** – for there to be a contract of employment the worker must agree to provide his own services rather than those of another. However, an independent contractor is also perfectly free to agree to provide his own services and many will do so, for example artistes such as opera singers.
- **Control and organisation** – the greater the degree of control that can be exercised by the business over the worker in terms of how, when and where he performs the task and how he organises himself, the more likely the contract is to be one of employment. Conversely the more autonomy the worker has the more likely he is to be an independent contractor: *Addison v London Philharmonic Orchestra* [1981] ICR 261.
- **Form of documentation** – the form, as distinct from the content, of the documentation recording the terms of the contract may suggest the type of contract. The fact that an agreement is called a 'Consultancy Agreement' or 'Agreement for Services', avoids use of the terms 'employer' and 'employee' and contains terms consistent with a contract for services will be evidence that it is indeed such a contract. On the other hand, any of the following documents will be evidence of a contract of employment: an agreement entitled 'Service Agreement' in a form consistent with a service agreement; a statement supplied pursuant to Section 1 Employment Rights Act 1996 and a memorandum under Section 318(1) Companies Act 1985.
- **Reimbursement of expenses** – such a term is generally indicative of a contract of employment; an independent contractor normally agrees an all-inclusive price for his work. However, as with personal service, (see above) reimbursement of expenses is not inconsistent with a contract for services.

1(d) Status of the contract – a question of fact or law?

2.17 The answer to this question is critically important because in a tribunal case it determines the scope for a disgruntled litigant's ability to appeal. Does an individual whose unfair dismissal claim has been rejected by an employment tribunal on the grounds he was not an employee have a real chance to wrest that decision from the employment tribunal? Additionally can greater certainty be gained from reported cases for those constructing contracts, or are all authorities of limited use because each case turns on its own facts? The question has been the subject of much debate over the years. However comparatively recently it has been decided that subject to one exception the question of the status of a contract is a question of fact: *O'Kelly v Trusthouse Forte plc* [1983] IRLR 369 (CA): *Nethermere (St Neots) Ltd v Taverna and Gardiner* [1984] ICR 612 (CA): *Lee Ting Sang v Chiung Chi-Keung* [1990] ICR 409 (PC) and *Clifford v Union of Democratic Mineworkers* [1991] IRLR 518 (CA) but see *Express and Echo Publications Ltd v Tanton* [1999] IRLR 370 referred to at paragraph 2.19. The exception is where the contract is wholly contained in documents. In such a case the interpretation of those documents is a question of law: *Davies v Presbyterian Church of Wales* [1996] IRLR 194 and see *McMeehan v Secretary of State for Employment* [1995] ICR 444.

2.18   The consequence of the general rule is that where the appellate body is the EAT, it will only be able to entertain an appeal on the status of the contract where the employment tribunal had misdirected itself in law, for example, in applying the wrong test to determine status or on a perversity argument: that no reasonable tribunal properly directed on the facts could have reached the conclusion come to by the initial tribunal. In practice this means that it will normally be very difficult to overturn an initial decision on status and that very little binding authority will be available to assist those putting together contracts in determining their likely status which is an unfortunate consequence of the courts' approach.

2.19   For a recent example of a successful appeal see *Express and Echo Publications Ltd v Tanton* [1999] IRLR 370. In that case, both the employment tribunal and the EAT were found to have erred in law by concluding that a contract which included a term inherently inconsistent with a contract of employment was nonetheless a contract of employment. The 'inconsistent term' was the ability of Mr Tanton to provide the services through a substitute rather than having to provide them personally. In *Express and Echo* the Court of Appeal also gives useful guidance on the approach tribunals/courts should take in determining whether a contract is one of employment and the scope for potential appeals under the *Edwards (Inspector of Taxes) v Bairstow* principles.

The approach for tribunals/courts to take was described by the Court of Appeal as follows:

- Establish the terms of agreement between the parties – a question of fact;
- Consider whether any of the agreed terms are inherently inconsistent with a contract of employment – a question of law;
- In the absence of any terms inherently inconsistent with a contract of employment, determine whether the contract is one of employment or for services having regard to all the terms – a question of mixed law and fact.

In *Express and Echo* the error occurred at the second stage. The Court of Appeal in *Express and Echo* departed without specifically addressing the point from the categorisation of the status of the contract being a question of fact: see paragraph 2.17. The approach in *Express and Echo* to determining the status of the contract also underlines the importance to be attached to the terms agreed between the parties, as distinct from how the contract was performed. In *Express and Echo* the Court of Appeal found that where the tribunal Chairman had gone wrong was by focusing predominantly on how the contract had been performed rather than the agreed terms of the contract. The consequence of his doing so produced a result, untenable in law, namely that a contract was one of employment even though it did not require personal service by Mr Tanton.

1(e)   The power of the parties to dictate the status of the contract

2.20   There are clear advantages to both parties if the contract under which the individual works is a contract for services. The individual will normally gain the benefit of being taxed under Schedule D whereas the business will avoid having to operate PAYE and will have none of the obligations imposed by statute exclusively on an employer (although obligations applicable to the broader concept of 'worker', for example to give paid holiday, may still be applicable). The temptation therefore for parties to describe their contracts as contracts for services is great. However, describing a contract in this way will be ineffective if the contract is really one of employment – the parties cannot avoid the legal consequences of the employment relationship merely by attaching a different label to the contract: *Young and Woods Ltd v West* [1980] IRLR 201. However, where the contract could genuinely be either a contract of employment or a contract for services then it is quite legitimate for the parties to so organise themselves as to make their relationship fall into which category they choose: *Massey v Crown Life Insurance Co* [1978] ICR 590. Parties considering treating their relationship as a contract for services when it is obviously one of employment should exercise caution. Contracts which defraud the Revenue, as such a contract may be found to do, are illegal and void and normally cannot be relied on as the basis of any claim even where either or both parties are ignorant of the illegal character of the agreement: *Miller v Karlinski* (1945) 62 TLR 85 (CA) applied recently in *Salveson v Simons* [1994] IRLR 52 in which the EAT conducted a useful review of the authorities on illegality. The exception is where the contract is found to be illegal as performed, as distinct from illegal as formed, and one party is innocent of the illegal purpose: *Newland v Simons and Willer (Hairdressers) Ltd* [1981] ICR 521 (EAT); or at least substantially less culpable than the other: *Hewcastle Catering Ltd v Ahmed and Elkamah* [1991] IRLR 473 (CA). In those circumstances the innocent or less culpable party may be able to enforce the contract. Whilst it is arguable that wrongly electing to treat a contract of employment as a contract for services only means that the contract is illegal as performed, where both parties are equally culpable of perpetrating the fraud on the Revenue, as often they will be, the exception will not assist. In cases where there is doubt about the proper status of the contract, the prudent course is to avoid the risk of an illegality argument by making full disclosure of the relevant facts to the Revenue and obtaining their prior approval to treating the worker as self-employed as had been done in *Young and Woods Ltd v West* [1980] IRLR 201. The 'employer' who fails to take this step faces the possibility of being unable to enforce the contract, in particular the restrictive covenants.

2.21 Similarly tax saving (as distinct from evasion) schemes other than the 'independent contractor route' should also only be adopted after careful thought. Whilst a scheme will not necessarily be unlawful because its only purpose is to reduce tax: *Lightfoot v D & J Sporting Ltd* [1996] IRLR 64 (EAT) such schemes will almost inevitably come under careful scrutiny by the courts and tribunals. So, for example, in *Salveson v Simons* [1994] IRLR 52 after some years of employment at Simons' suggestion his (then) employer agreed to pay him a reduced salary but pay an amount equal to the reduction to a partnership of Simons and his wife. That partnership declared and paid tax on the sums it received but provided no services to Simons' employer. Unsurprisingly, the arrangement was found to be illegal with the result that Simons could not pursue an unfair dismissal claim. For obvious reasons, pure tax evasion schemes under which for example sums are paid but never declared to the Revenue should never be contemplated.

2.22 For the use of personal service companies as vehicles to secure independent contractor status see paragraph 2.32.

1(f) Directors as employees

2.23 The term 'director' in this book is used to refer to a person who holds office as a director of a company in accordance with the provisions of the Companies Act 1985 which include a shadow director as defined in Section 741 of that Act. It does not include those given the courtesy title of director who are not members of the Board. To the experienced reader this may seem a rather obvious point to make but it is surprising how often it is wrongly assumed that someone called a director is in fact a director under the Companies Act 1985. The office of director is held subject to the provisions of the company's Memorandum and Articles of Association and the Companies Act 1985.

2.24 A director is an office-holder of a company. He may also be an employee of the company but that does not by any means follow automatically from his directorship. To be an employee the director must be able to show an express or implied contract of employment between himself and the company: *Eaton v Robert Eaton Ltd* [1988] ICR 302. To determine whether such a contract exists, the process described above of considering all the facts and balancing those in favour of a contract of employment against those not in favour must be carried out. The factors outlined above will be relevant but there are certain points, peculiar to directors that need to be considered in connection with those factors.

1(f)(i) CONTROL AND ORGANISATION

2.25 The degree of control exercised over a director may be minimal; this is particularly so in small family companies. A minimal degree of control does not prevent the director being an employee: *Trussed Steel Concrete Co Ltd v Green* [1946] Ch 115. Even the virtual absence of control, such as occurs when the director owns a controlling interest in the company, will not prevent the director from being an employee if there is a bona fide contract of employment between the company and the director: *Nottingham Egg Packers and Distributors Ltd v McCarthy and Haslett* (1967) 2 ITR 223, 2 KIR 302. There is no rule of law that precludes an individual who holds a controlling interest in a company from being an employee of that company: *Secretary of State for Trade and Industry v Bottrill* [1999] IRLR 326 (CA) adopting the comments of the Court of Session in *Fleming v Secretary of State for Trade and Industry* [1997] IRLR 682 and disapproving as unsound the EAT's earlier decision in *Buchan v Secretary of State for Employment* [1997] IRLR 80. Consequently, whilst the holding of a controlling interest will always be a relevant factor and in many cases a decisive one in determining whether an individual is an employee it remains only one of the factors to be taken into account in reaching that decision. So, for example, in *McLean v Secretary of State for Employment* ((S) EAT 672/91) IRLB 455 14 it was the absence of any documentation recording any contract between McLean and the company and the fact that McLean had taken out a second mortgage on his home to raise money for the company which defeated his claim that he was an employee, not the fact that he held a majority shareholding in the company.

1(f)(ii) METHOD OF PAYMENT

2.26 The traditional method of remunerating directors, who are not employees, is through fees. Normally the company's Articles of Association provide for an annual figure to be voted on, and that figure will usually be a fairly nominal amount compared to what the individual may expect to earn by way of salary. The fact that a director's remuneration was treated as 'fees and emoluments' was one of the factors which led the Court of Appeal to conclude that a director was not an employee in *Albert J Parsons & Sons Ltd v Parsons* [1979] ICR 271. In contrast, a director who is required to work full time for a company in return for a salary is likely to be an employee: *Folami v Nigerline (UK) Ltd* [1978] ICR 277 (EAT).

1(f)(iii) Form of contractual documentation

2.27 Section 318(1) Companies Act 1985 imposes on a company an obligation, subject to certain exceptions, to keep copies of any written contracts of employment between itself and its directors or, if any such contract is not in writing, a written memorandum setting out its terms. The company is under the same obligation where the director is employed by a subsidiary of the company (Section 318(1)(c)) and shadow directors are treated as directors for the purposes of the Section (Section 318(6)). The documentation is open to inspection by members of the company (Section 318(7)). It is always important, when deciding whether or not a director is an employee, to bear the provisions of this Section in mind. If, for example, a written memorandum has been produced in accordance with Section 318(1) then that will be evidence to support the existence of an employment relationship.

2.28 The principal exception to Section 318(1) is where the contract will expire or can be determined by the company within the next twelve months without the company incurring a liability for compensation Section 318(11). Compensation is not a defined term and consequently it is unclear whether it is limited to compensation under the contract or also includes for example unfair dismissal damages. Because of this element of doubt the prudent advice to a company is always to err on the side of caution in terms of compliance with its Companies Act obligations unless there are good commercial reasons in a particular case for doing otherwise.

2.29 In the event of a dispute/potential dispute between a director and his employing company, Section 318(7) can provide a director/employee who has lost his contract, and does not want to arouse suspicion by asking for a copy, an alternative means of access to it, provided he can find a 'tame' member to do the inspecting for him. It must, however, be remembered that the member's right is only to inspect the document and not to take a copy of it; transcribing the document is also probably not allowed. Where the employing company is listed, Rule 16.9 of the Stock Exchange Listing Rules, January 1999 (the Yellow Book) provides an additional right of inspection to Section 318(7). The right is subject to a similar, but rather clearer, exception to that in Section 318(11) in that it only applies to directors' service contracts which are for a period of or require notice of termination of one year or more or which include provisions for pre-determined compensation on termination which equals or exceeds one year's salary and benefits. However, the categories of those entitled to inspect are, predictably, broader extending to 'any person' including, for example, potential investors and the press. Whilst the right remains only to inspect, and not copy, the listed company director does not have to find the 'tame' member to do his inspecting for him.

1(g) Ex-employees as independent contractors

2.30 It is convenient to deal here with this special category of individuals. The most common circumstances in which an ex-employee of a business may become an independent contractor to that business are:

● Where one, or both, of the parties to the contract perceive the advantages of the change in status and agreement is reached on the change: *Massey v Crown Life Insurance Co* [1978] ICR 590; or
● The business has had to dispense with the services of a full-time employee but wishes to retain some access to their services. Most often nowadays the individual will have been made redundant and the 'consultancy' position will be offered as part of the termination package. These arrangements can have definite advantages for both parties but they are not without their pitfalls.

2.31 That an individual can continue to do the same work and be properly treated as employed one day and self-employed the next by reason only of an agreement between the parties is accepted: *Massey v Crown Life Insurance Co and Inland Revenue Commissioners v Duke of Westminster* [1936] AC 1. However, such arrangements are open to close scrutiny, particularly by the Inland Revenue, and if the reality of the situation is that the continuing relationship is one of employment, applying a contract for services label to it will make no difference. Furthermore, the tax treatment of any payment made in connection with the purported termination of the employment may also be called into question. Where the employer treats all or the first £30,000 of such a payment as tax free relying on Section 188 Income and Corporation Taxes Act 1988 (under which the first £30,000 of any payment made in connection with the termination of employment may be paid without deduction of tax subject to certain conditions being satisfied) he may well face a successful challenge from the Inland Revenue, and a consequent tax liability. Detailed consideration of these types of arrangement is beyond the scope of this book but suffice to say that great care needs to be taken, particularly with the tax treatment of such arrangements. Seeking approval from the Inland Revenue is prudent and careful thought should also be given to whether there is any need for indemnities in relation to potential liabilities for tax and national insurance contributions.

2.32 Because of the real difficulties in making an ex-employee an independent contractor in his personal capacity it is common practice to hire the ex-employee through his service company. By introducing a separate legal entity into the arrangements the parties hope to avoid PAYE and national insurance contributions and, from the ex-employer's perspective, minimise the risk of employment protection claims. In real terms the ex-employee is often doing exactly what he did as an employee and simply using the service company as a post box for monies. In such cases from a tax perspective the effectiveness is now likely to be short lived. In the March 1999 Budget the Government announced that it will be introducing legislation to combat this route of what it describes as tax avoidance. The proposed legislation is to be effective from April 2000 but, as yet, no drafts have been published. In its Budget announcement – Inland Revenue 35, the Government said that the proposed legislation is only to be aimed at 'engagements with essential characteristics of employment' and that there was no intention to re-define the existing boundary between employment and self employment. However, a document published by the Inland Revenue following the Budget

Announcement entitled 'Proposed new rules on the provision of personal service companies – addressing some concerns' suggests that the proposed new legislation may go well beyond the original announcement. Rather than addressing concerns the document has actually given rise to significant concern and opposition particularly on the part of small businesses. It remains to be seen what the final scope of the new legislation will be. However, even if it is in line with the original Budget Announcement it is likely to lead to a subtle re-definition of the existing boundaries between employment and self employment if only because the payment of PAYE tax is one of the factors to be taken into account in determining the status of a contract.

2. The creation of the contract of employment

2.33 The creation of a contract of employment is subject to the normal rules of the law of contract. There must be an offer made which is accepted without qualification; there must be consideration; and there must be an intention to create legal relations. While it is not always easy to analyse precisely how the facts of a particular case conform to these criteria, conform they must otherwise no contract exists as a matter of law.

2(a) Commencement of the employment relationship

2.34 The date of commencement of employment may be:

- The date specified in the contract of employment; or
- The date on which the employee first undertakes work for the employer; or
- The date the contract of employment was entered into, determined in accordance with the normal contractual principles relating to offer and acceptance.

Sometimes there is a significant gap between the date of entering into the contract of employment and the date employment actually begins, for instance, because of the length of notice required to determine the current contract of employment.

2.35 The commencement of the employment relationship is not to be confused with the commencement of the period of continuous employment for the purposes of calculating statutory employment protection rights. The two dates may be coincident but will not always be the same. For the purposes of this book, the date of commencement of employment will usually be the important date, for example where the length of notice required to terminate or the duration of the covenants increases with length of employment.

2(b) The form of the contract

2.36 With the exception of a very few categories of employee, for example apprentices and crews of merchant ships, the provisions of Section 1 Employment Rights Act 1996 and of Section 318(1) Companies Act 1985 there is no requirement that terms of employment should be recorded in writing. Moreover, failure to follow the provisions of Section 1 and Section 318(1) respectively will not affect the validity of the contract. It follows that a contract of employment can be a purely oral agreement between the parties. Nowadays, however, this is unusual. Partly written and partly oral agreements are much more common with only the major terms being reduced to writing. The type of documentation and degree of formality varies from industry to industry. However, as a rule of thumb the more senior the employee the more formal the documents are likely to be with the possible exception of employees who have risen through the ranks, whose only documentation is often a rather brief initial letter of appointment. The existence of a foreign parent company may also dictate the style of the documentation, for example certain American corporations issue voluminous documentation.

2.37 It is difficult to generalise about the format of documentation issued to employees but the following are the usual categories in descending order of formality:

- Service Agreements;
- Short Form Service Agreements;
- Letters of Engagement sometimes incorporating Staff Handbooks/Employee Manuals or parts of Collective Agreements with recognised Trade Unions;
- Written statements of particulars of employment under Section 1 Employment Rights Act 1996 and amendments thereto pursuant to Section 4 of the same Act (but see paras 2.43-2.44 on the status of these) sometimes incorporating the documents referred to in the previous bullet point.

2.38 With the increased emphasis on collectivism stemming from the provisions relating to automatic union recognition in the Employment Relations Act 1999 (although these provisions are yet to be brought into force); the emphasis on informing and consulting with any recognised trade union in the Collective Redundancies and Transfer of Undertakings (Protection of Employment) (Amendment) Regulations 1999; the imminent requirement for relevant UK companies to comply with the European Works Council Directive 94/45/EC it will be interesting to see what impact collectivism has on individual employment terms over the next few years. Certainly lawyers will in future have to be much more aware of the collective aspect and in construing a contract of employment check whether there are any collective terms that are incorporated into the contract. It is predictable that some terms such as pay and arrangements regarding working time under the Working Time Regulations 1998 will become increasingly the subject of collective negotiations. In contrast, collectivism is unlikely to have any significant impact on restrictive covenants which, by their very nature, have to be tailored to the individual circumstances of each employee.

2(c)   The terms of the contract

2.39 The basic rule is that the parties are free to agree whatever terms they choose subject only to specific statutory and common law restraints. For the purposes of this book the most relevant restraints are the statutory restraint against providing for notice periods shorter than those specified in Section 86 Employment Rights Act 1996 and the common law restraint against an employer seeking to obtain, by way of restrictive covenant, more than adequate protection for his legitimate interests.

2.40 In practice it is always advisable for the parties to a contract of employment to reach agreement on all relevant matters and to record at least the most important terms of their agreement in writing. To do so minimises the likelihood of dispute. In reducing the terms to writing it is, however, vital to ensure that the written terms accurately reflect what was agreed. This is particularly important where the document is intended to express the entire agreement between the employer and the employee. The parole evidence rule applies as much to a contract of employment as to any other contract so that a party will not normally be able to adduce oral or written evidence to contradict or vary the express terms of the contract. Although there are exceptions to the parole evidence rule (see *Chitty on Contracts* (27th edn) Vol I paras 12-081–12-090) and the rule does not apply to an application to rectify the agreement: *Lovell and Christmas Ltd v Wall* (1911) 104 LT 85, both parties are better off investing time in ensuring the accuracy of the written agreement rather than risking the cost and uncertainty of seeking to rely on these exceptions.

2.41 Types of term – there are two basic types of term: express terms and implied terms. Express terms are those explicitly agreed between the parties, for example where the parties discuss the employee's salary and agree a figure of £30,000 per annum. Implied terms are those which the parties have not specifically agreed on but which nonetheless form part of the contract of employment. Implied terms fall into two broad categories: those which are implied as a matter of common law (these insofar as they are directly relevant to the subject of this book are dealt with in detail in Ch 3); and those that are imposed as a matter of statute, for example equality clauses under Section 1 Equal Pay Act 1970. Collectively negotiated terms may be incorporated into a contract either expressly or impliedly.

2(d) Written statement of particulars of employment

2.42 Section 1 of the Employment Rights Act 1996 provides that, subject to certain exceptions, within two months of an employee commencing employment the employer must provide a written statement of certain particulars of the employment. The particulars to be provided are no more than the basic terms applicable to the everyday operation of the employment. They include matters such as rates of pay; normal hours of work (if any); arrangements for holidays and holiday pay; job title and notice. Also to be included are details of any collective agreements that affect the employee's terms and conditions (Section 1(4)(j)) such agreements may become more important in the future in the light of the increased emphasis on collectivism discussed above (see para 2.38). By virtue of Section 4 Employment Rights Act 1996 the particulars provided must be kept up to date and changes notified to the employee within one month of the change.

2(d)(i) STATUS OF THE WRITTEN PARTICULARS

2.43 A document which does no more than provide the particulars required by Section 1 is not, as a matter of law, a contractual document. It is persuasive, but not conclusive, evidence of the terms of the contract of employment: *Moore v RH McCulloch Ltd* [1966] 1 ITR 484 and *Robertson v British Gas Corporation* [1983] ICR 351 (CA). The importance of this is that a party seeking to argue that the written particulars are inaccurate can do so unfettered by the parole evidence rule. Evidence of discussions that took place, for example before the employee joined, can be used to show the inaccuracy of the written particulars. However, an employer wishing to dispute the accuracy of such a document will face an uphill struggle. Issue of the document was his unilateral act and if the terms are not accurately recorded that is no-one's fault but his own. Perhaps somewhat unusually, bearing in mind the frequent divergence of view on employment law between the European Court and our domestic courts/tribunals, the UK's interpretation of the status of Section 1 Statements is consistent with the ECJ approach as expressed in the recent case of *Kampelmann v Landschaftsverbrand Westfalen-Lippe* C235/96 [1998] IRLR 333.

2.44 The fact that an employee has signed acknowledging receipt of written particulars will not alter the status of the document: *Robertson v British Gas.* However, where a statement contains particulars other than those required by Section 1 or where the employee is required to sign the document not only to acknowledge receipt but also to confirm his agreement to the terms, that may be enough to persuade a tribunal/court that the document has contractual force: see *Gascol Conversions Ltd v Mercer* [1974] ICR 420.

2(d)(ii) FAILURE TO COMPLY WITH STATUTORY OBLIGATIONS

2.45 Section 11 Employment Rights Act 1996 sets out the remedies for breaches of Sections 1 and 4. Essentially the Section provides for an application to be made to the employment tribunal by the employee only, where the alleged breach is a total failure to comply with either Section or where the details given are incomplete, and by either party where the allegation is that the information given is inaccurate.

2.46 The tribunal's powers on an application under Section 11 were clarified by. the Court of Appeal in *Eagland v British Telecommunications plc* [1992] IRLR 323. The Tribunal is limited to recording terms covered by Section 1 which have been expressly or impliedly agreed between the parties. In the absence of any such agreement the tribunal is not empowered to 'invent' a term – the obiter dictum of Stephenson LJ to that effect in *Mears v Safecar Security Ltd* [1982] IRLR 183 was strongly disapproved.

2(d)(iii) RELEVANCE OF SECTION 11 APPLICATIONS

2.47 A Section 11 application can be a speedy and cost-effective way, in particular, for an employee, to obtain a determination of the terms of his employment. In the Tribunal in most regions such applications tend to be listed for hearing relatively quickly and the power to award costs against a party arises only where in bringing or conducting proceedings the party has acted 'frivolously, vexatiously disruptively, abusively or otherwise unreasonably' (Industrial Tribunal (Rules of Procedure) Regulations 1993 – Schedule 1, Rule 12). Such costs orders are comparatively rarely made.

2.48 In particular, Section 11 applications may be used to establish the period of notice the employee is required to give or receive to determine his employment. It is important, however, to remember that it will only be worthwhile making such an application where there is a reasonable prospect of showing that there was an agreement on the notice period, express or implied. In the absence of such an agreement as a matter of common law, a reasonable notice period will be implied and that will be all the tribunal can record: *Cuthbertson v AML Distributors* [1975] IRLR 228. Although Parker LJ suggested in an obiter comment in *Eagland v British Telecommunications plc* [1992] IRLR 323 (CA) at page 326 that the tribunal 'may also have power to decide, as would a court of law, the length of such notice'. The better view is that currently the tribunal has no such power under Section 11. Where the tribunal does have a power to determine the length of reasonable notice is in the exercise of its contractual jurisdiction of determining damages for wrongful dismissal. However, in the context of this book that jurisdiction is unlikely to be of any practical value.

Chapter 3

The implied duty of fidelity

Introduction

The duty of fidelity

3.1   Implied into every contract of employment is a term that the employee will serve his employer with good faith and fidelity: *Robb v Green* [1895] 2 QB 315 (CA); *Faccenda Chicken Ltd v Fowler* [1986] 3 WLR 288 (CA). The implied term is frequently augmented by express terms and typical examples are dealt with in Ch 4. For the purposes of this chapter we will assume that there are no relevant express terms.

3.2   The implied duty of fidelity is owed throughout the duration of the contract of employment including the employee's spare time: *Hivac Ltd v Park Royal Scientific Instruments Ltd* [1946] 1 Ch 169. The duty ceases only when the employment ceases. In the words of Hawkins J:

> 'The dividing line between [the employee] owing his master a duty and owing him none is that imperceptible period of time between the termination of his service and the moment he acquires freedom of service after his service has terminated.' *Robb v Green* [1895] 2 QB 1, 14.

3.3   This essential point was reaffirmed by the Court of Appeal in *J A Mont (UK) Ltd v Mills* [1993] IRLR 172 in which Simon Brown LJ stated (para 38):

> 'The duty of good faith, in my judgment, arises out of the obligation of loyalty inevitably owed by an employee to an employer. Once the employment relationship ceases, there is no occasion for loyalty. All that is left is a residual duty of confidentiality in respect of the employer's trade secrets.'

3.4   This is to be contrasted with the director or senior employee's fiduciary duty which may extend beyond termination of the directorship or employment: *Island Export Finance Ltd v Umunna* [1986] BCLC 460 and *Canadian Aero Service Ltd v O'Malley* (1973) 40 DLR (3d) 371 (Can SC).

3.5   What the duty of fidelity requires of the employee is honesty. The standard to be applied is that of the man of ordinary honesty and intelligence; if he would regard the employee's acts as dishonest towards his employer, the implied duty of fidelity will prohibit those acts: *Robb v Green* [1895] 2 QB 315 (CA).

3.6   The precise ambit of the duty of fidelity varies from one case to the next. It depends on matters such as the status and position of the employee and, in some cases, on the relationship of the employees inter se. As Lord Greene MR said in *Hivac* (page 174):

'The practical difficulty in any given case is to find exactly how far that rather vague duty of fidelity extends.'

3.7   The duty of fidelity is considered under the following headings:

1   Competition during employment;
2   Preparations during employment to compete after employment has ended;
3   Duty of disclosure to the employer;
4   Duty not to make a secret profit; and
5   Confidential information: this is dealt with in Chs 5 and 6.

1. Competition during employment

3.8   While a contract of employment subsists the employee's time falls into two categories:

*   Working time when he has contracted to work for his employer; and
*   Spare time which he has kept free for his own purposes.

3.9   In some contracts the working hours are well defined, for example 'Your working hours will be 9.00 am to 5.00 pm Monday to Friday (inclusive)'; in others, particularly those of senior employees, there may be no agreed hours or merely a statement that the employee shall 'devote his whole time and attention to the business of the employer'. Even in the case of 'whole time and attention' clauses, however, the employee is entitled to some spare time: if the proper construction were otherwise, the result would be ludicrous.

3.10   The distinction between working time and spare time is important for three reasons:

*   Because it is a breach of contract for an employee to do anything other than work for his employer during the hours he has contracted to work for him, except with the employer's consent; and
*   Because although the implied duty of fidelity subsists during both working and spare time (*Hivac*), the extent of the duty may be less onerous during the employee's spare time; and
*   For the purposes of determining working time under the Working Time Regulations 1998 (discussed at paragraphs 4.10 to 4.14).

3.11   An anomalous kind of 'spare time' arises from the practice of ex- employers, who have given or received notice to terminate the contract of employment of a (usually senior) employee, not to require (or permit) the employee to work during the notice period, but to pay the normal salary and benefits. It has been suggested (obiter by Scott J in *Balston Ltd v Headline Filters Ltd* [1987] FSR 330) that during this period of so-called 'garden leave' the duty not to compete may be less onerous than during normal working time. In our view this is not correct: see paragraph 3.29 below.

Working time

3.12 During the hours the employee has agreed to work for the employer he is not at liberty to do anything else without the employer's consent. To do so would be a breach of the agreement as to working time. Additionally it may be a breach of the implied duty of fidelity and will be where the employee is using the employer's time to compete with him: *Thomas Marshall (Exports) Ltd v Guinle* [1979] 1 Ch 227. See also the cases referred to in paragraphs 3.19 to 3.24.

Spare time

3.13 As a general rule there is no implied term prohibiting an employee working for another or for himself in his spare time, even where the work is in the same line of business as his employer. However, where the effect of the employee's spare time activities may be to inflict great harm on the employer the implied duty of fidelity will prohibit those activities: *Hivac Ltd v Park Royal Scientific Instruments Ltd* [1946] 1 Ch 169, page 178 and *Nova Plastics v Froggatt* [1982] IRLR 146. In *Hivac* both companies were engaged in the manufacture of midget valves which involved skilled manual work. Before Park Royal (which had recently been incorporated) started to trade, Hivac had had a monopoly of the manufacture of midget valves. Without the knowledge of Hivac, Park Royal employed a number of Hivac's skilled manual workers to work for Park Royal in their spare time. Hivac sought an interlocutory injunction against Park Royal to restrain the employment. The Court of Appeal granted an injunction. In doing so the Court said that, although reluctant to impose restrictions which would hamper the employees increasing their earnings in their spare time, the injunction was justified because:

> '... it would be deplorable if it were laid down that a workman could consistently with his duty to his employer knowingly, deliberately and secretly set himself to do in his spare time something which would inflict great harm on his employer's business.' (Lord Greene MR at page 178.)

3.14 In *Hivac* it was found that what the employees had done was to assist Park Royal to develop its business from the early stages to that of its becoming a competitor of Hivac. The following points should be noted from the judgments in that case:

● The court placed considerable weight on the fact that there was a significant risk that if the injunction were not granted Hivac's confidential information would be disclosed to Park Royal. The court found that no confidential information had been disclosed but there was almost an inevitability that it would be. Lord Greene MR rejected as impractical the idea that the employees would be able to ensure that Hivac's confidential information was not disclosed. It is clear that where the employee has access to confidential information and there is a real risk that in the course of his spare time activities he might, even inadvertently, disclose that information to a competitor, the implied duty of fidelity will prohibit him from working for that competitor.

● The court drew a distinction between different classes of employee: at one end of the scale were manual workers where a forceful argument could be presented that the implied duty of fidelity would not restrict them outside their working hours. At the other end of the scale were those where the very nature of the employment would be enough to make it clear that certain types of spare time activity would not be permissible. Given as an example was a solicitor's clerk who, the court said, would be prohibited from working for another solicitor in his spare time.

3.15 The decision in *Hivac* was applied in *Nova Plastics v Froggatt* [1982] IRLR 146. Confirming the decision of the employment tribunal, the EAT found that the implied duty of fidelity of an employee engaged as an odd job man did not prohibit him from working in a similar capacity for a rival company in his spare time. Consequently the employee's dismissal for doing so was unfair. The employment tribunal had concluded correctly that the work the employee was doing for the rival 'was not contributing very seriously to any competition'. The principle accordingly extracted from *Hivac* was that spare time activity which is competitive is not necessarily impermissible; it is only so where it may cause serious harm to the (full-time) employer. But see *Lancashire Fires Ltd v Lyons & Co and others* [1997] IRLR 113 (CA) (discussed at para 3.21) where spare time activities were held to be in breach of the duty of fidelity: the Court of Appeal stated that any employee with technical knowledge and experience can expect to have his spare time activities in the field in which his employer operates carefully scrutinised as to whether they amount to a breach of fidelity.

2. Preparations during employment to compete after employment has ended

3.16 As a general rule, in the absence of a valid restrictive covenant, an employee is free once his employment has terminated to join a competitor or to establish a rival business. An employee choosing either of these options will normally make some preparations for the future before his employment ends. For him, leaving a secure employment will inevitably involve a degree of risk and it is only human nature to want to minimise that risk before he hands in his notice to his employer. Preparatory activity by the employee may, however, amount to a breach of the duty of fidelity.

3.17 It is impossible to provide an exhaustive list of the preparatory steps prohibited by the duty of fidelity; the ambit of the duty varies depending on the facts of each case. However, the following is a summary of the preparatory steps that have been considered by the courts. The first category are those which have been prohibited by the courts, the second, those which have been permitted. This is summarised in the table in the Appendix to this Chapter.

2(a) Prohibited activities

2(a)(i) PREPARATORY STEPS IN THE EMPLOYER'S TIME

3.18 The employee is not entitled to make preparations for his future during the hours he is contracted to work for his employer. To do so would be a clear breach of the term of the contract as to hours. It may also be a breach of the implied duty of fidelity: see *Thomas Marshall (Exports) Ltd v Guinle* [1979] Ch 227.

2(a)(ii)   SOLICITING THE EMPLOYER'S CUSTOMERS (OR SUPPLIERS)

3.19 An employee may not solicit the custom of his employer's customers. The meaning of 'solicitation' is considered in paragraph 10.30. It is irrelevant that the solicitation takes place only very shortly before the employment ends and that the employee is only seeking custom from a time after his employment has ended. In *Wessex Dairies Ltd v Smith* [1935] 2 KB 80 on the last day of his employment the defendant, Smith, informed the customers to whom he delivered milk that he would cease to be employed by Wessex on that day, that he was setting up his own business and that in future he would be able to supply their milk. A number of customers placed orders with Smith. Greer LJ at page 84 stated that Smith was:

> '... under the ordinary implied obligation existing between master and servant – namely, that during the continuance of his employment he will act in his employers' interests and not use the time for which he is paid by the employers in furthering his own interests.'

The Court of Appeal held that Smith was in clear breach of his duty of fidelity and upheld Wessex's claim for damages. Although the solicitation took place during Smith's working time, the case was discussed by the Court of Appeal in *Hivac Ltd v Park Royal Scientific Instruments Ltd* [1946] 1 Ch 169 where the Court concluded that the solicitation would have been a breach of Smith's duty of fidelity even if it had been done in his spare time. See also *Marshall v Industrial Systems & Control Ltd* [1992] IRLR 294 and the other cases discussed at paragraph 3.23 and 3.24.

3.20 Where an employee during employment places an order with his employer's supplier for goods to be supplied to the employee's intended business after termination of employment, this would probably only amount to a breach of fidelity where the suppliers only supply to a limited number of customers or supplies are limited: cf *Laughton and Hawley v Bapp Industrial Supplies Ltd* [1986] IRLR 245, discussed at paragraph 3.27.

2(a)(iii)   ENTERTAINING OFFERS FROM CUSTOMERS

3.21 In *Sanders v Parry* [1967] 1 WLR 753 an assistant solicitor, Parry, received a proposal from a client for whom he did work that if he set up his own practice the client would transfer his instructions to him. Havers J held that whilst employed, Parry was not in a position to consider or discuss the offer; instead his duty was to seek to retain the client for his employer, Sanders. The fact the offer was unsolicited was irrelevant. Likewise in *Lancashire Fires Ltd v Lyons & Co and others* [1997] IRLR 113 (CA) the employee was held to be 'well on the wrong side of the line' when during his employment (in addition to renting and equipping premises) he entered into a finance agreement with a potential customer (albeit one whose needs the employer was not at the time able to service) under which he agreed to become its sole supplier. He pursued this project during his spare time taking advantage of the finance provided. His duties to his employer included participating actively in the development of new projects and his activity for his new concern were directed to the same end with a view to competition with the employer. It is suggested that to arrange finance with a bank will not usually amount to impermissible preparatory activity – but here, the financing was not with a disinterested party – and the combination of the finance agreement and spare time working on a rival production process put the employee in clear breach of fidelity. This case is further discussed in Chapter 5 in relation to breach of confidence. The line was also crossed by the employee in *Adamson v B&L Cleaning Services Ltd* [1995] IRLR 193 where the EAT upheld as fair a decision by an employer to dismiss an employee (of a contract cleaning company) who refused to undertake not to tender for future work being currently undertaken by his employer when those contracts came up for renewal – his actions were held by the EAT to be more than 'testing the market' but amounted to actual competition during employment.

2(a)(iv) OFFERING WORK TO OTHER EMPLOYEES

3.22 It may be a breach of the duty of fidelity for an employee to offer employment to fellow employees even though that employment is to commence upon due termination of their contracts of employment. In *Sanders v Parry*, Parry was told by one of his employer's secretaries that she was dissatisfied in her employment. At the time Parry was making preparations to leave to set up his own practice and instead of reporting the matter to Sanders, Parry offered the secretary employment which she accepted. Havers J held that Parry was in clear breach of his duty of fidelity.

3.23 In *Marshall v Industrial Systems & Control Ltd* [1992] IRLR 294 Marshall, the managing director together with a manager intended to start a new company to replace Industrial Systems as distributors to Industrial Systems' best client. They had drawn up a business plan. Pursuant to that plan the two had already:

- Approached the client;
- Tried to induce another key employee to join the new company.

The EAT (Scotland) upheld the decision of the industrial tribunal that Marshall had breached his duty of fidelity and had been fairly dismissed. It was one thing, as in the case of the employee in *Laughton and Hawley v Bapp* (see para 3.27) to form an intention to set up in competition, and another (as held by the employment tribunal in this case) to form a plan with another important manager to try and persuade another to join them in order to deprive the company (of which Marshall was the managing director) of their best client. Further, it was not merely a plan, but concrete arrangements had been made to obtain business from the client.

3.24 See, however, *G D Searle & Co Ltd v Celltech Ltd* [1982] FSR 92 (CA) in which Cumming Bruce LJ commented (obiter) that there was nothing in the general law to prevent a number of employees in concert deciding to leave their employer and set themselves up in competition with him (see para 3.36). Also, in *Tithebarn Ltd v Hubbard* (Lexis 7 November 1991/IRLIB 449, unreported), the EAT held that it was not necessarily a breach of the employment contract for an employee to discuss his future with other employees and to invite them to join him in a new business which he was likely to set up (see para 3.27).

2(a)(v) COPYING OR MEMORISING TRADE SECRETS OR CONFIDENTIAL INFORMATION

3.25 Normally this involves the copying or memorising of customer information for use after employment has ended to solicit business. This is prohibited: *Robb v Green* [1895] 2 QB 315. In that case the copying by the employee was by transcribing the information from the claimant's order book; however, photocopying is equally offensive. See also *Louis v Smellie* (1895) 73 LT 226 (CA) and *Roger Bullivant Ltd v Ellis* [1987] ICR 464 (CA); cf *Coral Index v Regent Index Ltd* [1970] RPC 147 (no evidence of conscious memorising of customers and their addresses). A useful summary of what is permitted and what is forbidden appears in the judgment of Sir Donald Nicholls VC in *Universal Thermosensors Ltd v Hibben* [1992] 1 WLR 840, 850:

> '[the defendant ex-employees] were entitled [in the absence of express covenant to the contrary in the employment contract] to approach the [claimant's] customers, and seek and accept orders from them. Still further, they were entitled to use for their own purposes any information they carried in their heads regarding the identity of the [claimant's] customers, or customer contacts, or the nature of the customers' product requirements, or the [claimant's] pricing policies, provided they had acquired the information honestly in the course of their employment and had not, for instance, deliberately sought to memorise lists of names for the purposes of their own business. What the defendants were not entitled to do was to steal documents belonging to the [claimant], or to use for their own purposes information, which can sensibly be regarded as confidential information, contained in such documents regarding the [claimant's] customers or customer contacts or customer requirements or prices charged. Nor were they entitled to copy such information onto scraps of paper and take these away and then use the information in their own business.'

The same principles apply in relation to other types of trade secret or confidential information (see Ch 5).

2(b) Permitted activities

2(b)(i) SEEKING WORK WITH A COMPETITOR

3.26 An employee is free to seek work with a rival organisation and the fact he is doing so is not of itself a fair reason to dismiss him: *Harris & Russell Ltd v Slingsby* [1973] IRLR 221. He is only prevented from doing so if there are:

> 'reasonably solid grounds for supposing that he is doing so in order to abuse his confidential position.' (Sir Hugh Griffiths at page 222.)

2(b)(ii) INDICATING AN INTENTION TO COMPETE IN THE FUTURE

3.27 A mere indication of an intention to compete in the future is not on its own objectionable. In *Laughton and Hawley v Bapp Industrial Supplies Ltd* [1986] IRLR 245, Messrs Laughton and Hawley were employed as warehouse manager and deputy warehouse manager respectively. Bapp was a company engaged in the supply of nuts and bolts. The two employees decided to leave to set up a competing business in the same area. As part of their preparations, before their employment ended they wrote to a number of Bapp's suppliers saying that they intended to start a competing business and asking for details of the suppliers' products and the best terms the suppliers could offer them. Bapp obtained a copy of the letter and summarily dismissed the two employees. In their notice of appearance in the employment tribunal proceedings they gave as the reason for dismissal 'gross misconduct/breach of trust'. The EAT, overruling the employment tribunal, found the dismissals unfair. The EAT concluded that merely indicating an intention to set up in competition with the employer in the future, which they found was the central issue in the case (per Gibson J at page 247, para 11) was in itself not a breach of the duty of fidelity. If, however, the employer reasonably believed that in addition the employee had committed, or was about to commit, a wrongful act, then the two things together would be sufficient to justify dismissal. In our view what is permissible under the principle in *Laughton* is fairly limited. For example, the indication of an intention to compete made to a customer may easily be construed as an attempt to solicit custom and therefore be a breach of the implied duty. *Laughton* was cited with approval in *Balston Ltd v Headline Filters Ltd* [1990] FSR 385. *Laughton* was also applied in *Tithebarn Ltd v Hubbard* (Lexis 7 November 1991/IRLIB 449, unreported). In this case Hubbard, a senior sales trainer, invited a successful and important salesman in the company to join him in a venture which Hubbard was thinking of setting up, apparently in competition with Tithebarn. The employment tribunal (by a majority) decided that this did not amount to a breach of the terms of the contract of employment, since there was no attempt to induce the fellow employee to breach his contract of employment. The EAT held that, although one view of the evidence was that Hubbard was seeking to undermine the loyalty of, or entice away his fellow employee, nonetheless the industrial tribunal was entitled to form the view that this was a mere discussion for the future, an intention by Hubbard to set up in business and an invitation that in due course his colleague might care to join him. *Laughton and Tithebarn* should be contrasted with *Marshall* (para 3.23) in which the employee's acts went beyond a mere intention to compete. As to what the departing employee can lawfully tell clients about his future intentions see paragraphs 10.30 to 10.31 where the meaning of the word 'solicitation' is discussed.

2(b)(iii) OTHER PREPARATIONS

3.28 The employee who wishes to set up his own business may carry out preparatory acts such as acquiring premises, ordering stationery and purchasing an off-the-shelf company. In *Robb v Green* [1895] 2 QB 1, 15 Hawkins J in a celebrated (although in some respects unhelpful) passage said:

> 'In what I have said I do not mean to convey that while the contract of service exists a person intending to enter into business for himself may not do anything by way of preparation, provided only that he does not, when serving his master, fraudulently undermine him by breaking the confidence reposed in him. For instance, he may legitimately canvass, issue his circulars, have his place of business in readiness, hire his servants etc. Each case must depend on its own circumstances.'

The passage appears too broadly stated. Maugham LJ in *Wessex Dairies Ltd v Smith* [1935] 2 KB 80, 87 (CA) said that he did not know what Hawkins J meant by 'legitimately canvas'. This seems to have been a reference to canvassing persons other than the employer's customers: *Balston v Headline Filters Ltd* (per Falconer J at page 414). Likewise it would seem that Hawkins J was not intending to sanction the sending during employment of circulars to customers of the employer.

PREPARATORY ACTIVITY DURING GARDEN LEAVE

3.29 In our view there is no lessening of the duty not to compete in the case of the employee who is not actively working, but is spending his notice period at home. In *Balston Ltd v Headline Filters Ltd* [1987] FSR 330 Scott J held that there was no reason why an employee should not while on garden leave establish a company (intended to compete with the employer after the end of the notice period), arrange for premises, order materials preparatory to the intended commencement of business and arrange for colleagues (not very many) to commence employment with the intended company. We agree that there could be no complaint as regards any of the activities referred to, even if the employee is working out his notice, except (possibly) the arranging of colleagues to commence work with the intended company – the question of soliciting colleagues has been referred to in paragraphs 3.22 to 3.24. In relation to solicitation during garden leave of orders from a customer (to be placed at the end of that period) Scott J suggested (at page 340) that there might be a distinction between an employee actively working and one on garden leave. We do not believe that there is any basis for such a distinction. Indeed at the trial of the action (*Balston Ltd v Headline Filters Ltd* [1990] FSR 385) Falconer J held (at page 416) that the competitive activity of the employee amounted to a breach of the duty of fidelity notwithstanding that he was on garden leave at the time. The position is different in relation to positive aspects of the duty of fidelity – once on garden leave the employee was not under an obligation to take steps to advance the business of the employer (Falconer J at page 416). In *Hutchings v Coinseed* [1998] IRLR 190, unusually the Court of Appeal held that it was not a repudiatory breach for a member of the 'sales support telephone staff' (who gave one month's notice, as was required under her contract of employment) to assume during the garden leave period a position with a rival of her employer. The case seems to have turned very much on its own facts. A letter by the employer was held to have varied her contract of employment – and the contract so varied was held not to contain any express or implied prohibition on the employee working for anyone else during the period of garden leave. Further, there was no allegation of breach of confidence against Miss Hutchings. Accordingly, she was entitled to maintain her claim for salary against Coinseed for the month in question.

Preparations by director employees: special case?

3.30 It should also be noted that, generally speaking, employees who are also directors are under no greater duty by virtue of that directorship with regard to preparatory activities than ordinary employees. There is no conflict of interest under the principle of *Phipps v Boardman* [1967] 2 AC 46 as long as there is no actual competitive activity during the subsistence of the directorship: *Balston Ltd v Headline Filters Ltd* [1990] FSR 385, 412, cited with approval by Blackburne J in *Framlington Group plc v Anderson and others* (unreported: Chancery Division 6 February 1995, at page 50) and by Jonathan Parker J in *Saatchi & Saatchi Company plc and others v Saatchi and others* (unreported: Chancery Division 13 February 1995, at page 33): in the latter case there was no breach when a director entered into 'heads of agreement' to acquire shares in a competing venture which would only come into full force when the director 'was free to do so', that is, free from all restrictions arising from the employment contract or directorship.

3. Duty of disclosure to the employer

3.31 During employment an employee will be the recipient of a whole variety of information which is relevant to his employer. In the majority of instances the employee will pass on the information to the employer without hesitation and therefore the question of whether or not there was a duty to do so will be irrelevant. Inevitably, however, there are times when information is not passed on, as a result of which the employer suffers a detriment of some sort and one of the issues in the ensuing litigation is whether or not a duty to disclose existed. Surprisingly, there are comparatively few authorities on the duty to disclose. Those there are concern three categories:

1   Information concerning misconduct on the part of fellow employees in which the employee himself may or may not be implicated;
2   Information relevant to the employer which the employee uses to his own advantage. This type of information is sometimes in the form of business opportunities which the employee seeks to divert to himself: diversion of business opportunities is discussed in paragraphs 3.54 to 3.64;
3   Inventions and discoveries made in the course of employment.

3(a) Misdeeds/misconduct

3.32 A contract of employment is not a contract of the utmost good faith (uberrimae fidei). An employee is not, therefore, under a duty to disclose his own misconduct: *Bell v Lever Bros Ltd* [1932] AC 161 (HL) and *Sybron Corporation v Rochem Ltd* [1983] 3 WLR 713 (CA). There is no general duty on employees to report a fellow employee's misconduct or breach of duty but an employee may have such a duty; whether or not he does depends on the circumstances of each particular case: *Swain v West (Butchers) Ltd* [1936] 3 All ER 261 (CA) applied in *Sybron*. Swain was the general manager and was found to be under an obligation to disclose unlawful orders given to him by the managing director. In *Sybron* the information was the establishment and operation by a number of employees of *Sybron* of rival businesses in competition with the company. The employee found to be under a duty to disclose was the European zone controller who was in de facto control of the European operation of Sybron and had a duty to report on the state of his zone every month. Factors of significance were: the position of the employee in question in the hierarchy, the recognised reporting procedure, and that there was a continuing fraud on the employer. Employees in managerial positions with reporting responsibilities and/or responsibilities for discipline are likely to be under a duty to disclose misdeeds of subordinate or superior colleagues. The seriousness of the conduct in question is important: where this is not obvious the employer may need to draw to the attention of the workforce the seriousness which he attaches to the particular conduct. In *Distillers Company (Bottling Services) Ltd v Gardner* [1982] IRLR 47 Gardner, a loader who was employed together with other loaders, was dismissed for not reporting pilfering and abuse of alcohol by colleagues. The EAT appear to have regarded Gardner as being obliged to report the matter to his employer and that his failure to report an earlier incident of pilfering warranted a final warning. However, in relation to a later incident which led to dismissal, the EAT (inconsistently) said that it was asking a lot of an employee to report misdemeanours of his colleagues, and if this was to be the rule it should be clearly spelt out.

3.33 Express terms in the contract of employment may alone or in conjunction with the implied duty give rise to the duty to disclose. Indeed the express term may impose a wider obligation to disclose than the implied duty. In *Swain* the contract provided that Swain would 'do all in his power to promote, extend and develop the interests of the company'. Greer LJ said that this imposed on Swain an obligation to report to the Board 'any acts not in the interest of the company'. In other words the duty was not limited to the misdeeds of his fellow employees.

3.34 An employee under an obligation to disclose the misdeeds of his fellow employees must do so even if he thereby incriminates himself: *Swain* and *Sybron*. In *Sybron* Kerr LJ (at page 729) was of the view that the principle in *Bell v Lever Bros Ltd* that an employee is under no duty to disclose his own misdeeds did not necessarily extend to cases of fraudulent concealment of misdeeds, since the absence of fraud was stressed in the speeches in the House of Lords (the jury having negatived fraud); see also: *Horcal v Gatland* [1984] IRLR 288. As to the duty to declare own misdeeds, in our view a fiduciary such as a director is not in a different position from the ordinary employee – indeed *Bell v Lever Brothers* was a case involving a director (albeit of a different company in the group).

3(b)   Information relevant to the employer concealed and used to the employee's advantage

3.35 Two examples of this arose in *Sanders v Parry* [1967] 1 WLR 753. In that case (see paras 3.21 and 3.22) Parry was an Assistant Solicitor employed in the practice of Sanders. Parry received an unsolicited offer from one of Sanders' clients, Tully, for whom he worked, that if he left and set up his own practice, Tully would transfer the bulk of his work to Parry. After Parry had decided to accept Tully's offer and was making plans for his departure one of Sanders' secretaries mentioned to Parry that she was dissatisfied with her job. Parry offered her employment with him which she accepted. In considering Parry's conduct Havers J ruled that Parry should have disclosed to the claimant the dissatisfaction of the secretary, thereby affording the claimant an opportunity to retain her services. On what Parry should have disclosed, if anything, in relation to Tully's offer Havers J said at page 765:

> '... if Mr Tully had expressed any dissatisfaction as to the position the defendant should have found out any grievance which Mr Tully thought he had and should have gone to the [claimant] ...'

3.36 An interesting question arises on the duty of disclosure, if any, of employees who intend to leave in concert. The question arose in *GD Searle & Co Ltd v Celltech Ltd* [1982] FSR 92 but since the injunction sought was confined to restraining activities after employment had ended the Court did not have to consider the implied duty of fidelity. Cumming Bruce LJ commented:

> 'In the absence of restrictive covenants, there is nothing in the general law to prevent a number of employees in concert deciding to leave their employer and set themselves up in competition with him.'

That comment was obiter. Whether there is a duty to disclose in any particular case depends on a number of factors, primarily:

- Whether the employees' plans involve any misdeeds by them (such as removal of confidential information);
- Whether the employee whose conduct is in question has reporting duties in relation to the other employees who are party to the plan. In practice this will mean that normally only senior staff will be at risk of breaching the duty of fidelity (or express reporting duties) although not necessarily only

in relation to their subordinates: in *Swain* a general manager was held to be under a duty to disclose the misdeeds of the managing director;
● Whether the impact of the departure on the employer is likely to be significant, as for example where an entire team is leaving.

3.37 A director-employee is not under an obligation to disclose to the company (legitimate) preparatory steps which he is taking to compete with the company after termination of his employment or directorship: *Framlington* (at page 50) relying on *Balston* (Falconer J) at page 412: see paragraph 3.30.

3(c) Inventions, discoveries and copyright

3.38 Until 1978 it was uncontroversial that an employee was required to disclose to his employer inventions and discoveries which he, the employee, makes in the course of employment. In the absence of agreement to the contrary these belonged to the employer: in *Triplex Safety Glass Co Ltd v Scorah* [1938] Ch 211 Farwell J stated that this was the position where the invention or discovery was made in the course of employment by an employee during working hours and using the employer's materials. The decision in *British Syphon Co Ltd v Homewood* [1956] 2 All ER 897 was on a different basis. In that case Roxburgh J held that it was contrary to the duty of fidelity for an employee who was employed as a technical adviser to advise on all aspects of the business, including the manufacture of soda water syphons, during employment to make an invention (an improved form of soda syphon) and dispose of it as he saw fit. No consideration was given to whether the invention was made during working hours or using the employer's materials or confidential information; further, the ex-employee only sought to exploit the invention after termination of the relevant employment. The reason for the decision was that the employee should not put himself in a position in which he would have personal reasons for not giving to his employers the best possible advice. However, the Patents Act 1977 (in this paragraph all references to section numbers refer to the 1977 Act) introduced an element of uncertainty into the law. By Section 39(1) all pre-existing common law rules are either swept away completely or are to be applied with great caution: *Harris's Patent* [1985] RPC 19. An 'invention' (not defined in the 1977 Act) either belongs to the employer by virtue of two separate two-stage tests respectively applicable to employees who, in brief, are 'paid to invent' and employees who, by virtue of their (higher) responsibilities, have a special obligation to further their employer's undertaking. All other inventions belong to the employee: Section 39(2) of the 1977 Act; see further paragraph 3.46 below. 'Invention' means much more than 'patentable invention': *Viziball's Application* [1988] RPC 213 and may indeed in suitable fields such as electronics and software encompass things also covered by copyright, compare 'all other purposes' in Section 39(1); and generally see Section 39(3) combined with Section 43(4). Finally, by Section 42(2) a term in a contract is unenforceable to the extent that it diminishes the employee's rights in an invention.

3.38a Hence a duty to disclose to the employer inventions which by Section 39(2) belong to the employee might be seen as a diminution of rights, given possibly wide interpretation of 'rights'. How then can an employer claim rights in an invention if he is unaware of its existence? One practical solution may be based on the implied term of the employee's duty of fidelity which in this context may mean a requirement to disclose for the initally limited purpose of determination of ownership; and also on the need to give the contract of employment business efficacy. Employers requiring such disclosure should bear in mind the need to maintain the confidentiality of the employee's submission pending determination of its ownership; see *Prout v British Gas* [1992] FSR 478, from the neighbouring field of suggestion schemes where an employee's submission was held to give rise to a contractually enforceable obligation of confidence or alternatively an equitable obligation arising from the fiduciary relationship between the employee and the employer. There is also the possibility of a claim for unfair constructive dismissal by failure to treat the employee reasonably.

3(c)(i) EMPLOYEE WORKS AND INTELLECTUAL PROPERTY RIGHTS IN THEM: STATUTORILY IMPLIED TERMS

3.39 While the protection of intellectual property rights in the context of employment covenants goes beyond the scope of this book, employers should be aware of the effect of legislation which effectively implies into the contract of employment provisions as to the ownership of intellectual property generated during the employment relationship.

3(c)(ii) COPYRIGHT WORKS

3.40 Copyright exists in a very wide range of material, from illustrations and computer programs to internal memoranda written for an employer by employees and others. Section 11(1) of the Copyright, Designs and Patents Act 1988 provides that the author of a work is the first owner of copyright in it. Without more, this would mean that an employee engaged to write software for a software house employer would own copyright in any software written by him for the employer (but note that by Section 9(3), for computer-generated works the 'author' is taken to be the person who made the arrangements necessary for the creation of the work).

3.41 However, Section 11(1) is made subject (so far as is relevant to employment) to Section 11(2), which provides as follows: where a literary, dramatic, musical or artistic work is made by an employee in the course of his or her employment, the employer is the first owner of copyright in the work, subject to any contrary agreement between them.

3.42 But Section 11(2) applies only to those who are employed under contracts of service or apprenticeship: Section 178 of the 1988 Act. The difference between a contract of employment and one for services is dealt with in paragraphs 2.4 to 2.26. The employer and freelancer/consultant may, however, expressly agree that the employer shall be the first owner of the copyright.

3.43 Assuming an employer can show that the worker concerned was an employee, another hurdle that the employer must overcome is to show that the work concerned was generated in the course of that employee's employment. This might seem an obvious point, and one that is easily disposed of by the employer. Unfortunately, this is not always so. In the leading case on this point, *Byrne v Statist Co* [1914] 1 KB 622, Mr Byrne, the employee, was on the permanent editorial staff of *The Financial Times*. His regular working hours were 11.00 am to 6.00 pm. He was asked by *The Financial Times* to translate, for a separate fee, the text of a speech from Portuguese to English. The English version was to be printed in *The Financial Times*. Mr Byrne prepared the translation in his own time, that is, outside his normal working hours. The court decided that he had not produced the translation within his ordinary duties as an employee of *The Financial Times*. In other words, the work was not produced in the course of his employment and, consequently, Mr Byrne was the owner of the copyright in the translation.

3.44 It follows that employers should, wherever possible, make specific provision in contracts with consultants and other freelancers for ownership of, and dealings with, works created by those consultants and freelancers. It is prudent for employers, too, to make similar provision in their standard contracts of employment. Outline provisions are suggested in paragraph 4.31. For a detailed account of the law of copyright and associated moral rights under Chapter IV of Part I of the Copyright, Designs and Patents Act 1988 in the context of employment, readers are referred to Laddie, Prescott and Vitoria, *The Modern Law of Copyright and Designs* (2nd edn, 1995) Butterworths, Ch 4.

3(c)(iii) OTHER EMPLOYEE WORKS AND INTELLECTUAL PROPERTY RIGHTS IN THEM

3.45 Design rights – Section 213 of the Copyright, Designs and Patents Act 1988 established a new, unregistered, design right in the original design of an article. Ordinarily, the designer is the first owner of the design right: Section 215(1) of the 1988 Act. However, in contrast to the position of literary or artistic works enjoying copyright protection, where a design is created in pursuance of a commission, the commissioner is the first owner of any resulting design right: Section 215(2). For example, where an employer engages a freelance worker to produce a design, the employer as commissioner will be first owner of the design. Where a design is created by an employee in the course of his employment, the employer will be first owner of any resulting design right: Section 215(3). (Note that by Section 214(2) of the 1988 Act, the 'designer' of the commercially increasingly important computer-generated work is taken to be the person who made the arrangements necessary for the creation of the design.) The principles determining whether or not a worker is an employee and issues such as whether the design was created in the course of employment will be similar to those applicable to the creation of copyright material by employees in the course of their employment. The ownership of registered designs is dealt with by Section 2 of the Registered Designs Act 1949, as amended by Section 267 of the Copyright, Designs and Patents Act 1988. Ownership of registered designs follows the pattern of ownership of unregistered design rights, as outlined above.

3.46 Employee inventions – Section 39 of the Patents Act 1977 sets out an all-embracing code to determine who, as between employer and employee, owns rights in inventions arising out of their relationship. There are two situations addressed by Section 39.

3.47 The first deals with inventions made in the course of the normal duties of the employee or in the course of duties falling outside his or her normal duties, but specifically assigned to him, and where, in either case, the circumstances suggest that the invention might reasonably have been expected to result from the carrying out of those duties: Section 39(1)(a) of the 1977 Act. In effect, this situation covers junior employees and those in middle-management positions.

3.48 The second situation deals with inventions made in the course of the employee's duties and where, at the time of making the invention, because of the nature of the employee's duties and the particular responsibilities arising from the nature of those duties, he has 'a special obligation to further the interests' of the employer's business: Section 39(1)(b). Because of the need for the special obligation mentioned in this provision, this situation effectively covers senior employees and directors.

3.49 In each of these situations, any inventions covered will belong to the employer: see, generally, *Harris' Patent* [1985] RPC 19. In any other situation, inventions arising out of the employment relationship will belong to the employee: Section 39(2).

3.50 Having provided for the ownership of inventions, the Patents Act 1977 goes on to give inventive employees the right in certain circumstances to compensation for the 'outstanding' benefit gained by the employer from the *patent* derived from the invention: *Memco-Med's Patent* [1992] RPC 403: Section 40(1). More particularly, compensation will be paid where a patent has been granted for the employee's invention which, by virtue of Section 39(1) of the 1977 Act always belonged to the employer, the patent itself is (taking into account such factors as the size and nature of the employer's business) 'of outstanding benefit' to the employer, and it is just that the employee should be awarded compensation. There is also provision for compensation where by Section 39(2) the employee (and not the employer) is the first owner of the patented invention, the employee then sells the ownership in the patent or grants an exclusive licence under it to the employer, but the employee's benefit from the sale or licensing of his or her rights is 'inadequate' in comparison to the benefit derived by the employer from the patent: Section 40(2). There are detailed provisions for determining the level of compensation payable by the employer. Employers cannot in the employment contract (or, indeed, in any other contract) require employees, before the employees create any invention, to contract out of the benefits provided for by this statutory code in relation to those inventions and the patents for them: Section 42(2). This is made even more explicit in Section 40(4) in relation to inventions originally belonging to the employee and subsequently covered by Section 40(2). However, this rule against contracting out does not derogate from any duty of confidentiality owed by the employee to his or her employer: Section 42(3). In other words, while employees may benefit from the inventions they create for their employers, they must still preserve their employers' trade secrets and other confidential information.

3(c)(iv)   SUMMARY

3.51 The above account of the law relating to designs and inventions created by employees is necessarily brief, and readers are advised to consult specialist texts on industrial and other designs and patents. The law of designs and employee inventions is complex and, as in the case of copyright, contains many traps for the unwary. Employers should seek specialist legal advice in this area (as well as in the copyright area). In addition (and having taken such advice) employers should in their standard contracts of employment make specific provision for the ownership and use of registered and unregistered design rights, copyright, patents and all other intellectual property rights that arise out of employment (in the latter case, taking into account the mandatory nature of the Patents Act 1977 as regards employee inventions). An outline of certain, basic, provisions is suggested in paragraph 4.31.

4. Duty not to make a secret profit

3.52 An employee is under a duty not to make a secret profit for himself from the use of assets of the company, including its information and opportunities: *Boston Deep Sea Fishing and Ice Co v Ansell* (1888) 39 Ch D 339. In that case Ansell, on behalf of his employer, Boston, made purchases from another company in which (unknown to his employer) he held shares. Ansell was held liable to account to Boston for commission received by him from the seller on those sales. Although this was a case of a (managing) director breaching his fiduciary duty, in our view the principle is equally applicable to breaches of fidelity: see *Reading v Attorney General* [1951] AC 507, 516, 517 (where an army sergeant was held liable to account for bribes received). See also *British Syphon Co Ltd v Homewood* [1956] 2 All ER 897 (para 3.38) where the invention made by the employee was held to belong in equity to the employer because the employee had breached his duty of fidelity by placing himself in a position of conflict between duty and personal interest. (See below, however, the position in relation to exploitation of corporate opportunities after termination of employment.)

3.53 It should be noted that not only director-employees of companies may be regarded as fiduciaries. Senior employees who are not directors may be under a fiduciary duty not to make secret profits: *Canadian Aero Services Ltd v O'Malley* (1973) 40 DLR (3d) 371 (Can SC).

4(a) Diverting business opportunities

3.54 It is a breach of fiduciary duty for directors to take for themselves the benefit of a contract which they have ostensibly been negotiating on behalf of the company whose interests they ought to have been protecting, and if they do so, they hold the benefit in trust for the company: *Cook v Deeks* [1916] 1 AC 554 (PC).

3.55 The employer has to establish:

• That what the directors did was so related to the affairs of the company that it can properly be said to have been done in the course of their management and in utilisation of their opportunities and special knowledge as directors; and

• That what they did resulted in a profit to themselves: *Regal (Hastings) Ltd v Gulliver* (decided in 1942 and reported at [1967] 2 AC 134 (HL) per Lord MacMillan at page 153).

3.56 In the same case Lord Russell explained the wide implications of the rule as follows:

'The rule of equity that insists on those who by use of a fiduciary position make a profit, being liable to account for that profit, in no way depends on proof of fraud or absence of bona fides; or upon such questions or considerations as whether the profit would or should otherwise have gone to the [claimant]; or whether the profiteer was under a duty to obtain the source of the profit for the [claimant]; or whether he took a risk or acted as he did for the benefit of the [claimant]; or whether the [claimant] has in fact been damaged or benefited from his actions. The liability arises from the mere fact of a profit having, in the stated circumstances, been made.'

See also *Boardman v Phipps* [1967] 2 AC 46 and contrast *Peso Silver Mines Ltd (NPL) v Cropper* (1966) 58 DLR (2d) 1 (Canadian Supreme Court), in which it was held that a director who exploited a corporate opportunity which the company had bona fide rejected was not in breach of fiduciary duty. Accordingly, it is unwise for a director to exploit knowledge or opportunities learnt in his capacity as a director, unless (possibly) the company has bona fide rejected that opportunity. Even in the latter case there may be a duty to disclose the exploitation of the opportunity, for example, if it involves an interest in a competing venture.

4(b) Exploiting maturing business opportunities after termination of employment

3.57 Here a distinction must be made between executive directors and possibly senior employees (on the one hand) who are subject to a fiduciary duty and on the other hand (more junior) employees who are not subject to a fiduciary duty.

4(b)(i) DIRECTORS (AND SENIOR EMPLOYEES)

3.58 W here an employee who is a fiduciary resigns in order to exploit a corporate opportunity of the employer, he may in certain circumstances be held liable to account for all profits made. In *Canadian Aero Services Ltd v O'Malley* (1973) 40 DLR (3d) 371 Laskey J (at page 391) identified the factors relevant to the question of whether there was a breach of duty as including:

- The position or office held;
- The nature of the corporate opportunity;
- Its ripeness;
- The specificity of the opportunity;
- The officer's relation to the opportunity;
- The amount of knowledge possessed;
- The circumstances in which it was obtained and whether it was special or indeed even private;
- The factor of time in the continuation of fiduciary duty where the alleged breach occurs after termination of the relationship with the company;
- The circumstances in which the relationship was terminated, for example, whether by resignation or termination by the employer.

3.59 The circumstances in which liability may be incurred are illustrated by the well-known case of *Industrial Development Consultants Ltd v Cooley* [1972] 2 All ER 162. Cooley had been the managing director of IDC under a contract which contained no express covenants. As part of his duties he entered into negotiations with the Gas Board for IDC to provide architectural services in relation to certain projects. IDC's proposal was rejected. The Gas Board contacted Cooley and made it clear to him that he had a good chance of getting the work but that the Gas Board were only interested in employing Cooley privately and that they did not want any trouble with his employers. Cooley realised that in order to obtain this work it was necessary to free himself from IDC as soon as possible. He accordingly made false representations about the state of his health to IDC who accordingly agreed to release him within a matter of days from his employment. Five days after Cooley ceased to be managing director the Gas Board offered him employment as project manager of four projects. This work was in substance the same work which IDC had unsuccessfully attempted to obtain. Roskill J held that Cooley had acted in breach of fiduciary duty in that he had failed to pass on to IDC all information which he had received in the course of his dealings with the Gas Board. Instead he had embarked on a deliberate course of conduct which had put his personal interests as a potential contracting party with the Gas Board in direct conflict with his pre-existing duty as managing director. He was accordingly in breach of his fiduciary duty in failing to pass to IDC all relevant information received in the course of his negotiations with the Gas Board and in guarding it for his own personal purposes and profit. He was held liable to account to IDC for all the benefit he had received and would receive under the contract with the Gas Board.

3.60 The following points from *Cooley* are worthy of emphasis:

● It was irrelevant that:
   – IDC would never itself have been able to obtain the benefit of the contracts in question;
   – The approach was made by the Gas Board to Cooley and not the other way round;
   – The contract was obtained after the termination of Cooley's employment–because he obtained the contract as result of work carried out by him while he was managing director and he resigned in order to obtain the contract for himself.
● It was significant that:
   – Cooley was employed to obtain the contract in question for IDC: he was still managing director when he met the representative of the Gas Board in connection with their approach to him and when he prepared a document in order to get the work for himself;
   – IDC was very interested in the work which ultimately went to Cooley.

3.61 See also *Cranleigh Precision Engineering Ltd v Bryant* [1964] 3 All ER 289 and *Thomas Marshall (Exports) Ltd v Guinle* [1979] 1 Ch 227 in which Sir Robert Megarry VC granted interlocutory non-solicitation/dealing injunctions inter alia on the basis that there was a good arguable case that the effect of the director's fiduciary duty was that where he resigned his employment he could not claim instant freedom to use his relationship with suppliers and customers (which he had established on behalf of the company) for his own benefit (pages 245B–E and 247D–E).

3.62 Also in *Island Export Finance Ltd v Umunna* [1986] BCLC 460 (broadly following *Canadian Aero Services*) Hutchinson J held that a director's fiduciary duty does not necessarily come to an end when he ceases to be a director: he was precluded from diverting to himself a maturing business opportunity which his company was actively pursuing even after his resignation, where the resignation was prompted or influenced by a desire to acquire the opportunity for himself. On the facts the ex-employer's claim failed because:

● The company's hope of obtaining further orders was not a maturing business opportunity;

- The company was not actively pursuing further orders either when the defendant resigned or subsequently when he obtained the orders;
- The employee's resignation was not prompted or influenced by a wish to acquire for himself the orders in question.

Hutchinson J was of the view (page 481) that it went too far to hold that former directors were liable to account for profits wherever information acquired by them as such led them to the source from which they subsequently, perhaps as a result of prolonged fresh initiative, acquired business:

> 'It would, it seems to me, be surprising to find that directors alone, because of the fiduciary nature of their relationship with the company, were restrained from exploiting after they had ceased to be such any opportunity of which they had acquired knowledge while directors. Directors, no less than employees, acquire a general fund of knowledge and expertise in the course of their work, and it is plainly in the public interest that they should be free to exploit it in a new position.'

(The actual decision was reversed in the Court of Appeal on fresh evidence: 8 January 1989 unreported: *Palmer Company Law* (25th edn) para 8.538 footnote 41.)

3.63 It is accordingly necessary to look at all the facts of the case, in particular the factors listed by Laskey J in *Canadian Aero Services* (see para 3.58) when deciding whether or not there has been a diversion of a business opportunity for which the ex-employee is liable to account.

3.64 Finally, a director or senior employee is in breach of fiduciary obligation in respect of business opportunities which come to him in his capacity as a director or which he is employed (as in *Industrial Development Consultants Ltd v Cooley*) to obtain for the benefit of the company. It is unlikely that (except where he is employed to obtain such opportunities for the benefit of the company), he would be precluded from exploiting for his own benefit opportunities which come to him in a private capacity.

4(b)(ii) OTHER EMPLOYEES

3.65 Apart from express restrictions in the contract of employment, the only bar on activity by an employee (who is not a fiduciary) after employment is that he may not use trade secrets of the employer: *Faccenda Chicken Ltd v Fowler* [1986] 3 WLR 288 (CA) and *J A Mont (UK) Ltd v Mills* [1993] IRLR 172. Further, if the information constituting the corporate opportunity does not itself qualify as a trade secret, it will not assist the claimant to argue that this information is protected by virtue of it being a corporate opportunity: *Ixora Trading Incorporated v Jones* [1990] FSR 251. In this case Mummery J held that the information contained in a feasibility study was not a trade secret, being merely information of an organisational nature and of the day to day management of the claimant's business (see Ch 5). The claimant's attempt to salvage this part of its case by referring to the feasibility study as a maturing business opportunity within the meaning of the *Canadian Aero Services Ltd* and *Island Export Finance Ltd* cases failed in that the study was held to be too vague and unspecific to be caught by any fiduciary duty.

5. Pre-employment disclosure of confidential information

3.66 Interesting problems may arise in the pre-employment period, particularly in relation to the imparting of confidential information by the proposed employer or employee during discussions about the possible appointment. The employer who is proposing to employ a high status employee may reveal confidential information about the business, for example confidential financial information, in order to enable the proposed employee to value a share option offered by way of a 'sweetener'. On the other hand the prospective employee may reveal confidential information regarding the identity and volume of business received from customers of his present employers whom the proposed employee expects will follow him to his new employment. This may amount to a breach of confidence and a breach of the duty of fidelity vis-à-vis the present employer, except in the unlikely event of his having consented to disclosure, and may therefore render the prospective employer vulnerable to proceedings. The usual principles governing the definition and the protection of such information (which are dealt with in Ch 5) will apply.

3.67 For the proposed employer contemplating disclosing important confidential information it is well worth his considering entering into a written confidentiality agreement with the potential employee before any confidential information is revealed. Such an agreement will be particularly important where the potential employee is currently working for a competitor who could cause significant damage to the proposed employer were he aware of the confidential information. The confidentiality agreement should include the following elements:

• Identify the information to be treated as confidential
• Limit the use of that information by the potential employee solely to the pre-employment negotiations and employment if it results
• Prohibit disclosure of the information to any third party other than financial and legal advisers in confidence
• Require delivery up of documents and all copies containing the information and irrevocable deletion of the information incorporated into any computer system immediately upon the breakdown of the negotiations.

Where the negotiations result in employment the employer should also ensure that the contractual obligations on confidentiality and return of property are sufficiently widely drawn to catch information disclosed pre-commencement of employment. For further detail on suggested contractual provisions on confidentiality and return of property see paragraphs 4.30 and 4.88 to 4.91.

3.68 It is not appropriate for there to be a confidentiality agreement along the lines suggested above where it is the potential employee intending to disclose a current employer's confidential information. Such an agreement would be strong prima facie evidence of a breach of the duty of fidelity by the potential employee and possibly also of an inducement of breach of contract by the proposed employer. Hardly the sort of evidence either of those parties would want to create.

Preparatory activity during employment to compete after employment

The following table sets out the main types of permitted and prohibited activity (where there is no express prohibition).

Permitted (in employee's own time)	Prohibited
Seeking work with a competitor;	Anything in employer's time;
Indicating an intention to compete in the future;	Soliciting employer's customers;
Arranging premises;	Soliciting employer's exclusive suppliers (or other suppliers to employer of scarce commodities);
Ordering stationery;	
Purchasing off-the-shelf company;	Entertaining offers from customers;
Hiring staff (query excluding fellow employees);	Possibly, offering work to other employees;
Arranging finance with a disinterested third party;	Copying or memorising trade secrets or confidential information.
Entering into heads of agreement to takes shares in a competing company when free of restraints (of contract or as a director).	

Chapter 4

Express terms of the contract of employment

Introduction

4.1 Chapter 3 examined the various aspects of the duty of fidelity which restrict competitive activities during employment. While those aspects of the duty of fidelity are important – indeed often claims against employees are based solely on breach of the implied duty – they are no substitute for properly drafted express terms. Through such terms not only can the employer gain additional protection against competition, he also acquires the advantages that:

- The employee is fixed with notice of his obligations; and
- There is far less uncertainty surrounding the enforcement of express terms.

The use of express terms may also be of benefit to the employee, in the sense that he knows precisely what is and what is not permitted.

4.2 In this Chapter we look at the various types of express term available to protect the employer from competition until the contract of employment terminates (express terms applicable after termination are dealt with in Chapters 9 to 11). The employer should give careful consideration to inclusion of these express terms. There will, of course, be cases where particular terms would be inappropriate or commercially unacceptable. However, some of the terms, particularly those which deal with termination and matters connected with termination, are universally advisable and an employer ignores them at his peril. There are three basic categories of express term:

- Those which record obligations included within the implied duty of fidelity or extend those obligations;
- Those which define the employee's role; and
- Those which pertain to termination of employment.

1. Terms recording/extending obligations included within the duty of fidelity

4.3 One of the inherent problems with implied terms is their imprecision and the consequent uncertainty of their scope. As a result, arguments as to whether or not a particular activity is a breach of the employee's implied obligations are commonplace. Furthermore, trends change so that predicting the precise ambit of a term to be implied in years to come is a difficult and rather precarious task. Because of this uncertainty it is now common, and generally thought to be desirable, to translate into express terms a general statement of the employee's duty of fidelity and at least some of the specific aspects implied by that duty. In addition, in some instances those obligations may be extended; see for example express terms in relation to outside activities: see paragraphs 4.16 to 4.22.

4.4   An employer contemplating this course of action, which we recommend, should bear two general points in mind:

● The relationship between the express terms he includes and the terms implied by the duty of fidelity. In particular, can the inclusion of an express term mean the employer is deprived of relying on a corresponding or lesser obligation imposed by the duty of fidelity? This question was answered in the negative by Farwell J in *Triplex Safety Glass Co Ltd v Scorah* [1938] 1 Ch 211 pages 216–217. See also *Provident Financial Group plc v Hayward* [1989] 3 All ER 298 where the express term was struck down but the employer was nonetheless held to be entitled to rely on the implied duty of fidelity. As a matter of caution, however, some draftsmen do specifically provide that the express terms are incorporated without prejudice to the implied duty of fidelity. Although in our view this practice is not strictly necessary, such a provision cannot be harmful and may be of some benefit in putting the issue beyond argument. For the draftsman who wishes to include a provision of this sort the following is a sample clause:

PRECEDENT – SENIOR EXECUTIVE

*For the avoidance of doubt the terms set out in Clauses [**insert clause numbers**] are included without prejudice to the Executive's implied duty of fidelity.*

● The doctrine of restraint of trade can, in exceptional circumstances, apply during the contract of employment. This point was acknowledged by Lord Reid in *Esso Petroleum Co Ltd v Harper's Garage (Stourport) Ltd* [1968] AC 269 [HL] at page 294. More recently it arose in the case of *Electronic Data Systems Ltd v Hubble* (Lexis 20 November 1987, unreported) where the Court of Appeal allowed an appeal against an order for summary judgment for repayment of training expenses on the ground that Hubble had an arguable case that the terms of repayment amounted to a restraint of trade. Mustill LJ delivering the judgment of the Court relied on the general principles enunciated in *Macaulay v Schroeder Music Publishing Co Ltd* [1974] 1 WLR 1308. The exceptional circumstances that are likely to give rise to the doctrine applying are either that the effect of the contract is to sterilise rather than utilise the employee's skills and abilities or, as in the case of *Electronic Data Systems Ltd v Hubble*, where the employee is left with no option but to continue working for the employer.

4.5   The employer should consider including express terms covering the following:

● A general statement of the employee's duty of fidelity;
● Working hours;
● Control of the employee's outside activities during employment;

- A prohibition on encouraging other employees to leave;
- Disclosure of information and reporting procedures;
- Confidentiality and the protection of trade secrets; and
- Patents, copyright and certain other intellectual property.

In every case the precise drafting of the express term will depend on the circumstances and in particular the role and status of the employee. Included in the following paragraphs are precedent clauses appropriate for a senior employee engaged on the terms of a Service Agreement. While the precedents will require changes to style where they are to appear, for example, in a Staff Handbook appropriate to a more junior employee, the basic principles will remain substantially the same.

4.6   In each of the precedent clauses references to the 'Group' should only be included in appropriate cases and the term should be defined carefully to reflect the organisations for which the employer is seeking protection. For example, the 'Group' may consist exclusively of companies or partnerships or it may be a mix of those two or include, perhaps, a local authority. The mere fact the 'Group' consists only of companies does not obviate the need for a carefully drawn definition of which companies are included. In English law there is no single definition of 'Group' which could operate as a default option. By omitting a definition the employer will not have identified which companies he intended be encompassed by the term thereby leaving scope for argument by the employee. For the purpose of the precedents included in this Chapter we have assumed that the 'Group' consists only of companies.

1(a)   A general statement of the duty of fidelity

4.7   Although this duty is implied into every contract of employment there are three reasons why a general statement of the duty should be expressly incorporated. First, it draws the matter specifically to the employee's attention, a deterrent to competitive activities in itself; secondly, where only certain aspects of the implied duty are expressly incorporated, it puts it beyond argument that there was no intention to exclude the entire duty in favour of those particular aspects; thirdly, if formulated in a negative as well as a positive way it may found the basis of an injunction: *Provident Financial Group plc v Hayward* [1989] 3 All ER 298.

PRECEDENT – SENIOR EXECUTIVE

At all times during the continuance of this Agreement the Executive shall use his best endeavours to promote and protect the interests of the Company [and the Group] and shall faithfully and diligently perform such duties and exercise such powers as may from time to time be assigned to or vested in him and shall not do anything that is harmful to the Company [or any other company in the Group].

Note: The word 'Group' should be defined in the Service Agreement; see paragraph 4.6.

1(b)   Working hours

4.8   As we saw in Ch 3 when considering the implied duty of fidelity, there is a distinction between the hours the employee has contracted to work for the employer and the employee's spare time. In the former case there is an absolute prohibition on any competitive activity whilst in the latter case the employee is merely prohibited from doing anything which may cause serious damage to the employer.

4.9   A commonly encountered problem is identifying what hours are the employer's time and what is the employee's spare time. This is particularly so in the case of senior executives and those on flexitime. Section 1(4)(c) Employment Rights Act 1996 requires the employer to notify the employee of any terms and conditions relating to hours of work including 'normal working hours'. There is an exception to this: Section 2(1) Employment Rights Act 1996 provides that the employer may simply state that there are no particulars under Section 1(4)(c). In most cases, however, some details can be given and because of the distinction between the employee's working time and his spare time, from the perspective of limiting competition it is desirable to have the most specific working hours provision possible.

4.10   In addition, with the maximum average 48-hour week (Regulation 4, Working Time Regulations 1998) applying to most employees, from 1 October 1998 the identification of working hours became much more important. To enforce the limit, the Working Time Regulations impose stringent record-keeping requirements which apply even where an employee has agreed to opt out of the 48-hour week (Regulations 5 and 9 respectively). To comply with these record-keeping obligations some employers have already tightened up their working hours provisions and others are in the process of doing so.

4.11   One particularly knotty problem that arises in the context of senior employees is whether the employer wants to try and take advantage of their being excluded from the majority of the Working Time Regulations 1998 on the ground that their working time is 'not measured or pre-determined or can be determined by the worker himself' (Regulation 20(a)). The advantages to the employer of the employee falling within this exception are threefold (1) the employer does not have to concern himself with the bulk of the Working Time Regulations (2) he does not have to obtain an opt out agreement from the employee nor (3) contend with the risk of the employee giving notice to terminate such an agreement. The disadvantage, in the context of limiting competition, is that to support the contention that the employee is within the excluded category, his hours of work clause will need to be drawn very widely. The hours of work clause will probably be on the basis that there are no normal working hours and that the employee is required to devote such hours to the business of the employer as are necessary to discharge his duties.

4.12   In short, the employer will have to choose between clarity on working hours thereby enhancing his chances of a successful claim based on breach of the employee's contractual obligations and/or duty of fidelity or escaping the rigours of the Working Time Regulations. Bearing in mind the subject matter of this book, we favour the first option coupled, where possible, with an opt out agreement under Regulation 5 of the Working Time Regulations. Our remaining comments on working hours proceed on the assumption that the first option is being pursued. However, it must be noted that there is currently a proposal to relax some aspects of the Working Time Regulations 1998 through the, currently in draft, Working Time Regulations 1999. The final extent of those later Regulations and how they will impact on drafting hours of work clauses cannot be predicted at the moment. For the time being, the safest course is for employers to proceed only on the basis of the 1998 Regulations.

DRAFTING

4.13 Drafting hours of work clauses can be difficult. The key to success is careful thought as to what the basic hours are likely to be and the degree of flexibility the employer wants to incorporate. Employers should be realistic about what they expect, particularly bearing in mind the constraints imposed by the Working Time Regulations 1998. Clauses which appear to require the employee to spend his entire time at work are clearly unrealistic and will be of no assistance in any dispute as to whether something was done in the employer's or the employee's time. Furthermore, hours of work clauses need to be kept up to date to ensure that they accord with the employer's current practice. For employees for whom overtime is appropriate, the employer needs to decide whether overtime will be compulsory or voluntary. If it is to be compulsory, it is normally best to provide for a short period of notice to be given of the requirement to work overtime, save in the case of emergency or exceptional needs of the business.

PRECEDENT – SENIOR EXECUTIVE

The Executive shall devote the whole of his time and attention and abilities during normal business hours and at such other times as the Company or his duties may reasonably require to the business and affairs of the Company [and the Group].

Note: The phrase 'normal business hours' and the term 'Group' should be defined in the Service Agreement; on the later point see paragraph 4.6.

4.14 Finally one associated point arising from the Working Time Regulations which is relevant in the context of working time is holidays. For the first time in English law the Working Time Regulations give employees a right to paid holidays (Regulation 13). The Working Time Regulations also set out 'a procedural mechanism' for the taking of holiday from which the parties can 'opt out' through a 'relevant agreement' as defined in the Working Time Regulations. Since the periods of notice the employee must give of his wish to take holiday are very short, basically twice the length of the holiday to be taken, employers would be well advised to ensure that they have a 'relevant agreement' permitting more commercial time frames. The relevance of the issue of when holiday can be taken in the context of limiting competitive activity is that anything that weakens the employer's position in terms of controlling working time is potentially disadvantageous.

1(c) Control of outside activities

4.15 Having defined what the employee's working hours are, the employer has taken the first step in controlling the employee's activities. Provided the drafting of the provision is correct, he has ensured that it would be a breach of the employee's implied duty of good faith to do anything of a competitive nature during those hours: *Thomas Marshall (Exports) Ltd v Guinle* [1979] 1 Ch 227. In addition, by providing that the employee must devote his whole time and attention to the employer's business during those hours the employer has also prohibited non-competitive activities.

4.16 What additional steps the employer takes to control the employee's outside activities will largely depend on the status of the particular employee, the access he has to confidential information and the likelihood of his being a serious threat either as a competitor or working with a competitor. In assessing the latter point employers should always bear in mind the possibility that the employee may set up in competition with fellow employees or may work for a competitor with other of the employer's employees. The employer should not look at the employee only as an individual. It is not clear to what extent it is permissible to prevent an employee from undertaking preparatory competitive activity (for example, purchasing an off-the-shelf company) which would not amount to a breach of the duty of fidelity (see paras 3.26 to 3.30). Arguably, such a prohibition might be struck down as being an unlawful restraint of trade.

4.17 In every case the employer should consider the inclusion of an express term restricting the employee's spare time activities. That term may be a total prohibition on outside business activities or a ban on certain defined activities only. It may also provide that activities are permissible where the prior consent of the employer is given and that such consent will not be unreasonably withheld. On these formulations two questions arise:

- Should the employer choose a total or partial ban?
- Should a consent provision be included?

TOTAL V PARTIAL BAN?

4.18 As a general rule, where the employee works full time for the employer (full time in the colloquial sense and not as used in the Employment Rights Act 1996 context of 16 hours per week or more) a blanket ban on outside business activities is normally unobjectionable. Such an employee is not normally faced with the alternative of starving or complying, although if he were, the clause will be struck down: *Young v Timmins* (1831) 1 Cr & J 331 approved by Lord Reid in *Esso Petroleum Co Ltd v Harper's Garages (Stourport) Ltd* [1968] 2 AC 269. It is on the same reasoning that such a clause in a part-time employee's contract may be objectionable. An outside activities clause is valid and would probably be enforced by injunction in circumstances such as arose in *Hivac Ltd v Park Royal Scientific Instruments Ltd* [1946] Ch 169 where the employees were working for a competitor in their spare time. There may, however, be an advantage in having a partial ban only where it is contemplated that a garden leave injunction may be sought. Garden leave injunctions are considered in Ch 14.

4.19 Where the employer adopts a total ban on outside business activities it is common practice, and clearly sensible, to include a proviso permitting investment up to a particular ceiling in listed companies. Precedents of both total and partial ban clauses appear below.

CONSENT PROVISION

4.20 From the employer's point of view there is no disadvantage in including a provision whereby outside business activities are permissible with his consent.

Such a provision will, however, obviously be of limited value where the ban on outside business activities is partial. In such cases the banned activities will normally be precisely those for which the employer would refuse consent in any event. To avoid disputes it is sensible to specify the title of the officer (rather than the name of an individual) who will give consent on behalf of the employer, provide that consent must be given before the activity is undertaken and that consent must be in writing. Having taken these steps it is important that the procedures are adhered to.

4.21 Providing that the consent will not be unreasonably withheld is less advantageous to the employer. Whilst it is unlikely to cause difficulty in the context of activities which are clearly competitive, where withholding of consent would be reasonable, it may lead to disputes in other areas. Where possible the employer should resist such an inclusion but by the same token it is to the employee's advantage to press for it. Where the ban on outside activities is partial, provided the banned activities are those which are likely to harm the employer, which is normally the case, there is little point in including a provision that consent will not be unreasonably withheld. As the employer has gone to the trouble of identifying those activities that may cause him harm it should always be reasonable for him to withhold consent.

4.22 Where the outside activities clause is otherwise unreasonable it is highly unlikely that the inclusion of a consent provision will validate it. The cases in which this point has been considered all relate to post-termination restraints but in our view the same principles apply to a clause controlling activities during employment. In both *Chafer Ltd v Lilley* [1947] LJR 231 and *Technograph Printed Circuits Ltd v Chalwyn Ltd* [1967] 84 RPC 339 a consent provision did not validate an otherwise unreasonable restraint but cf *Kerchiss v Colora Printing Inks Ltd* [1960] RPC 235 where Danckwerts J found such a provision was one of the factors validating the covenant.

PRECEDENTS – SENIOR EXECUTIVES

Total ban:

Except as a representative of the Company [or with the prior written approval of ***[insert title of Company officer]]*** *[which approval shall not be unreasonably withheld] the Executive shall not during his employment by the Company be directly or indirectly engaged or concerned or interested in any other trade or business [or the setting up of any business] save as a holder of the legal or equitable interest in the shares or securities of a company any of whose shares or securities are quoted or dealt in on any recognised Stock Exchange provided that any such holding shall not exceed [3%] of the whole or any class of the issued share capital of the company concerned.*

Partial ban:

The Executive shall not [except with the prior written approval of the ***[insert title of Company officer]]*** *[which approval shall not be unreasonably withheld] during his employment by the Company be directly or indirectly engaged or concerned or interested in any other trade or business [or the setting up of any business] which is similar to or in competition with the business carried on by the Company [or any other company in the Group] or any part of such business* *save as a holder of the legal or equitable interest in the shares or securities of a company any of whose shares or securities are quoted or dealt in on any recognised Stock Exchange provided that any such holding shall not exceed [3%] of the whole or any class of the issued share capital of the company concerned.*

Note: The word 'Group' should be defined in the Service Agreement; see paragraph 4.6.

1(d) Non poaching of employees

4.23 As we have seen from Ch 3 (paras 3.22 to 3.24) there is considerable uncertainty as to the scope of the implied duty of fidelity when it comes to employees leaving in concert or one employee encouraging another to join a competitor with him. To cure that uncertainty we suggest that the employer includes an express prohibition along the lines of the following precedent.

PRECEDENT – SENIOR EXECUTIVE

The Executive shall not at any time during the continuance of the Agreement directly or indirectly and whether on his own behalf or on behalf of any third party entice or encourage or seek to entice or encourage any other employee of the Company [or any other company in the Group] to leave their employment.

Note: The word 'Group' should be defined in the Service Agreement; see paragraph 4.6.

4.24 There are no reported cases in which the courts have considered the enforceability of a clause of this kind. However, the courts have now clearly accepted the stability of the workforce as a legitimate interest protectable after termination of employment: *Ingham v ABC Contract Schemes Ltd* CA (unreported – Lexis 12 November 1993), applied in *Alliance Paper Group v Prestwich* [1996] IRLR 25 Ch D and most recently *Dawnay Day & Co Ltd v De Braconier D'Alphen* [1997] IRLR 422 CA. In the circumstances, it is difficult to see on what grounds a provision such as this could be challenged, save perhaps, that unlike a post-termination covenant it is not limited to specific categories of employee: all employees are caught. In our view the distinction is justified but an employer wanting to 'play safe' could easily refine the clause to limit it to particular categories of employee in the same way as a post-termination non entitlement covenant would be limited. For further guidance on that issue see paragraphs 11.49 to 11.53 and the Appendices to Ch 11.

1(e) Disclosure of information and reporting procedures

4.25 The implied duty of fidelity imposes on an employee an obligation to disclose certain information to his employer. The extent of the obligation is considered in paragraphs 3.31 to 3.34. The implied duty of fidelity does not have the effect of making the contract of employment a contract of utmost good faith. There is no general obligation on an employee to disclose the misdeeds of his fellow employees. However, such a duty can arise where the employee is in a managerial position with reporting obligations and responsibility for disciplinary matters: *Swain v West (Butchers) Ltd* [1936] 3 All ER 261 (CA) and *Sybron Corporation v Rochem Ltd* [1983] 3 WLR 713.

4.26 Therefore, preliminary steps for employers to take are to ensure that those employees charged with managerial duties have this fact reflected in their contracts, and that reporting procedures should be clearly set out including the intervals at which reports are to be made and an overriding provision requiring matters of particular significance to be reported to the employer forthwith. Furthermore, employees with responsibility for disciplinary matters should be given those responsibilities subject to an obligation to report and in, certain cases, consult.

4.27 In addition, careful consideration should be given to the inclusion of a positive obligation on the employee to disclose certain information including the misdeeds of his fellow employees. While it is unrealistic for the employer to expect that this will necessarily result in his being made aware of any competitive activities of his employees, it may nonetheless be sufficient to deter some competitive activities and, if the sanction for breach is clearly stated to be dismissal, would entitle the employer to dismiss an employee who did not disclose, without giving him notice. An obligation on an employee to disclose his own misdeeds is of no practical value. The employee will, of course, not comply and his breach will make no significant difference to the remedies already available to the employer as a result of the employee's misdeeds.

4.28 The difficulty is how to frame an express obligation to disclose. In *Swain v West (Butchers) Ltd* [1936] 3 All ER 261 the court found that it was Swain's position as general manager, by virtue of which he was given general control of the company subject to the overriding power of the Managing Director, coupled with the obligation in his contract to '... do all in his power to promote, extend and develop the interests of the company' which gave rise to the obligation to report the unlawful orders of the Managing Director to the Board. Although such an express term will be relevant, it would not be sufficient to impose an obligation of disclosure on an employee with no managerial responsibilities. In such cases an express term in clear language is advisable: *Distillers Company (Bottling Services) Ltd v Gardner* [1982] IRLR 47. In *Distillers* the Scottish Employment Appeal Tribunal dealt ambiguously with the company's contention that Mr Gardner who had been employed to load goods onto container trailers was under an obligation to report theft of the company's goods by his fellow employees. While accepting that a final warning was justified in connection with an earlier failure to report theft by fellow employees, in relation to a second incident which led to dismissal Lord McDonald MC at paragraph 17 responded to an argument that the tribunal had attached insufficient weight to the company's need to prevent misappropriation and misuse of alcohol in the following way:

> 'If, however this is a matter of great importance to the appellants, it would be reasonable to expect in their rules not merely a specific prohibition against misappropriation but a clear obligation placed upon employees who witness such behaviour to report it immediately. It is asking a lot of an employee to require him to report the misdemeanours of his colleagues, but if this is to be the rule it should, in our view, be very clearly spelled out.'

DRAFTING

4.29 In all cases a general obligation along the lines of the clause in *Swain*, which is simply a general statement of the implied duty of fidelity, should be included (see para 4.7 for a precedent). In addition, the employer can either include a general obligation to disclose misdeeds, perhaps with a non-exhaustive list identifying matters of particular concern or simply an obligation to disclose specified matters. Examples of both formulae are set out below.

PRECEDENT – SENIOR EXECUTIVE

Specific obligation to disclose

*The Executive shall promptly disclose to **[insert title of company officer]** any of the following information which comes into his possession: the plans of any employee to leave the Company (whether alone or in concert with other employees), the plans of any employee (whether alone or in concert with other employees) to join a competitor or to establish a business in competition with the Company [or any other company in the Group], any steps taken by any employee to implement either of such plans, the misuse by any employee of any confidential information belonging to the Company [or any other company in the Group] **[insert other examples]**. This clause shall not oblige the Executive to disclose information pertaining to his own activities but the Executive shall be obliged to make disclosure under this clause notwithstanding that to do so would involve disclosure of information pertaining to the Executive's own activities, including breaches by him of his contract of employment.*

General obligation with non-exhaustive list

*The Executive shall promptly disclose to **[insert title of company officer]** any information which comes into his possession which affects adversely or may affect adversely the Company [or any other company in the Group] or the business of the Company [or any other company in the Group]. Such information shall include, but shall not be limited to the plans of any employee to leave the Company (whether alone or in concert with other employees), the plans of any employee (whether alone or in concert with other employees) to join a competitor or to establish a business in competition with the Company [or any other company in the Group], any steps taken by any employee to implement either of such plans, the misuse by any employee of any confidential information belonging to the Company [or any other company in the Group] **[insert other examples]**. This clause shall not oblige the Executive to disclose information pertaining to his own activities but the Executive shall be obliged to make disclosure under this clause notwithstanding that to do so would involve disclosure of information pertaining to the Executive's own activities, including breaches by him of his contract of employment.*

Note: The word 'Group' should be defined in the Service Agreement; see paragraph 4.6.

1(f) Confidentiality and the protection of trade secrets

4.30 The information the employer is entitled to protect by express covenant is considered in detail in Chapter 5. In broad terms, during employment the employer can protect most kinds of information, whereas once employment has ended he is limited to two categories: trade secrets and mere confidential information which the employer has protected by express covenant. However, in practice the employer will normally want to protect the same types of information both during and after employment and for this reason it is normal for there to be an express covenant applying to both situations which identifies by non-exhaustive list, to allow for change, particular types of information which the employer wants to protect. The advantage of this approach is that it ensures the employer has addressed the question of what information should be treated as confidential but without excluding other possible types of information that may arise and may be confidential.

PRECEDENT – SENIOR EXECUTIVE

The Executive shall not make use of, divulge or communicate to any person (save in the proper performance of his duties under this Agreement) any of the trade secrets or other confidential information of or relating to the Company [or any other company in the Group] which he may have received or obtained as a result of or in any way in connection with his employment by the Company [or any other company in the Group]. This restriction shall continue to apply after the termination of his employment without limit in point of time but shall cease to apply to information ordered to be disclosed by a Court of competent jurisdiction or otherwise required to be disclosed by law. For the purposes of this Agreement confidential information shall include, but shall not be limited to [insert types of confidential information].

Note: In our precedent we have not exempted information which comes into the public domain. Whilst such an exception is common, in our view it is dangerous to include it. It is at least arguable that information which comes into the public domain does not always automatically cease to be protectable: see paragraphs 6.2 to 6.5. The word 'Group' should be defined in the Service Agreement: see paragraph 4.6.

1(g) Patents, copyright and certain other intellectual property

4.31 Questions connected with patent and copyright and the like raise complex issues which are beyond the scope of this book. However, the following is an outline of some of the most important terms dealing with certain types of intellectual property which it is prudent to include in a contract of employment.

- Subject to the cautionary note relating to 'inventions' in paragraph 3.38 above, the employee should disclose to the employer any discovery or invention or improvement to an existing invention or process used by the employer. Subject to the relevant legislation (not least the Patents Act 1977), the employer should be first owner of the discovery, invention or improvement.
- All other intellectual property (including copyright, design, trade marks created 'in the course of employment' and, where appropriate, similar or other rights in jurisdictions outside the United Kingdom) created by the employee in the course of his or her employment, together with the right to apply for such rights, will be owned by the employer. Employers will need to give consideration to the meaning of the phrase 'in the course of his or her employment', as situations will vary, making a wider formulation necessary in some cases, such as where it is contemplated that the employee will spend time outside normal working hours engaged on the employer's business.
- Consideration should be given to a suitable waiver of moral rights associated with copyright, under Chapter IV of Part I of the Copyright, Designs and Patents Act 1988.

- There should also be a 'further assurances' provision, under which the employee undertakes to do everything necessary to vest in the employer all the intellectual property which, by virtue of the employment contract, is to vest in the employer. Sometimes, this may even extend to the employee granting a power of attorney to the employer to carry out all necessary actions in the employee's name, for example, the completion of necessary filings with trade mark registries and formal assignments of copyright and other intellectual property. It should be noted that by Section 30(6) of the Patents Act 1977 assignments, mortgages and assents relating to patents or patent applications are void unless they are (1) in writing and (2) signed by *both* parties; while similar transactions in respect of trade marks, copyright, registered designs and unregistered design rights require writing and the signature of the transferor or grantor.

- In express confidentiality covenants contained in the contract of employment, the employer should consider whether special treatment is required in relation to software products where the employer is a software supplier (so that the software is itself treated as confidential information). Similarly, special treatment will be required for 'paid to invent' employees for ensuring that technical information, test or experimental detail, technical trade secrets, formulae, embryonic inventions etc, are not taken or passed into the public domain by the departing employee.

- On termination of the employment, the employee should return to the employer all material that belongs to the employer. Care should be taken to ensure that data and other intangible property is returned as well. Information that cannot be returned, such as data held in a computer, should be deleted from the computer memory and from all other data storage devices.

- Finally, employers will need to ensure that employees can, legally, comply with the above provisions. In some cases, because of undertakings given to a previous employer, an employee might not be able, say, to agree to the vesting of certain intellectual property in his new employer. It would be prudent to establish whether any such restrictions bind the employee before employing him.

- Those employers who employ consultants, designers of logos, graphic artists, software writers or other freelancers should ensure that similar provision is contained in the contracts under which those consultants and freelancers are engaged. Particular care is required in relation to copyright works because the commissioner does not by virtue of the contract of commission alone acquire ownership by implication: express transfer of ownership is required.

2. Terms which define the employee's role

4.32 The term 'role' is used here in the broadest sense to encompass not only the employee's job title but also what his duties are, how and where he performs those duties and his status in the hierarchy of the employing organisation.

4.33 In the context of competitive activities it is in the employer's interests (although not necessarily the employee's) to define the employee's role for two reasons. First, the precise ambit of the implied duty of fidelity is governed in each case by the employee's role. Second, by identifying the employee's role the employer will simultaneously have focused on the employee's potential as a competitor and therefore have a good idea of the risks against which he should seek protection through the contract.

4.34 In defining the employee's role the employer must be sure to include a considerable degree of flexibility. One of the most common defences to an action by an employer to enforce post-termination restrictive covenants is that the employer has repudiated the contract and cannot therefore rely on any term of the contract. (Repudiatory breach is considered in Chapter 8). The employee frequently bases his claim of repudiatory breach on matters such as loss of status, change of duties, withdrawal of work or change of place of work.

4.35 Such arguments are significantly more difficult to sustain where the contract allows for flexibility on these points. Flexibility can be achieved either by the employer reserving the right to make specified changes or by the contract expressly contemplating certain events. What the employer should never do is rely on a clause which purports to give him 'carte blanche' to vary the contract. Such clauses are not effective: *United Association for the Protection of Trade v Kilburn* (17 September 1985, EAT 787/84, unreported) where a clause which read:

> 'This Handbook constitutes your contract of employment. The Association reserves the right to make alterations to the contract of employment. Such changes will be notified to you ...'

was held by the EAT to permit only the most minor of changes and nothing more. The clause did not override the general principle that variations to a contract of employment normally require consent.

4.36 In defining the employee's role the employer needs to deal with the following issues:

- Job title and duties.
- Garden leave.
- Joint appointments.
- Mobility.

2(a) Job title and duties

4.37 Section 1(4)(f) Employment Rights Act 1996 requires the employer to give the employee written notification of his job title or a brief description of the work he is employed to do. While technically, therefore, the employer can be silent on duties it is undoubtedly good practice, and indeed increasingly common, for a list of duties to be drawn up by the employer. In deciding on the employee's title and duties some caution must be exercised.

4.38 Where a contract of employment is very specific about the employee's job title and/or duties then there is very little scope for alteration without the employee's consent. Virtually the only qualification to this is that there is an obligation on employees to adapt to new methods and improved technology, provided that the employer arranges any necessary training in the new skills and the nature of the work does not alter so radically that it is outside the contractual obligations of the employee: *Cresswell v Board of Inland Revenue* [1984] ICR 508. In that case the introduction of a computerised PAYE system, appropriately referred to throughout the case as 'COP', was found not to be a variation of the duties of tax officers and clerical assistants.

4.39 How then does the employer obtain the necessary flexibility? First of all he should give careful thought to the choice of job title. Some job titles are necessarily restrictive, for example 'Senior Manager – Overseas Department'; others are more general, allowing the employer greater flexibility: for example, simply 'Manager'. For senior employees unspecific job titles such as the commonly used 'Executive' should be adopted with caution. The preferred way of obtaining flexibility for these employees, who may well be the potential competitors, is to have a reasonably specific job title but coupled with a provision whereby the employer can require the employee to do another job. Prospective employees will normally agree to such clauses particularly where the other job is to be of a comparable status and there is an obligation on the employer to act reasonably.

4.40 The second point for the employer to consider is the definition of the employee's duties. As a general rule the best course is to provide a reasonably specific list but with a general 'safety-net' provision requiring the employee, in addition to the duties specified, to do such other duties which in the opinion of the employer are connected with or incidental to the duties set out in the description. Where the employer has incorporated a right to change the employee's job, a right to change the employee's duties must be expressly reserved.

PRECEDENT – SENIOR EXECUTIVE

1.1 The Company shall employ the Executive and the Executive shall serve the Company as [insert job title] or in such other [comparable] capacity as the Company may from time to time [reasonably] require.

1.2 The Executive's duties for the Company shall be those specified in the Schedule to this Agreement or in the event of a change in the capacity in which the Executive is employed by the Company pursuant to Clause 1.1 such other duties as are in the [reasonable] opinion of the Company appropriate to and consistent with such new capacity.

[1.3 The Executive may be required to perform duties for and accept office in other companies in the Group without additional remuneration].

Note: The word 'Group' should be defined in the service agreement, see paragraph 4.6.

Schedule

The Executive's duties shall be

[Set out specific duties]

In addition the Executive will perform such other duties, appropriate to his position as [insert job title], as the Company may from time to time require.

2(b) Garden leave

4.41 Garden leave is considered in paragraphs 4.79 to 4.87.

2(c) Joint appointments

4.42 Very senior employees may argue that any attempt to appoint another employee to act jointly with them amounts to a reduction in their status and consequently a repudiatory breach of the contract. To avoid this argument being available to the employee it is sensible for the employer to include an express term permitting such an appointment. In the case of corporate employers when dealing with board level positions, for example, a managing director, the draftsman should always check that the Articles of Association would permit a joint appointment. If a joint appointment is not permissible then the employer will either have to revise his plans or the Articles will have to be altered.

PRECEDENT – SENIOR EXECUTIVE

The Company may from time to time appoint any other person or persons to act jointly with the Executive in his appointment.

2(d) Mobility

4.43 Section 1(4)(h) Employment Rights Act 1996 requires the employer to give the employee written notification of his place of work or where the employee is permitted or required to work at various places an indication of that fact and the address of the employer.

4.44 To avoid arguments of repudiatory breach the employer should endeavour to include flexibility in the place of work provision. That flexibility can be achieved either by providing for an initial place of work with a power on the part of the employer to require a change or that the employee work at various places usually within a defined territory. Examples of both types of clause which are usually referred to as mobility clauses are set out below. Which one the employer chooses should be based on the factual background and the employer should also take into account the points in paragraph 4.45.

PRECEDENT – SENIOR EXECUTIVE

Right to Change Workplace

*The Executive's normal place of work shall initially be the Company's premises at **[insert address]** but the Company reserves the right to require the Executive to change his normal place of work to such other premises of the Company [or any other company in the Group] [within the United Kingdom] as the Company may from time to time require.*

Note: The word 'Group' should be defined in the Service Agreement; see paragraph 4.6.

PRECEDENT – SENIOR EXECUTIVE

Flexible Workplace

The Executive may be required in pursuance of his duties hereunder to work at such places within the United Kingdom as the Company may from time to time require.

Note: The word 'Group' should be defined in the Service Agreement; see paragraph 4.6.

4.45 Employers should be aware that retaining flexibility in place of work clauses is not risk-free and has some potential disadvantages. The key risk is that the clause may be struck down on the ground it constitutes indirect sex discrimination if it cannot be justified on grounds other than sex: *Meade-Hill and NUCPS v British Council* [1995] IRLR 478 CA. In the case of senior executives it may be possible to justify the provision irrespective of sex. However, if there is any doubt at all the only safe course is to include a proviso that the employee shall not be required to move if their personal circumstances preclude it.

4.46 The employee's rights to move an employee must not be exercised in a way likely to destroy trust and confidence: *Woods v WM Car Services (Peterborough) Ltd* [1981] IRLR 347 or capriciously: *United Bank v Akhtar* [1989] IRLR 507. Finally the employee must not act in a way that renders it impossible for the employee to comply with the obligation: *White v Reflecting Roadworks Ltd* [1991] IRLR 331 EAT. Obviously having gone to the trouble of including the clause in the first place it would be unfortunate were the employer to fall foul of an argument of repudiatory breach on implementation.

4.47 Finally, following the Court of Appeal's decision in *High Tables Ltd v Horst* [1998] ICR 409, where an employee has worked at one place or moved only very infrequently the employer will not be able to rely on a mobility clause to defeat a claim of redundancy. Interestingly, however, there will still be scope for a fair dismissal for refusal to relocate, that is, refusal to obey a lawful order.

4.48 Notwithstanding the potential problems outlined above associated with retaining flexibility in the place of work it remains our view that such flexibility should be retained. Properly drafted and applied a mobility clause will still avoid a successful repudiatory breach claim by an employee.

3. Terms pertaining to termination

4.49 There are six important issues that should be covered by express terms:

- What justifies summary dismissal;
- The notice required to terminate the contract;
- How that notice may be served;
- Garden leave;
- The return of property; and
- Resignations from directorships/offices held as a result of the employment.

3(a) What justifies summary dismissal

4.50 Having formulated the express terms to prohibit competitive activities the employer should specify what justifies summary dismissal of the employee without notice or a payment in lieu of notice. By doing so, an employer who dismisses summarily adhering strictly to the terms of the contract will minimise the risk of a successful wrongful dismissal claim and may, but not necessarily will, reduce the risk of an unfair dismissal claim. Remember that there is a sharp distinction between the hurdles the employer has to get over to resist these two types of claim. In wrongful dismissal claims the employer must simply show that he acted in accordance with a contractual term. In unfair dismissal claims the employer must establish that his reason for dismissal was one of those specified in Section 98(1) and (2) Employment Rights Act 1996, and that he acted reasonably in treating that reason as a sufficient reason for dismissal (Section 98(4) Employment Rights Act 1996). The existence of a contract term will be only one, among many, of the factors taken into account by the employment tribunal.

4.51 How should an employer frame his summary dismissal provisions? Traditionally, driven largely by the low level of the cap on the compensatory award for unfair dismissal (currently £12,000), but also by the comparatively low cost of paying during short notice periods, there has been a significant difference in style between senior executives contracts and those of more junior staff. The former, focusing on avoiding a wrongful dismissal claim, have tended to consist of a combination of several fairly general provisions justifying summary dismissal, for example, 'any serious breach of this Agreement' and 'bringing the Company into disrepute' and some very specific provisions such as conviction of an indictable offence or becoming a patient under the Mental Health Act 1983. In contrast, contracts for more junior staff have focused more on the possibility of an unfair dismissal claim. These contracts often only allow for summary dismissal in the event of gross misconduct which is either a defined term or, and this is undoubtedly better practice, explained by reference to a non-exhaustive list of examples. In short, the two types of contract have each focused on only one of the two potential types of claim.

4.52 With the raising of the cap on the compensatory award for unfair dismissal to £50,000 looming on the horizon (Section 34(4) Employment Relations Act 1999 – yet to be brought into force), the contracts of senior executives are likely to change to encompass a clearer focus on what gross misconduct amounts to. In our view, that need not be at the expense of the more traditional general terms relating to conduct although the employer will have to accept that these more general terms will be of little use in contesting an unfair dismissal claim. For the future, we expect to see a greater alignment of summary dismissal provisions between senior executive contracts and those of more junior staff. We recommend that in each case the summary dismissal provisions should include the following:

- A right to dismiss for gross misconduct defined by reference to a non-exhaustive list. Note: failure to include an item as an example of gross misconduct will not prejudice the employer's right to terminate summarily where the conduct is clearly gross misconduct; *CA Parsons & Co Ltd v McLoughlin* [1975] IRLR 65; *The Distillers Company (Bottling Services) Ltd v Gardner* [1982] IRLR 47, but see *Lock v Cardiff Railway Co Ltd* [1998] IRLR 358 where the employer's failure to identify any specific examples of gross misconduct resulted in a dismissal for a particular offence being held by the EAT to be unfair;
- Relevant generally-drawn terms such as 'bringing the employer into disrepute'; and
- Relevant specific terms such as a right to dismiss where the employee has been off sick for a specific period or, in appropriate cases, where the employee has voluntarily resigned as a director.

4.53 In drawing up summary dismissal provisions it is worth remembering the following:

- General definitions of grounds for summary dismissal are unlikely to have any deterrent effect. Nor are they likely to assist in the defence of an unfair dismissal claim in the sense of the employer being able to show that the employee knew without doubt what the consequences of his conduct would be. Where, however, the employer can establish the employee knew the likely consequences of his actions, barring procedural problems, the dismissal would stand a good chance of being fair even if the conduct would not, apart from its express inclusion in the definition of gross misconduct, normally be gross misconduct: *Meyer Dunmore International Ltd v Roger* [1978] IRLR 167.
- Consistency of application both to the employee and to all employees will be critical in the defence of an unfair dismissal claim.

4.54 In recent years it has become common for employers to provide specifically that disciplinary procedures do not form part of the contract of employment. The reason for this practice was a string of cases where employers were successfully sued for breach of contract in failing to follow their disciplinary procedure. In some instances the employee was awarded damages for the period it would have taken the employer to comply: *Dietmann v The London Borough of Brent* [1987] ICR 737 affirmed [1988] ICR 842 (CA); in another case the Court granted an injunction to keep the contract alive while the procedures were properly complied with: *Robb v London Borough of Hammersmith and Fulham* [1991] ICR 514. The courts have also been willing to restrain the employer by injunction from using an incorrect disciplinary procedure: *Peace v City of Edinburgh Council* [1999] IRLR 417. Where the practice making the disciplinary procedure non-contractual is adopted the employer must make sure that the examples of gross misconduct are given contractual status so that there is no problem in relying on them to terminate the contract summarily.

SUSPENSION

4.55 It is recommended that employers include in their contracts a right to suspend while investigations into the employee's conduct are made. The circumstances in which the right to suspend is exercisable should be clearly stated as should the terms on which suspension is permitted. In particular, it must be clear what entitlement the employee has to pay and benefits while suspended. Commonly, pay and benefits are simply continued, although some employers suspend the right to pay but provide that the employee will not suffer any loss of salary in the event of his being reinstated following the suspension. In rare cases the employer reserves the right to suspend without pay. However, such provisions are disliked by the courts, and in *McLory v Post Office* [1992] ICR 758 the fact that the Post Office had reserved the right to suspend without pay was a significant factor in the court's decision that the Post Office's right to suspend was subject to an implied term that it could only suspend where there were reasonable grounds for doing so and only continue the suspension so long as those reasonable grounds continued. (For a fuller discussion of *McLory* see para 16.13. The subject of suspension (and in particular the position where there is no express right to suspend) is further considered in paragraphs 16.12 and 16.14 and 16.15.

PRECEDENT – SENIOR EXECUTIVE

The Company may at any time by written notice suspend the Executive for the purpose of investigating any allegation of misconduct or breach by him of this Agreement. The period of such suspension shall not normally exceed one month and whilst suspended the Executive shall continue to be entitled to his salary and all other contractual benefits. During any period of suspension pursuant to this Clause the Executive (a) shall not, except with the prior written consent of [insert title of company officer] attend at any premises of the Company [or any other company in the Group] conduct any business on behalf of the Company [or any other company in the Group] or contact any employee or customer of the Company [or any other company in the Group] (b) shall ensure that [insert title of company officer] has a postal address at which the Executive is residing and at which he can be contacted and shall, in any event contact [inserted title of company officer] by telephone at intervals of not more than three working days on such telephone number and at such times as he shall be informed at the commencement of his suspension.

Note: This precedent presupposes that the Executive does not receive any form of variable pay. Where he does, express provision should be made either in the clause or in the documentation setting out the details of the variable pay as to what the employee will receive while suspended. The word 'Group' needs to be defined in the Service Agreement; see paragraph 4.6.

3(b) Notice required to terminate the contract

4.56 The majority of contracts of employment can be determined by notice. The main exceptions are contracts for a fixed term where there is no provision for early termination by notice (and which therefore simply expire by effluxion of time) and contracts for life, see for example: *McClelland v Northern Ireland General Health Services Board* [1957] 2 All ER 129.

4.57 In the context of prohibiting competitive activities, agreeing the period of notice required to terminate the contract is advantageous to the employer for two reasons:

- It avoids arguments of repudiatory breach of contract based on insufficient notice having been given. (For the question of repudiatory breach see Ch 8.)
- It enables a realistic and enforceable garden leave provision (see paras 4.79 to 4.85) to be agreed to operate during all or part of the notice period.

4.58 Subject to two limitations, the parties can agree whatever length of notice they wish. The limitations are:

- The notice cannot be shorter than the minimum periods specified in Section 86 Employment Rights Act 1996. The effect of Section 86 is to substitute automatically the statutory minimum periods for any shorter periods agreed.
- In the case of directors, Section 319 Companies Act 1985 provides that any contract for more than five years must be approved by the shareholders in General Meeting. Where such approval is not obtained the contract is deemed to be terminable by reasonable notice: Section 319(6) Companies Act 1985. For the purposes of Section 319 a 'shadow director' is treated as a director: Section 319(7).

THE IMPLIED TERM OF REASONABLE NOTICE

4.59 If the parties fail to agree a notice period, which is surprisingly common even nowadays, the law implies a term that the contract is determinable on reasonable notice: see for example, *Adams v Union Cinemas Ltd* [1939] 3 All ER 136; *Richardson v Koeford* [1969] 3 All ER 1264 (CA). What is reasonable notice in any particular case is a matter to be determined by the court: *Cuthbertson v AML Distributors Ltd* [1975] IRLR 228.

WHAT IS REASONABLE NOTICE?

4.60 What amounts to reasonable notice is a question of fact and will depend on the circumstances of the particular case; reported authorities are of limited value only. However, factors considered relevant by the courts have included the employee's seniority and level of responsibility; the level of salary and frequency of pay days; the employee's length of service; the importance of the employee in the organisation; the difficulty the employer will face in replacing him; and local, trade or professional customs. See *Hill v CA Parsons & Co Ltd* [1971] 3 All ER 1345 (CA) for an example of how reasonable notice has been determined relatively recently. While reasonable notice will never be less than the statutory minimum, in the case of senior employees it will frequently be considerably more. It is *not* correct that Section 86 Employment Rights Act 1996 applies automatically where the parties have failed to reach agreement. That Section only applies automatically where the parties to the contract have purported to agree a shorter notice period than that specified as the minimum.

4.61 In agreeing provisions relating to notice an employer seeking to limit the risk of competitive activities should ensure two things. First that where commercially possible too lengthy a notice period is avoided and second that there is an express reservation of the right of the employer to make a payment in lieu of notice or of any unexpired period of notice.

LENGTH OF THE NOTICE PERIOD

4.62 We advise employers against long periods because they cause both commercial and legal difficulties. On the commercial side once notice has been given it is extremely unusual for either party to want the contract to continue for any length of time. That in turn leads to the legal difficulty that unless the parties are able to agree a variation to the notice period or comply with a garden leave clause for a lengthy period, both must face the unpalatable choice of continuing with a relationship for which neither has any great enthusiasm or acting in breach of their obligations and facing the consequences which in the employer's case are the potential invalidating of any restrictive covenants which may exist. Where it is the employee who breaches his obligation by, for example, going to work for a competitor before the end of his notice period this can work to the employer's advantage. He then does not have to take the risk of invalidating the restrictive covenants by breaching the terms of the contract as to notice. However, often the employer is the first to find the strain intolerable and therefore risks his legitimate protection against competition. For this reason, wherever commercially possible, employers should agree a notice period of around six to nine months, or in appropriate cases less, coupled with a garden leave clause which allows the relationship to continue for the notice period but gives the employer the option to keep the employee away from the business for some if not all of that period. (See paras 4.79 to 4.85 for garden leave clause.) By this route the employer gains the best chance of keeping the contract alive and therefore of keeping the employee bound by the implied duty of fidelity with the added option of excluding the employee from the business and thereby devaluing his worth as a competitor. Nowadays it is increasingly common for the notice required to be given by the employee to be shorter than that required from the employer. It is obviously to an employee's advantage to reach such an agreement. It may also be advantageous to an employer except in those cases where the effect is to reduce the period of garden leave below that which a court is likely to enforce.

4.63 Finally on the question of length of notice employers should always reconsider this point when an employee's job duties are altered in any significant way and in particular on a promotion. If the notice period is to remain the same that should be expressly stated to pre-empt any argument that the existing notice period became obsolete on promotion and that therefore reasonable notice should apply thereafter in the absence of an agreed term. Equally, if a new notice period is required by the employer, that should be specifically included as part of the offer and the employee's written agreement to it obtained.

PAYMENTS IN LIEU OF NOTICE

4.64 Once notice has been given by either the employer or the employee, it is very common for the employer to want the contract terminated immediately, even though sending the employee on garden leave may be a better option. This is particularly so where the employee is joining a competitor or has been found to have been busy taking steps to set up in competition with his employer.

4.65 If the employer wants to bring the contract to an end, either at the time notice is given, or indeed at any time during the notice period by making a payment in lieu to the employee, he must expressly reserve the right to do so. If he does, there is no breach if the required payment is made and therefore the post-termination restrictive covenants survive the payment: *Rex Stewart Jeffries Parker Ginsberg Ltd v Parker* [1988] IRLR 483. If he does not reserve the right to terminate the contract with a payment to the employee he is (in the absence of agreement by the employee) obviously in breach of the contract: *Dixon v Stenor Ltd* [1973] IRLR 28 (NIRC). The breach may, and often will, be a repudiatory breach. (See paras 8.29 to 8.31). Where the breach is repudiatory, an employee who accepts it as terminating the contract is automatically released from all future obligations, including restrictive covenants; *General Billposting Co Ltd v Atkinson* [1909] AC 118 (HL) and see further Ch 8. Because of this risk an employer who includes restrictive covenants in his contracts intending to rely on them should always consider also including a right to make a payment in lieu. Although there are potential disadvantages to such provisions (see paras 4.66 to 4.67) an employer who wants to preserve his covenants but equally have the flexibility to terminate without notice, rather than, for example, relying on a garden leave clause to distance the employee from the business's clients and confidential information must reserve the right to make a payment in lieu.

4.66 From the employer's standpoint there are two disadvantages in reserving the right to make a payment in lieu of notice. First, any payment made pursuant to the right is taxable under Schedule E as an emolument from employment *EMI Group Electronics Ltd v Coldicott (Inspector of Taxes)* [1999] STC 803 (CA). Consequently, the employer loses the advantage of being able to treat up to

£30,000 in payment in lieu of notice as tax free under Sections 148 and 188 Income and Corporation Taxes Act 1988. The commercial significance of the loss of this advantage arises in the context of negotiating any termination agreement with the employee. Employers who do not reserve the right to make a payment in lieu of notice can 'enhance' the value of their offers of compensation to an employee by taking advantage of Sections 148 and 188 Income and Corporation Taxes 1988 to make the first £30,000 of any damages for failure to give notice as tax free. In contrast, employers whose contracts include payment in lieu of notice provisions and who make payments in accordance with the provisions cannot avail themselves of the benefits of Sections 148 and 188 unless they are making other compensation payments, for example to compromise statutory employment claims, which can legitimately be made tax free under those Sections. For an employer dealing with a departing employee who is a higher rate tax payer on current rates this can make a difference of up to £12,000 (ie, 40% of £30,000) to the value of the employer's compensation proposals. Undoubtedly, there will be cases where this difference is commercially unacceptable to the departing employee so that the effect of reserving the right to make a payment in lieu of notice will be to make any settlement more expensive for the employer.

4.67 The second and more serious disadvantage of reserving a right to make payment in lieu of notice is the risk that the payment becomes a contractual entitlement of the employee which is not subject to the normal rules of mitigation that apply to damages claims and the employer cannot escape making the payment by wrongfully dismissing the employee. Assessing how real this risk is and the extent to which payment in lieu provisions can be formulated to avoid, or at least minimise, the risk is no simple task. The difficulty arises primarily from a very recent, and in our view erroneous decision of the EAT in *Cerberus Software Ltd v Rowley* [1999] IRLR 890 and to a much lesser extent from gauging the impact of the Court of Appeal's decision in *EMI Group Electronics Ltd v Coldicott (Inspector of Taxes)*; see paragraph 4.66.

4.68 Prior to *Cerberus* and *EMI* there were two Court of Appeal decisions which dealt with the question whether a payment in lieu of notice constituted a contractual debt. In *Abrahams v Performing Rights Society* [1995] IRLR 486 (CA) the ex-employee succeeded in establishing that his particular payment in lieu provision was a contractual debt. In *Gregory v Wallace* [1998] IRLR 387 (CA) a differently constituted Court of Appeal, quite correctly in our opinion, distinguished *Abrahams* on its facts and ruled that the payment in lieu provision applicable to *Gregory* did not create a contractual debt. Although in *Cerberus* the EAT in referring to *Abrahams* and *Gregory* (as well as the House of Lords decision in *Delaney v Staples* [1992] IRLR 191) said '... we have not been persuaded that these cases bear directly on the point at issue ...' (Morrison J at page 891). In the authors' view the EAT was fundamentally wrong to reach that conclusion. For that reason, before the case of *Cerberus* is considered and the conclusions of the 'contractual debt' risk and possible ways of avoiding it are summarised, *Abrahams* and *Gregory* will be looked at in some detail.

4.69 The pertinent facts were that beginning on 1 April 1987 Mr Abrahams was employed by Performing Rights Society ('PRS') on a five-year fixed-term contract. Part way though that contract PRS became aware that the expiry of a fixed-term contract constituted a 'dismissal' for the purposes of the Employment

Rights Act 1996. PRS therefore decided through its Staff Committee to introduce notice provisions into the fixed-term contracts of Mr Abrahams and others. These notice provisions were to the effect that, save in cases of gross misconduct, 'two years notice of termination (or salary in lieu)' would be given by PRS. By letter of 28 March 1989 to Mr Abrahams, PRS's Chief Executive referred to the Committee's decision and then explained his understanding of the variation to Mr Abraham's contract in the following way '… in the event of termination of your employment by the Society either at the end of the fixed-term contract period or at any time during the final two years of such period you would be entitled, other than in the case of dismissal for gross misconduct, to a period of notice of two years or an equivalent payment in lieu.' Mr Abrahams accepted that variation by signing a copy of the letter 'agreed'. In early 1992 negotiations began for the renewal of Mr Abrahams' contract. Those negotiations were not successful. Instead an agreement was reached, and made public by a staff announcement of 12 March 1992, that Mr Abrahams was to remain in post until 31 March 1994 'under the terms of his existing contract'. Both parties accepted that the staff announcement accurately recorded the agreement. Notwithstanding this agreement on 14 September 1992 Mr Abrahams was summarily dismissed without justification. Mr Abrahams claimed an entitlement to two years pay in lieu of notice in accordance with the 1992 Agreement to which he alleged he was entitled as a contractual debt. PRS defended the claim on the basis that they had wrongfully dismissed Mr Abrahams and that his entitlement to damages was based on the unexpired portion of a fixed-term contract due to expire on 31 March 1994 which they alleged was the proper effect of the 1992 Agreement. PRS lost comprehensively, the Court of Appeal first found that the 1989 variation as to notice was incorporated into Mr Abrahams' contract and that therefore he was entitled to two years' notice. The Court also ruled that Mr Abrahams' summary dismissal was not a wrongful dismissal but simply, as Mr Abrahams' Counsel put it 'deciding not to serve notice' leaving Mr Abrahams with the ability to claim 'the alternative contractual remedy available to him', that is, to sue for the payment in lieu. The report does not record in detail the argument on whether the dismissal was wrongful. However, the Court did specifically reject an argument for PRS that to infer that PRS was electing to make a payment in lieu of notice there would have to have been a tender of money due or at the very least an assurance of a willingness to pay. The final blow for PRS was the Court's finding, unsurprising on the facts and particularly the use of the word 'entitlement', that Mr Abrahams was not obliged to mitigate. In reaching this conclusion, the Court relied on *Rex Stewart Jeffries Parker Ginsberg Ltd v Parker and Another* [1988] IRLR 488.

4.70 Following *Abrahams*, some commentators took the view that all payment in lieu provisions created contractual debts. However, although this was probably true in some cases, it is our view that this was incorrect and that there are two primary grounds on which *Abrahams* could be 'contained'. The first relates to the formulation of the pay in lieu of notice clause and the second to the manner of the dismissal. In *Abrahams* the formulation of the clause was on the basis of an entitlement, as it was in *Rex Stewart Parker*. Where the provision is formulated as an option of the employer, particularly one exercisable at the employers' absolute discretion, failure to serve notice cannot be said to give rise to an enforceable entitlement. This point has recently been confirmed by the Court of Appeal in *Gregory v Wallace* [1998] IRLR 387. Mr Wallace was entitled to two years notice from his employer. Under the contract upon the giving of that notice the employer became 'entitled' to terminate the agreement immediately by making a payment or payments to Mr Wallace which Mr Wallace could elect to receive either in monthly instalments over the two year period or as a single lump sum subject to a reduction for accelerated receipt. In 1992, Mr Wallace's employers ran into financial difficulties. Administrative receivers were appointed and Mr Wallace was summarily dismissed on 3 August 1992, a decision confirmed in writing on 5 August 1992. Distinguishing the case from *Abrahams* the Court of Appeal held that Mr Gregory had been wrongfully dismissed and that therefore his remedy lay in damages. The Court ruled that the giving of two years' notice was a pre-condition to the employers' entitlement to make a payment in lieu of notice. Furthermore distinguishing *Rex Stewart Parker* it was a condition that could not be waived by Mr Gregory since it was not for his benefit alone. The Court found that in order to succeed Mr Gregory would have to show that his summary dismissal had been effected by his employers under the contractual provision and that, in turn, had to be preceded by the giving of two years' notice. On the facts, although the Court expressed a general willingness to construe the employer's actions as 'consistent with rather than repudiatory of the contract' (Peter Gibson LJ para 23) in this case it was not possible. In short, by inserting the 'hurdle' of the giving of notice and expressing the provision as an option only the Abrahams arguments were defeated.

4.71   The decision in *Gregory* was greeted with considerable relief by employers. Undoubtedly it prompted some variations to the drafting of payments in lieu of notice clauses, most notably the insertion of the various 'hurdles' that had successfully defeated Mr Gregory's 'contractual debt argument', but the general consensus was that *Abrahams* had been correctly and sensibly limited. For the future it was anticipated that subject to sensible precautions payment in lieu clauses could safely be included in contracts of employment.

4.72   In July 1999 the EAT's decision in *Cerberus* upset the equilibrium once more. The facts of *Cerberus* were very straightforward, Mr Rowley's contract of employment provided that it could be terminated by not less than six months' notice and that *Cerberus* '... may make a payment in lieu of notice to the employee'. Mr Rowley was summarily dismissed but within weeks of his dismissal found alternative and higher paid employment. Notwithstanding this, he brought a claim in the Employment Tribunal for damages for wrongful dismissal. The Tribunal upheld his claim of wrongful dismissal and, applying *Abrahams*, ruled that Mr Rowley was entitled to the full sum due under the pay in lieu of notice clause with no account being taken of his mitigation. *Cerberus'* appeal to the EAT was unsuccessful. The EAT concluding that because the contract included a right to make a pay in lieu of notice, albeit at the employer's election, the contract could only be terminated either by notice or Cerberus make the full payment in lieu. The EAT's reasoning is extremely difficult to follow. The judgment contains a series of material inconsistencies not least in some instances in treating debt and damages as though they are subject to the same principles. The EAT questioned the House of Lords' analysis in *Delaney v Staples* [1992] IRLR 191 of situations where an employer makes a payment in lieu of notice. The EAT also took the opportunity, albeit obiter, to doubt the validity of pay in lieu clauses generally in so far as they purport to deprive an employee of the statutory minimum periods of notice laid down in Section 86 Employment Rights Act 1996. The EAT took this line notwithstanding that Section 80 expressly permits employer and employee to effectively 'contract out' by a payment in lieu being made – a point acknowledged by the Court of Appeal in *EMI*. Furthermore, in the authors' view, it is not without significance that the EAT does not in any way seek to comment on or distinguish either *Abrahams* or, more importantly, *Gregory*.

4.73 In short, the decision in *Cerberus* is an anomaly and in our view the case is wrongly decided. However, an appeal is not being made to the Court of Appeal and consequently, for the time being at least, it is likely to be a focal point of debate in negotiations relating to an emploee's entitlement on termination. Can *Cerberus* be circumvented or is the combined effect of *Cerberus* and *EMI* that an employer who reserves the right to make a payment in lieu not only cannot have the benefit of any mitigation but also cannot make any payment attributable to the notice period tax free? In the authors' view, this is an unduly pessimistic outlook at least as far as mitigation is concerned. In principle there are two possible ways in which an employer can circumvent the effect of *Cerberus*. The first, and undoubtedly the only really safe course, is for the payment in lieu provision to expressly require the ex-employee to seek alternative work during the period for which payment in lieu is made and for any remuneration earned to be offset against the payments in lieu. For this to work in practice the payment in lieu would have to be made in a series of tranches. Immediately before each tranche became payable the ex-employee would have to be under an obligation to disclose the extent of his 'mitigation' in terms of effort made and results achieved and the payment would then have to be reduced to reflect any 'mitigation' achieved. An alternative formulation of this principle, although far less satisfactory for the ex-employer, would be to make an immediate and sinle lump sum payment but for the provision to include a right of clawback in relation to remuneration received from the alternative work. These formulations are not, however, risk-free and suffer three possible dis-advantages. They are potentially time-consuming in terms of administration, policing the disclosure obligations is by no means simple and there is a risk that the ex-employee dilutes the effect of his 'mitigation' in the short term, eg by taking a lower salary in favour of non-quantifiable benefit, eg a share option or simply deferring payments. However, for a key employee where it is critical to protect the covenants, the degree of effort required may well be worthwhile particularly in the case of a lengthy notice period.

4.74 The following precedent is an example of how this type of payment in lieu may be formulated using a stage payment system. As with previous precedents in this Chapter, the precedent needs to be used with care and some thought needs to be given to particular issues, for example, the type of work the employee is obliged to find and whether or not non-cash benefits and deferred consideration are to be included in the deductions to be made from the payment in lieu. Both these issues are difficult ones in principle and in terms of drafting. In our precedent, assuming the notice period would not exceed a year, we have taken the view that the employer should be obliged to try and find a comparable alternative job, largely on grounds of reasonableness and to reflect the general principles of mitigation in damages claims. We have also included non-cash benefits and deferred compensation in the sums to be deduced. While this can create uncertainties and valuation difficulties it seems to us that to omit them would enable the ex-employee to avoid the effect of the clause with considerable ease.

PRECEDENT – SENIOR EXECUTIVE

*1.1 Once notice to terminate has been given by either party in accordance with Clause **[insert number of Clause dealing with notice]** the Company reserves the right, exercisable in its absolute discretion, to terminate the Executive's employment forthwith by making payments, or where appropriate a payment, calculated and payable in accordance with this Clause in lieu of the notice period required by Clause **[repeat number of Clause dealing with notice]** ('the Notional Notice Period') or any unexpired portion of the Notional Notice Period.*

1.2 During the Notional Notice Period the Executive shall use his best endeavours to secure alternative work commensurate with his skills and abilities and providing an income and benefits comparable to those provided by the Company under this Agreement. Five working days before any payment is due to be made to the Executive under this Clause, the Executive shall delivery to the [Company Secretary] a written statement together with all relevant documents (where available) detailing in respect of the period to which the payment relates (1) all efforts made by him to secure alternative work and, (2) all sums or benefits (including any entitlement to deferred compensation or benefits) earned whether or not received in respect of work undertaken by him for any third party (collectively 'Sums Earned'). In relation to non-cash benefits the Execuitve shall provide sufficient information to enable the Company to place a financial value on the benefits. The Company's valuation of the benefits shall be final and binding on the parties.

*1.3 Subject to the Executive complying with his obligation under Clause 1.2 the Company shall continue to pay the Executive at the rate of his base salary as at termination together with **[insert method of valuation of variable compensation and benefits as a monthly figure]** throughout the Notional Notice Period less, in the case of each payment: (a) any deductions which the company is obliged to make, including but not limited to tax, and (b) any Sums Earned attributable to the period to which the payment relates.*

4.75 The alternative formulation is to draft a payment in lieu provision incorporating those aspects of the provisons in *Gregory* which successfully defeated the contractual debt argument and also including some administrative mechanism in the pay in lieu of notice provision to make clear how that right will be exercised to ensure that it is not deemed to have been exercised by default. The Precedent which follows reflects this formulation of a pay in lieu of notice provision. It also addresses the key elements which should always be included in a single lump sum payment in lieu provision, namely:

• That a payment in lieu can be made whether notice is given by the employer or the employee. Many clauses are silent or at best ambiguous on this point;
• That a payment in lieu can be made of either the entire notice period or any unexpired part of it;
• Precisely how the payment in lieu will be calculated, thereby avoiding arguments about whether or not benefits such as cars, bonus schemes etc are included or excluded. In practice, valuing non-cash benefits for payment in lieu clauses can be extremely difficult and therefore it is common practice for a payment in lieu clause to refer to salary only or salary and other cash benefits, for example commission or profit share schemes. The employer

should also ensure that there are no conflicts between the terms of contract on pay in lieu and any scheme documentation, for example, for bonus/profit share or indeed any other schemes.

PRECEDENT – SENIOR EXECUTIVE

Once notice to terminate has been given by either party in accordance with Clause [insert number of Clause dealing with notice] the Company reserves the right, exercisable in its absolute discretion, to terminate the Executive's employment by making a payment in lieu of the notice required by Clause [repeat Clause number dealing with periods of notice] or any unexpired period of such notice. Any payment in lieu of notice shall consist solely of a sum equivalent to the Executive's Base Salary (at the rate applicable at the date notice is given) for the notice period required by Clause [repeat Clause number dealing with periods of notice] or any unexpired period of such notice and shall be subject to such deductions as the Company is required [or authorised in writing by the Executive (pursuant to the terms of the Agreement or otherwise)] to make. Any exercise of the Company's rights under this Clause shall be made by notice in writing to the Executive which such notice shall be substantially in the form of Appendix [ ].

Appendix [   ]

In accordance with Clause [ ] of the Service Agreement dated [   ] the Company hereby confirms that it is exercising its rights to make a payment to you in lieu of the [entirety]* [unexpired portion]* of your notice period. Accordingly, we [enclose a cheque in the sum of £   ]* or [have today transferred the sum of £   into your account with [insert name of Bank]]*. This sum has been calculated as follows:

Base Salary at date of termination x [notice period]* [unexpired period of notice]*   =£

Less: [Specify each item of deduction	£	
by description and amount]	£	
	£_____	
Total Deductions:	£	
		£_____
Net Sum Due:	£_____	

For and on behalf of [insert Company name]

*   *Delete as appropriate*

Note: The precedent presupposes that the employee will receive salary only and that the notice period is the same whether given by employer and employee. On the first point, the clause is not favourable to the employee and it is sensible for the employee to identify the additional benefits he receives and endeavour to have some payment in respect of them included or, where possible, for those benefits to be continued during what would have been the notice period. The precedent permits deductions the employer is required to make for example currently tax (see paragraph 4.66) and has the option to permit deductions authorised by the employee in writing. It is vital to remember that in the latter case the written authorisation must precede the deduction if it is to be a permitted, as distinct from an unlawful, deduction within Section 13(1)(b) Employment Rights Act 1996.

4.76 As indicated at the outset of this section on payments in lieu of notice, the prime, and only, purpose of their being included in a contract of employment is to avoid the risk of an employee being able to claim successfully that he is released from his restrictive covenants where the employer terminates without notice. Because of the disadvantages of payment in lieu provisions outlined in paragraphs 4.66 and 4.67 it is now the case that payment in lieu of notice clauses should probably only be included in contracts where it is critical to the employer to protect the restrictive covenants or in the less usual case where for some other reason it is necessary to be able to terminate lawfully without giving notice, for example to prevent valuable share rights accruing. Where a pay in lieu provision is included, the formulation which expressly addresses the ex-employee securing alternative remuneration during what would have been his notice period had notice been given, is recommended. This formulation seems to successfully circumvent the contractual debt arguments of *Abrahams* and *Cerberus*. The alternative formulation suggested should also do so, but it is undoubtedly less certain that it will, in view of the breadth of the judgment in *Cerberus*. With regard to tax, as indicated in paragraph 4.66, where payment is made in accordance with the payment in lieu provision there is no escape from *EMI*. However, it is certainly arguable, and indeed expressly contemplated within the judgment of Chadwick LJ that if an employer in fact makes a lesser payment than that required by the payment in lieu of notice clause in compromise of the contingent liability such a payment could be made taking advantage of Sections 148 and 188 Income and Corporation Taxes Act 1988.

4.77 Under the common law there are three important rules on the service of notice.

- Oral notice is perfectly valid unless the parties have agreed otherwise: *Latchford Premier Cinema Ltd v Ennion* [1931] 2 Ch 409; and
- Notice cannot be said to have been given until such time as it is actually communicated to the other party or the other party has a reasonable opportunity of learning of it: *Brown v Southall and Knight* [1980] IRLR 130 [1980] ICR 617 applied in *Hindle Gears Ltd v McGinty* [1985] ICR 111 see also *McMaster v Manchester Airport plc* [1998] IRLR 112.
- Where notice is given orally on a day when work is carried out, the notice period does not begin to run until the following day: *West v Kneels Ltd.* [1986] IRLR 430.

4.78 To avoid common problems associated with these rules it is sensible for the contract to include a provision which contains the following points:

- That notice should be given in writing (the employer can in any event probably waive the benefit of the written provision and accept an unequivocal oral resignation if necessary).
- By what method written notice can be delivered, that is, personally, by post (stating method, for example, first class post or recorded delivery), facsimile

or nowadays e-mail. For each method of delivery there should be a deemed delivery date or time (as appropriate).

- Where notice can be served on the employer.
- To whom notice should be addressed at the employer: the contract should specify a position rather than give the name of a current employee.
- Where notice can be served on the employee.

PRECEDENT – SENIOR EXECUTIVE

*Any notice to be given under this Agreement shall be given in writing and shall be duly served on the Company if it is handed to **[insert title of Company officer]** or left at or sent by first class or recorded delivery post to the Company's registered office for the time being marked for the attention of **[insert title of Company officer]**. Any notice shall be duly served on the Executive if it is handed to him personally or left at or sent by first class or recorded delivery post to his address given in this Agreement or such other address as he may notify to the **[insert title of Company officer]** in writing. Any notice left for either the Company or the Executive at premises in accordance with this Agreement shall be deemed to have been served on the day on which it was so left. Any notice sent by recorded delivery post shall be deemed to have been served 48 hours after it was posted.*

3(c) Garden leave

4.79 An employee is said to be on garden leave where he is required not to attend his employer's premises and not to perform any duties for his employer but he nonetheless remains an employee entitled to receive full salary and benefits. Most importantly, by remaining an employee the individual is precluded from engaging in activities which are competitive with his employer's activities. The employer will normally seek to send an employee on garden leave where it has become apparent that the employee is intending to leave and to compete or occasionally where the employee is already competing. The purpose is to keep the employee out of circulation for a period of time, thereby breaking his links with customers, other employees and contacts and removing his access to confidential information. The first case on the subject, *Evening Standard Co Ltd v Henderson* [1987] ICR 588, was not, strictly speaking, a garden leave case at all. In that case Henderson, a production manager for the *Evening Standard*, was subject to a notice period of 12 months. He sought to terminate his employment on two months' notice in order to join a rival paper. The *Evening Standard* sought to keep the contract of employment alive, rather than accepting Henderson's conduct as bringing the contract to an end. In seeking the court's assistance to keep Henderson to the period of his notice the *Evening Standard* offered undertakings to the court to pay Henderson his full salary and benefits during the notice period, whether or not he worked, and also not to seek damages against him for his failure to work (which would otherwise, of course, have cancelled out the benefit of the undertaking to pay salary and benefits). The *Evening Standard* were granted an injunction because they were not seeking to force Henderson to work, which is not permitted (see para 14.3), nor were they refusing him the right to work. The *Evening Standard* were quite prepared to have Henderson work out his notice period. It is this rather unusual factor which makes this case not, strictly speaking, a garden leave case. Usually, where an employee is making plans to join a rival the last thing the employer will wish to do is to have him remain on the premises, where he may do harm to the employer pending his departure. A true garden leave case was that of *Provident Financial*

Group plc v Hayward [1989] ICR 160 where Hayward, a financial director of an estate agency gave six months' notice in accordance with his contract. After working for two months he agreed to take four months' pay on the basis that he would be on garden leave during the period (that is, not work at all) and keep his duty of confidentiality for two years. Hayward then sought to commence employment with another estate agency. The Court of Appeal refused an injunction sought by Provident to prevent him from doing so. The key reason for the refusal was the finding that Hayward's new employment was such that it was unlikely that Provident's position would be seriously affected by it. Contrast with *Provident, GFI Group Inc v Eaglestone* [1994] IRLR 119 and *Euro Brokers Ltd v Rabey* [1995] IRLR 206. In those cases, garden leave injunctions were granted to protect the employer's customer connections which had been secured by lavish entertainment expenses and which, the court found, were likely to be significantly damaged were some injunctive relief not granted.

4.80 It is possible for an employer to send an employee on garden leave, and obtain a garden leave injunction, relying only on the notice provisions in the contract, the implied duty of fidelity and the absence on the part of the employee of a right to work: *Provident Financial Group plc v Hayward* and *GFI Group Inc v Eaglestone* (above). However, sending an employee on garden leave without an express right to do so has always carried the risk of a challenge from the employee that the employer's acts amount to a repudiatory breach of the contract releasing the employer from all future obligations: *General Billposting v Atkinson* [1909] AC 118. Invariably this argument is based on the employee's contention that he has a right to work, a contention which in many cases will have been materially improved by the recent Court of Appeal decision in *William Hill Organisation Ltd v Tucker* [1998] IRLR 313 which is considered at paragraph 4.77.

4.81 The traditional view on right to work stems from cases such as *Turner v Sawdon & Co.* [1901] 2 KB 653 and *Collier v Sunday Referee Publishing Co Ltd* [1940] 2 KB 647 which established that the employee's right is not to work but simply to receive pay or as Asquith J put it in *Collier* 'provided I pay my cook, she cannot complain if I choose to take any or all of my meals out'. For many years certain exceptions have been recognised to this principle primarily the cases of pieceworkers where earnings are entirely dependent on the amount of work done: *Devonald v Rossers & Sons* [1906] 2 KB 708 and performance artists whose careers depend on working: *Herbert Clayton & Jack Waller Ltd v Oliver* [1930] AC 209 HL. Very gradually, as social conditions have changed, the courts began to hint at a willingness to extend the categories of those with a right to work. So, for example, in *Langston v AUEW No 2* [1974] IRLR 182 NIRC both Denning MR and Stephenson LJ thought it arguable that a welder had a right to work. Similarly in *Provident* supra, Dillon LJ in the context of exercise of discretion of the court as to the appropriate length of any restraint (there was an express negation of any right to work in the contract) expressed the view that 'The employee has a concern to work and to exercise his skills' and that concern extended to 'skilled workmen and even to chartered accountants'. In contrast, there is the case of *Spencer v Marchington* [1994] IRLR 392 where the employee, Mrs Marchington based her contention that she had a right to work primarily on the fact that she was remunerated on a profit share basis. She alleged that the employer's request that she not work for the final two months of a fixed-term 12-month contract amounted to a repudiatory breach. The court found that the breach was 'not quite important enough, even in the context of a

12-month contract, to amount to a fundamental breach' (John Mowbray QC sitting as a Deputy High Court Judge, at page 395). However, in *Spencer* there were circumstances which justified the result, most notably that there was no evidence that Mrs Marchington (the employee) had accepted the alleged repudiatory breach and, although she was remunerated on a profit share basis, she had agreed to a compromise figure for the two months of garden leave. However absent these special factors, it would be dangerous to rely on the decision in *Spencer*. (For a fuller discussion of what amounts to a repudiatory breach of a contract of employment see Ch 8).

4.82 In the *William Hill* case the Court of Appeal had to address directly the question of whether Mr Tucker had a right to work. Mr Tucker was responsible for initially investigating and then establishing a spread betting business for William Hill. In 1995 he was appointed to the position of senior dealer. Initially his contract was terminable on one month's notice but that was subsequently increased by agreement to six months' notice. The contract was silent on whether Mr Tucker had a right to work and contained no garden leave clause. In February 1998 Mr Tucker resigned to join a competitor of William Hill and purported to give one month's notice. William Hill reminded Mr Tucker that the required notice was six months and purported to send him on garden leave for that period. Mr Tucker declined to comply and William Hill sought a garden leave injunction. Unsuccessful at first instance, William Hill persisted but again lost in the Court of Appeal, the Court finding that Mr Tucker had a right to work. The Court of Appeal ruled that the question of whether there is a right to work is a matter of construction of the contract in the light of the surrounding circumstances. In Mr Tucker's case he had a right to work arising from four factors (the first two of which arise from the surrounding circumstances):

- Mr Tucker's position was both in substance and form a specific and unique post;
- Mr Tucker's skills required frequent exercise;
- The following contract terms:
  - The identification of days and hours of work and an obligation to work the hours necessary to carry out his duties in a full and professional manner;
  - A declaration in the Staff Handbook that William Hill will 'invest in its staff to ensure that they have every opportunity to develop their skills';
  - An express power of suspension to investigate serious allegations of breach of discipline.
- There was no express garden leave provision.

The Court also 'observed' that there was little likelihood of an implied term permitting garden leave arising (Morritt LJ page 318, para 24).

4.83 The *William Hill* case undoubtedly reflects the growing trend in favour of a right to work. However, it must be said that there are certain aspects on which the Court relied which are, at the very least, surprising. Quite why, for example, (what was prior to the Working Time Regulations) a standard hours of work clause or a standard suspension provision are now to be key factors in determining a right to work is unclear. For a post-*William Hill* case in which on the constitution of the contract a 'Divisional Director' of an insurance broker (not a Companies Act Director) was held to have no right to work even though there was 'garden leave' provision see *S B J Stephenson Ltd v Mandy* (unreported) 30 July 1999. What is clear, however, is that the only safe course following the Court of Appeal decision is to include an express right to send an employee on garden leave in the contract of employment. Additionally, as a 'belt and braces' measure (because albeit obiter the *William Hill* case raises issues as to how flexible the Courts will be in interpreting garden leave clauses in future see Morritt LJ para 25) wherever commercially possible the contract should include a provision to the effect that the employer has no obligation to provide work nor has the employee any right to perform services.

Precedent – Senior Executive

'Nothing in the Agreement shall mean or be deemed to mean that the Company is obliged to provide work to the Executive or that the Executive has the right to perform services for the Company [or any other company in the Group]'.

Note: The word 'Group' should be defined in the Service Agreement, see paragraph 4.6.

Where the employee is a director, particularly one with specific responsibilities such as a managing director or finance director, some thought will need to be given to the interaction of such a clause with the individual's responsibilities as a director. In practice, directors may well resist the inclusion of this sort of term precisely because of the tension it could create with their directorships.

4.84 Drafting a garden leave clause requires some care. The essential features of the clause should be as follows:

- The right should only operate once notice has been given by either party.
- In our view the maximum period of garden leave should be relatively short. This might be the entirety of the notice period, or in the case of a long notice period a maximum of six months with the employer having the power to elect when the garden leave is to be taken. It is right to say that there is an alternative view that the garden leave clause can be for a much longer period. This view relies on the Court of Appeal's indication in *Crédit Suisse Asset Management Ltd v Armstrong and Others* [1996] IRLR 450 that garden leave of 12 months may be acceptable coupled with the fallback position of the Courts' willingness to grant garden leave injunctions for periods shorter than the notice period: *GFI Group v Eaglestone* (above) and see the comments of the Court of Appeal in *Provident* (above) – although an injunction was refused in that case on grounds unconnected with the length of the garden leave provision. Both views on the recommended length of garden leave are sustainable on the current state of authorities. However, we favour the shorter view because:
  - It gives the parties greater certainty
  - It takes into account the Court of Appeal's views in *Provident* to the effect that skilled workmen and 'even chartered accountants' have a concern to work (Dillon LJ page 304d) and that the effect of garden leave should not be that skills 'atrophy'. (Taylor LJ 305(h))
  - It reflects a reasonable approach of the type the courts are seeking and finally

- Although arguably less flexible than the longer period – it will almost certainly achieve the same result. It is worth noting that notwithstanding the Court of Appeal's view in *Crédit Suisse* that a 12-month garden leave would be acceptable, there is not a single reported case in which the courts have upheld such a period.

- It should relieve the employer of any obligation to provide work for the employee.
- It should permit the employer to exclude the employee from the workplace(s).
- It should allow the employer to prohibit contact between the employee and (1) customers/clients (2) suppliers.
- It should provide for the continuation of salary and benefits throughout the garden leave period with a fixed formula operating in respect of variable pay, for example, bonuses/commissions. Where the variable pay is set out in a separate document, for example, bonus scheme which is renewed/amended annually there is no objection to setting out the amount(s) payable during garden leave in those documents rather than in the garden leave clause itself. The only important fact is that the issue is covered in documentation upon which the employer can rely as agreed by the employee.

PRECEDENT – SENIOR EXECUTIVE

1.   Once notice to terminate the Executive's employment has been given by the Company or the Executive, or in the event that the Executive purports to terminate in breach of those obligations the Company
1.1 shall be under no obligation to vest in or assign to the Executive any powers or to provide any work for the Executive and the Executive shall have no right to perform any services for the Company [or any other Company in the Group];
1.2 may prohibit contact and/or dealings between the Executive and clients and/ or suppliers of the Company [or any other Company in the Group];
1.3 may exclude the Executive from any premises of the Company [or any other company in the Group];

provided always that salary and all other contractual benefits shall not cease to be payable or provided by reason only of the Company exercising its rights pursuant to sub clauses 1.1 and/or 1.2 and/or 1.3 of this Clause. This Clause shall not affect the general right of the Company to suspend in accordance with Clause [insert Clause number of Suspension Clause] nor affect the rights and obligations of the parties prior to the service of such notice.

Note: This precedent is based on the assumptions (1) that both the Executive and the Company are required to give the same period of notice to terminate the contract; (2) that the notice period is not more than six months; and (3) that the employee does not receive any commission, profit share or similar performance related payments; suitable adjustments will be necessary where the facts are different. For example, say the notice period is two years, the options in those circumstances are either (1) provide that the employee may be sent on garden leave for a period or periods up to six months and leave it to the employer's discretion when during the notice period he can exercise his rights (2) to fix a period of, say, six months during which the employee may be sent on garden leave and make that the six months immediately preceding expiry of the notice. The first option gives greater flexibility and is the one we would recommend. In practice, it is highly unlikely that an employee would ever be sent on garden leave under the second option since it would presuppose that he had spent 18 months working out his notice. Having a shorter notice period is a neater solution for the employee but may not be commercially acceptable to the employer. The second proviso in the last sentence is designed to negate any argument that by expressly providing that the employee has no right to be given work or attend the workplace during garden leave, the employer is conceding that there are such rights prior to garden leave. This will not be necessary although, equally, it is unlikely to be harmful where an express provision negating any right to work along the lines of the Precedent in paragraph 4.83 is included in the contract. Finally, the word Group should be defined in the Service Agreement; see paragraph 4.6.

4.85 Previously in this Chapter we have referred to various express terms which we recommend should be included in the contract. A number of these terms are necessary to maximise the effectiveness of a garden leave clause and it is worth identifying them collectively, they are:

- A statement of the duty of fidelity phrased in both a positive and negative way (see para 4.7).
- A working hours clause (see para 4.13).
- A prohibition on the employee undertaking outside activities ideally limited to activities of a competitive nature at least during any garden leave period (see para 4.22). Following the recent decision in *Gregory v Wallace* [1998] IRLR (387) where the prohibition is partial so that, for example, non-competitive work is permitted it will be sensible to consider giving the employer a right of offset of any sums received by the employee from other employment during the garden leave period against sums due from the employer. In *Gregory* no such offset was allowed and although following his summary dismissal, *Gregory* was only entitled to damages, *Wallace* was not able to set-off by way of mitigation the sum *Gregory* was receiving from full time employment because that full time employment was expressly permitted by the contract.
- A confidentiality clause (see para 4.30).
- A notice period of sufficient length to make the garden leave meaningful (see para 4.62 to 4.63).

4.86 In addition, two issues not yet dealt with where a repudiatory breach argument could arise even in the context of an express garden leave clause, are the return of property and status as a director. An employer taking the trouble to include an express garden leave clause, and all the complimentary provisions identified above, should also include:

- An obligation on the employee to return property (excluding contractual benefits) on request or if this is too broad, and it may be particularly in the case of a director, at the very least on the employer exercising his rights to send the employee on garden leave.
- A right to call for the employee's resignation as a director at any time after the exercise of the right to send the employee on garden leave.

For further information on these issues see paragraphs 4.88 to 4.91 and 4.95 to 4.98 respectively.

4.87 Finally, following the EAT's decision in *Whittle Contractors Ltd v Smith* (unreported EAT 842/94) that holiday continues to accrue during garden leave it had become common practice to include a term negating that decision. Following the implementation in English law for the first time of a statutory right to holiday (Regulation 13 of the Working Time Regulations 1998) such a term can prudently no longer be included. However, there can be no objection to a term which provides that outstanding holiday as at the date of commencement of garden leave is, insofar as there is a sufficient garden leave period, deemed to be taken during that period. Employers may well want to consider amending their holiday clauses accordingly.

3(d) Return of property

4.88 Every contract of employment should include a term that the employee shall return all the employer's property when the relationship terminates. Where the contract includes a garden leave clause, as most will now do following the Court of Appeal's decision in *William Hill v Tucker* above (paras 4.82 to 4.83) it is prudent for the obligation also to be triggered by the employer exercising his right to send the employee on garden leave. Where such a provision is included care needs to be taken to exclude from the obligation any property provided as a contractual benefit, typically a car. If that type of property is not excluded there will be a conflict between the garden leave clause which will, and indeed must, provide that all contractual benefits are continued and the return of property clause.

4.89 Some employers omit an obligation to return property from their contracts on the ground that it is no more than a statement of their common law right to have their property returned on request. While an express clause will invariably incorporate that right it can also improve the employer's position in the following ways:

- By providing that property is to be returned automatically on the employee being sent on garden leave or on termination the employee is on notice of the position from the outset and therefore the need for a formal request for return from the employer is obviated. However, it is undeniably good practice for the employer to draw the obligation to the employee's attention once it is known that the employee is to be sent on garden leave or employment is to terminate.
- Where the Service Agreement provides that any property belonging to the individual but containing information belonging to the employer becomes the property of the employer, it can ensure that property is delivered up even if the actual physical property, for example, a computer disk, belongs to the employee.
- It can set out an administrative mechanism for dealing with return of property under which the employee lists the property returned and warrants that he has retained nothing in any form. Not only is this a useful reminder to ensure that the mechanics of return are gone through, but it can also be a significant practical deterrent to an employee proposing to keep, for example, a crucial customer list. Unless he is prepared to lie about documents returned, his only other option is to be evasive about the procedure, which in itself will alert the employer's suspicions. A clause incorporating all these features is set out below.

4.90 Since nowadays it is common for employees to use personal computers at home to work on their employer's business it is also worth including an obligation that the employee delete irrevocably any of the employer's information from the employee's computer systems.

1.1 Upon whichever is the first to occur of (a) the Company exercising its rights pursuant to Clause [insert clause number of garden leave clause] and (b) termination howsoever arising of this Agreement the Executive shall subject to Clause 1.2:

1.1.1 forthwith deliver up to [insert title of company officer] all property in his possession, custody or under his control belonging to the Company [or any other company in the Group] including but not limited to keys, security and computer passes, computer hardware, facsimile machines and all documents and other records (whether on paper, magnetic tape or in any other form and including correspondence, lists of clients or customers, notes, memoranda, software, plans, drawings and other documents and records of whatsoever nature and all copies thereof) made or compiled or acquired by the Executive during his employment hereunder and concerning the business, finances or affairs of the company [or any other company in the Group] or its [or their] clients or customers.

1.1.2 irrevocably delete any information belonging to the Company [or any other company in the Group] from any computer and/or word processing system in his possession or under his control.

1.2 Where the Company exercises its rights pursuant to Clause [insert clause number of garden leave clause] the Executive shall not be obliged to return any property provided to him as a contractual benefit. The Executive shall return such property forthwith on the termination of this Agreement to [insert title of company officer].

1.3 If so requested the Executive shall on each occasion he is obliged to deliver up property or delete information pursuant to this Clause provide to the [insert title of company officer] a signed statement confirming that he has fully complied with his obligations under this Clause.

Note: The word 'Group' should be defined in the Service Agreement; see paragraph 4.6.

4.91 There are two points to be made regarding this precedent. First, we have not used a common formulation namely that return of property shall be 'at any time on request and in any event on termination'. The reason we have not done so is because in our view that formulation does not adequately address the distinction that needs to be drawn as regards contractual benefits during garden leave. Second, this precedent pre-supposes that it is clear what items of property are provided to the Executive as contractual benefits. It is crucial that clarity is achieved on this point not only for the purposes of this clause but also to avoid any argument of breach where the employee is sent on garden leave. Employers should state clearly in the Service Agreements what benefits are contractual and where an additional item of property, for example, a mobile phone, is provided, after the Service Agreement has been signed the employer should make it clear at the time he first agrees to provide it whether or not it is being provided as a contractual benefit. To avoid arguments precisely on this point some Service Agreements now specifically provides that with the exception of benefits referred to in the Agreement all benefits are deemed to be non-contractual. While such a provision may not be determinative in every case it will certainly resolve most potential disputes and is worth including. Set out below is a sample clause.

Any benefits and/or property provided by the Company [or any other company in the Group] to the Executive [or his family] which are not expressly referred to in the Agreement shall be provided to and be enjoyed by the Executive [or his family] at the absolute discretion of the Company [or relevant Group company] and shall not form part of the Executive's contractual entitlements.

Note: The word 'Group' should be defined in the Service Agreement; see paragraph 4.6.

3(e) Resignation from directorships

4.92 Where an employee is also a director of the employing company or any other company within the same group and the Service Agreement includes a garden leave provision it is sensible to include a clause requiring him to resign from the office when he is sent on garden leave or, if he is not, on termination of employment and, in the event of default, entitling the company to appoint someone else to resign on his behalf. The obligation can be framed so that it operates automatically for example once the employee is sent on garden leave or is triggered by a request from the employer. Since there may well be circumstances in which it suits the employer to have greater flexibility we recommend the latter option.

4.93 Traditionally, a clause requiring a director to resign on termination of employment was included as a matter of administrative convenience. It enables a company to circumvent the procedural requirements of Section 303 Companies Act 1985 should the employee not tender his resignation, although in practice it is rare for an employee engaged in competing activities to withhold his resignation. Normally such an employee would prefer to at least attempt to divest himself of his fiduciary duty as a director at the earliest opportunity but delays doing so until termination because of the suspicion which earlier resignation would arouse. With the increasing popularity of garden leave clauses this type of clause has acquired two additional functions in the context of an employee sent on garden leave. First, by having the right to remove the employee as a director it deprives the employee of the argument that sending him on garden leave was a repudiatory breach. Second, assuming the employee is required to resign he is legitimately deprived of all access to up to date confidential information.

4.94 In the rare cases where the employee does not tender his resignation the second limb of the clause operates. It should, however, be remembered that like all other provisions in a Service Agreement it will not survive a repudiatory breach: *General Billposting v Atkinson* [1909] AC 118 (HL) which is considered in Chapter 8.

Upon termination of this Agreement howsoever arising or at any time after the Company has exercised its rights pursuant to Clause [identify garden leave clause] the Executive shall within three days of a request from the Company resign from office as a Director of the Company and all offices held by him in any other companies in the Group and his membership of any organisation acquired by virtue of his tenure of any such office, and should he fail to do so he hereby irrevocably authorises [the Company Secretary] in his name and on his behalf to sign any documents and do any thing necessary or requisite to give effect thereto.

Note: Since the Clause includes a power of attorney the Agreement needs to be executed as a deed by the employee: Section 4 Powers of Attorney Act 1971. Also, the word 'Group' should be defined in the Service Agreement; see paragraph 4.6.

4.95 When including a clause along the lines of the precedent the draftsman needs to think carefully how it will interact with other parts of the Agreement. It is common for a Service Agreement to provide either that resignation as a Director automatically triggers termination of the Agreement or that it gives the employer a power of summary dismissal. Bearing in mind that the primary function of this type of clause is in support of garden leave it would be very unfortunate if exactly the opposite effect were achieved as a result of the draftsman failing to ensure that a resignation under this type of clause did not trigger for example the automatic termination provisions. Also, where the employee's job title and description specifically reflects his position as a director, for example Managing Director, the employer should reserve the right to change the title at the same time as requiring the employee's resignation as a director. By doing so, not only is yet another alleged ground for repudiatory breach removed but also it allows the employer to appoint a replacement management director without risk of any breach of the Articles of Association.

Chapter 5

Confidential information

Introduction

5.1   In Ch 1 we referred to the potential conflict which is inherent in the relationship of employer and employee. In Ch 2 we defined the employment relationship and considered the contract of employment. In this Chapter we consider one of the aspects of the employment relationship which is often the key source of conflict between employer and employee, namely information which the employee acquires in the course of his employment.

Different kinds of business information

5.2   In the decisions of the courts dealing with information which an employee may acquire in the course of employment, reference is made to four kinds of business information. In descending order of significance to the employer they are information which:

(a) is especially confidential so as to amount to trade secrets or their equivalent;
(b) is merely confidential;
(c) amounts to general skill of the employee;
(d) is trivial or easily accessible from public sources.

Only information in categories (a) and (b) amounts to proprietary information of the employer.

Practical effect of the distinction between different types of information: summary

5.3   In view of the complexity of the law on this subject we set out an initial summary of the practical effect of the distinction between different types of business information.

- Trade secrets of the employer will be protected:
  - Even after termination of employment; and
  - Even though there is no express covenant relating to such information.
- Mere confidential information will only be protected during employment and not thereafter; to this there are two exceptions:
  - **Express covenants** – we suggest that the employer may obtain protection over such information after termination of employment by means of an express covenant (an area covenant, non-solicitation/dealing covenant or an express confidentiality covenant: see para 9.22) – provided the

information cannot fairly be regarded as part of the employee's general
skill and knowledge, that is, does not fall into category (c); or
- **Springboard injunctions** – where the employee has during his
employment misused confidential information so that after termination
he gains for himself a head start over others, even if the information is no
longer confidential (for example, because the information has been widely
published after the termination of employment) the employee may
nonetheless be prevented by injunction for a limited period from using
this head start – so placing him under a special disability (for a limited
period) from using this information. Typically, such a 'springboard'
injunction will apply to an ex-employee who during employment removed
a customer list for the purposes of competing with the ex-employer.
Somewhat illogically, the ex-employee may be prevented from dealing
after employment even with customers whose names he can remember
without using the list even though (but for having this list) he would have
been permitted to contact these customers after employment (that
information normally being merely confidential and not trade secret).
The decision in *Universal Thermosensors Ltd v Hibben* [1992] 1 WLR
840 suggests that the position described in the last sentence may be
reviewed by the courts in the future. Springboard injunctions are discussed
in detail in Ch 14.
● It is impermissible (as being against public policy) to seek to prevent the ex-
employee from using his general skill and knowledge after employment.

5.4   These principles are derived from, among others, the decisions of the Court
of Appeal in *Faccenda Chicken Ltd v Fowler* [1987] Ch 117, *Roger Bullivant
Ltd v Ellis* [1987] IRLR 491, *Johnson & Bloy (Holdings) Ltd v Wolstenholme
Rink plc* [1987] IRLR 499 and *PSM International plc v Whitehouse* [1992] IRLR
279.

WHEN IS IT NECESSARY TO DISTINGUISH BETWEEN TRADE SECRET, CONFIDENTIAL
INFORMATION AND SKILL AND KNOWLEDGE?

5.5   In practice it is necessary to distinguish between these categories of
information in two different situations:

● **Where there are no express restrictive covenants** – in the employment
contract, for example restraining competition or solicitation of clients by
the ex-employee after termination of employment, the question may arise
whether the ex-employee can be restrained from using or disclosing
information concerning the business of the ex-employer acquired by him in
the course of his employment in order to compete with the ex-employer; it
is generally only information which is so confidential as to amount to a
trade secret or which is equivalent to a trade secret which will be so protected;
● **Where there are such express restrictive covenants** – in the employment
contract the question is whether the employer can by way of these express
covenants gain protection over mere confidential information which the
general law would not otherwise protect after termination of employment.
There is some uncertainty as to whether an express covenant can achieve
this end, although the gathering consensus is that it can, except in relation to
information which can fairly be regarded as the employee's skill or
knowledge. In our view the employer cannot by express covenant prevent

the use by the employee after employment of information which amounts to general skill and knowledge on the part of the employee.

5.6   The existence and, if existing, the extent of the distinction between categories (a), (b) and (c) (para 5.2) are not universally apparent from the reported cases on the subject. While no-one would argue that general skill and knowledge must be distinguished from confidential information generally (that is, categories (a) and (b) taken together) there is often a blurring of the distinction between (b) (mere confidential information) and (c) (skill and knowledge). Equally there is often a lack of clear distinction between (a) (trade secrets) and (b) (mere confidential information).

5.7   It is often not too difficult to distinguish between genuine trade secrets of the employer, such as secret processes of manufacture, and general skill and knowledge acquired by the employee in the course of his employment, such as knowledge of general scientific and technical principles and methods. However, often between these two extremes there is an intermediate area of information, where it is extremely difficult to differentiate between that which is the employer's confidential information and that which the employee may properly regard as his own skill or knowledge. An example of this is the identity of the employer's customers or even manufacturing knowledge which, although particular to the employer's process, has become part and parcel of the employee's general knowledge. It is in this intermediate area that a controversy has developed, namely the extent to which an employer can by express covenant protect such information which would not, without such express covenant, be protected by the general law.

5.8   The law relating to both the kind of information which is automatically protected in favour of the employer and that which, absent such automatic protection, the employer can protect by means of express covenants is unduly complex and in need of clarification by the courts.

Guide to detail of this chapter

5.9   In the remainder of this Chapter we shall:

- Set out the requirements of confidential information generally.
- Distinguish between:
  - Trade secrets;
  - Mere confidential information; and
  - Skill or knowledge;
  dealing at the same time with the practical effects of the distinction between these types of information.
- Determine if, and to what extent, the employer can by express covenant protect his business information, which is not automatically protected by the general law.
- Deal with the requirement that the employer who seeks to have the court protect trade secrets or confidential information, must be able to identify precisely the information in question – this is often more difficult than would at first appear.
- Consider the duration of the duty of confidence.

- Lastly, consider the position of third parties such as a new employer to whom confidential information of the old employer is disclosed.

1. Requirements of confidential information: generally

5.10 In order to found an action for breach of confidence information must satisfy three requirements to qualify as confidential:

- It must have the necessary quality of confidence.
- It must have been imparted in circumstances importing an obligation of confidence.
- There must be an unauthorised use of that information to the detriment of the party communicating it.

Saltman Engineering Co Ltd v Campbell Engineering Co Ltd (1948) 65 RPC 203 (CA); *Coco v A N Clark (Engineers) Ltd* [1969] RPC 41, 47 (Megarry J); *Attorney General v Guardian Newspapers Ltd (No 2) (*the *Spycatcher* case*)* [1988] 3 All ER 545 (HL) by Lord Griffiths at pages 648–649.

1(a) Quality of confidence

5.11 This element is difficult to define in the abstract, although inaccessibility is always an important feature. Confidentiality may reside in a simple idea: *Under Water Welders & Repairers Ltd v Street and Longthorne* [1968] RPC 498, 506; equally the mere size of the body of information does not make it confidential: *Yates Circuit Foil Co v Electrofoils Ltd* [1976] FSR 345, 393. Something which has been constructed solely from materials in the public domain may possess the necessary quality of confidentiality, for something may have been brought into existence by the application of skill and ingenuity: *Coco v Clark* at page 47. Confidentiality will often reside not in individual items but in a compilation of those items, such as a list of customers: *Roger Bullivant Ltd v Ellis* [1987] IRLR 491. A significant distinction is drawn between confidential or secret information and general skill and knowledge of the employee which cannot be the subject of a duty of confidentiality, and this is discussed below. That which is initially confidential may lose that quality through dissemination, and this is discussed in the context of the defence of publication (Ch 6) and also in Ch 14 in the context of springboard injunctions.

1(b) Circumstances importing an obligation of confidence

5.12 In the employment contract this element is chiefly concerned with the identification by the employer and communication to the employee of what the employer (properly) regards as confidential. This is commonly done by way of express term of the contract of employment. Sometimes even without such identification the circumstances, for example, the employer's method of treatment of the information, will make it clear that the information is regarded as confidential. For a recent relevant case (but outside the employment field) see *Mars UK Ltd v Teknowledge Ltd* 11 June 1999 (unreported) in which Jacob J held that the fact of encryption of information did not render the encrypted information confidential or necessarily render someone who de-encrypted the information subject to a duty of confidence. This element is considered under the definitions of trade secrets and confidential information (in particular: see paras 5.17 to 5.22).

1(c) Detrimental breach

5.13 The element of detriment is controversial. The better view is that in the case of private or commercial confidences it is not a separate element: for example, the anonymous donor whose identity is revealed against his wishes may suffer no specific detriment but should still be able to claim protection of the law of confidence. On the other hand, where the Crown seeks to restrain the disclosure of information (as in the *Spycatcher* case) it must (since it has no private life to protect) show likely harm to the public interest: *Attorney General v Guardian Newspapers Ltd (No 2) (*the *Spycatcher* case*)* [1988] 3 All ER 545, 639-642 (per Lord Keith) (and see also page 657) but see the contrary view of the *Spycatcher* case of Lord Griffiths (at page 650). Lord Goff preferred to keep the question open (page 659). However, in the case of breaches of confidence by an employee or ex-employee the detriment to the employer will usually be clear, rendering the question of whether it is necessary to demonstrate detriment academic.

2. Distinction between trade secrets, confidential information and skill and knowledge: detail

5.14 In the leading case of *Faccenda Chicken Ltd v Fowler* [1984] ICR 589 (upheld in the Court of Appeal at [1987] Ch 117) Goulding J classified confidential information in the field of employment contracts as falling into two categories, namely information which:

- The employee must treat as *confidential* (either because he is told it is confidential or because from its character it is obviously so) but which once learnt necessarily remains in the employee's head and becomes part of his own skill and knowledge applied in the course of his employer's business. So long as the employment lasts he cannot otherwise use or disclose such information without infidelity and therefore breach of contract. However, when he leaves his employment he may use his full skill and knowledge for his own benefit in competition with his ex-employer. Goulding J was of the view (with which the Court of Appeal did not agree, but which has been supported by subsequent court decisions) that if an employer wants to protect information of this kind, he can do so by express covenant restraining the employee from competing with him (within reasonable limits of time and space) after the termination of employment. Examples of this category are manufacturing processes and lists of customers. It is in our view clear from the examples he was here quoting that Goulding J was referring to information which is proprietary in character, ie relates to the particular employer's business and not to general skill or knowledge of the employee acquired in the course of the employment: an employee could not after termination of his employment, it is suggested, be prevented from using general skill or knowledge.
- Amounts to *trade secrets* which even though they have been learnt by heart, they may not, even after termination of the employment contract, be used for anyone's benefit except that of the ex-employer, for example, secret processes.

5.15 The Court of Appeal in *Faccenda* also drew a distinction between trade secrets and mere confidential information, stating that the implied term which imposes an obligation on the ex-employee after termination of employment was restricted in its scope: it might cover such information as secret processes of manufacture such as chemical formulae or designs or special methods of construction and 'other information which is of a sufficiently high degree of confidentiality as to amount to a trade secret'. It did not extend to all information which is only 'confidential' in the sense that an unauthorised disclosure of such information to a third party while the employment subsisted was a clear breach of the duty of good faith. It is not clear to what extent the Court of Appeal had in mind in its category of mere confidential information the distinction between proprietary information of the employer and skill or knowledge of the employee, since use or disclosure during employment of either kind of information for the benefit of a third party would, it is suggested, be a breach of the duty of good faith.

5.16 Since information which is so confidential as to be regarded as trade secret will enjoy protection after termination of employment even without an express restrictive covenant, it is vital to understand what is meant by trade secret in contradistinction to mere confidential information.

2(a) Definition of trade secrets

5.17 In order to determine whether any particular item of information falls within the implied term so as to prevent its use or disclosure even after the termination of employment the Court of Appeal in *Faccenda Chicken Ltd v Fowler* [1987] Ch 117 listed (non-exhaustively) the following factors.

2(a)(i) THE NATURE OF THE EMPLOYMENT

5.17a Employment in a capacity where 'confidential' information was habitually handled might impose a high obligation of confidentiality because the employee could be expected to realise its sensitive nature to a greater extent than if he were employed in a capacity where such material reached him only occasionally or incidentally.

2(a)(ii) THE NATURE OF THE INFORMATION ITSELF

5.17b The information would only be protected if it can properly be classed as a trade secret or as material which, while not properly to be described as a trade secret, is in all the circumstances of such a highly confidential nature as to require the same protection as a trade secret: examples were secret processes of manufacture but there were innumerable other pieces of information capable of being trade secrets, though the secrecy of some information might be short-lived. In addition the fact that the circulation of certain information is restricted to a limited number of individuals might throw light on the status of the information and its degree of confidentiality.

2(a)(iii) WHETHER THE EMPLOYER IMPRESSED ON THE EMPLOYEE THE CONFIDENTIALITY OF THE INFORMATION

5.17c Though the employer cannot prevent the use or disclosure of information merely by telling the employee that it is confidential, the manner in which the employer treats the information may be significant; in *Bjorlow (Great Britain)*

Ltd v Minter (1954) 71 RPC 321 the ex-employers' claim for an injunction failed principally because of their failure to show that they had impressed on the employee during employment that the information was confidential. On the other hand, in *Poly Lina v Finch and Another* [1995] FSR 751, 762 the way in which the information in question was treated by both the employer and the employee during the course of the latter's employment was held to be a crucial factor in determining whether that information warranted protection as a trade secret. On the facts of the case, it was held that the employee had been well educated as to the confidential nature of the information the employer sought to protect.

5.17d See also the decision in *Lancashire Fires Ltd v S A Lyons & Co Ltd* [1997] IRLR 113 where the Court of Appeal held that the judge below had erred in holding that the duty of confidence ended on termination of employment because the claimants had not precisely defined and pointed out those aspects of the production process which they sought to protect as trade secret. It was not incumbent on the employer to point out to the employee the precise limits of what he sought to protect as confidential. Plainly each case turns on its own precise facts.

2(a)(iv) Whether the information can be easily isolated from other information which the employee is free to use or disclose

5.17e The separability of the information is not conclusive but the fact that the 'confidential' information is part of a package and that the remainder of the package is not confidential is likely to throw light on whether the information in question is really a trade secret.

5.17f Of the four elements referred to in *Faccenda*, element number 2 (the nature of the information) is easier to state than to apply in practice, while 4 (separability) also tends to have an elusive quality. It is therefore valuable to consider other formulations by the courts of the definition of trade secrets.

2(a)(v) Recent applications of the above principles

5.17g For a fairly straightforward application of the above principles see *Brooks v Olyslager O M S (UK) Ltd* [1998] IRLR 590 in which the Court of Appeal refused to treat as trade secrets subject to an implied term of confidentiality (after termination of employment on the part of an ex-managing director) information regarding the claimant's solvency, its ability to carry on business for a period of time and its relationship with its holding company. There was no evidence that the information was not widely known or that its 'confidentiality' had ever been impressed on the employee, nor could this information be easily separated from other information which he was free to use.

5.17h *Brooks* should be contrasted with the decision in *Poly Lina v Finch and Another* [1995] FSR 751. It was held that profit margins, costs, sales and development plans all represented confidential information equivalent to a trade secret. This was despite the fact that much of the information could be gleaned at least partially by alternative means - for example market research. The judge found that the alternatives would have been expensive and only partially successful in obtaining the information in question. He also placed emphasis on the degree of damage that would be done to the claimant if the information was released.

2(b) Other definitions of trade secrets

5.18 In *Lansing Linde Ltd v Kerr* [1991] 1 All ER 418 Staughton LJ defined a trade secret (in the context of that case) as information:

- Used in a trade or business.
- Which if disclosed to a competitor would be liable to cause real (or significant) damage to the owner of the secret.
- In respect of which the owner has sought to limit its dissemination or at least has not encouraged or permitted widespread publication.

Trade secrets would cover not only secret formulae for the manufacture of products but also in an appropriate case the names of customers and the goods which they buy. Butler-Sloss LJ also favoured a broader definition of trade secrets 'to be interpreted in the wider context of highly confidential information of a non-technical nature or non-scientific information which may come within the ambit of information the employer is entitled to have protected, albeit for a limited period' (page 435).

5.19 In *Printers & Finishers Ltd v Holloway* [1965] 1 WLR 1 Cross J put forward the test of what is a trade secret as being whether a man of average intelligence and honesty would think that there was anything improper in his putting his memory of the matters in question at the disposal of his new employers.

5.20 In *Thomas Marshall (Exports) Ltd v Guinle* [1979] Ch 227 (a case relating to breach of confidence during the subsistence of the employment contract) the Vice Chancellor Sir Robert Megarry identified four elements which might be of assistance in identifying confidential information and trade secrets:

- The owner of the information must believe that the release of the information would be injurious to him or of advantage to his rivals.
- The owner of the information must believe that the information is confidential or secret.
- His belief under the first two points must be reasonable.
- The information must be judged in the light of the usage and practices of the particular industry or trade concerned.

In *FSS Travel & Leisure Systems Ltd v Johnson* [1998] IRLR 382 the Court of Appeal stated (at para 33) that in identifying whether there were trade secrets which could fairly be regarded as the employer's property there needed to be examined the nature of the employment, the character of the information, the restrictions imposed on its dissemination, the extent of use in the public domain and the damage likely to be caused by its use and disclosure in competition with the employer.

5.21 The above definitions are helpful in focusing on the elements of:

- The likelihood of harm to the employer if disclosure is made.
- Ordinary notions of honesty and fair dealing as being the touchstone of secrecy or confidentiality.

5.22 Again, however, these definitions are often difficult to apply in practice.

Each case has to be carefully considered on its own merits and in this context *Faccenda* provides a useful case study.

2(c) Case study on trade secrets: Faccenda in detail

2(c)(i) THE FACTS

5.23 Faccenda were in the business of breeding, rearing and preparing chickens for sale. Fowler was the former sales manager of Faccenda who had built up a large van sale operation whereby fresh chickens in travelling refrigerated vehicles were offered to the trade. The van salesmen each operated in a different area and after a few weeks knew well the following sales information which Faccenda claimed as confidential:

- The names and addresses of their customers in the particular sector.
- The general limits of the area and the detailed routes taken day by day for supplying the customers.
- The customers' usual requirements both as to quantity and quality.
- The times of delivery.
- The prices paid – which varied with individual circumstances.

5.24 After resigning from the employ of Faccenda, Fowler set up a similar competing business with eight ex-employees of Faccenda. None of the contracts of employment contained express covenants against the use of confidential information or trade secrets gained by the employees while in the employ of Faccenda. Goulding J refused to grant an injunction, regarding the information as falling within the category of mere confidential information which was automatically protected by the implied duty of fidelity during employment and there was no express covenant applying thereafter. The Court of Appeal refused the appeal by Faccenda on the basis that the sales information in question fell into a class of information acquired and remembered by the employee which, while the employment continued the employee might not use or disclose otherwise than in his employment, even though it became part of his own skill and knowledge. However, on leaving his employment the ex-employee was free to use this information for his own benefit.

2(c)(ii) THE ARGUMENTS

5.25 Before the Court of Appeal Faccenda argued that the confidentiality of the sales information resided in its entirety (as a 'package') and that the pricing information was in itself confidential on the basis of the judge's findings that:

- It would be of value to competitors.
- Persons outside the claimant's employment could only obtain approximate knowledge of the prices to individual customers.
- Even a slight price difference might be important in the competitive trade.

It was further argued that the judge below was wrong, in that there was only one class of confidential information (and not trade secrets and confidential information); in holding that information in his second category (mere confidential information) could be protected by express covenant; and in that a clear distinction could be drawn between the skill and general knowledge of trade or business which an employee might obtain in the course of the ex-employer's business and which he was entitled to use in subsequent employment, and the special knowledge of his ex-employer's business which he could not use thereafter.

5.26 In drawing a distinction between trade secrets and confidential information the Court of Appeal stated in *Faccenda* that the implied term which imposes an obligation on the ex-employee after termination of employment was restricted in its scope. It might cover such information as secret processes of manufacture such as chemical formulae or designs or special methods of construction and 'other information which is of a sufficiently high degree of confidentiality as to amount to a trade secret'. It did not extend to all information which is only 'confidential' in the sense that an unauthorised disclosure of such information to a third party while the employment subsisted was a clear breach of the duty of good faith. Examples of this latter class of information were: identity of suppliers, and printing instructions (used in a printing factory) remembered (but not memorised or copied for the purposes of post-employment competition with the ex-employer–which was not permissible). Applying the above criteria to the sales information in question the Court of Appeal held that neither the pricing information nor the sales information as a whole had the degree of confidentiality for it to be regarded as trade secret because:

- The sales information contained some material which was not confidential when looked at in isolation.
- The information about the prices was not clearly separable form the rest of the sales information.
- Neither the sales information in general nor the pricing information could be regarded as plainly secret or sensitive.
- The sales information including the pricing information was necessarily acquired by the salesmen to do their work and each salesman could quickly commit the whole of the sales information relating to his area to memory.
- The sales information was generally known among the van drivers and the secretaries at quite a junior level.
- There was no evidence that Faccenda had ever given any express instructions that the sales information was to be treated as confidential.

5.27 One cannot help having some sympathy in particular with Faccenda's submission that the information in question was more in the nature of special knowledge of the ex-employer's business than general skill or knowledge, but the factors listed in paragraph 5.26 outweighed this.

2(c)(iii) SPECIAL CASE: WHERE THE EX-EMPLOYEE WISHES TO SELL THE INFORMATION

5.28 The Court of Appeal in *Faccenda* also left open for future decision whether additional protection should be afforded to an employer where the ex-employee is not seeking to earn his living by making use of the body of skill, knowledge and experience which he has acquired in the course of his career, but is merely selling to a third party information which he acquired in confidence in the course of his former employment. In *Mainmet Holdings plc v Austin* [1991] FSR 538 Mainmet alleged that its former managing director, Austin, had leaked certain potentially embarrassing information to customers regarding problems being experienced with equipment installed by Mainmet – not in order to compete with Mainmet, but out of malice. Lionel Swift QC (sitting as a deputy High Court Judge) held that the principles concerning the protectability of (mere) confidential information after termination of employment were applicable even though the defendant was allegedly using the information for purposes other than competing with the ex-employer. We suggest, however, that the need for the ex-employer to use his knowledge to earn a living is a compelling reason for marking the moment of termination of employment as the point where the employer is no longer entitled to protection against the use by the employee of mere confidential information or knowledge against the interests of the employer. Where confidential information is to be divulged not for the purpose of enabling the ex-employee to earn a livelihood, whether in his own or someone else's business, but for some other purpose, the court ought to approach the matter more strictly and be prepared to protect even (mere) confidential information.

2(c)(iv) Particular example: pricing information

5.29 A recurring question which arises in practice is whether pricing information amounts to a trade secret. The Court of Appeal in *Faccenda* accepted that there may well be circumstances where pricing information would be regarded as a trade secret or its equivalent. Examples were:

- The price put forward in a tender document.
- The price to be charged for a new model of car or some other product.
- Prices negotiated in a highly competitive market in which it is known that prices are to be kept secret from competitors.

Other pricing information may be protected by express covenant (see below).

2(d) Conclusion regarding the distinction between trade secrets and confidential information

5.30 The elements referred to above under the definition of trade secrets are equally helpful in defining what is (mere) confidential information as they are helpful in defining trade secrets, but they do not necessarily assist in distinguishing between trade secrets and confidential information. Indeed, somewhat startlingly (in the light of the decisions of the Court of Appeal in *Faccenda Chicken v Fowler*, *Roger Bullivant Ltd v Ellis* and *Johnson & Bloy (Holdings) v Wolstenholme Rink plc*) Staughton LJ in *Lansing Linde v Kerr* [1991] 1 All ER 418 (at page 425 h–j and 426d) questioned whether there was a difference at all between trade secrets and confidential information! While it is true that the distinction between trade secret and confidential information is often difficult to draw in practice, the distinction is fundamental, and the claim of an employer (absent an express restrictive covenant) will often depend entirely (as it did in *Faccenda*) on whether the information in question falls into one or the other category. Yet there does not appear to be any difference in principle between the two categories of confidential information, the difference being a matter of degree: (see *Faccenda* at page 299f per Neill LJ and *PSM International plc v Whitehouse* [1992] IRLR 279 (CA) at page 282).

5.31 The employer who wishes to allege that his information is trade secret and not merely confidential must (even in obvious cases, such as secret processes) provide the court with proper details justifying this higher categorisation (see para 5.45). We suggest that in seeking to identify what is a trade secret it is helpful to bear in mind the distinction between general skill and knowledge of the employee and (proprietary) information which relates to the specific business of the employer: the court ought to be careful not to raise to the status of trade secret that which is more in the nature of general skill or knowledge of the ex-employee than knowledge of the employer's specific business. Thus in *Lancashire Fires Ltd v SA Lyons & Co Ltd* [1997] IRLR 113, 117 Sir Thomas Bingham MR stated that the distinction between mere confidential information and trade secrets may often be on the facts very hard to draw

> '.... but ultimately the court must judge whether an ex-employee has illegitimately used the confidential information which forms part of the stock-in-trade of his former employer either for his own benefit or to the detriment of the former employer, or whether he has simply used his own professional expertise, gained in whole or in part during his former employment.'

2(e) Distinction between general skill/knowledge and confidential information

5.32 The courts have long distinguished between (1) confidential or secret information and (2) general skill and knowledge of the employee. In a well-known passage in *Herbert Morris Ltd v Saxelby* [1916] AC 688, 709 Lord Parker stated:

> 'Wherever such covenants have been upheld it has been on the ground not that the servant or apprentice would, by reason of his employment or training, obtain the skill and knowledge necessary to equip him as a possible competitor in the trade, but that he might obtain such personal knowledge of and influence over customers of his employer, or such an acquaintance with his employer's trade secrets as would enable him, if competition were allowed, to take advantage of his employer's trade connection or utilise information confidentially obtained.'

(See also *Wessex Dairies Ltd v Smith* [1935] 2 KB 80.)

5.33 The distinction between (1) general skill and knowledge and (2) confidential information or trade secrets often lies at the heart of disputes relating to confidential information, yet despite recourse to the above-mentioned definitions of trade secrets and confidential information it often remains very difficult to decide on which side of the line particular information falls. In particular, it is often extremely difficult to say whether a specific item of information forms part of the employee's skill and knowledge or amounts to special knowledge of the ex-employer's business (*Faccenda* provides a good example of this difficulty). However, the mere fact that the ex-employee has retained information in his memory (even though he did not deliberately memorise it to compete with his employer after termination of employment) does not mean that this information is not secret: *Amber Size & Chemical Company Ltd v Menzel* [1913] 2 Ch 239. The employer cannot restrict the use by the employee of his skill or knowledge after employment. Thus the decision of the Court of Appeal in *F S S Travel & Leisure Systems Ltd v Johnson* [1998] IRLR 382 serves as a reminder that the employer must adduce sufficiently cogent relevant evidence to identify a separate body of objective knowledge qualifying for protection by means of a restrictive covenant. It was not sufficient for the employer to assert that he was entitled to an accumulated mass of knowledge which he regarded as confidential. In this case the employer failed to justify a 12-month UK wide covenant when the confidential information relied on comprised a computer program in relation to its computerised booking system for the travel industry. It was not established that the defendant took with him or memorised any software programs. The only evidence relied on related to problems encountered and solutions to problems in the computer system and knowledge that 'something could be done': this was held to be too vague and the employers were in fact seeking to restrict the ex-employees' use of their skill, know-how and general experience, inevitably gained while employed as a computer programmer by the ex-employers. However, information amounting to proprietary information of the employer may be automatically protected after employment if it amounts to trade secrets, or by express covenant if it is merely confidential. In order further to illustrate the distinction between (1) confidential information and (2) skill and knowledge, examples from the decided cases are set out by way of an Appendix to this Chapter.

2(f) Non-confidential information

5.34 That which is not confidential the employee is free to use. The starting point is, of course, the other way round, namely that of freedom of speech. The principle of freedom of speech is set out in Article 10 of the Convention for the Protection of Human Rights and Fundamental Freedoms (Rome, 4 November 1950; TS 71 (1953); Cmd 8689) (ratified by the United Kingdom): see *Attorney General v Guardian Newspapers Ltd (No 2)* (the *Spycatcher* case) (1988). In the Court of Appeal [1988] 3 All ER 545, Sir John Donaldson MR said at page 596:

> 'The starting point of our domestic law is that every citizen has a right to do what he likes, unless restrained by the common law, including the law of contract, or by statute. If therefore, someone wishes to assert a right to confidentiality, the initial burden of establishing circumstances giving rise to this right lies on him. The substantive right to freedom of expression contained in Article 10 is subsumed in our domestic law in this universal basic freedom of action.'

Freedom of speech is limited (principally) by the law of defamation and the law relating to confidential information.

5.35 In *Faccenda Chicken Ltd v Fowler* [1984] ICR 589 Goulding J indicated (in the employment context) that this category of information should not be interpreted too broadly; for instance it is perfectly possible to have a document which is the result of work done by the maker on materials which may be readily accessible to the public, but what makes it confidential is that the maker of the document has used his brain and thus produced a document which can only be produced by someone who has gone through the same process.

5.36 Occasionally an employer will seek to protect even non-confidential information. For example, sometimes an employee will agree in a severance agreement in consideration of the payment of money (a 'golden handshake') not to disclose or publish any information whatsoever regarding the employer's affairs. For taxation consequences of such an arrangement see paragraphs 12.20 to 12.21. Even in relation to non-confidential information such an agreement can be effective : *Attorney General v Barker* [1990] 3 All ER 257 (CA), subject to the defence of just cause: see Chapter 6; although conceivably, if the vow of silence inhibits the employee from earning his living, such an agreement might be void as being an unreasonable restraint of trade: cf the discussion above (para 5.28) in relation to the distinction made by the Court of Appeal in *Faccenda* between the ex-employee who uses mere confidential information in the course of new employment and one who seeks to sell it. See also *Femis-Bank (Anguilla) Ltd v Lazar* [1991] 2 All ER 865 in which the Vice Chancellor, Sir Nicholas

Browne-Wilkinson, emphasised the public interest in maintaining freedom of speech.

2(g) Can (mere) confidential information be protected by express covenant?

5.37 Until the decision of the Court of Appeal in *Faccenda* it was always assumed that confidential information could be protected by express covenant. Thus, in *Littlewoods Organisation Ltd v Harris* [1977] 1 WLR 1472 Lord Denning MR said (at page 1479):

'It is thus established that an employer can stipulate for protection against having his confidential information passed on to a rival in trade. But experience has shown that it is not satisfactory to have simply a covenant against disclosing confidential information. The reason is because it is so difficult to draw the line between information which is confidential and information which is not: and it is very difficult to prove a breach when the information is of such a character that a servant can carry it away in his head. The difficulties are such that the only practicable solution is to take a covenant from the servant by which he is not to go to work for a rival in trade. Such a covenant may well be held to be reasonable if limited to a short period.'

Lord Denning referred to the judgment in *Printers & Finishers Ltd v Holloway* [1964] 3 All ER 731 where Cross J said:

'Although the law will not enforce a covenant directed against competition by an ex-employee it will enforce a covenant reasonably necessary to protect trade secrets. ... If the managing director is right in thinking that there are features in the [claimants'] process which can fairly be regarded as trade secrets and which their employees will inevitably carry away with them in their heads, then the proper way for the [claimants] to protect themselves would be by exacting covenants from their employees restricting their field of activity after they have left their employment, not by asking the court to extend the general equitable doctrine to prevent breaking confidence beyond all reasonable bounds.'

See also *Lawrence David Ltd v Ashton* [1989] IRLR 22, 27 (CA).

2(h)(i) FACCENDA

5.38 This was not a case where there was an express covenant. Nonetheless, the question of whether the information which the employers were seeking to protect could have been protected by an express covenant was considered by Goulding J and the Court of Appeal. The type of sales information in question was exactly the sort which ex-employers will often wish to protect as against ex-employees. (The trial judge, Goulding J, found that the sales information was clearly of value to a competitor). Although upholding the decision of Goulding J the Court of Appeal disagreed with the judge that his category of mere confidential information could be protected by express covenant. It is that part of their judgment (probably obiter) that is most controversial.

2(h)(ii) DEVELOPMENTS POST FACCENDA

5.39 In *Balston Ltd v Headline Filters Limited* [1987] FSR 330 the correctness of the proposition that mere confidential information as referred to by Goulding J could not be protected by an express covenant was doubted by Scott J (page 347), who thought that the Court of Appeal could not have intended to exclude all such information from possible protection by restrictive covenant. Scott J referred to the passage from the judgment of Cross J in *Printers & Finishers Ltd v Holloway* [1965] 1 WLR 1 (see para 5.37) quoted with approval by the Court of Appeal in *Faccenda* as to the necessity for employers to protect their trade secrets – by exacting express covenants from their employees. Scott J pointed out that an express covenant would not be needed to protect trade secrets – they would fall within the terms of the implied covenant between employer and employee. Thus the Court of Appeal in *Faccenda* must have been contemplating the protection by an express covenant of confidential information in respect of which an obligation against use or disclosure after determination of the employment could not be implied. He accordingly did not understand the *Faccenda* judgment as meaning that mere confidential information could not be protected by a suitably worded covenant.

5.40 In *Systems Reliability Holdings plc v Smith* [1990] IRLR 377 (a case treated by Harman J on the basis that the covenants were truly vendor and purchaser type covenants and not employer-employee covenants, as to which see para 9.8) Harman J agreed with Scott J's reservations and regarded (what were in his view) the obiter remarks of the Court of Appeal in *Faccenda* as not binding him to hold that there could be in an express restrictive covenant no restriction on the information held by an ex-employee which was not of the type of a trade secret or similar sort of information. These remarks of the Court of Appeal were 'improbable as being the law'.

5.41 In *Lansing Linde Ltd v Kerr* [1991] 1 All ER 418 the Court of Appeal supported the move away from the excessively narrow view of confidential information of the Court of Appeal in *Faccenda* and the type of information which may be protected by express covenant. In this case an ex-director of housing had a contract of employment which included a term that for a period of 12 months after termination of the contract he would not be engaged in any business which competed with Lansing or its associated companies. Staughton LJ regarded the question of whether Goulding J's category of mere confidential information could be protected by express covenant as a matter of definition of trade secrets and whether they differ (if at all) from confidential information. Further, in *Lancashire Fires Ltd v SA Lyons & Co Ltd* [1997] IRLR 113, 116-117, the Court of Appeal (obiter) supported the view that 'mere' confidential information could be protected by a non-competition covenant (para 16 of the judgment of Sir Thomas Bingham MR).

5.42 Thus (by way of example) it may now be expected that the kind of information referred to in *Thomas Marshall (Exports) Ltd v Guinle* [1979] Ch 227 will be capable of being protected by way of express covenant. In that case the Vice Chancellor, Sir Robert Megarry (at page 248), regarded the following categories of trade information as being potentially confidential:

- Names and telex addresses of the company's manufacturers and suppliers and their individual contacts;
- The negotiated prices paid by the company;
- The names of some overseas buying agents through whom the company dealt;
- The company's new ranges actual or proposed;
- Information as to the requirements (such as styles) of the company's customers;

- Details of the company's current negotiations;
- Negotiated prices paid by customers to the company;
- The company's samples;
- The company's current fast-moving lines.

See also *Spafax Ltd v Harrison* [1980] IRLR 442, 447 where the court regarded as confidential such matters as names and addresses of customers, names of buying agents, recent selling history (dates of recent calls and details of recent purchases) computer print-outs containing details regarding customers and price lists.

5.43 It is only what can truly be regarded as skill or knowledge which cannot be protected by an express covenant – where the information is proprietary or more in the nature of proprietary information of the employer than skill and knowledge of the employee, the employer has a legitimate interest which he may protect by restrictive covenant. For example, in *Routh v Jones* [1947] 1 All ER 758 (a covenant by a medical practitioner) Lord Greene MR said (at page 761) that a covenant might be taken to protect for the employer the employee's knowledge of the clients of the practice and their peculiarities, but not his skill or reputation. The cases set out in the Appendix to this chapter help to indicate how the courts have tended to draw the line between the two types of information.

3. Express confidentiality covenants

5.44 Because of the difficulty of drawing the line between confidential information of the employer and general skill and knowledge of the employee and also the difficulty of policing breaches of confidence, most employers prefer to protect their trade secrets and confidential information by means of area covenants. However, most contracts of employment contain also express covenants requiring the employee to maintain confidentiality during and after employment. These covenants are helpful provided that they define and communicate to the employee the kinds of proprietary information for which the employer seeks protection. It follows from our view of *Faccenda* referred to above that it is also our view that the employer can by such a covenant obtain protection after the termination of employment over mere confidential information, but not over skill or knowledge of the employee. In *Ixora Trading Incorporated v Jones* [1990] FSR 251 Mummery J held (at page 258–259) that the contents of a feasibility study and two manuals (alleged to constitute a fund of technical knowledge and experience) was in fact organisational and day-to-day management information which was part of the employee's skill and knowledge and not confidential, even if this information was acquired in the course of employment and was useful in setting up a similar operation after termination of employment. This was so, despite express contractual obligations not to disclose any of the employer's affairs or trade secrets during or after employment and that any information acquired in the course of employment would remain confidential and would not be used for the benefit of the employee. The express covenants were too wide to be enforceable for the protection of confidential information.

3(a) Confidential information must be properly identified

5.45 A common problem which faces employers (and their advisers) is to define with sufficient precision the confidential information which the employer wishes to protect as against ex-employees. The problem may arise because the court regards the employer's view of what is confidential as exaggerated but also because the affidavits or witness statements filed on behalf of the employer do not move away from generalities: see for example *Mainmet Holdings plc v Austin* [1991] FSR 538. Part of the reason for the insistence on particularity is that an injunction must be framed with sufficient precision to enable the person enjoined to know what he is prevented from doing: *Lawrence David Ltd v Ashton* [1989] IRLR 22 (CA) or to prepare properly for trial: *Ocular Sciences Ltd v Aspect Vision Care Ltd* [1997] RPC 289. However, in *Lawrence David* Balcombe LJ (relying on *Littlewoods Organisation Ltd v Harris* [1977] 1 WLR 1472, 1479 (CA)) regarded (at page 27) the difficulty of defining confidential information with sufficient precision for the purposes of a confidential information injunction as one of the reasons justifying the taking of an area covenant. See also *Turner v Commonwealth & British Minerals Ltd* (CA) 19 October 1999 (unreported) to similar effect. Accordingly, while the Court of Appeal refused an injunction prohibiting the disclosure of confidential information on the ground of insufficient identification of the information, it upheld (seemingly inconsistently) the area covenant which was justified principally (but not exclusively) on the basis that it protected confidential information. Unless the court is satisfied that the ex-employee is at the time of making the contract of employment potentially exposed to confidential information, the covenant (if it is taken to protect such information) ought not to be enforced. This means that the employer must identify at least some of this information. It is noteworthy that the Court of Appeal (at page 27) accepted that the employer had identified items of information which were capable of amounting to confidential information (for the purpose of showing that they would suffer damage if their trade secrets were disclosed). Thus it would be safe to assume that in order to justify a restrictive covenant taken to protect confidential information the employer must always make out an arguable case of confidentiality in relation to at least some items of confidential information. See also *Channel Tunnel Group Ltd v Balfour Beatty Construction Ltd* [1992] 2 WLR 741 in which Staughton LJ (at page 760C–E) referred to a relaxation in practice in the last 20 years, at any rate in commercial cases, in the requirement that there should be a high degree of precision in the framing of injunctions, but specifically excepting employees leaving and proposing to use their employer's trade secrets. It is also noteworthy that in adopting a strict approach to the definition of confidential information the Court of Appeal in *Lawrence David* (at page 27) declined to follow the decision of Sir Robert Megarry VC in *Thomas Marshall (Exports) Ltd v Guinle* (referred to above) where he was apparently prepared to grant an injunction restraining the ex-employee from using confidential information without defining the information (although it is fair to say that the report of that case does not set out the terms of the injunction which was actually granted). See also *Lock International plc v Beswick* [1989] 3 All ER 373 and *PSM International plc v Whitehouse* [1992] IRLR 279 (CA). Contrast, however, *Amber Size & Chemical Company Ltd v Menzel* [1913] 2 Ch 239 (see para 5.33). Note also *FSS Travel & Leisure Systems Ltd v Johnson* [1998] IRLR 382 in which the Court of Appeal (at para 34 per Mummery LJ) referred to lack of precision in pleading (and absence of solid proof) of trade secrets as being frequently fatal to enforcement of restrictive covenants and see to similar effect *Ocular Sciences*. The safer course in the light of these recent decisions is to assume that the court will now require precision in identifying confidential information in both classes of case, ie, action to enforce confidentiality and action to enforce restrictive covenants which depend on the existence of confidential information.

3(b)   Restricted shelf life of confidential information

5.46 Confidential information or trade secrets do not normally maintain their confidentiality forever. It is a question of fact in each case for how long protection is merited. Once the information no longer has the quality of confidence, in particular because it has lost the attribute of inaccessibility or has become obsolete, it will no longer be protected as confidential. In *Balston Ltd v Headline Filters Ltd* [1987] FSR 330, 348 Scott J thought that the implied duty of confidentiality would always be unlimited in time (and probably in area as well). However, once the information loses the attribute of inaccessibility or is obsolete it will no longer be confidential and therefore the duty to be implied might preferably be said to last until the information is no longer confidential. In *Prout v British Gas plc* [1992] FSR 478 it was held by the Patents County Court that the duty of confidence (in relation to information placed by an employee under an 'employee's suggestion scheme' would ordinarily have come to an end when the suggestion was publicly used for the employer's purposes without objection from the employee. However, if the employee gave notice that he intended to seek patent protection, the employer was under a duty to continue to respect the confidence at least until the employee's rights had been safeguarded by the filing of a patent application on his behalf. Where the parties have entered into express covenants for a limited period (for example, an area covenant) for the protection of confidential information, the court will often take that agreed period as marking the duration of the duty of confidence (express or implied): *Systems Reliability Holdings plc v Smith* [1990] IRLR 377; *Roger Bullivant Ltd v Ellis* [1987] IRLR 491. The circumstances under which publicity can destroy confidentiality are further discussed in Ch 6 (in the context of the defence of publication) and in Ch 14 (when dealing with the duration of springboard injunctions).

3(c)   Confidential information in the hands of third parties

5.47 A third party who knowingly receives confidential information may be restrained from using it: *Prince Albert v Strange* (1849) 64 ER 293; *Schering Chemicals Ltd v Falkman Ltd* [1981] 2 All ER 321. He will also be liable to account for profits derived from using the information, or for damages. A third party who 'turns a blind eye' where the circumstances are suspicious will be taken to have knowledge: *London & Provincial Sporting News Agency Ltd v Levy* (1928) MacG Cop Cas 340 (1923–28). It may be enough to impute knowledge on the part of the third party that (on the basis of an objective test of reasonableness) he ought to have known that he was receiving information in breach of confidence: *Ansell Rubber Co Pty Ltd v Allied Rubber Industries Pty Ltd* (1966) [1972] RPC 811, 821, and see Gurry *Breach of Confidence* (1984) page 274. A third party who receives confidential information not knowing that it is confidential may be restrained from using it after notice of impropriety: *Malone v Commissioner of Police of the Metropolis (No 2)* [1979] 2 All ER 620; *Printers & Finishers Ltd v Holloway* [1964] 3 All ER 731; *Fraser v Evans* [1969] 1 All ER 8. This would appear to be subject to two provisos, namely that it has not lost its quality of confidence by becoming too widely disseminated and the third party has not provided value for it.

5.48 This is a controversial area of the law (for a detailed treatment of the subject see Gurry *Breach of Confidence* [1984] pages 269 to 283). Some clarification is to be found in certain of the judgments in the *Spycatcher* case (*Attorney General v Guardian Newspapers Ltd (No 2)* [1988] 3 All ER 545). Lord Griffiths said (page 652):

> 'In a case of commercial secrets ... a third party who knowingly receives the confidential information directly from the confidant ... is tainted and identified with the confidant's breach of duty and will be restrained from making use of the information. If, however, before the confider can act, his confidential information has spread far and wide and is read in, say, some trade magazine by a rival manufacturer, that manufacturer is in no way tainted or associated with the original breach of confidence, and he will not be restrained from making use of the confidential information that is now public knowledge even though he may realise that the information must have been leaked in breach of confidence ... That is not to say that the original confidant may not be restrained or even a third party in the direct chain from the confidant. Each case will depend on its own facts and the decision of the judge as to whether or not it is practical to give injunctive protection and whether the third party should, as a matter of fair dealing, be restrained ...whether the conscience of the third party is affected by the confidant's breach of duty. There is certainly no absolute rule even in the case of a breach of a private confidence that a third party who receives the confidential information will be restrained from using it.'

5.49 In the judgment of the Court of Appeal in the *Spycatcher* case Sir John Donaldson MR described the position of the third party as follows (page 596):

> 'Since the right to have confidentiality maintained is an equitable right, it will ..."bind the conscience" of third parties, unless they are bona fide purchasers for value without notice (per Nourse LJ on 25 July 1986 in the interlocutory proceedings: *Attorney General v Observer Ltd*).'

3(d) Confidentiality injunctions affecting vested rights of third parties

5.50 Often the ex-employer will wish to enjoin not only the ex-employee but also the new employer (to whom the ex-employee has transferred his loyalties) from using the ex-employer's trade secrets or confidential information. Thus the court may grant an injunction preventing the ex-employee from continuing with a contract of employment where to enter into such employment would be in breach of covenant as against the ex-employer. The effect may be to deprive the new employer (who may be entirely innocent) of his contractual rights to the services of the employee. Although the court will be readier to restrain the entering into of future contracts it may even deprive the third party of acquired contractual rights. Thus in *P S M International plc v Whitehouse* [1992] IRLR 279 the Court of Appeal (while reiterating that the Court should be wary of granting equitable remedies which would interfere with the contractual rights of innocent third parties) upheld the grant of an injunction restraining the new employer (a company controlled by the ex-employee) from proceeding with or fulfilling orders which had been placed by a former customer of the claimant in circumstances in which it was arguable that in obtaining these orders the ex-employee had used trade secrets of the claimant.

3(e) Confidential information disclosed in pre-employment period

5.51 This is dealt with in paragraphs 3.66 to 3.68.

3(f) Jointly owned confidential information

5.52 In the absence of any contractual relationship a claimant who co-owned a package of confidential information put together to facilitate a business project was held to be powerless to protect the information after a decision taken by his co-owner to exclude him from participating in the project. The use of the information to the detriment of the claimant could not be relied on to found an action for breach of confidence: *Murray v Yorkshire Fund Managers Ltd* [1998] 1 WLR 951.

Examples of cases showing the difference between confidential information and skill and knowledge

Non-technical information

1. In *Island Export Finance Ltd v Umunna* [1986] BCLC 460 Hutchinson J held (at page 483g) that knowledge of a potential market which could be exploited was something which became part of the director-employee's own skill and knowledge and which he could use for his own benefit in competition with the employer after termination of his appointment. Here the alleged confidential information was of a requirement for a large number of caller boxes in the Cameroons and that there was a manufacturing source in the United Kingdom. It was held that directors (no less than employees) acquire a general fund of knowledge and expertise and will not, where such knowledge and expertise in truth becomes part of their stock in trade, be precluded from exploiting it merely because they came by it solely because of their position as directors (page 482b–e). It is of course entirely different where the ex-director uses his knowledge of a business opportunity which was being actively pursued by the company (see diverting business opportunities: paras 3.54 to 3.56): we suggest that this type of information could have been protected by an express covenant. See *E Warsley & Co Ltd v Cooper* [1939] 1 All ER 290 (a case in which there were no express covenants) in which Morton J held that the names of suppliers (of paper to the employers who were paper merchants) amounted to knowledge, skill and experience, although this information was treated by the employers as confidential.

2. In *Stephenson Jordan and Harrison Ltd v MacDonald and Evans* [1952] 1 TLR 101 the compilation and application of certain (well-known) accounting principles to a particular business were held to be general skill and knowledge and not confidential information. We suggest that this type of information could not have been protected by an express covenant.

3. In *Baker v Gibbons* [1972] 1 WLR 693 the name and address of a particular employee of the employer or the names of the employer's selling agents were not (apart from the case where a list was taken or memorised) regarded as confidential: we suggest that this type of information could have been protected by an express covenant.

4. In *G D Searle v Celltech* [1982] FSR 92 (CA) the Court of Appeal held that names, aptitudes, characteristics or fields of specialisation of employees (in the absence of express covenants relating to such matters) were not confidential. In the absence of restrictive covenants, there was nothing to stop a number of employees in concert deciding to leave their employer and

set themselves up in competition with him. However, Brightman LJ (dissenting on this point) was prepared to accept (at page 106) that an employee leaving one commercial organisation for another was not prima facie at liberty to divulge to his new employer the identity of the skilled workforce of his former employer in order to enable his new employer to poach such workforce, if such information was in the possession of the ex-employee only because of his former employment.

5. In *Sir W C Leng & Co Ltd v Andrews* [1909] 1 Ch 763, 774 Farwell LJ held that details of office organisation, general organisation and management of the business of the employer, were not capable of protection by express covenant: the employer's claim failed for the same reason in *Herbert Morris Ltd v Saxelby* [1916] AC 688; and see also *Commercial Plastics Ltd v Vincent* [1964] 3 All ER 546, 551 (CA), *Amway Corporation v Eurway International Ltd* [1974] RPC 82, and *Ixora Trading Incorporated v Jones* [1990] FSR 251 referred to at paragraph 5.44. On the other hand in *Littlewoods Organisation Ltd v Harris* [1977] 1 WLR 1472, 1484 (CA) Megaw LJ accepted that knowledge obtained by Harris as chairman of the Littlewoods Organisation of such matters as the trend of mail order sales, the percentage and identity of the returns, and the sources of manufacture, plans for future catalogues and the results of market research were confidential.

6. In *Berkeley Administration Inc v McClelland* [1990] FSR 505 (related to the litigation in *Ixora Trading Incorporated v Jones* referred to above) Wright J held that financial information in a business plan, namely the average operating profit per bureau de change operated by the employer, the average profit in the first year of operation expressed as a percentage of the full year's profit, the average capital cost per bureau, the average number of annual transactions per bureau and the average value per transaction, was not confidential, since the information was either well known or part of the general knowledge and experience of the employees. This finding was made despite the fact that most of the information was contained in a book marked confidential, of which a limited number of copies were produced, each copy being numbered, a record being kept of all recipients and confidentiality firmly impressed on anyone who had anything to do with it. There were apparently also express contractual confidentiality covenants, although they are not considered in the judgement, the question of confidentiality being dealt with on general principles. The decision of the court can be justified on the basis of the key factual finding that figures contained in the book were not genuine historical or forecast figures, but were merely assumptions for the purpose of supporting any proposal to raise a particular sum of money. Further, some of the information had actually been advertised by Berkeley in the press.

7. In *F S S Travel & Leisure Systems Ltd v Johnson* [1998] IRLR 382 a computer program in relation to computerised booking systems for the travel industry was held not to be trade secret. Problems encountered and solutions to problems in the computer system and knowledge that 'something could be done' was held to be too vague: the employers were in fact seeking restrict the ex-employees general skill and knowledge.

Technical information

1. In *Printers & Finishers Ltd v Holloway* [1964] 3 All ER 731 in a well-known passage Cross J in putting forward a reasonable man test of honesty to distinguish between the employee's knowledge and confidential information of the employer put the onus squarely on the shoulders of the employer to take express covenants so as to enable the employee to distinguish between the two categories: the employer failed principally because:

    *   The employee might not realise that a particular feature of the employer's process was peculiar to the employer's process; and
    *   Even if he did, the knowledge in question was not readily severable from his general knowledge of the flock printing process and his acquired skill in manipulating a flock printing plant (page 736D–F).

2. In *Under Water Welders & Repairers Ltd v Street and Longthorne* [1968] RPC 498 a novel process for the cleaning of ships' hulls was held (for purposes of an interlocutory injunction against ex-employees) to be confidential even though the claimant's evidence did not provide details of the process which gave it a confidential character, the court basing its decision on the fact that there was strong evidence that the information was treated by the claimant and both defendants (and others) as confidential and that the defendants' case did not sufficiently negate confidentiality. It is unlikely in today's atmosphere of greater scepticism regarding claims of confidentiality that an injunction would have been granted in these circumstances.

3. In contrast to *Under Water Welders*, in *United Sterling Corporation Ltd v Felton and Mannion* [1974] RPC 162, where Brightman J undertook a useful review of the earlier authorities bearing on the distinction between general knowledge and confidential information, he held that in the absence of an express covenant the knowledge of an ex-employee gained during employment as to a new process for producing polystyrene was know-how and not the employer's confidential information. He sought to explain (at pages 172-173) the differing decisions in *Printers* and *Under Water Welders*. In both cases the claimant company had operated the process in question under licence from a third party imposing a duty of confidence. Further, in both cases the employee was aware of the employer's duty of confidence and had either expressly or impliedly been under instruction to preserve confidence. The difference was, however that:

    *   In *Printers* there was no secret feature of the process readily separable from Holloway's general knowledge and skill. This led Cross J to conclude that a reasonable man would not have thought there was anything improper in his using that information post employment for the benefit of another employer. In contrast in *Under Water Welders* the judge concluded that the process did involve some secret characteristic readily distinguishable from the managing director's general knowledge of the business of cleaning ships' hulls;
    *   *Printers* was decided after full trial with full opportunity to debate the principles involved, whereas *Under Water Welders* was decided in interim proceedings.

The latter point is significant: it may be considerably more difficult to persuade a judge at trial on all the evidence that the process is truly confidential than to set up an arguable case of confidentiality on paper for the purposes of obtaining interim relief. Thus in *Lawrence David Limited v Ashton* [1989] IRLR 22 (CA) the Court of Appeal (in emphasising that the principles of *American Cyanamid Co v Ethicon Ltd* [1975] AC 396 (HL) (see Ch 13) were normally applicable to applications for interim injunctions in restrictive covenant cases) held that all the claimant must establish was that there was a serious issue to be tried as to confidentiality, and held (following *Cranleigh Precision Engineering Ltd v Bryant* [1964] 3 All ER 289) that various manufacturing techniques (as well as customer connection and knowledge of their requirements in a highly specialised field) were arguably confidential so as to support an area covenant.

See also *Diamond Stylus Company Ltd v Bauden Precision Diamonds Ltd* [1973] RPC 675.

4. In *Balston Ltd v Headline Filters Ltd* [1987] FSR 330 the court followed the strict approach of the Court of Appeal in *Faccenda* towards the definition of what was a trade secret. While Scott J regarded it as arguable that the claimant's specific blend of fibres (for the glass microfibre tubes which it sold) was a trade secret, he regarded a claim to be entitled to restrain the ex-employee from using blends substantially the same as the specific blends as a claim to prevent him from using his knowledge and experience of mixing grades of fibres to produce filter tubes with particular specifications. The ex-employee's knowledge of the mixes necessary to meet particular specifications included knowledge of the claimant's mixes which could not be separated from the sum total of the ex-employee's knowledge of the manufacturing process. In the absence of an express non-competition covenant the ex-employer was not entitled to protection against anything more than its specific fibre mixes. At trial – [1990] FSR 385 – Falconer J appeared to accept that the fibre mix recipes were confidential (at page 420) although not highly secret, but was of the view that the sort of recipes which would be likely to produce a particular filter tube was part of the knowledge and expertise of the ex-employee. Accordingly, while the specific recipes were confidential, the knowledge of the general area in which a recipe must lie to produce a particular result was part of the ex-employee's expertise or know-how.

5. In *Johnson & Bloy (Holdings) Ltd v Wolstenholme Rink plc* [1987] IRLR 499 (CA) Fox and Parker LJJ held (at pages 501 and 502) that to limit any restraint to the precise details of the ex-employer's precise formulae was not adequate since it would or might enable the restraint to be avoided by small variations in the percentages of the constituents or otherwise. In this case the claimant alleged that the combination of the ingredients and the particular proportions in which they were used in the drying agent utilised in the manufacture of one of the inks was unique and amounted to a trade secret. The Court of Appeal upheld the employer's claim for an injunction preventing the use of this information on grounds (among other things) that there was an arguable case that the information amounted to a trade secret. Unlike *Balston* this was a case where the ex-employee had improperly removed

documents containing information relating to the ex-employer's formulae. The fact that the ex-employee might by the injunction be prevented from using his general chemical knowledge was accordingly regarded as a problem of his own making. Although the illicit removal of documentation is primarily relevant to the second ground of the decision of the Court of Appeal, namely the application of the springboard doctrine (see Ch 14), the ex-employee's conduct may also have encouraged the Court of Appeal to take a wider view of what amounted to trade secrets.

6.   At the interim stage the claimant need only establish an arguable case of confidentiality (see *Graham v Delderfield* [1992] FSR 313) and it may be a tempting course for the judge in a case involving complicated scientific data to say that the matters can only be properly investigated at trial and that for interim purposes the claimant must be treated as having an arguable case. However, in *Lock International plc v Beswick* [1989] 3 All ER 373 Hoffmann J refused to '... allow the [claimant] to blind the court with scientific banalities', and held that (save in one respect) the claimant did not have even an arguable case in relation to technical information relating to metal detectors manufactured by the claimant. Hoffmann J distinguished between a case where the employee has general familiarity with the claimant's product (which was pre-eminently the kind of skill and knowledge which the honest employee cannot help taking away with him) and one where the ex-employee is shown to have detailed knowledge of the employer's trade secrets. See also *Mainmet Holdings plc v Austin* [1991] FSR 538.

7.   See also: *Morison v Moat* (1852) 21 LJ Ch 248 and *Reid & Sigrist Ltd v Moss Mechanism Ltd* (1932) 49 RPC 461.

8.   In *Systems Reliability Holdings plc v Smith* [1990] IRLR 377, 384 Harman J held that in the case of vendor and purchaser type covenants it was proper that the vendor should be prevented from using or disclosing confidential knowledge in his head concerning the business or services supplied by the company.

9.   In *Lancashire Fires Ltd v SA Lyons & Co* Ltd [1997] IRLR 113 the Court of Appeal held that that the claimant's production process was a trade secret even though the employer had not pointed out to the employee the precise limits of what he sought to protect as confidential.

Chapter 6

Confidential information: defences

6.1   In Ch 5 we considered the circumstances in which business information of an employer will be protected by the law as secret or confidential. In this Chapter we look at the circumstances in which information which is on the face of it confidential can be said to have lost that quality. In particular, we consider the two principal areas of defence which an employee or ex-employee may raise when faced with a breach of confidence action by the employer or ex-employer, namely:

- Publication;
- The defence of just cause.

1. Publication

1(a) When will publication destroy confidentiality?

6.2   It is very difficult to describe the degree of publication that is necessary to destroy confidentiality. This matter was the subject of much debate in the notorious *Spycatcher* case. In that case (*Attorney General v Guardian Newspapers Ltd (No 2)* [1988] 3 All ER 545 (CA)) Sir John Donaldson MR said in the Court of Appeal (page 595):

> 'As a general proposition, that which has no character of confidentiality because it has already been communicated to the world, ie made generally available to the relevant public, cannot thereafter be subjected to a right of confidentiality ... However, this will not necessarily be the case if the information has previously only been disclosed to a limited part of the public. It is a question of degree.'

In the same case Bingham LJ said (page 624):

> 'The information must not be 'public knowledge' (*Seager v Copydex* [1967] 1 WLR 923, 931G per Lord Denning MR), nor in the public domain: *Woodward v Hutchins* [1977] 1 WLR 760, 764D per Lord Denning MR. To be confidential, information must have what Francis Gurry recently called the basic attribute of inaccessibility. See Gurry, *Breach of Confidence* (1984) page 70.'

6.3   If the claimant publishes the confidential information before he brings proceedings, for example by including it in the specification for the purposes of a patent application, that will ordinarily destroy the confidentiality: *Mustad & Son v Allcock & Co Ltd and Dosen* [1963] 3 All ER 416; *Franchi v Franchi*

[1967] RPC 149. However, that is not the case where the employer was not responsible for publication: *Cranleigh Precision Engineering Ltd v Bryant* [1964] 3 All ER 289 and see Ch 14 in relation to springboard injunctions. The same is true (all the more so) where it is the confidant who is responsible for its publication: *Speed Seal Products Ltd v Paddington* [1986] 1 All ER 91 and see *Attorney General v Guardian Newspapers Ltd (No 2)* [1988] 3 All ER 545 (per Lord Griffiths at page 649). However Lord Goff (at pages 661–662) expressed doubts in this regard, saying that once confidential information has ceased to exist as confidential information the duty of confidence must be destroyed no matter who destroyed it – the confidant who so destroys the confidential information may, however, be put under a special ('springboard') disability.

6.4   The law may still treat as confidential information which is quite widely available: *Exchange Telegraph Company Ltd v Central News Ltd* [1897] 2 Ch 48 and see also *Spycatcher* (page 643) per Lord Keith.

1(b)   How management can protect confidential information which needs to be circulated to the workforce

6.5   Confidentiality is not lost where information is disclosed to a limited number of people who have an interest to receive it. In *Sun Printers Ltd v Westminster Press Ltd* [1982] IRLR 292 Donaldson LJ said:

> 'There is nothing, in my judgment, to prevent the fullest communications between management and the workforce under a seal of confidentiality.'

The claim for an injunction failed in that case because the employer failed to stamp 'confidential' on each document and to make it clear that the widespread distribution of information to the workforce did not mean that the report in question ceased to be confidential.

2. Defence of just cause or excuse

6.6   The public interest which requires that (in general) confidences should be upheld sometimes dictates the opposite, namely that confidences be broken: as, for example, where the alleged confidence relates to the commission of a crime or civil wrong. This is most commonly expressed by the statement of Wood VC in *Gartside v Outram* (1856) 26 LJ Ch 113: 'there is no confidence as to the disclosure of iniquity'. From this has developed the (broader) defence of just cause or excuse: *Attorney General v Guardian Newspapers Ltd (No 2)* [1988] 3 All ER 545 (HL) (per Lord Griffiths at page 649).

6.7   In *Initial Services Ltd v Putterill* [1968] 1 QB 396 Lord Denning MR stated (page 405) that the defence:

> '... should extend to crimes, frauds and misdeeds, both those actually committed as well as those in contemplation, provided always, and this is essential, that the disclosure is justified in the public interest.'

See also: *Beloff v Pressdram Ltd* [1973] 1 All ER 241, 259-260.

6.8   The defence was broadened in *Lion Laboratories Ltd v Evans* [1985] QB 526 in which Griffiths LJ expressed it as follows (at page 550):

> 'I can see no sensible reason why this defence should be limited to cases in which there has been wrongdoing on the part of the [claimants] ... [I]t is not difficult to think of instances where, although there has been no wrongdoing on the part of the [claimant], it may be vital in the public interest to publish a part of his confidential information.'

In the same case Stephenson LJ formulated the defence in this way (at page 536):

> 'The courts will restrain breaches of confidence ... unless there is just cause or excuse for breaking confidence. The just cause or excuse with which this case is concerned is the public interest in admittedly confidential information. There is confidential information which the public have a right to receive and others, particularly the press, now extended to the media, may have a right and even a duty to publish, even if the information has been unlawfully obtained in flagrant breach of confidence and irrespective of the motive of the informer.'

A useful summary of the cases on the just cause defence is contained in the judgment of Rose J in *X v Y* [1988] 2 All ER 648.

2(a)   Distinction between public interest and what may be interesting to the public

6.9   As to what is to be regarded as in the public interest it is relevant to bear in mind the words of Lord Wilberforce in *British Steel Corporation v Granada Television Ltd* [1981] 1 All ER 417, 455 e–f:

> '...there is a wide difference between what is interesting to the public and what is in the public interest to make known.'

As Stephenson LJ said in *Lion Laboratories* at page 537 C:

> 'The public are interested in many private matters which are no real concern of theirs and which the public have no real pressing need to know.'

2(b)   Examples of matters of wrongs which may be disclosed

6.10   Examples of (the narrower category of) wrongs which may be disclosed are:

- Accounting and business information which indicated that the employer was defrauding his customers: *Gartside*;
- (Arguably) information of breach of the claimant's duty to register a pricing agreement under the Restrictive Trade Practices Act 1956: *Initial Services.*

2(c)   The broader category

6.11   In *Fraser v Evans* [1969] 1 QB 349 Lord Denning MR said that 'iniquity' was merely an instance of 'just cause or excuse for breaking the confidence'. There are, however, difficulties in defining this broader category of matters which may be disclosed in the public interest. The broader approach:

> '... involves the judge in balancing the public interest in upholding the right to confidence, which is based on the moral principles of loyalty and fair dealing, against

some other public interest that will be served by publication of the confidential material ... I have no doubt ... that in the case of a private claim to confidence, if the three elements of quality of confidence, obligation of confidence and detriment or potential detriment are established, the burden will lie on the defendant to establish that some other overriding public interest should displace the [claimant's] right to have his confidential information protected.' (*Attorney General v Guardian Newspapers Ltd (No 2)* (the *Spycatcher* case) [1988] 3 All ER 545, 649 (per Lord Griffiths) and see Lord Goff (page 659).

EXAMPLES OF THE BROADER CATEGORY

6.12 Examples of the broader category of information which may be disclosed are:

- Internal memoranda casting doubt on the accuracy of breathalyser instruments relied on in prosecutions: *Lion Laboratories*.
- Matters regarded by the court as constituting a threat to the health or welfare of the community: *Hubbard v Vosper* [1972] 1 All ER 1023 and *Church of Scientology of California v Kaufman* [1973] RPC 635 (information regarding scientology), but not where the threat has passed: *Schering Chemicals Ltd v Falkman Ltd* [1981] 2 All ER 321 (allegedly dangerous drug already withdrawn from the market).
- Conduct misleading to the public: *Initial Services*: (arguably) wrongly claiming to the public that a price increase was because of tax and *Church of Scientology* (that large fees were being charged for what was 'mumbo-jumbo').
- In *Woodward v Hutchins* [1977] 1 WLR 760, Lord Denning MR said that there should be 'truth in advertising' so that the public should not be misled (private lives of pop musicians could be disclosed by their former public relations officer). This decision seems to stretch the limits of the just cause defence to extraordinary limits: it should, it is suggested, be applied with the greatest circumspection: exaggeration should be distinguished from fraud on the public. Further, this was surely a case of information which, although of interest to the public, was hardly required in the public interest to be disclosed.
- Not evidence of homosexual acts between consenting adults: *Stephens v Avery* [1988] Ch 449.

2(d) On what evidence may the employee disclose?

6.13 There must be reasonable grounds for the employee to suspect that the misdeed has been or will be committed. It must not be 'upon a mere roving suggestion ... or even perhaps on a general suggestion' (*Gartside*).

6.14 In *Attorney General v Guardian Newspapers Ltd (No 2)* (the *Spycatcher* case) [1988] 3 All ER 545, 644 Lord Keith of Kinkel was of the view that there must at least be a prima facie case that the allegations have substance. Lord Goff said (at page 660):

'... a mere allegation of iniquity is not of itself sufficient to justify disclosure in the public interest. Such an allegation will only do so if, following such investigations as are reasonably open to the recipient, and having regard to all the circumstances of the case, the allegation in question can reasonably be regarded as being a credible allegation from an apparently reliable source.'

6.15 In *Re a Company's Application* [1989] 3 WLR 265, 270 Scott J said (referring to Lord Keith's remark) that it was made in the context of a disclosure threatened to be made to the world at large, a disclosure which would have taken place in the national press. He said that where the disclosure which is threatened was no more than a disclosure to a recipient which has a duty to investigate matters within its remit, it was not, in his view, for the court to investigate the substance of the proposed disclosure unless there was ground for supposing that the disclosure went outside the remit of the intended recipient of the information.

2(e) Disclosure to whom?

6.16 Disclosure of what would otherwise be confidential information in order to be justified by the defence of just excuse must be to a person with a proper interest to receive such information. In *Initial Services* (at page 405) Lord Denning MR said that the disclosure must be to one who has a proper interest to receive the information. Thus it would be proper to disclose a crime to the police, or a breach of the Restrictive Practices Act to the registrar. There might be cases where the misdeed was of such a character that the public interest might demand, or at least excuse, publication on a broader field, even to the press.

6.17 Put differently (in the words of Sir John Donaldson MR) in the *Spycatcher* case (page 596):

'... the nature and degree of the communication must be proportionate to the cause or excuse.'

See also page 649 (per Lord Griffiths). In cases of civil misdeeds the appropriate person to whom disclosure should be made is the victim and in cases involving the community, disclosure to the press might be appropriate.

6.18 The significance of the nature and extent of the proposed disclosure is illustrated by the decision in *Re a Company's Application* [1989] 3 WLR 265 in which Scott J refused to grant an injunction against a former employee of a company providing financial services restraining him from informing FIMBRA (the appropriate regulatory body) of alleged breaches of the regulatory scheme. Likewise the ex-employee was not restrained from informing the Revenue of confidential information relating to fiscal matters. Scott J doubted that an employee's duty of confidence extended to not disclosing information to the regulatory authority or not to disclose fiscal matters to the Revenue. If the ex-employee had threatened general disclosure of the company's information there would have been no answer to an injunction (page 269 C). Accordingly, the court would probably have granted an injunction restraining the ex-employee from communicating to anyone other than his legal advisers the fact that he had instigated the relevant investigations – but the defendant proffered an appropriate undertaking to that effect to the court. See also *W v Egdell* [1989] 2 WLR 689.

2(f) Bad faith on the part of the employee

6.19 Generally, where the defence of just cause exists the motive of the employee will not be relevant: *Lion Laboratories* at page 536 and *Re a Company's Application* [1989] 3 WLR 265. However, in doubtful cases bad faith may tip the balance against the employee: see *Schering Chemicals Ltd v Falkman Ltd* [1981] 2 All ER 321, 338-9; *Weld-Blundell v Stephens* [1919] 1 KB 520. Of course, bad faith may also go to the strength of the defence of just cause indicating that it may have been 'dreamt up' by the defendant. See *Re a Company's Application* at page 269.

2(g) Distinction between defence of just cause (breach of confidence) and defence of justification in defamation

6.20 In a defamation case the court will not (except in the rarest cases) grant an injunction to prevent publication where the defence of justification is raised. The public interest in freedom of speech will be upheld but the court will restrain the publication of obvious lies: *Harakas v Baltic Mercantile and Shipping Exchange Ltd* [1982] 1 WLR 958. In the case of breach of confidence there is, however, a competing public interest in the duty of confidence being upheld and it is for the defendant to show a prima facie defence of just cause.

In *Lion Laboratories* Griffiths LJ said (at page 550):

'But if the same approach [as in defamation] was adopted in actions for breach of confidence it would ... indeed be a mole's charter. There is a public interest of a high order in preserving confidentiality within an organisation ... When there is an admitted breach of confidence, there will usually be a powerful case for maintaining the status quo by the grant of an interlocutory injunction to restrain publication until trial of the action. It will, I judge, be an exceptional case in which a defence of public interest which does not involve iniquity on the plaintiff will justify refusing an injunction. But I am bound to say that I think this is such a case.'

6.21 Thus, where there are possible defences of just cause or justification, the claimant who can sue either for breach of confidence or defamation is usually in a stronger position to obtain an interlocutory injunction relying on breach of confidence: see the discussion in *Lion Laboratories* at page 538 where earlier authorities to the contrary are doubted. The decision of the Court of Appeal in *Woodward v Hutchins* [1977] 1 WLR 760 in which an injunction based on breach of confidence was refused essentially because it was interwoven with a claim based on libel appears to have been wrongly decided in this respect. The approach in *Lion Laboratories* is to be preferred.

3. Whistleblowing

6.22 Under the Public Interest Disclosure Act 1998 since 2 July 1999 specific rights are introduced for those who disclose information to a third party about an alleged wrongdoing in defined circumstances. The Act does not provide a general 'whistleblowers' charter' but provides instead for the channeling of disclosures through specific sources. It is essential first to ascertain whether the relevant disclosure relates to one of the six specific categories of subject matter set out in the Act and secondly whether the disclosure has been made by one of the six procedures specified by the Act. The Act introduces a new section 43B to the Employment Rights Act 1996 which provides that a 'qualifying disclosure' means any disclosure of information which in the reasonable belief of the employee making the disclosure tends to show one or more of the following things:

- That a criminal offence has been committed, is being committed or is likely to be committed;
- That a person has failed, is failing or is likely to fail to comply with any legal obligation to which he or she is subject;
- That a miscarriage of justice has occurred, is occurring or is likely to occur;
- That the health or safety of any individual has been, is being or is likely to be endangered;
- That the environment has been, is likely to be damaged; or
- That information tending to show any matter falling within any one of the preceding paragraphs has been, is being or is likely to be deliberately concealed.

The first method of disclosure which will be protected is a good faith disclosure by the employee to his employer. In the case of exceptionally serious breaches the specified procedures may in limited circumstances be bypassed. A new section 103A of the Employment Rights Act 1996 renders a dismissal unfair if the reason for the dismissal was that the employee made a protected disclosure. It is not necessary for the employee to have the normal period of qualifying time to claim unfair dismissal. The Act contains extremely detailed provisions which are beyond the scope of this book: see Harvey on Industrial Relations and Employment Law Vol [281]–[410].

6.23 For an analogous case pre-dating the Public Interest Disclosure Act 1998 see *Camelot v Centaur Communications Ltd* [1998] IRLR 80. The draft accounts of Camelot were leaked to a journalist in Centaur – Camelot sought an order for delivery up of the draft accounts to enable it to identify the source of the leak. Applying Section 10 of the Contempt of Court Act 1981 (enacted to give effect to certain aspects of Article 10 of the European Convention on Human Rights) the Court of Appeal held that the Judge (who had ordered delivery up and will become law under the Human Rights Act 1998 currently scheduled to be brought into effect in October 2000) had correctly concluded that the public interest in enabling employers to discover the disloyal employee was greater than the public interest in enabling him to avoid detection. Significantly, the Court of Appeal said that this was not a true 'whistleblowing' case, since the information disclosed would in any event have become legitimately available to the public some five days after its actual disclosure. The premature disclosure apparently served a private purpose rather than the public interest.

Chapter 7

Practical steps to protect the employer's interests

Introduction

7.1 The purpose of this Chapter is to look at the key practical steps the employer can take, during the subsistence of the employment relationship, to protect his business from competition from its employees. These practical steps can afford significant additional protection to that given by the various legal safeguards considered in Chs 3, 4 and 5.

7.2 The practical steps require no more of the employer than a degree of foresight, together with the investment of time and some resources. None of the steps can be said to be unduly onerous and all are based on straightforward common sense. It is therefore surprising how infrequently employers take them.

7.3 The steps fall into two broad categories: those designed to ensure that the employee is motivated and properly rewarded and those designed to maximise the possibility of detecting any competition during employment or acts in preparation for competition once employment has ended.

1. Steps designed to ensure the employee is motivated and properly rewarded

7.4 A motivated and properly rewarded employee is far less likely to engage in competitive activities than an employee who feels 'taken for granted' and exploited at every opportunity. By treating the employee fairly and honourably and showing that his interests have been considered, even if they have not prevailed, the employer will often gain the allegiance of the employee. That allegiance may in itself be enough to stop the employee from competing with the employer. The employee may feel under a moral obligation to treat his employer in the same fair and honourable way as he has been treated, and the strength of that moral obligation should not be underestimated. In many cases, although clearly not all (there are as many unscrupulous employees as there are unscrupulous employers), it will obviate the necessity for time-wasting and expensive litigation and on that ground alone is of considerable benefit to the employer. Additionally, an employer with a reputation for fair treatment of his employees will find recruitment and retention of employees easier, and such a reputation may be enough to give the employer the edge over a rival, where both are competing for the services of a valuable individual.

7.5   There are eight basic steps to ensure that an employee is motivated and properly rewarded. They are as follows:

1(a) Recognise the value of the employee

7.6   Many employers make the error of not finding the time to show their appreciation of an employee until he resigns. Invariably the employer's excuse is that he was too busy with day-to-day problems and just getting the work done, leaving no time for anything else and particularly not something that was working well. Such a reaction is understandable but short-sighted in the extreme. The time necessary to make a short telephone call or dictate a congratulatory memorandum or send a short e-mail is minimal, yet the satisfaction it will give to the employee is significant. More tangible signs of appreciation such as performance-related bonus schemes are also important.

1(b) Recognise the employee's need for leisure time

7.7   'All work and no play makes Jack a dull boy' – it also makes him very ineffective. The employer should ensure that each employee has adequate leisure time, and repeated short deadlines on tasks which result in the employee working long hours continuously should be avoided. The employer should allocate work considerately, spreading the load evenly amongst the workforce. The constant allocation of urgent work to a particular employee will result in that employee being exhausted and, ironically, other employees feeling resentful at not being given the opportunity to show their skills and commitment. It may also involve breaches of the Working Time Regulations 1998.

1(c) Recognise the employee's family commitments

7.8   The majority of employees have family commitments of one sort or another. The good employer will ensure, without being intrusive, that he is aware of those commitments and the demands they make on the employee. For example, on a relocation, employees with school-age children will have to consider what is in the best interests of those children.

7.9   Where an employee is having problems reconciling his work and family commitments, the employer should not automatically adopt the stance that the employee's work is more important. To do so will only put the employee in the difficult position of having to decide between his family and his job. The employer should talk to the employee and see if there is a compromise that would assist which is reasonable as far as the business is concerned. Even if no compromise can be achieved, the willingness to look for one will earn the gratitude of the employee. Furthermore, the issue will become more important when the Human Rights Act 1998 becomes part of English law which is currently expected to be on 2 October 2000. The Act will incorporate into English law a right to family life (Article 8) directly enforceable in the English courts against specified entities and indirectly enforceable generally through the obligation to interpret legislation consistently with Convention rights where possible.

1(d) Keep the employee challenged

7.10   Most employees perform better when given interesting and challenging work to do. They raise their standards to meet the challenge. The employee who is constantly overlooked when good quality work is allocated will eventually become bored and look elsewhere for job satisfaction. The employer should bear this in mind when allocating work and avoid the tendency to give the 'plum jobs' to tried and tested employees.

1(e) Provide a proper career structure

7.11 The majority of employees will be looking for promotion at appropriate times in their careers and it is important that the employer provides a proper career structure where possible. Obviously, the more senior the employee the more difficult it becomes to provide a career structure; promotion may depend on another employee leaving or being redeployed. However, the employer should be inventive – traditional pyramid structures, although tried and tested, are not always the best. The employer should consider division of responsibilities and reorganising corporate structures.

1(f) Review the employee's terms and performance regularly

7.12 The terms of employment of all employees should be reviewed regularly. How often, depends on the size and administrative resources of the business, but reviews should be at least annual. The employer should not delay a review because he is too busy, except in a genuine emergency. To do so is bad time management and will give the employee the impression that he ranks low in the employer's priorities. Regular reviews are important for the following reasons:

- They remind the employer to check that the employee is being properly rewarded for his efforts. Is he receiving the market rate for the job? The most common reason for an employee competing with his employer during his spare time, is to earn extra cash. The employee may need that cash to support an expensive hobby but more commonly it is necessary for basic expenditure such as mortgage repayments.
- They mean the employee knows that his position is being looked at and that his work is not being taken for granted.
- They provide an opportunity for a formal discussion between employer and employee, at which the expectations of both can be discussed. Prior exchanges of view in writing make the process more productive.
- They provide a useful opportunity for the employer to check that the terms of the contract and in particular the restrictive covenants are still appropriate and reflect the current facts. A common problem with restrictive covenants is that the underlying facts have changed but the covenants have not been altered and therefore they provide either limited or, worse still, no protection to the employer.

1(g) Consider the use of long-term incentives for the employee

7.13 Such incentives, frequently referred to as LTIPs are commonplace nowadays and are actively encouraged for senior employees whose remuneration shareholders expect to be geared to the performance of the employing company.

7.14 Long-term incentives are particularly useful where it is important to retain the employee for a particular period or until a task is completed. A recent example would be information technology personnel whom it is essential to retain to deal with issues relating to the millenium. The most common incentive in this context is a 'one off' bonus representing a significant percentage of the employee's salary.

An employer considering these incentives needs to avoid two pitfalls. First, the employee should not have to wait too long before receiving the bonus, otherwise a competitor's offer of a larger salary now may be sufficient to tempt the employee away. Secondly, it should be made clear that the incentive is only payable if the employee remains until the payment date. If this is not done, the employee may have a claim based on quantum meruit or under the Apportionment Act 1870 for part of the monies due notwithstanding that he leaves before the payment date. It should be noted that where the same incentive is appropriate to more than one employee, the employer might consider staggering the payment dates to avoid the risk of those employees leaving at the same time. However, unless the payments can be staggered over a significant period this may only give the employer a limited period of security as, subject to his notice provisions, there is nothing to prevent each employee leaving once his payment date has passed.

7.15 Where an employer introduces a long-term incentive scheme he should review it regularly to ensure that it offers a real incentive to employees. For example, many employers have used share option schemes as long-term incentives. In principle that is fine but there have been a number of instances where, compared to the market price of the employer's shares, the exercise prices of the options are so high that the options will never produce any value for the employee and consequently will not motivate him.

1(h)   Involving the employee in management

7.16 Where appropriate, this is a useful step to secure the loyalty of the employee. As a manager the employee faces a much greater dilemma in reaching a decision to compete with his employer than an employee of non-managerial status. As we saw in Chapter 3, the implied duty of fidelity imposes more onerous requirements on the employee of managerial status than other employees. Consequently, this duty acts as a deterrent to managerial staff competing with their employers. Normally the only disadvantage of giving an employee managerial status, apart perhaps from his demanding higher pay, is that it may necessitate his having greater access to trade secrets and confidential information with the attendant risk of misuse of that information.

2.   Steps designed to maximise the possibility of detecting competitive activities

7.17 Frequently the employer is the last to know that an employee is competing with him while still employed or making preparations to do so once employment has ended. The employee has an obvious interest in concealing his activities. He may well go to considerable lengths to do so, thereby making detection difficult. However, usually detection will be possible if the employer is vigilant and has taken the time to implement basic safeguards.

7.18 We do not suggest that the employer spies on his employees nor that he implements procedures which are unduly onerous or time consuming for the employees. What we do suggest is that the employer assesses the risk of competitive activity (including the likely degree of damage it will cause) and then takes a sensible commercial decision as to the time, energy and money he is prepared to spend on limiting that risk. In every case there will be a happy medium between doing nothing (the course often taken until the employer becomes a victim of competition) and taking steps that are reasonable and which will either deter competitive activities or at the very least provide the evidence that it has occurred. Obtaining proof that competitive activity has taken place can be extremely difficult and any safeguards that can assist in providing evidence are very useful.

7.19 Once the employer has made a decision in principle to take steps to maximise the chances of detecting competitive activities, precisely what steps he takes will be governed by four factors.

- The nature of the business.
- How the business operates.
- The nature of the likely competitive activity.
- The time and money the employer has decided to invest.

7.20 These four variables make it impossible to provide an exhaustive list of the steps each employer can take. However, set out below are some of the more common steps available to employers. Most of them are applicable to all types of business and grades of staff with the exception of manual workers and some support staff, who will not usually be a significant competitive threat. In the main, the steps are simply means of ensuring that the employer is aware of what is happening in his business and can therefore exercise proper control over it.

7.21 In implementing the steps he decides to take, the employer should never appear unduly distrustful. To do so may deter some would-be competitors but it can create an unpleasant working atmosphere and those whom it does not deter will simply become more furtive in their activities, thereby reducing the prospects of detection.

7.22 Finally before considering the steps the employer might take, it is important to consider the potential impact on those steps of the developing law in relation to employee's rights to privacy. At present that law is very embryonic but there are two important developments on the horizon. First, there is the Human Rights Act 1998 which the Government currently intends to bring into effect from 2 October 2000. Second, there is the awaited Code of Conduct on employee surveillance from the Data Protection Registrar, a draft of which has yet to be published. The Human Rights Act 1998 will incorporate into English law, key individual rights from the European Convention of Human Rights, including a right to privacy. The extent of the proposed Code on employee surveillance is not yet clear although there are certainly suggestions that it may cover the use of closed circuit television and the interception of e-mails. A detailed consideration of how these proposed privacy rights will interact with the employer's legitimate interests to discover competitive activity is beyond the scope of this book, and could in any event only be somewhat speculative bearing in mind the new rules are not yet in place. Suffice to say that any employer considering steps that might be said to infringe privacy, for example, listening to phone calls, inspecting property or monitoring e-mails, should in our view retain an express right to do so in the contract of employment. As long as such a provision is included and surveillance is used only for legitimate purposes, that, for the moment at least, should be sufficient. Although in relation to telephone monitoring, guidance (which is not legally binding) issued by Oftel in August 1999 does also suggest that there are sufficient telephone lines at the place of work, possibly payphones, that the employees can use with an assurance that they are genuinely private. Furthermore, the Government has indicated an intention to change the existing law (Consultation Paper – 'Interception of Communication in the United Kingdom') so that telephone monitoring which takes place in the course of lawful business practice may only take place where the employer has taken reasonable steps to inform the employees that monitoring may occur. An employer who fails to take this course may well find in future that he faces arguments of breach of privacy rights. For a case in which the UK Government unsuccessfully defended a claim of breach of privacy or rights based on the interception of telephone calls on a 'private phone' used by the employee at her employer's premises, see: *Halford v United Kingdom* [1997] IRLR 471.

2(a) Institute proper reporting procedures

7.23 It is straightforward good management for the employer to have proper reporting procedures which are adhered to. Such procedures are particularly important where much of the employer's business is conducted away from the business premises, for example where the employee spends much time travelling to customers.

7.24 The employee should know to whom he reports. He should also know what the reporting requirement entails. Usually the best formula is to have a general requirement to report on a day-to-day basis with an express obligation to report matters of consequence forthwith and more formal reports at regular intervals. The employer needs to consider what information he requires in writing. In reaching his decision the employer should bear in mind that evidentially a written report may be more valuable. If the employee has been dishonest in that report, or if the report is misleading that in itself will be misconduct. There may be disputes about the interpretation of a written report but unlike an oral report the employee cannot deny what he has written.

7.25 Reporting requirements should always include progress reports on the matters on which the employee is working and the way in which he has spent his time since the last report, unless this is available from another source, for example through time sheets or other similar records. Interestingly, an indirect effect of the record keeping obligations under the Working Time Regulations 1998 may well be to provide an employer with a much clearer picture than he has had hitherto of at least when the worker claims to be working. Although note the Government's proposals to 'water down' the recording obligations in the draft Working Time Regulation 1999.

2(b) Ensuring proper controls are kept on which employees have access to confidential information

7.26 In many businesses there are virtually no controls over which employees have access to trade secrets and confidential information. In others, matters are taken to the opposite extreme. Unnecessary and cumbersome procedures are adopted which impede the efficient operation of the business. Neither of these situations is ideal and the employer is well advised to spend time devising the correct system of control for his business.

7.27 The employer should devise his system of controls by reference to three questions:

- What information needs to be subject to control?
- Who is to have access to it?
- How is that access to be limited to those entitled to it?

2(b)(i) WHAT INFORMATION NEEDS TO BE SUBJECT TO CONTROL?

7.28 The categories of information which should be subject to control are trade secrets and confidential information. Identifying what amounts to a trade secret or confidential information is by no means straaightforward. Guidance can be gained from paragraphs 5.10 to 5.43, but this is an area of law which is regrettably very unclear. The best advice that can be given to the employer is to identify those pieces of information which he regards as confidential, and are not publicly available, to treat those as confidential and impress upon the employees who have access to them their confidential nature.

2(b)(ii) WHO IS TO HAVE ACCESS TO IT?

7.29 Deciding who has access to each trade secret and piece of confidential information on his list can be a difficult task for the employer and it is often at this stage he goes wrong. Some employers, fearful of the information being leaked to a competitor, restrict access to such an extent that even those who need the information to do their work properly are not allowed access. Others, and this is particularly true of larger organisations, simply permit access to all employees of a particular status and above irrespective of whether or not they really need the information. A prime example of the 'over-protective' employer would be one who did not include the Finance Director on the circulation list for information concerning new product lines. Without this information obviously the Finance Director's budgets and financial projections will be inaccurate and unnecessarily so.

7.30 Who is to have access to any trade secret or piece of confidential information is primarily a commercial decision, but the employer should always ensure that, apart from exceptional circumstances, access is only given to those who genuinely need the information to do their work efficiently, and that he can justify the inclusion of every person, not just every category of person, given access.

7.31 Sometimes the result will be that virtually all the workforce will have access. This does not mean, as some employers believe, that the information is not properly confidential, merely that many employees need access to it to do their jobs.

7.32 The employer needs to make it clear what is to happen if an employee with access is absent: for example, does his deputy thereby become entitled to the information? The access list should be reviewed regularly and always when there are changes in circumstances such as a group re-organisation.

2(b)(iii) HOW IS ACCESS TO BE LIMITED TO THOSE ENTITLED TO IT?

7.33 The answer to this question will depend very much on the number of employees who are to have access. Where there are only a very few, stringent and detailed procedures will need to be put in place – the employer is protecting the information not only from third parties but also from other employees working side by side with those who have access. By contrast, if virtually all the work force are to have access, it will be necessary to include a section in the staff handbook or to issue a general memorandum setting out steps to be taken by employees to avoid disclosure. For cases between these two extremes it will be a matter of adapting either of the two approaches mentioned to suit the situation.

7.34 Employers wishing to limit access to a fairly small number of employees often seek guidance as to how best to do it. In the Appendix to this Chapter we have therefore included some basic guidelines which can be adapted to meet most situations.

2(c) Monitoring correspondence

7.35 Employees engaged in competitive activity use correspondence as a means of communication only as a last resort for obvious reasons. However, monitoring correspondence is something each employer should consider. It can deter employees from competitive activity and for those it does not and who do resort to correspondence the chances of being caught are high.

7.36 The usual form of monitoring is to require that all incoming correspondence, including faxes and telexes, are seen by at least two employees and outgoing correspondence is either seen by an employee other than the author before it is despatched, or a copy is sent to that other employee on the same day. The employer should also keep records of all documents created on his word processing system and a log of all faxes sent and received, recording the identity of sender and recipient, the time of despatch/receipt and the number of pages. Employees with word processors and fax machines at home should be required to keep similar records relating to work documents. These records will provide a useful way of cross-checking that, with the exception of incoming correspondence, any file of correspondence is complete. One key advantage to the employer of implementing a monitoring system of the type outlined above is that he should always have a second employee with knowledge of each matter to take it over if the employee with primary responsibility is unable to continue. This can be particularly useful where an employee leaves to set up in competition. Unless the second employee also leaves, the employer has someone in a position to help the customer immediately and consequently the customer is not faced with the alternatives of transferring his business or starting from scratch with an employee ignorant of the particular transaction. In transactions where speed is vital this can mean the difference between the employer retaining the customer and losing him.

2(d) Monitoring e-mails

7.37 Nowadays many businesses conduct much of their internal and, to a slightly more limited extent, their external communications by e-mail. For reasons which are not clear to us it is a common misconception that once deleted from a particular employee's personal computer an e-mail is irrevocably destroyed. Because of this misconception e-mail is a popular way for those competing and intending to compete to communicate. An employer is well advised to keep an eye on the use of e-mail both as a means of detecting competitive activity and of ensuring that confidential information is not being wrongly disclosed or misused. The majority of employers who have e-mail systems have fairly stringent policies covering the use of e-mail. These policies almost invariably include a right on the part of the employer to carry out checks on what is being sent on the e-mail system.

While it is highly arguable that an employer would have that right of access in any event, expressly reserving the right puts the point beyond argument it also, for the moment at least, will be sufficient to counter claims of breach of privacy rights (see para 7.22). We recommend that any employer who has an e-mail system should have a clear policy relating to its use and that policy should reserve the right of access to the employer.

2(e) Monitoring telephone calls

7.38 Nowadays there are various ways in which employers can monitor the telephone calls made and received at their business premises. Alternatives range from monitoring the telephone numbers to which outgoing calls are made and the duration of those calls to full tape recordings of all external conversations conducted on telephones at business premises. Monitoring can be for selected numbers/extensions only or all telephones at the business premises. Monitoring of selected numbers/extensions is particularly useful where competitive activity is suspected.

7.39 The tape recording of all external telephone conversations is an extreme option but it is common in certain types of business such as stockbroking and foreign exchange dealing where much of the business is conducted by telephone, instructions received have to be acted on more or less immediately and considerable sums of money may be at stake.

7.40 Some employers regard any sort of monitoring as distasteful but it can prove extremely useful, for example in detecting employees actively competing with their employer. In one case an employee's illicit activity was discovered when scrutiny of the employer's telephone records showed that in a six-month period he had made an average of 18 calls per day to a rival business. Every employer should at least consider the question of monitoring.

7.41 Employers who adopt any sort of monitoring need to decide what, if anything, they tell their employees about it. While there is no direct authority on the subject, in our view there is no obligation on the employer to inform the employee although nowadays it is undoubtedly prudent for the employer to reserve in the contract of employment the right to monitor phone calls because of the developing law on an employee's right to privacy (see para 7.23). In addition, before October 2000 the Government needs to legislate to comply with Article 5 of the EU Telecommunication Data Protection Directive (No 97/66) which deals with the monitoring of phone calls. That implementation too may bring about some additional changes.

2(f) Monitoring expense claims

7.42 The employer should have a clear expenses policy and proper procedures for accounting for expenses incurred. Employees should be required to submit expense claims regularly and in those claims identify the amounts spent and on what they were spent. Scribbled claims on scraps of paper and descriptions such as 'business lunch' should be automatically rejected.

7.43 Employers should look carefully at the expenses being incurred by their employees. Money advanced to employees for expenses should be properly accounted for and expense claims checked before being authorised. The use of company credit cards should also be carefully watched. Employers who pay an employee's home telephone bill or make a contribution to it or provide a mobile telephone for the employee should insist on itemised telephone bills.

7.44 Apart from being good practice the steps outlined above can help in the detection of competitive activity. For example, an employee may suddenly start taking customers out to lunch when he had never previously done so or may arrange an overseas trip with an unusual itinerary or make an inordinate number of telephone calls to suppliers. While there may be a perfectly innocent explanation for any of these occurrences there may also be a sinister one. A vigilant employer will detect the sinister one and thereby either avoid the illicit activities altogether or 'nip them in the bud'.

7.45 A measure of subtlety is called for. If employees know that every expense claim will be scrutinised they are unlikely to be 'careless' as to what they include on their claims.

2(g)   Monitoring the use of photocopiers on business premises

7.46 In virtually every case of competitive activity by an employee the employer's photocopiers will have been misused. The most common example is where the employer's confidential information is photocopied for use in a rival business. Whether the employee is already engaged in that rival business or merely has plans to join it once his employment has ended, he frequently cannot resist the temptation of photocopying significant amounts of his employer's confidential information which he then uses to his advantage in his competitive activities. Other examples include employees already engaged in a rival business who simply find it convenient to photocopy documents relating to that business, and employees preparing to set up in competition who economise on their 'start-up' expenses by producing their new business's introductory leaflets and circulars on their employer's photocopier, often they will also have been typed on the employer's word processing system by a 'loyal' secretary!

7.47 The cost to the employer of these types of misuse normally far exceeds the secretarial time or price per sheet of the photocopying. This is particularly so where the employee is photocopying confidential information for use in a rival business. The information he photocopies may often have taken his employer many working days to compile and yet the employee obtains it at no cost at all, not even the price of the photocopying.

7.48 An employer cannot, unless he has only a very few employees, realistically hope to prevent completely the misuse of his photocopiers by his employees engaged in competitive activity. What he can do, however, is deter the would-be misuser by adopting safeguards to increase the chance of misuse being detected. The safeguards will vary from business to business, and some employers may decide it is not commercially viable to adopt any, but each employer needs to consider three basic issues.

NUMBER AND TYPES OF PHOTOCOPIER

7.49 The more photocopiers an employer has and the more reliable and sophisticated they are, the greater the temptation to the would-be misuser. Employers should consider carefully the number and types of photocopier they really need. If the normal demand for photocopying is not high it may be practical to have fairly basic machines generally available throughout the premises, for example one per floor, with the more sophisticated machinery in a self-contained room possibly with one or more designated members of staff to operate that machinery.

POSITIONING OF PHOTOCOPIERS

7.50 Photocopiers available for general use should, where possible, be positioned in a place where there are likely to be other employees around to observe what is happening. Frequently, because of the noise they make, photocopiers are tucked away in side rooms without windows, so that only other employees in the room at the same time as the misuser can see what he is doing.

RECORDS OF USE

7.51 There are various ways in which an employer can have available a record of the use being made of his photocopiers. Some employers use photocopiers which operate on a 'pass card' system under which the machine can only be activated by inserting specially designed cards similar to the card keys for hotel rooms. The employer issues each authorised user with a card which that person uses when taking copies and the number of copies are logged on the machine against the card. Less sophisticated are manual records where, on each occasion, the user writes his name, the number of copies taken and, in some cases, the customer or account to which the copies are attributable. Whatever record system the employer chooses, abuse is always possible, but the employer should not discount the idea on that basis alone. Even a manual record with only minor cost implications may be enough to deter a would-be misuser.

2(h) Monitoring removal of the employer's property from business premises

7.52 The employer should always consider carefully what controls, if any, he keeps on the removal of physical property from his premises. Sometimes a complete ban is appropriate, but often that is not commercially expedient, either because the employee needs particular items of property to do his work away from the employer's premises or it is convenient for him to have that property, for example so he can do more work at home in the evening.

7.53 Controlling removal of property can be extremely difficult. In practice the employer has only two options. The first option is simply to identify any property which is never to be removed, for example highly sensitive confidential information, such as unpublished plans of new products, and to inform the employees who have access to that property accordingly. At the very least, the employer should adopt this option even if it is difficult to enforce. The second option is to go one stage further and identify a second category of property which can be removed subject to certain procedures. The procedures might include prior authorisation and the employee signing to say what property he has removed, when and for what purpose. Such procedures can be very laborious and often the employer, quite justifiably, discounts this second option on the basis that it is too time consuming and impossible to police. Alternatively, he adopts a watered-down version, for example through a general statement in the Staff Handbook that property should only be removed where to do so is necessary for the employee's work. Such statements obviously do no harm, but nor do they do much good.

2(i) Monitoring use of home computers

7.54 Nowadays quite a number of employees have computers, sometimes supplied by their employer, in their homes. Generally this is a beneficial arrangement for the employer since it allows the employee to continue working, for example in the evenings or at weekends, without having to be physically in the employer's premises. Home computers linked in to the employer's system via a modem are doubly useful. An employee with this facility often need not even worry about taking information home with him since he will be able to access it from his desk at home.

7.55 Useful though home computers are, employers need to be vigilant about the use made of them. For example, an employee may produce a highly confidential report on a home computer. Unless the employer ensures that that report is deleted from the employee's system the employee will have access to it at any time. Furthermore, where the home computer is linked to the employer's system, the employer should give very careful thought to the information to which the employee can gain access through the system and how that access can be monitored. While the employee is working for the benefit of the employer extensive access may be no problem, but the situation is rather different where the employee is engaged or is about to engage in competitive activities.

7.56 An important point for employees to remember is that if their home computer is linked to their employer's system, often the link works both ways so that the employer can find out what is on the employee's computer. This can be a useful way of detecting competitive activity. For example, employees engaged in competitive activities have been caught when the home computer has been used to prepare such things as business plans and letters to the employer's clients soliciting their business the creation dates of which precede the date of termination of employment.

2(j) Ensuring employees take proper holidays

7.57 Employers should require each employee to take at least one unbroken period of ten working days' holiday each calendar year. As well as ensuring that the employee has one decent break per year, this allows the opportunity for illicit competition to come to light. Surprisingly, it is not unusual for illicit competition, particularly the operation of a rival business during employment, to be uncovered in the employee's absence. Often discovery is through a telephone call from a customer or supplier normally used to dealing with the employee at his employer's telephone number. Colleagues taking over matters and speaking to the employee's customers may also discover competition, for example that the absent employee has been soliciting their custom for himself.

2(k) Ensuring customers deal regularly with a number of employees

7.58 Where practical, and we recognise that there are circumstances when it is not, it is a good idea that more then one employee deals regularly with each customer, particularly the most important ones. There are two reasons for this. First, it can limit the risk of an employee being able to solicit the customer away to a rival business. Customers who deal with only one employee with whom they have a good working relationship have a tendency to transfer their business with the employee when he moves. For them, their businesses are better served by staying with the 'tried and tested' employee than building up a relationship with an unknown employee. Second, and more importantly in the context of this Chapter, it minimises the chances of soliciting by the employee going undetected. A customer is unlikely to make the effort to report an attempt to solicit his custom by an employee if he knows no-one else at the business, but he may well mention it in passing to another employee with whom he deals. Having two employees looking after a customer is not without danger, however, since it may increase the likelihood of the employer losing two employees to a competitive business and not just one. Usually the more senior employee decides to leave but takes the second employee with him to maximise the chances of securing 'his customer' for the competitive business. For this reason, it is inadvisable for the employer to let employees simply work in pairs, particularly where he recruited the employees as a pair. Where it is unavoidable and both employees do indicate their intention to leave, the employer should think carefully about the prospects of retaining the more junior employee by offering him a promotion. See further Ch 16.

Guidelines for maintaining confidentiality

These guidelines assume the information is in written form, either in hard copy or on a computer/word processing system, since that will usually be the case. However, they are easily adaptable for oral information.

(1)   Impress on any secretaries or other support staff engaged in producing or handling the information that it is confidential. It should be made clear to them that (i) they should not disclose the information to or discuss it with anyone other than the employee who has asked them to produce the information or for whom they are handling the information without that employee's consent, and (ii) they should keep the information secure at all times. Keeping the information secure includes not leaving dictating machine tapes containing the information nor drafts of it out on their desks, nor leaving word processors unattended when the information is on the screen even if the screen automatically goes off after a short period. Where the information is very sensitive but it is necessary, for example, for a number of reports containing it to be produced, the employer might consider using an outside agency. A typical example of this would be where there was a proposed takeover of the business. If this step is taken, necessary confidentiality undertakings should be obtained from the outside agency.

(2)   Production of the information on a computer/word processing system should be done in such a way that other employees cannot gain access to it.

(3)   Only the number of paper copies required for circulation should be made and no extras. All paper copies should be numbered and the number attributed to an identified recipient. Any spare copies should be shredded. They should not be put in a waste paper bin from which they can simply be picked out.

(4)   Where information is in documentary form it should be circulated in sealed envelopes – re-usable internal envelopes or, worse still, opaque plastic folders should not be used. Ideally the envelope should only be opened by the employee given access to the information. However, frequently secretaries open all mail for their 'bosses' and if that is to be permitted, the confidentiality of the information should be impressed on the secretary also.

(5)   For highly confidential information some businesses use special coloured paper reserved only for that purpose, so that anyone taking an additional copy of it is likely to be noticed.

(6)   The employees to whom access is given should be told (i) that the information is confidential; (ii) the identity of the other employees who have access to it (a circulation list on the document or word processor job will usually suffice); (iii) that they are not at liberty to discuss it with or disclose it to anyone other than those named at (ii), nor are they entitled to use it other than for the benefit of the employer; (iv) that any discussions they have about the information with other employees on the circulation list should be out of earshot of anyone else and, where possible, the use of telephone systems for discussion should be avoided; (v) that they should not make any additional copies; and (vi) that the document or, where the information is on a disk or word processing system, the disk/system should be kept secure, away from prying eyes, when not being used. Employees should also be warned against reading the information either in paper copy or on a portable word processor in public places (the favourite is commuter trains) and leaving them unattended outside business premises, for example in a pub or unattended vehicle. For very sensitive information a ban on removing it from office premises is appropriate.

There are various ways in which employees can be advised of the points mentioned above. Some employers have a special standard form covering memorandum which they circulate with each item of confidential information. Others simply have a general memorandum which they issue to the relevant employees at regular intervals. The employer who adopts the latter course should always make it clear to which pieces of confidential information the general memorandum applies. The employer should avoid marking the document 'private and confidential' unless those words are specifically reserved for genuinely confidential information. In some organisations the word is greatly over-used.

Chapter 8

Termination of employment

Introduction

8.1 This Chapter considers two critically important issues connected with termination of employment: when the contract of employment comes to an end; and in what circumstances termination is the result of a repudiatory breach of the contract.

8.2 The question of when employment ends is looked at from the common law perspective only. Because of the way in which Section 95 Employment Rights Act 1996 defines the effective date of termination for statutory employment protection purposes it is arguable that in some cases, particularly constructive dismissal claims, the date of termination at common law will be different from the effective date of termination in an unfair dismissal claim. Consideration of the statutory aspects of termination are beyond the scope of this book but the issue is well covered in most of the general texts including *Harvey on Industrial Relations and Employment Law* and *Tolley's Employment Law*.

1. When does employment end?

1(a) Significance of the date of termination

8.3 This book focuses on the competing interests of employer and employee and of ex-employer and ex-employee. In this context it is important to define the precise date of termination of the employment relationship for the following reasons:

- The date of termination of employment marks the end of the duty of fidelity: *J A Mont (UK) Ltd v Mills* [1993] IRLR 172 (CA). In an instant the now ex-employer is deprived of the protection from competition afforded by the duty of fidelity (see Ch 3 for the scope of the duty). So in *Faccenda Chicken Ltd v Fowler* [1986] 3 WLR 288 (CA) after termination of employment the ex-employee was free to use for the purposes of his new business mere confidential information (but not trade secrets) of the ex-employer which he was prevented from using for his own benefit during employment. Similarly, in the absence of an express covenant prohibiting contact with clients, former employees of a firm of solicitors were free to seek the custom of those clients for a new firm they had established: *Wallace Bogan v Cove* [1997] IRLR 453 (CA). Termination of employment does not, however, absolve the ex-employee from breaches of the duty of fidelity during employment nor, in appropriate cases, from breach of a fiduciary duty which may, in any event, continue beyond termination of employment (see paras 3.54 to 3.64). The ex-employer retains all his remedies in relation to those breaches including the potentially powerful springboard injunction for misuse of confidential information (see Ch 14).

- All contractual obligations cease on termination other than those stated to operate after employment has ended; for example covenants restricting the freedom of the ex-employee to compete with his former employer. Unlike other contractual terms these types of covenant are subjected to rigorous scrutiny by the courts and are only upheld in limited circumstances (see Chs 9 and 10).
- Where there are express restrictive covenants operating after the termination of employment, these are usually drafted to run for a specified period from the date of termination of employment. To determine the period during which those covenants operate, it is necessary to establish the date of termination of employment.

8.4   The question of the exact date of termination of employment often arises where the employer has dismissed the employee with payment of a sum equal to the salary he would have received during the contractual notice period. In *Berkeley Administration Inc v McClelland* [1990] FSR 505, 510 the employer sought in these circumstances to argue that since McClelland had used confidential information (acquired by him in the course of his employment) during the period for which he received a payment in lieu, he had done so during employment. Wright J rejected this contention, on the basis of the evidence it was plain that Berkeley had wished to get rid of McClelland as soon as possible and that a payment was made in lieu of notice. In those circumstances, there was no question of McClelland having misused confidential information while he was still an employee: see also paragraphs 8.8 to 8.15.

1(b) Methods of termination

8.5   The contract of employment may be terminated in various different ways including:

- By notice by the employer;
- By notice by the employee;
- As a result of a repudiatory breach of the contract;
- Consensually;
- By expiry of a fixed term;
- Through frustration of the contract (for instance where some supervening event which was not reasonably foreseeable renders further performance under the contract impossible or something radically different from what was originally envisaged);
- Other supervening events, such as compulsory winding up of the employer, appointment of a receiver by the court, cessation of trading, or death of the employer.

8.6   Most contracts of employment are terminated by notice or following breach and it is in such cases that it is often difficult to establish the precise date of termination. In contrast, where the contract of employment is terminated consensually or on expiry of a fixed term the date of termination will normally be clearly agreed by the parties. Similarly, where the contract is terminated through frustration or other supervening events, the date of termination does not normally present particular difficulties. Because it is in cases of termination by notice or following a repudiatory breach that identification of the date of termination of employment is often problematic the remainder of this Chapter focuses on those methods of termination.

1(c) Notice: general principles

8.7   Before looking at precisely when notice brings employment to an end it is worth drawing together the following key principles about notice.

- Where no notice period is specified in the contract it is terminable on reasonable notice: *Adams v Union Cinemas Ltd* [1939] 3 All ER 136. See paragraphs 4.60 and 4.61 for a discussion of how reasonable notice is determined. For an employer/employee wishing to terminate a contract with no agreed notice period deciding what notice to give is no simple task. For an employer, particularly one wishing to avoid an allegation of repudiatory breach, the best advice is to err on the side of generosity. In contrast an employee who wants to be free of the contract as soon as possible, for example, to join a competitor, can risk giving the minimum notice he feels he can get away with simply to test the employer's reaction. In practice, the employer may well reject the employee's minimum period but put forward an alternative period which the employee can accept or challenge. In most cases provided the period proposed by the employer is sensible the parties compromise around the level of the employer's proposal. In the remainder of this Chapter we have assumed that there is no issue on the period of notice.
- Notice may be given orally unless the contract requires it to be given in writing: *Latchford Premier Cinemas Ltd v Ennion* [1931] 2 Ch 409. Nowadays contracts commonly provide for written notice, a requirement which in practice is often waived.
- Notice must be unambiguous and *Morton Sundour Fabrics Ltd v Shaw* [1966] 2 ITR 84 is authority for the proposition that notice by the employer must state the date of termination or enable it to be inferred. Warnings of possible redundancy do not constitute notice.
- Notice once given effectively cannot be unilaterally withdrawn: *Riordan v War Office* [1959] 3 All ER 552 1 WLR 210 (CA) and *Harris Russell Ltd v Slingsby* [1973] 3 All ER 31 (NIRC). Both were cases where it was the employee who gave notice but there is no reason in principle why the position should be different where notice is given by the employer.
- For unfair dismissal purposes at least, words of dismissal or resignation spoken in anger in the heat of the moment may be withdrawn within a short cooling off period: *Martin v Yeoman Aggregates Ltd* [1983] ICR 314. The position at common law is likely to be the same. Similarly an anticipatory repudiatory breach, for example, a threat to act in breach of contract, can be withdrawn at any time before acceptance: *Harrison v Norwest Holst Group Administration Ltd* [1985] ICR 668.
- Where notice is given orally, the notice period runs from the day after the oral notice is given if any work is done on that day: *West v Kneels* [1986] IRLR 430.
- Where notice is given in writing the notice runs from the day the employee

becomes aware of the dismissal: *McMaster v Manchester Airport plc* [1998] IRLR 112 or ought to have been aware of it had he not been deliberately avoiding becoming aware of the dismissal: *Brown v Southall Knight* [1980] IRLR 130.

1(d) Date of termination: notice by the employer

8.8 An employer can 'give notice' in a number of different ways. For example, he may give the employee notice and require him to work throughout the notice period or alternatively to work for part only of the notice period. At the other end of the scale the employer may simply give the employee a lump sum payment in lieu of notice or dismiss him summarily. When the employment comes to an end will depend, broadly speaking, on which method is chosen and whether it is a method contemplated by the contract and which is appropriate on the facts.

8.9 The date of termination may also depend on whether the employee has a right to give a shorter notice period than the employer. An employee who has such a right can validly advance the termination date simply by giving notice in accordance with the contract. In the following paragraphs under this heading we have assumed that the notice period required from employer and employee are the same. Nowadays that will not always be so and it is vital to check the contractual position in each case.

8.10 Where the employer gives notice of termination in accordance with the contract, continues to pay salary at the normal intervals and requires the employee to work out his notice, the employment will terminate at the end of that notice.

8.11 Where the employer gives notice of termination in accordance with the contract, continues to pay salary at the normal intervals but the employee is told that he need not work during the notice period, the employment will terminate at the end of the notice: *Brindle v H W Smith (Cabinets) Ltd* [1972] IRLR 125; except where the employer's action amounts to a repudiatory breach which the employee accepts: see paragraphs 8.18, 8.25 to 8.36 and 8.37 to 8.39.

8.12 Where the employer dismisses the employee with a lump sum payment ('wages in lieu of notice') there are a number of possibilities: *Delaney v Staples* [1992] IRLR 191 (HL), although note, the *Delaney* classification has recently been questioned by the EAT in *Ceberus Software Ltd v Rowley* [1999] IRLR 890: see paragraph 4.72. The possibilities envisaged by *Delaney* are as follows:

- The employer gives the employee proper notice but tells him he need not work it out. In this case the payment is an advance of wages, the position is the same as under paragraph 8.11, subject to any argument of repudiatory breach the employment terminates at the end of the notice period.
- Payment is made pursuant to an express provision of the contract of employment entitling the employer to make a payment in lieu of notice. In this case the employment will end on the date the employee ceases working, rather than the end of the notice period: *Rex Stewart Jeffries Parker Ginsberg Ltd v Parker* [1988] IRLR 483 (CA).
- If the contract of employment contains no right to make a payment in lieu of notice and the employee tenders such payment, it will be seen as payment of damages for breach of contract: *Dixon v Stenor Ltd* [1973] IRLR 28, and the

employment ends when the employee accepts the repudiatory breach as bringing the contract to an end.

Of course, if the employer and employee agree that employment shall end on payment of a sum in lieu, employment ends on the agreed date.

8.13 There is a fine line between the positions in the first and last bullet points. Where (in the absence of an express payment in lieu of notice clause) the employer terminates the contract of employment and pays the employee a sum to cover the notice period while dispensing with the employee's services it may be that either:

- The employee has been given notice with payment in lieu of working out the notice – in which case the contract terminates at the end of the notice period; or
- That the employee has been dismissed with a payment in lieu of damages – in which case the contract of employment terminates on acceptance of the breach by the employee.

It is a question of construction of the employer's letter or oral intimation of termination in all the circumstances of the case as to the category into which the termination falls: *Adams v GKN Sankey Ltd* [1980] IRLR 416; *Chapman v Letherby & Christopher Ltd* [1981] IRLR 440 and *Leech v Preston BC* [1985] IRLR 337. The court may lean towards finding the latter category of termination: *Berkeley Administration Inc v McClelland* [1990] FSR 505: see paragraph 8.4. In practical terms for the employer who wants to maintain that the contract remains in existence throughout the notice period there is no legal advantage to making a single lump sum payment he would be best advised to continue to pay salary at the normal intervals and, in the absence of an express garden leave provision, allow the employee to continue to work, thereby avoiding an argument of 'premature' termination.

8.14 Where the employer dismisses the employee summarily in accordance with the contract the employment will terminate immediately. Where the dismissal is in repudiatory breach of the contract, the date the employment ends will be the date of acceptance by the employee of the employer's repudiatory breach. This applies also to other forms of repudiatory breach by the employer which the employee accepts as bringing the contract to an end. For a discussion of when breach of notice provisions might constitute a repudiatory breach by the employer: see paragraphs 8.29 to 8.31.

8.15 It is always open to the parties to waive the requirement of notice or to agree to shorten the period.

1(e) Date of termination: notice by the employee

8.16 Where the employee gives notice in accordance with the contract the employer may respond in any of the various ways identified in paragraph 8.8, that is, let the employee work out his notice, make a lump sum payment in lieu of notice and so on. In principle, (subject to express contractual provisions) there is no reason why the analysis of when the employment ends should be any different simply because it is the employee who has taken the first step to termination. Consequently, determining when the employment ends involves the same process outlined in paragraphs 8.8 to 8.14. On a practical note, where the employee gives notice it is much more common for there to be discussions about the termination date and for a mutually satisfactory arrangement to be reached. For example, where the contract includes a lengthy notice period and no garden leave provision the employer may agree to release the employee for part of the notice period in return for the employee agreeing to take garden leave until his employment ends. Where such arrangements are reached there is no need to resort to the analysis referred to above.

8.17 Where the employee purports to resign in breach of a notice provision, as frequently happens when the employee is planning to join a competitor, there are a number of options open to the employer. The date of termination of employment will be dictated by which route the employer elects to take. The employer can hold the employee to his contractual obligations (albeit that he cannot force the employee to perform further services) in which case employment ends when the contractually required notice would expire: *Thomas Marshall (Exports) Ltd v Guinle* [1979] 1 Ch 227 and *Evening Standard Co Ltd v Henderson* [1987] ICR 588 (CA). Alternatively, the employer can release the employee early on a mutually agreed date which then becomes the termination date. Lastly, where the purported notice amounts to a repudiatory breach the employer can accept the breach, terminating the contract from the date of acceptance. Whether the purported resignation amounts to a repudiatory breach needs to be considered very carefully by the employer. Not every resignation that departs from the strict terms of the contract will be a repudiatory breach: see paragraphs 8.29 to 8.31 for further discussion on this point. An employer who treats a purported resignation as a repudiatory breach, accepts it as terminating the contract but does so wrongly may himself have committed a repudiatory breach with all the attendant consequences of having done so: see paragraphs 8.19 to 8.24. In the context of limiting competition the first option of holding the employee to his full notice period is often the best course. This is particularly so where the contract of employment includes a garden leave provision that the employer can activate.

1(f) Date of termination: repudiatory breach

8.18 A repudiatory breach of the contract of employment does not bring the contract of employment to an end automatically. The innocent party has the option either to waive the breach or to accept it. It is only where the innocent party accepts the breach as bringing the contract to an end that it does so *Gunton v Richmond upon Thames London Borough Council* [1980] ICR 755 (CA) applied, albeit with some reluctance, *Boyo v Lambeth London Borough Council* [1994] ICR 727 (CA). Acceptance of the breach will, however, be readily inferred from the conduct of the innocent party: *Gunton*. Particularly, in view of the court's willingness to infer acceptance, the need for acceptance is sometimes said to be a rather esoteric point. However, it may on occasion have great practical significance. Since the contract of employment continues in existence until acceptance of the repudiation, then activities by the parties pending such acceptance may amount to breaches of contract, whereas if the contract were to end immediately on repudiation, they would ordinarily not: cf paragraph 8.3. Likewise, questions as to whether the contract may be specifically enforced: see pararaph 14.3: may depend on the precise moment of termination.

2. Repudiatory breach

2(a) Effect of a repudiatory breach

8.19 It is the effect of a termination as a result of repudiatory breach that makes the whole issue of repudiatory breach so critically important in the context of this book. In broad terms that effect is to discharge the innocent party (normally the employee) who accepts the breach, from all his future obligations under the contract: *General Billposting Co Ltd v Atkinson* [1909] AC 118 (HL). So, for example, where the employee accepts the breach, from the moment of acceptance he is discharged from his obligations under the contract including any post-termination restrictive covenants. The only protection which remains for the now ex-employer is that afforded to him by the duty of confidence owed by his ex-employee, insofar as that duty exists in equity or as a property right of the employer and, in some instances ongoing fiduciary duties: see paragraphs 3.54 to 3.65. In our view, no contractual duty of confidence (express or implied) continues after the acceptance of the repudiatory breach. An employee seeking to escape the bonds of a restrictive covenant will often endeavour to find a repudiatory breach on which to rely, and may indeed indulge in tactics designed to invite such a breach. It is for this reason that it is vital for an employer to understand what conduct can amount to a repudiatory breach and to bear the risk of an allegation of repudiatory breach in mind at all times, not least when reacting to an employee's resignation.

8.20 In recent years some doubt has been raised as to whether *General Billposting* remains good law. In our view there are no real grounds for that doubt. However, because the point is raised quite frequently in the context of restrictive covenants it is a point which requires some consideration. The foundation of the doubt arises from two House of Lords decisions in which provisions of commercial contracts were held to survive termination as a result of repudiatory breach. In neither case was *General Billposting* referred to. In *Heyman v Darwins Ltd* [1942] AC 356 the surviving provision was an arbitration clause. In *Photo Productions Ltd v Securicor Ltd* [1980] AC 827, the more significant case of the two, the relevant provision was an exclusion clause limiting the liability of Securicor for certain acts of its employees.

8.21 In *Rock Refrigeration Ltd v Jones and Seward Refrigeration Ltd* [1996] IRLR 675 Philips LJ, obiter, at paragraphs 61 to 68 sought to extend the categories of clause that survive termination as a result of a repudiatory breach. In his view 'General Billposting accords neither with current legal principle nor with the requirement of business efficacy' (para 63) and, while not having to decide the point he thought it 'at least arguable' that not every restrictive covenant would be discharged by a repudiatory breach. Similarly Simon Brown LJ, again obiter, questioned whether *General Billposting* was unaffected by *Photo Productions*.

8.22 In advancing his argument Philips LJ referred for support in principle to *Haynes* and *Photo Productions*. However, what he did not even attempt to do was to reconcile the concept of a restrictive covenant surviving a termination as a result of repudiatory breach with the analysis of the effect of such a breach in the *Haynes* and *Photo Production* cases. Had he tackled this task he may have realised the flaw in his argument because there are fundamental differences between the surviving clauses in those two cases and restrictive covenants. The surviving clauses in *Photo Productions* and *Haynes* related (respectively) to the responsibility for or resolution of disputes arising from previous breaches of the contract, that is, matters that have already occurred at the time of termation whereas restrictive covenants will be a purely future obligation at the time of termination. Both *Haynes* and *Photo Productions* expressly recognise this distinction. For this reason we remain firmly of the view that *General Billposting* continues to be good law; a view reinforced by the fact that notwithstanding Philips LJ's propositions, the argument has not advanced in the three years that have elapsed since the *Rock* decision.

8.23 It is important to remember that it is only future obligations under the contract of employment that are discharged by a repudiatory breach, not arrangements which are clearly separate from that contract. So in *Pearce v Roy T Ward (Consultants) Ltd* EAT 11.10.96 (180/96) IDS Brief 585/March 1997 an employer who had wrongfully summarily dismissed an employee was still able to recover interest free loans made to the employee which the EAT found to be clearly separate from the contract of employment. While this case is understandable on its facts it does not in our view open the floodgates to arguments that restrictive covenants contained in separate documents, for example, deeds survive a repudiatory breach. Such covenants will almost invariably form part of the contract of employment. For further analysis see paragraphs 12.24 to 12.27.

8.24 Where the employee was in breach of contract before the employer's fundamental breach it will be open to the employer to pursue the employee in damages notwithstanding his own repudiatory breach. The victim of a repudiatory breach remains liable for his own breach committed before the contract is brought to an end: *Gill & Duffus SA v Berger & Co Inc (No 2)* [1984] AC 382. Difficult questions arise as to whether an employer who has committed a repudiatory breach can obtain injunctive relief against an employee/ex-employee in respect of that (ex-) employee's own conduct. While the court is unlikely to look with great favour on the (ex-) employer, there may be instances, for example for breach of property rights, where interim relief would be granted (see further Ch 14).

2(b) What amounts to a repudiatory breach?

8.25 A repudiatory breach is a breach which is so serious that it entitles the innocent party to elect to treat himself as discharged from future obligations under the contract. According to Lord Denning MR in *Western Excavating (ECC) Ltd v Sharp* [1978] ICR 221 (CA) the normal rules of contract apply so that, as he put it at page 226,

> 'If the employer is guilty of conduct which is a significant breach going to the root of the contract of employment, or which shows that the employer no longer intends to be bound by one or more essential terms of the contract, then the employee is entitled to treat himself as discharged from any further performance ... [The] conduct must ... be sufficiently serious to entitle him to leave at once.'

8.26 Whether there has been a repudiatory breach of contract is a question of mixed fact and law: *Pedersen v Camden London Borough Council* [1981] IRLR 173 (CA). Consequently, where the appellate body is the EAT the decision of the employment tribunal will be determinative unless the EAT finds either that the tribunal has misdirected itself in law or that on the facts as found no reasonable tribunal could have come to the conclusion reached. The position on appeal from a court to the Court of Appeal is different since the latter court is a court of appeal in respect of issues of law and fact.

8.27 In the context of the subject matter of this book certain types of conduct are regularly argued to constitute repudiatory breach, for example breach of notice provisions and sending employees on garden leave. These, together with other examples, are considered below. However, the categories considered below are by no means exhaustive, any breach which meets the criteria outlined by Lord Denning MR will be a repudiatory breach.

8.28 Before looking at specific examples of repudiatory breach there are a few general points worthy of note. Firstly it is irrelevant that the employer genuinely believes that his breach is not repudiatory: *Milbrook Furnishing Industries Ltd v McIntosh* [1981] IRLR 309. Although there remains some uncertainty on the point, it is probable that a genuine, but nonetheless incorrect, interpretation of the contract will not be a repudiatory breach where the employer has not taken up an entrenched position and where the time for performance of the term in dispute has not yet arisen: *Financial Techniques (Planning Services) Ltd v Hughes* [1981] IRLR 32 (CA); *Blyth v Scottish Liberal Club* [1983] IRLR 245 and *BBC v Beckett* [1983] IRLR 43 (EAT) and *Bliss v South Thames Regional Health Authority* [1985] IRLR 308 (CA) Cf *Frank Wright & Co (Holdings) Ltd v Punch* [1980] IRLR 217 and *Brigdens v Lancashire County Council* [1987] IRLR 58 (CA). For further detail see Harvey on Industrial Relations and Employment Law D 486-507.

2(b)(i) BREACH OF NOTICE PROVISIONS

8.29 The wrongful summary dismissal of an employee is a repudiatory breach: *General Billposting*; payment in lieu of notice in accordance with the terms of the contract is not: *Rex Stewart Jeffries Parker Ginsberg Ltd v Parker* [1988] IRLR 483. Within these two extremes the position is not entirely settled. For example, compare the decisions of the National Industrial Relations Court in *Dixon v Stenor Ltd* [1973] ICR 157 with the first instance decision of Neville J in *Konski v Peet* [1915] 1 Ch 530. In both cases the employees were dismissed with payments in lieu of notice where there was no contractual right to make such a payment. In *Dixon* the court found that the payment amounted to damages for breach of contract and that by accepting it the employee was discharged from his obligations. In *Konski* the payment was held to be consistent with the contract on the basis that the employer was not obliged to find work for the employee, merely to pay her. Nowadays with the increasing trend towards employees having a right to work (see *William Hill Organisation Ltd v Tucker* [1998] IRLR 313 (CA)) it is doubtful whether the result in *Konski* would be the same; arguably *Dixon* is to be preferred.

8.30 The Court of Appeal has made it clear that not every dismissal of an employee without proper notice will amount to a repudiatory breach: *Lawrence David Ltd v Ashton* [1989] IRLR 22. Mr Ashton's contract provided that he was entitled to one month's notice in writing. On 2 March 1988 he was informed orally that his contract was being terminated at the end of March but that he would be paid and could keep the company's car until the end of April. The main substance of what Mr Ashton had been told was confirmed by letter dated 7

March handed to him on 9 March. In an action by the company to enforce the restrictive covenants in the contract of employment it was conceded by the company that they were in breach of contract in that the notice was not written nor was the necessary period of one month given. However, at first instance Whitford J concluded that the case was not one 'in which one can come to the conclusion that this quite plainly was a repudiatory breach'. In confirming that there was a serious question to be tried the Court of Appeal referred to the first instance decision of *W Dennis & Sons Ltd v Tunnard Bros & Moore* (1911) 56 Sol Jo 162 as suggesting that there are cases where failure to give proper notice may not be a repudiatory breach.

8.31 Where an employer considers it necessary to breach the employee's notice provisions, other than by wrongful summary dismissal, the best advice that can be given is that all available steps should be taken to minimise the effect of the breach. In *Lawrence David Ltd v Ashton* (above) the net effect of the company's actions was that Mr Ashton had 29 days' actual notice of the termination of his employment *and* received an additional 30 days' salary and benefits for which he did not have to work. Overall, it was arguable that Mr Ashton benefited rather than suffered from the company's breach, a fact clearly taken into account by both courts in concluding that the company's application to enforce the restrictive covenants in the contract of employment did not automatically fail on Mr Ashton's argument of repudiatory breach.

2(b)(ii) SENDING THE EMPLOYEE ON GARDEN LEAVE

8.32 On this scenario the contract of employment is not terminated immediately. Instead, the employee is required not to perform any duties and to remain at home idle until the contract expires. Garden leave is a course commonly adopted where the employee has resigned to join a competitor business. Can such an instruction amount to a repudiatory breach? The answer is clearly yes, where the employee can show he has a right to work and the garden leave proposed represents a sufficient infringement of that right.

8.33 The old authorities such as *Turner v Sawdon & Co* [1901] 2 KB 653 held that an employee has no right to work, merely a right to be paid. Exceptions to this have long been recognised for pieceworkers: *Devonald v Rosser & Son* [1906] 2 KB 728, and for those like artists and singers whose careers depend on publicity: *Herbert Clayton & Jack Waller Ltd v Oliver* [1930] AC 209. The modern trend is towards extending those exceptions; so, for example, in *Provident Financial Group plc v Hayward* [1989] IRLR 84 the Court of Appeal recognised that Mr Hayward as an accountant had an interest in working. In the words of Dillon LJ:

'The employee has a concern to work and a concern to exercise his skills. That has been recognised in some circumstances concerned with artists and singers who depend on publicity, but it applies equally, I apprehend, to skilled workmen and even to chartered accountants.'

8.34 Most recently in *William Hill Organisation Ltd v Tucker* [1998] IRLR 313 the Court of Appeal ruled that Mr Tucker, a senior dealer in William Hill's spread betting business, had a right to work and to exercise his skills. It is fair to say that several of the aspects relied on by the Court of Appeal as giving rise to the right to work are common features of many employment contracts. This leads inevitably to the conclusion that in future many employees can legitimately claim to have a right to work. For a detailed analysis of the *William Hill* case see paragraphs 4.82 to 4.83.

8.35 Where the employee can establish that he has a right to work, there comes a point at which depriving him of that right is a repudiatory breach. In *Spencer v Marchington* [1988] IRLR 392 the court held that asking the manager of a recruitment agency to spend the last two months of her twelve-month fixed-term contract on garden leave 'was not quite important enough' to amount to a repudiatory breach notwithstanding that part of her remuneration was a 50% share of profits. In our view this decision seems a little harsh, but can be explained by the fact that the parties reached agreement on the amount to be paid for the balance of the contract and because the court was unable to find any evidence that the employee had accepted the repudiation. Since acceptance of the breach is a necessary pre-condition, the argument was doomed from the outset.

2(b)(iii) OTHER BREACHES

8.36 The two categories mentioned above are the most common 'traps' for the employer but there are others of which he should be aware of which the following are some examples. The dissolution of a partnership amounts to the repudiatory breach of contracts of employment with the partnership, except where there is an express or implied agreement that it will not do so: *Brace v Calder* [1895] 2 QB 253, applied in *Briggs v Oates* [1991] 1 All ER 407. Also, the compulsory winding up of a company is a repudiatory breach: *Measures Brothers v Measures* [1910] 2 Ch 248; as is even a small unilateral reduction in pay: *Industrial Rubber Products v Gillon* [1977] IRLR 389; or a failure to pay the tax element associated with a promise to provide tax free loans, even though the sums in dispute were not a significant part of the overall remuneration package: *Cantor Fitzgerald International v Callaghan* [1999] IRLR 234. A repudiatory breach can also arise from fundamental and unwelcome changes in the employee's duties: *Pedersen v London Borough of Camden* [1981] IRLR 173 and *Coleman v Baldwin* [1977] IRLR 342 or even in the manner in which a restructuring permitted by the contract is handled: *Dairy Crest Ltd v Wise* 24 September 1993 IRLB 491 at page 14. More recently in *Greenaway Harrison Ltd v Wiles* [1994] IRLR 380 (EAT) a threat to give lawful notice under a contract of employment to an employee if she refused to accept changes to her hours of work was held to be a repudiatory breach. The correctness of this decision is doubted. The employer should always take care with his general conduct and ensure that he respects the employee's rights. While single minor infringements will not amount to a repudiatory breach, several such infringements together may be enough at least to give the employee an arguable case, being together a breach of the implied obligation of trust and confidence: *Lewis v Motorworld Garages Ltd* [1985] IRLR 465. As Glidewell LJ explained the principle in that case page 469 paragraph 36 '... the last action of the employer which leads to the employee leaving need not itself be a breach of contract; the question is does the cumulative series of acts taken together amount to a breach of the implied term?'

2(c) Acceptance of repudiatory breach

8.37 As already explained (para 8.18) a repudiation does not in itself terminate the contract of employment. The contract will only come to an end on the acceptance of the repudiatory breach by the innocent party, although such acceptance will be readily inferred: *Gunton v London Borough of Richmond upon Thames* [1980] ICR 755 (HL) applied *Boyo v Lambeth London Borough Council* [1994] ICR 727 (CA). (See also para 14.2.)

8.38 In addition, it is only where the contract of employment terminates as a result of acceptance of the repudiatory breach that the innocent party is discharged from future contractual obligations. Much of the case law on whether acceptance of the repudiatory breach is the operative cause of termination derives from claims of constructive dismissal by employees under the Employment Rights Act 1996 and its predecessors. Nonetheless, in general terms the authorities are equally applicable in the common law context and provide useful general guidance on the strength of an argument of discharge by repudiatory breach. The innocent party will usually be the employee but in broad terms, and where appropriate on the facts, the principles will also apply to employers as innocent parties.

8.39 The following broad principles can be gathered from the authorities:

- **Timing** – The timing of the employee's resignation will be critical. There are no hard and fast rules as to how long an employee has to accept a repudiatory breach but time is undoubtedly limited. As Lord Denning MR explained the position in *Western Excavating* the employee 'must make up his mind soon after the conduct of which he complains; for if he continues for any length of time without leaving he will lose the right to treat himself as discharged'. The right may be lost on the basis that the employee has simply waived the breach or in some cases because he has expressly or impliedly accepted a variation to the contract which the employer had been seeking to impose. A common question posed to solicitors is 'how long do I have to take a decision?' No single answer will fit every case because the length of time will be governed by the particular facts including length of service, nature of the breach and whether the employee has objected to the breach. Where the breach has an immediate and significant impact on the employment, for example, a reduction in pay or a change in status the time frame may be fairly short. In contrast, where for example the breach involves remedying working conditions the time the employee has to decide may be longer. See: *Waltons & Morse v Dorrington* [1997] IRLR 488 (EAT) where the delay was approximately two months. As a general point, in the more recent cases there is a perceptible trend towards a recognition of an employee's dilemma in having to choose between waiving the breach and having no job. See *Jones v F Sirl & Son (Furnishers) Ltd* [1997] IRLR 493 (EAT) below and *Waltons & Morse* (above). At least from an employee's perspective this has been reflected in slightly more generous time frames than hitherto applied. One tactic that may buy the employee, or indeed the employer, a little more time to decide is giving the other party an opportunity to remedy the breach. In *W E Cox & Toner (International) Ltd v Crook* [1981] IRLR 443 the breach consisted of the issuing of a letter of censure to the employee, Mr Crook. He responded by inviting the employer to withdraw the letter, an invitation which was declined. Although not finally deciding the point the EAT intimated there was no affirmation of the contract until Mr Crook's invitation had been declined. Unfortunately for Mr Crook he ultimately lost because the EAT found that by wasting a further four weeks before resigning Mr Crook had forfeited his right to rely on the breach. A similar course to that taken in *W E Cox* might be for the employee to register a formal grievance under the employer's grievance procedure. For further examples of authorities on the issue of timing see: *Air Canada v Lee* [1978] IRLR 392; *Marriott v Oxford and District Co-Operative Society Ltd* (No 2) 1970 1 QB 186; *G W Stephens & Co v Fish* [1989] ICR 324 (EAT); *Bashir v Brillo Manufacturing Co* [1979] IRLR 295 (EAT); *Sheet Metal Components Ltd v Plumridge* [1974] IRLR 86. See also *Jones v F Sirl & Son (Furnishers) Ltd* [1997] IRLR 493 (EAT) below.

- **Post breach conduct** – Where the innocent party has waived the breach or expressly/impliedly accepted a variation to the contract which the other party (usually the employer) was seeking to impose, the innocent party can no longer rely on that breach to discharge the contract. Consequently, the conduct of the innocent party after the breach will be critical. In every case the innocent party should as an absolute minimum consider making an appropriate written protest about the breach. Where the innocent party is the employee, as already suggested in the preceding bullet point, he should also consider lodging a formal grievance with his employer. An illustration of how a combination of comparatively 'innocent acts' can defeat the right to rely on a repudiatory breach can be found in *Normalec Ltd v Britton* [1983] FSR 318. In that case, Britton's delay in leaving, coupled with the fact that he gave notice in accordance with his contract meant that he had affirmed the contract. One interesting but unresolved issue on affirmation is whether an employee can affirm if he is unaware that, as a matter of law, he could elect to accept the employer's conduct as repudiating the contract. In *Peyman v Lanjani* [1984] 3 All ER 703 (CA), a case not concerning employment but a property transaction May J thought an affirmation could not take place in these circumstances. In the employment sphere May J's view has thus far only been considered once in *Bliss v South East Thames Regional Health Authority* [1985] IRLR 308 (CA). In that case Dillon LJ (at paras 56 to 57) thought the argument a 'formidable' one but found it unnecessary to express a view on it in the particular case. It remains to be seen whether the argument will gather any greater force in the employment law context in years to come.

- **Express reliance not essential** – An employee need not expressly state that he is resigning because of the repudiatory breach. Whether there has been acceptance of a repudiation of a contract of employment is a matter to be determined on the facts and evidence of each case: *Weathersfield Ltd t/a Van & Truck Rentals v Sargent* [1999] IRLR 34 (CA) overruling *Holland v Glendale Industries Ltd* [1998] ICR 493 (EAT). However, notwithstanding its ruling the court in *Weathersfield* recognised that if, at or around the time of leaving, the employee does not indicate he is relying on the repudiation there is a greater likelihood that the repudiation will not be found to be the cause of the resignation. On a practical note a party seeking to rely on a repudiatory breach as terminating the contract should make his position crystal clear in writing as soon as practically possible, ideally at the time of resignation.

- **Effective cause of resignation** – The repudiatory breach need not be the only reason for the employee leaving but it must be the 'effective cause of the resignation': *Jones v F Sirl & Son (Furnishers) Ltd* [1997] IRLR 493 (EAT). Mrs Jones had been an employee of F Sirl & Son for nearly 30 years. Over several months in 1990 the employer made a series of adverse unilateral changes to her contract. Within one month of the final change Mrs Jones was approached by another furnishing company and offered a position with them which she accepted. She resigned from F Sirl & Son and brought unfair dismissal proceedings. Mrs Jones' claim failed in the Tribunal who found that notwithstanding the serious breaches her resignation had been 'prompted' by the alternative employment. Allowing the appeal the EAT recognised that 'in today's labour market' there may well be concurrent causes of a resignation – presumably an oblique recognition of the fact that many individuals cannot afford to be out of work. In those cases the job of the tribunal/court was to find which was the effective cause. In *Jones* the EAT had no hesitation in finding that the effective cause of Mrs Jones' resignation 'was the very serious and fundamental breaches of her contract by the employers'. In cases where the employee has alternative employment to go to it will be essential to establish how and when that employment was secured. An employee who can show, for example, that he was not actively engaged in looking for alternative employment until after the repudiatory breach occurred will usually have strong grounds for arguing that the repudiatory breach was the effective cause of his resignation.

- **Clear and unequivocal acceptance** – Acceptance of the repudiatory breach must be clear and unequivocal. In *Harrison v Norwest Holt Group Administration Ltd* [1985] ICR 668 (CA) a response to a repudiatory breach which was contained in a letter marked 'without prejudice' was found not to be sufficiently unequivocal.

Chapter 9

Legitimate protection for the ex-employer

1. Implied duties after termination of employment: trade secrets/confidential information

9.1   After the duty of fidelity has come to an end on termination of the contract of employment (paras 3.2 and 3.3) the only restrictions on competition by the ex-employee (in the absence of express restrictive covenants) are as follows:

- The ex-employee may not use or disclose trade secrets of the ex-employer gained by the employee in the course of his employment: *Faccenda Chicken Ltd v Fowler* [1986] 3 WLR 288 (CA); *Roger Bullivant Ltd v Ellis* [1987] IRLR 491 (CA); *Johnson & Bloy (Holdings) Ltd v Wolstenholme Rink plc* [1987] IRLR 499 (CA); (possibly) the ex-employee may not use or disclose even 'mere' confidential information of the ex-employer where the ex-employee intends to sell or use or disclose the information otherwise than for the purpose of his business or new employment: *Faccenda*.
- Where the employee in the course of his employment takes or makes extracts from the employer's documents or copies them with a view to competing with his employer after the end of his employment or deliberately memorises his employer's confidential information for this purpose the employee may not use such information after termination of employment: *Robb v Green* [1895] 2 QB 315 (CA); *Universal Thermosensors Ltd v Hibben* [1992] 1 WLR 840; this is so even though:
  - The ex-employee would have been free after employment to use the information, had he not copied, extracted or memorised it as described;
  - That information has lost its quality of confidentiality by virtue of the ex-employee's use or disclosure of it, so that others may use it. The ex-employee is (for a limited period) placed under a special disability in relation to the use of such information: *Roger Bullivant v Ellis*, and see further the discussion on springboard injunctions in Ch 14.

The above paragraph is by way of summary of points which have already been covered in some detail in Chs 3 and 5.

9.2   The position is potentially stricter in relation to directors who have fiduciary duties (and possibly other senior employees who may have such duties) which continue after employment so as to limit certain types of competitive activity by them: see paragraphs 3.54 to 3.65. An ex-employer who has not obtained an express restrictive covenant will often seek to show that for some reason he falls outside the rules referred to in paragraph 9.1. For example, in *Wallace Bogan & Co v Cove and others* [1997] IRLR 453 the Court of Appeal rejected an attempt by a firm of solicitors to prevent four of its former assistant solicitors from canvassing or soliciting its clients when there was no express restrictive covenant preventing such activity. The Court of Appeal overturned the finding by the judge that there was arguably an implied term in the contract of service between solicitors and the firm employing them restricting post employment soliciting or canvassing of clients. The Court of Appeal held that there was no distinction in this regard between solicitors taking advantage of their professional connections and any other trade or profession.

9.3   In paragraphs 5.41 to 5.42 we expressed the view that (apart from the automatic protection referred to in para 9.1) an ex-employee may be prevented from using 'mere' confidential information by express covenant in the contract of employment. We now turn to consider express covenants in the contract of employment which restrict competitive activity by the ex-employee with the ex-employer.

2. Express covenants in the contract of employment affecting the ex-employee

2(a) General statement of the doctrine of restraint of trade

9.4   The starting point is that covenants restricting the freedom of the ex-employee to compete with his ex-employer are void for illegality. However, the covenants will be upheld if the employer can show that the covenants:

- Are designed to protect his legitimate interests; and
- Extend no further than is reasonably necessary to protect those interests:

Mason v Provident Clothing & Supply Co Ltd [1913] AC 724 (HL); *Herbert Morris Ltd v Saxelby* [1916] AC 688 (HL); *Stenhouse Australia Ltd v Phillips* [1974] 1 All ER 117 (PC).

9.5   In the case of an employer/employee covenant the employer is not entitled to protect himself against competition in itself (applying after termination of employment a covenant purely to prevent competition sometimes being referred to as a 'covenant in gross') but only against unfair exploitation of the ex-employer's trade secrets or trade connection: *Stenhouse v Phillips*. Further, the reasonableness of the restriction is to be judged at the date the contract was made: *Rex Stewart Jeffries Parker Ginsberg Ltd v Parker* [1988] IRLR 483, 486 (CA).

2(a)(i) PUBLIC INTEREST

9.6   It is often said that the covenant must not be unreasonable with regard to the public interest (but that it is for the employee to show that a covenant which is reasonable as between the parties is unreasonable with regard to the public interest): for example, *Mason v Provident* at page 733; *Nordenfelt v Maxim Nordenfelt Guns and Ammunition Co* [1894] AC 535, 565. However, except in the case of a monopoly, a restraint which is reasonably necessary to protect the legitimate interests of the ex-employer will very rarely be regarded as unreasonable with regard to the public interest. The fact is that once it is established that a covenant is reasonable as between the parties the court will not normally look further. It is for this reason that in some of the recent decisions on the subject, reference to the public interest requirement is absent: see for example *Rex Stewart Jeffries Parker Ginsberg v Parker* [1988] IRLR 483, 486.

2(a)(ii) INTERESTS OF THE EMPLOYEE

9.7   It is also said that regard must be had to the interests of the ex-employee: for example, *Herbert Morris Ltd v Saxelby* [1916] AC 688, 716 (HL) (where the interests of the covenantee are equated with the public interest); *Attwood v Lamont* [1920] 3 KB 571, 589 (CA); *Fitch v Dewes* [1921] 2 AC 158, 163 (HL). It would, however, be an extremely unusual case where, while the protection offered by the restraint went no further than was necessary to protect the legitimate interests of the ex-employer, the restraint was nonetheless to be struck down as being unreasonable having regard to the interests of the ex-employee. It is suggested that this requirement is otiose: see for example *Rex Stewart Jeffries Parker Ginsberg Ltd v Parker* [1988] IRLR 483, 486 (CA). This is of course not to say that the interests of the ex-employee are irrelevant: when it comes to deciding whether or not to grant an injunction (both at the interim and the trial stage) the effect of enforcement of the covenant on the ex-employee (eg whether he will thereby be precluded from earning a living) is of fundamental importance. See the discussion of the relevance or otherwise of the adequacy of the consideration in paragraphs 10.12 to 10.22.

2(a)(iii) EMPLOYMENT CONTRACTS V BUSINESS SALE AGREEMENTS

9.8   The courts are more likely to strike down covenants which restrict competition contained in employment contracts than in business sale contracts. In business or share sale (and other types of business agreements) the court will regard these covenants more favourably (inter alia because of an assumed equality of bargaining power of the parties): *Mason v Provident Clothing & Supply Co Ltd* and *Attwood v Lamont*. See also *Systems Reliability Holdings plc v Smith* [1990] IRLR 377, *Alliance Paper Group plc v Prestwich* [1996] IRLR 25, *Dawnay Day v De Braconier D'Alphen* [1997] IRLR 442 and TSC *Europe UK Ltd v Massey* [1999] IRLR 22.

2(a)(iv) PRE-1913 CASES

9.9   Prior to 1913 the courts had tended to favour the principle of freedom of contract (and hence the enforceability of restrictive covenants) above the principle of freedom of trade (see *Attwood v Lamont* and in particular the judgment of Younger LJ at page 588ff). Accordingly, decisions of the courts (including the House of Lords) before 1913 have to be treated cautiously.

2(b) Legitimate interests of the ex-employer

2(b)(i) MEANING OF LEGITIMATE INTEREST

9.10   'Legitimate interests' means some interest of a proprietary nature – not merely an interest in avoiding competition. In the words of Lord Wilberforce in *Stenhouse Australia Ltd v Phillips* [1974] 1 All ER 117, 122:

'The employer's claim for protection is based on the identification of some advantage or asset inherent in the business which can properly be regarded as, in a general sense, his property, and which it would be unjust to allow the employee to appropriate for his own purposes, even though he, the employee, may have contributed to its creation. For while it may be true that an employee is to be entitled – and is to be encouraged – to build up his own qualities of skill and experience, it is equally his duty to develop and improve his employer's business for the benefit of his employer. These two obligations interlock during his employment: after its termination they diverge and mark the boundary between what the employee may take with him and what he may legitimately be asked to leave behind with his employers.'

2(b)(ii) THE MAIN TYPES OF PROTECTABLE INTEREST

9.11 There are two principal types of business interest which the employer is entitled to seek to protect:

- His trade connection or goodwill; and
- His business secrets or confidential information.

Restrictive covenants are upheld not on the basis that the employee:

'... would, by reason of his employment or training, obtain the skill and knowledge necessary to equip him as a possible competitor in the trade, but that he might obtain such personal knowledge of and influence over the customers of his employer, or such an acquaintance with his employer's trade secrets as would enable him, if competition were allowed, to take advantage of his employer's trade connection or utilise information confidentially obtained.'(per Lord Parker in *Herbert Morris v Saxelby* [1916] 1 AC 688, 709).

See also *Spafax v Harrison* [1980] IRLR 442, 446. In this connection the decision in *Cantor Fitzgerald (UK) Ltd v Wallace* [1992] IRLR 215 was something of an oddity. Judge Prosser QC (sitting as a Deputy Judge of the Queen's Bench Division) held that an ex-employer could not protect a customer connection which rested solely on the personality, temperament and ability of the employees to get on with people. The ex-employer was a firm of Eurobond brokers operating in the inter-dealer market. The employees were 15 brokers whose jobs did not require them to have technical or financial skills. Their success depended on their personality and ability to get on with traders. However, this is exactly the kind of case in which in numerous decisions the courts (including the House of Lords and Court of Appeal) have repeatedly held that the ex-employer may seek protection. Thus, in *Mason v Provident Clothing & Supply Co Ltd* [1913] AC 724 (HL) (a case of a travelling salesman) the House of Lords referred to the employer's right to protect himself against the employee's obtaining personal knowledge of and influence over the customers of his employer during employment. Indeed, Viscount Haldane LC said that:

'The capacity of the servant must obviously, from the character of the business as I have described it, be due mainly to natural gifts as a canvasser, and only in a secondary degree to special training.' (page 731)

9.12 Insofar as *Cantor* suggested that the employer may only protect himself against the employee whose influence over customers arises from his general skill and knowledge, it could not be supported – if anything, it is in the latter case that it could be argued that the employer should not be able to obtain protection. Indeed, in the very cases referred to in *Cantor*, namely *Marion White Ltd v Francis* [1972] 1 WLR 1423 (CA) (a case of a hairdresser) and *Home Counties Dairies Ltd v Skilton* [1970] 1 WLR 526 (CA) (a case of a milk roundsman) the Court of Appeal emphasised that the employer was entitled to protect his customer connection against the employee who may by virtue of his personality acquire influence over customers with whom his employment brings him into contact. Unsurprisingly, *Cantor* was doubted by Robert Walker J in the first instance decision in *Dawnay Day v de Braconier d'Alphen* [1997] IRLR 285 (at para 34). See also *Scorer v Seymour-Johns* [1966] 3 All ER 347, 350-351 and *London & Solent Ltd v Brooks* (IDS Brief 389 January 1989, unreported) (CA). The position is, of course, different where there is limited recurrence of customers: in *Bowler v Lovegrove* [1921] 1 Ch 642, 653 an area covenant given by an employee of an estate agent was struck down. Customers were such for only one transaction, and there was therefore no client connection to protect.

9.13 Where trade connection is relied on to justify a covenant in restraint of trade the ex-employer must accordingly show:

- The existence of the trade connection of the ex-employer – usually customers. Often, it is not difficult to identify who is a customer: essential to the concept is the recurrence or likelihood of recurrence of the purchase or use of the ex-employer's goods or services. In other cases the question may be quite complex – and it may be necessary in drafting the covenant to define who is a customer: see paragraph 11.9. The question of who is a customer is more fully dealt with below (paras 10.37 to 10.42) under non-solicitation covenants. Trade connection may also include suppliers (*Thomas Marshall (Exports) Ltd v Guinle* [1979] 1 Ch 227);
- That the ex-employee is likely to be able to take advantage of his ex-employer's trade connection – by means of the ex-employee's personal knowledge of and influence over customers or suppliers: the question of the required quality and degree of connection between the employee and the customer is more fully dealt with below (paras 10.37 to 10.63) under non-solicitation covenants.

2(b)(iii) OTHER TYPES OF PROTECTABLE INTEREST

9.14 Confidential information and business connection are not the only interests which the law will recognise. In *Dawnay Day & Co v De Braconier D'Alphen* [1997] IRLR 442 (CA) the claimant investment bank sought to enforce area covenants and non-solicitation covenants in the heads of agreement setting up a joint venture business with the defendant managers. The business was developed and carried on by a jointly owned limited company which employed the managers as inter-dealer brokers in the Eurobond market and owned the goodwill of the business. The Court of Appeal held that the fact that the claimants were neither the purchasers of the business from the defendants, nor their employers, did not mean that they did not have a legitimate or lawful interest in enforcing the covenants. The Court of Appeal emphasised that covenants in restraint may be enforced when the covenantee has a legitimate interest of whatever kind to protect and enforcement was not restricted as a matter of law to established categories of vendor/purchaser of a business or employer/employee cases. The established categories are not rigid or exclusive. The approach of the courts has developed away from such rigidity. In *Dawnay Day* the claimant's undertaking to contribute the capital for the joint business, and the contribution after it was made, gave it a clear commercial interest in safeguarding itself against competition from the managers. Likewise, in *Office Angels Ltd v Rainer-Thomas and O'Connor* [1991] IRLR 214 the Court of Appeal recognised as a protectable interest an employment agent's connection with its pool of temporary workers. Further, an employer has a legitimate interest in protecting the stability of his workforce (which he may seek to protect by a covenant preventing the enticement by the ex-employee of his former colleagues). In *Dawnay Day* the Court of Appeal settled the differing views expressed in two earlier Court of Appeal decisions (*Hanover Insurance Brokers Ltd v Shapiro* [1994] IRLR 82 and *Ingham v A B C Contract Services Ltd* (12.11.93) as to whether covenants covering non-poaching of employees could be justified on the basis of a legitimate interest of the employer in maintaining the stability of his workforce: in principle it may; see also *T S C Europe UK Ltd v Massey* [1999] IRLR 22. The employer is entitled to seek to protect himself against the personal influence which the employee may (while on the employer's payroll) gain over other members of staff. The position may be different where the interest in maintaining a stable workforce is sought to be protected by contract between prospective employers. In *Kores Manufacturing Co Ltd v Kolok Manufacturing Co Ltd* [1959] Ch 108 a non-poaching agreement between two rivals was struck down on the basis that the maintenance of the stability of the workforce was not an interest which could justify such an agreement. This basis for the decision is probably wrong in the light of the *Dawnay Day* decision referred to above in this paragraph.

2(b)(iv) INALIENABLE RIGHTS OF THE EX-EMPLOYEE

9.15 The law will not allow the ex-employer to protect himself against pure competition by the ex-employee. The position is set out in the classic statement by Lord Wilberforce in *Stenhouse Australia Ltd v Phillips* [1974] 1 All ER 117, 122:

'... the employee is entitled to use to the full any personal skill and experience even if this has been acquired in the service of his employer: it is this freedom to use to the full a man's improving ability and talents which lies at the root of the policy of the law regarding this type of restraint.'

9.16 The law will prevent the ex-employer from seeking by way of a confidentiality covenant or otherwise to expand the categories of confidential information so as to restrict the ex-employee's use of his skill or know-how: *Triplex Safety Glass Co Ltd v Scorah* [1938] Ch 211, 216 (per FarwellJ). See too, *F S S Travel & Leisure Systems Ltd v Johnson* [1998] IRLR 382 (CA) referred to in paragraph 5.45. As we have seen (in Chapter 5) there are considerable practical difficulties in distinguishing proprietary information of the employer from information which is to be regarded as the general skill or knowledge of the employee: see, for example, the judgment of Farwell LJ in *Sir W C Leng & Co Ltd v Andrews* [1909] 1 Ch 763, 773 (CA).

2(b)(v) PROTECTION FOR SUBSIDIARY/GROUP COMPANIES

9.17 The restrictive covenant must be for the protection of a business in which the employer is interested. Thus a group company is ordinarily entitled to protect its own business and not the separate interests of other group companies: *Henry*

Leetham & Sons Ltd v Johnstone-White [1907] 1 Ch 322, where each company carried on a separate business.

9.18 It will, however, often be possible to show that one company in a group has a legitimate interest in the business of another in the same group. That being said, it is an entirely different question whether, in the circumstances of the particular case, a covenant in relation to associated companies is necessary: such (parts of) covenants in restraint are often struck down, or more often severed (see paras 11.18 to 11.24), on the basis (for example) that the employee had no contact with customers of the associated companies. In *Hinton & Higgs (UK) Ltd v Murphy and Valentine* [1989] IRLR 519, 521 in which the Court of Session held that the covenant was too wide because it sought to restrict the employee from working not only for clients of the company but also those of other companies in the group: that in the absence of special circumstances it was not necessary for the protection of the interests of an employer that ex-employees be restricted from working for any client of any other company in the group. The decision in *Henry Leetham* may be justified also on the basis that the employee was a commercial traveller who by an area covenant would have been restricted from the whole of the United Kingdom, whereas he had been active in only a small part thereof. See also *Business Seating (Renovations) Ltd v Broad* [1989] ICR 729 and *Continental Tyre and Rubber (Great Britain) Co Ltd v Heath* (1913) 29 TLR 308, 310.

9.19 In *Stenhouse Australia Ltd v Phillips* [1974] 1 All ER 117, 125 (PC) a non-solicitation covenant extended not only to clients of the employer (a holding company) but also to clients of the subsidiaries of the employer. It was accordingly submitted on behalf of the employee that the interests to be protected were the interests of the subsidiaries as independent legal entities and therefore there was no legitimate interest of the employer to protect. The evidence was that the business of the group was controlled and co-ordinated by the employer company and all funds generated by each of the companies were received by the employer. The subsidiaries were mere agencies through which the employer directed its integrated business. Not only did the employer have a real interest in protecting the business of the subsidiaries, but the real interest of so doing was that of the employer. Its business was simply to some extent handled by subsidiaries. The Privy Council accordingly upheld the covenant distinguishing *Henry Leetham & Sons Ltd v Johnstone-White* [1907] 1 Ch 322 (see para 9.17). Following the decision of the Court of Appeal in *Dawnay Day & Co v De Braconier D'Alphen* [1997] IRLR 442 (see paragraph 9.14 above) it is to be expected that the courts will more readily accept that a holding company has a legitimate interest in the business of its subsidiary sufficient to amount to a legitimate interest justifying a covenant in favour of the holding company. However, the prudent draftsman will always seek to draw the covenants in a manner which deals specifically with this problem: see paragraph 11.61.

9.20 Similar principles should apply in relation to service companies, that is companies which are merely the administrative tools of other companies in a group of companies. A service company, although employing all or most of the employees of the group who are 'seconded' to the particular associate company for whom they are 'working', will normally have no clients or confidential information of its own. The service company should be entitled to reasonable protection over the interests of the associate company or companies for whom the employee is 'working' because the employment is in fact on behalf of the associate company or companies.

2(c) Reasonable protection of legitimate interests

2(c)(i) NO MORE THAN ADEQUATE PROTECTION

9.21 For any covenant in restraint to be treated as reasonable in the interests of the parties it must '... afford no more than adequate protection to the party in whose favour it is imposed.' (per Lord Parker in *Herbert Morris Ltd v Saxelby* [1916] AC 688, 707). It is for the court to decide as a matter of law whether a contract is in restraint of trade and, if so, whether it is reasonable. Whether a particular provision is or is not reasonable to protect the employer's legitimate interests is a matter of impression: (per Glidewell LJ in *Rex Stewart Jeffries Parker Ginsberg Ltd v Parker* [1988] IRLR 483, 486).

2(c)(ii) DIFFERENT TYPES OF RESTRICTIVE COVENANTS

9.22 The principal types of covenants taken to protect business secrets and trade connections after employment are:

- Area covenants: preventing the ex-employee from carrying on a similar business within a defined area often certain radius of the premises of the ex-employer; a similar type of clause is where an ex-employee is prevented from dealing with named competitors of the ex-employer: for example, *Littlewoods v Harris* 1 WLR 1472 (CA). In this book we have referred to 'area' covenants as encompassing this kind of 'non-competition' covenant.
- Non-dealing covenants: preventing the ex-employee from dealing with the customers (or suppliers) of the ex-employer.
- Non-solicitation covenants: preventing the ex-employee from soliciting the business of customers (or suppliers) of the ex-employer.
- Non-poaching covenants: preventing the ex-employee from enticing away his former colleagues.
- Confidentiality covenants: preventing the ex-employee from using or disclosing trade secrets or confidential information of the ex-employer.

2(c)(iii) WHICH TYPE OF COVENANT IS APPROPRIATE?

9.23 As we have seen, the law will only uphold covenants which extend no further than is necessary to protect the legitimate interests of the ex-employer. The first question which will often arise is whether the particular type of covenant used is suitable to protect the type of legitimate interest sought to be protected. For instance, an area covenant may be too blunt an instrument to protect customer connection because the ex-employee is thereby prevented from dealing with not only customers of the ex-employer but those who are not customers or in any sense part of his trade connection: therefore a non-solicitation/dealing covenant is more apt to protect this sort of interest. In *S W Strange Ltd v Mann* [1965] 1 All ER 1069 Stamp J held that an area covenant taken from a bookmaker's manager was not appropriate to protect the employer's trade connection because:

- The business was exclusively a credit business, so that the names and addresses of all the customers were known to him (that is, a non-solicitation/dealing covenant would have been effective); and
- The employee did not have such a personal relationship with customers

outside the town so as to make it likely that they would seek him out if he left his employment (that is, it was sufficient to prevent the ex-employee from seeking out customers).

9.24 In these circumstances the area covenant gave more protection than was necessary, while a non-solicitation covenant would have been appropriate. Stamp J, however, rejected the contention that an area covenant is necessarily inappropriate in relation to an exclusively credit business. See also *Mason v Provident Clothing & Supply Company Ltd* [1913] AC 724, 734. In *Office Angels Ltd v Rainer-Thomas and O'Connor* [1991] IRLR 214 Sir Christopher Slade said (at page 221):

> '... in considering the reasonableness or otherwise of a covenant such as this, the court is entitled to consider whether or not a covenant of a narrower nature would have sufficed for the covenantee's protection.'

In that case the area covenant was struck down since a properly drafted non-solicitation covenant would have provided sufficient protection to the ex-employer, the ex-employee's argument that an area covenant was necessary to 'police' infringements by the ex-employee being rejected by the Court of Appeal.

9.25 Hence, area covenants will have a better chance of survival when used to protect:

● The business connection of a business with a passing trade;
● Trade secrets.

(See the discussion in *Office Angels* at page 220).

9.26 Where an area covenant is justifiable as being reasonable to protect the employer's legitimate interests it may be upheld even where there is also a non-solicitation covenant – the area covenant is intended to avoid the problems of proving solicitation – being designed to ensure that the employee does not enter the 'danger area': *Specialist Recruiters International Ltd v Taylor* (RCJ 4 July 1989, unreported), but in these circumstances a non-dealing covenant may be a finer and therefore more suitable weapon.

2(d)   The effect of the Restrictive Trade Practices Act 1976

9.27 The Restrictive Trade Practices Act 1976 renders unenforceable restrictions which are contained in agreements which have not been registered pursuant to the Act. The Act relates to agreements to which at least two parties carry on business in the United Kingdom. It has separate but similar provisions relating to restrictions accepted in agreements relating to (i) goods and (ii) services. The Act may in principle apply to restrictions in the form of non-competition and non-solicitation/dealing covenants principally because Section 6(1)(f) of the Act includes as a restriction 'the persons or classes of persons to, or for whom, or the areas or the places in or from which, goods are to be supplied or acquired ...' (see Article 3(2)(e) of the Restrictive Trade Practices (Services) Order for a like provision in relation to services).

9.28 The Act applies only to agreements where restrictions are accepted by two or more parties (section 6(1) – goods; and Article 3(1)(b) of the Restrictive Trade

Practices Order 1976 – services). Thus the Act is not normally relevant to restrictive covenants in employment contracts because restrictions (such as area covenants or non-solicitation/dealing covenants) are normally accepted only by one party, the employee. It is usually only in partnership or joint venture agreements or agreements to which vendor-employees are parties that restrictions are likely to be accepted by more than one party under an agreement. However, such agreements will often be exempt by virtue of The Restrictive Trade Practices (Sale and Purchase and Share Subscription Agreements (Goods)) Order 1989 (SI 1989 No 1081) and The Restrictive Trade Practices (Services) (Amendment) Order 1989 (S.I. No 1082) in relation to goods and services respectively. Share sale agreements which qualify under the Orders are exempt from registration provided the restrictions accepted only limit the extent to which the vendor (or associated company or an individual) may compete with the business which is the subject of the sale, or be involved in or assist any business which so competes. Furthermore, the restrictions are only disregarded if they operate for a period not exceeding five years beginning with the date of the agreement or a period beginning with the date of the agreement and ending two years after the date of expiry or termination of the relevant employment or services contract, whichever is the later. Similar provisions apply to share subscription agreements. Further, Section 43(2) provides that (for certain purposes) 'any two or more interconnected bodies corporate, or any two or more individuals carrying on business in partnership with each other, shall be treated as a single person'. It is only where an employment agreement contains restrictions which are accepted by two or more unconnected persons that warning bells as to the possible application of the Act should ring. However, Section 9(6) provides that any restriction which affects or otherwise relates to the workers to be employed or not employed by any person or as to the remuneration, conditions of employment, hours of work or working conditions of such workers is to be disregarded. The exact meaning of this provision is not clear; in particular it is uncertain whether a non-competition or non-solicitation/dealing covenant contained in a contract of employment could be said to be part of the 'conditions of employment'. It may be stretching the meaning of this expression too far to regard it as covering covenants which apply post employment. It cannot be assumed that where there are such covenants given by more than one party under an agreement, the Act does not apply.

9.29 The statutory instruments referred to in paragraph 9.28 remain in force under the transitional arrangements set out in Sch 13 to the Competition Act 1998 pending commencement of that Act in March 2000. The Director General will have power under the Act to make block exemptions in respect of certain types of agreements. There are at present no definite plans to exempt share sale or share subscription agreements. Because of the limited application of the Act to employment contracts it is not appropriate to consider its provisions in detail.

2(e) The special position of the vendor-employee

9.30 It is not uncommon for the vendor of a business to remain in the business (often for a minimum fixed term) and so to enter into two sets of contractual obligations with the employer – those pertaining to the sale of the business (or the shares in the company) and those relating to employment. Often there will be a sale contract and an employment contract each containing covenants against competition and solicitation in substantially the same terms. In these circumstances the covenants will be less stringently tested for reasonableness –

the court being more concerned to uphold commercial bargains freely entered into, since it is assumed that there is greater equality of bargaining power than in a straightforward employment contract. This may be so even if the only covenants entered into are in the service agreement: *Alliance Paper Group plc v Prestwich* [1996] IRLR 25 and compare *Dawnay, Day & Co v De Braconier D'Alphen* [1997] IRLR 442 (CA) and *T S C Europe UK Ltd v Massey* [1999] IRLR 22.

9.31 In *Allied Dunbar (Frank Weisinger) Ltd v Weisinger* [1988] IRLR 60 a self-employed sales associate of the claimant, Weisinger sold his practice including goodwill to Allied Dunbar for £386,000. He agreed to act as consultant to the claimant ('Dunbar') for a minimum period and to be bound by a non-solicitation covenant (that is, not to solicit any existing customer for the purpose of selling a product competing with a product of Dunbar) and a non-competition covenant, (that for two years after termination of the consultancy he would not be involved in a business which competed with Dunbar or its parent company). The effect of the restraints was that after termination of the consultancy Weisinger would have to retire from the financial services industries for the agreed period. Millett J said that the question of whether the covenants were taken for the protection of the business sold to Dunbar by Weisinger, rather than for the protection of Dunbar's present and future business as employer under the consultancy agreement, was one of substance not of form – the fact that the covenants were in the sale contract was of very little weight. Since the purpose (or main purpose) of the consultancy agreement was to facilitate the transfer of the client connection which Weisinger had sold to Dunbar (Dunbar having no other business and Weisinger not being required to acquire any independent client connections apart from the practice), Millett J had no difficulty in deciding that the validity of the covenant fell to be determined by the less stringent approach adopted by the courts where the covenant is taken for the protection of a business sold by the covenantor to the covenantee rather than where it is taken by the employer from an employee. He accordingly upheld the covenants.

9.32 Similar considerations may arise in the case of employees who obtain what may be only a small shareholding in their company which on termination of their employment they sell to another. In some circumstances there may be difficulty in deciding which test is more appropriate. In *Systems Reliability Holdings plc v Smith* [1990] IRLR 377 the ex-employee who had during his employment acquired a total of 1.6% of the shares in the company sold these shares to Systems Reliability for £247,000. The share sale agreement contained covenants preventing competition (effectively for 17 months from the date of sale) with the company and its subsidiaries and the use of its confidential information. Harman J held that where a purchaser buys the whole of a business from a number of vendors, some of whom have only a small participation in the goodwill and business which is being sold but who are paid a price for their shares no different from that paid to other vendors and who thereby receive a substantial sum of money, this is a true vendor and purchaser situation (although he accepted that too much store ought not to be set by categorisation, the question being rather 'What is reasonable in this particular deal?' (page 382). Since there was no public policy which would prevent the ex-employee taking himself out of competition for the relatively short period of 17 months (which was on the evidence entirely reasonable) or to prevent the imposition of a worldwide restriction (which also was reasonable given that the business was completely international), the covenant was enforced.

Chapter 10

Reasonableness of express covenants

Introduction

In Ch 9 we considered the types of interest of the ex-employer which the law regarded it permissible for the ex-employer to seek to protect by restrictive covenant operating after the end of the employment relationship. We also considered the types of covenants typically entered into to protect such legitimate interests of the ex-employer. In this Chapter we consider the reasonableness of such covenants on the assumption that there is a legitimate interest to protect.

1. Criteria relevant to reasonableness of both area covenants and non-solicitation/dealing covenants

1(a) Position of the employee

10.1 The seniority of the employee and the nature of the occupation are significant. Often (although not always) the senior employee will have more opportunity to learn the trade secrets or confidential information of the employer or to gain influence over customers.

10.2 Where the employee is a junior, employed at a low wage, the court may be unwilling to enforce the covenant: *Sir W C Leng & Co Ltd v Andrews* [1909] 1 Ch 763, 771 and see *Kores Manufacturing Co Ltd v Kolok Manufacturing Co Ltd* [1959] 1 Ch 108 and *Spafax Ltd v Harrison* [1988] IRLR 442.

1(b) Nature of the business/activities of employee

10.3 The employee should only be restrained from carrying out the sort of business in which he was engaged as employee: *Attwood v Lamont* [1920] 3 KB 571 (CA) and *Commercial Plastics Ltd v Vincent* [1964] 3 All ER 546 (CA). Further, the ex-employee should not (over too wide an area or too long a period) be prevented from carrying out too wide a range of activities where all his expertise and experience lies in a restricted field: *Commercial Plastics* (at page 554) and *Herbert Morris Ltd v Saxelby* [1916] AC 688. The employee must be left with some reasonable means of earning a living: *Page One Records Ltd v Britton (trading as The Troggs)* [1968] 1 WLR 157: see paragraph 14.3. Covenants which express imprecisely the prohibited type of employment may be struck down: *Perls v Saalfeld* [1892] 2 Ch 149 (ex-employee prevented from accepting 'another situation as clerk or agent, nor to establish himself' in the particular area), but in some circumstances the covenant may be saved by a purposive construction: see paragraphs 11.12 and 11.14. The precise ambit of the activities prevented may be difficult to determine: in *Cullard v Taylor* (1887) 3 TLR 698, in which a solicitor was prohibited from operating in a certain area, he was held to be in breach when he sent letters to clients residing in that area. As to a prohibition against activities which are preparatory to competition (as distinct from actual competitive activities) see paragraph 10.5.

1(c) Nature of the business/activities of employer

10.4 The ex-employee should not be restrained from carrying on activities outside the area of business or practice of the employer: see *Routh v Jones* [1947] 1 All ER 758 (a doctor in general practice could not be prevented from practising in the restricted area as a consultant – which the court held could not injure the practice of the employers). In *Scully UK Ltd v Lee* [1998] IRLR 259 (CA) the covenant was struck down where it was held that the business embargoed was not limited to a business which was in competition with that of the claimant company. No intention to limit the restriction could be found in the words of the covenant and there was no reason for implying them. Another example is the case of an employee who has only been employed to provide his services on one side of the business, for example, wholesale, whereas the covenant prevents activity in both wholesale and retail. However, in *Rogers v Maddocks* [1892] 3 Ch 346 (CA) selling wholesale and retail were held not to be two distinct businesses, but only different modes of carrying on one business, so that the covenant was upheld. Contrast *Polymasc Pharmaceuticals plc v Charles* [1999] FSR 711 in which Laddie J upheld the covenant where it extended more widely than competing businesses which infringed the claimant's patents or confidential information to competitors using prior art techniques over which the claimant's techniques were an improvement. Merely to limit the ambit of the worldwide area covenant to competitors using the claimant's confidential information and patents would have rendered the covenant valueless. It was important that the ex-employee should not work for competitors in the same general field as the claimant, to ensure that there was no leakage of confidential information.

1(d) Duration

10.5 The period of the restraint is an important factor in determining the reasonableness of the covenant: *Sir W C Leng & Co Ltd v Andrews* [1909] 1 Ch 763, 771; *Haynes v Doman* [1899] 2 Ch 13,18; *Fitch v Dewes* [1921] 2 AC 158 (HL). In *Stenhouse (Australia) Ltd v Phillips* [1974] AC 391 (PC) Lord Wilberforce said:

> 'The question is not how long the employee could be expected to enjoy a competitive edge over others seeking the client's business. It is, rather, what is a reasonable time during which the employer is entitled to protection against solicitation of clients with whom the employee had contact and influence during employment and who were not bound to the employer by contract or by stability of association. This question their Lordships do not consider can advantageously form the subject of direct evidence. It is for the judge, after informing himself as fully as he can of the facts and circumstances relating to the employer's business, the nature of the employer's interest to be protected, and the likely effect on this of solicitation, to decide whether the contractual period is reasonable or not. An opinion as to the reasonableness of the elements of it, particularly of the time during which it is to run, can seldom be precise, and can only be formed on a broad commonsense view.'

Where the ex-employee is prohibited not merely from competing but also from preparing to do so, the overall effect may be to extend the duration of the covenant beyond the stated period. For example, the true effect of prohibiting preparatory activity for twelve months may be to prohibit competition for fifteen months where the time required to complete the preparations is three months. It is the fifteen-month duration which the court must consider.

10.6 Different considerations will apply according to the type of interest which is sought to be protected. In the case of covenants designed to protect customer connection the question is what is the minimum time required to protect the customer connection. This will normally be the time which it would take a replacement employee to establish a relationship with the customers such that the influence of the ex-employee will have been removed: *Middleton v Brown* (1878) 47 LJ Ch 411, 413. This of course depends substantially on the nature of the business and in particular the degree of customer loyalty, which may in turn depend on such factors as the nature and frequency of customer contact. The fact that the particular business is cyclical can be significant. For example, in the insurance industry where most policies are renewed annually a one year covenant may be more readily justifiable. Difficult issues arise when considering teams of employees. Often more junior employees subject to shorter notice and covenant periods will move first to a competing employer: see *G F I Group Inc v Eaglestone* [1994] IRLR 119. They are then able to keep the 'seat warm' for the more senior employees who were members of the same team – and who remain on the payroll of the (first) employer. To avoid such planned 'staggered' team moves, it may be appropriate to seek covenants of the same period for all team members. In our view a court would be likely, in such circumstances, to regard as reasonable a somewhat lengthier period in relation to a more junior employee than might otherwise be justifiable when considering him in isolation.

10.7 In the case of area or non-solicitation/dealing covenants designed to protect confidential information the principle factor will ordinarily be the 'shelf life' of the confidential information. Where there are secret (unpatented) processes which are expected to remain confidential for a long time, a long period (even an indefinite one) may be justified. In a world of rapidly developing technology it may be difficult to justify a long period even in the case of technical secrets. In the case of customer information such as prices, special requirements and the like, only short periods (usually in the 3 to 12 month range) will ordinarily be justifiable. Different considerations may apply according to whether the covenant is a non-solicitation/dealing covenant or an area covenant: in the former type of covenant a longer period may be tolerated. Lifetime restrictions will not normally be upheld: *Sir W C Leng and Co Ltd v Andrews* [1909] 1 Ch 763.

EXAMPLES OF PERIODS

10.8 Examples of periods recently permitted are:

- Milk roundsmen: two-year non-solicitation/dealing covenant: *Dairy Crest Ltd v Pigott* [1989] ICR 92 (CA); but two years was held to be too long in *Dairy Crest v Wise* (unreported QBD 24.9.93 – IDS Brief vol 515) in the light of evidence that the period had subsequently been reduced to 12 months for other roundsmen);
- Managing director of advertising agency: 18-month non-solicitation covenant: *Rex Stewart Jeffries Parker Ginsberg Ltd v Parker* [1988] IRLR 483 (CA);

155

- Branch manager and a salesman of company selling spare motor parts to the trade: two years' non-solicitation covenant (one year 'backstop' for the manager and six months 'backstop' for the salesman): *Spafax Ltd v Harrison* [1980] IRLR 442 (CA);
- A director and a senior designer of a high class shopfitting company: two-year non-solicitation covenants in relation to each: *John Michael Design plc v Cooke* [1987] 2 All ER 332 (CA);
- Sales representative of office furniture company: one-year non-solicitation covenant: *Business Seating (Renovations) Ltd v Broad* [1989] ICR 729;
- Accountant (salaried 'partner'): three years non-dealing too long but same period for non-solicitation upheld: *Taylor Stuart & Co v Croft* (unreported 7.5.97 ChD);
- Managing director of company manufacturing and selling paper: 12 months non-solicitation/dealing : *Alliance Paper Group plc v Prestwich* [1996] IRLR 25;
- Six months non-dealing and non-solicitation on top of six months' 'garden leave': *Credit Suisse Asset Management Ltd v Armstrong* [1996] IRLR 450.

Note: These examples are to be treated with caution, since each case depends on its own facts.

1(e)   Whether covenant usual

10.9   One of the main reasons in *Sir W C Leng & Co Ltd v Andrews* [1909] 1 Ch 763, 770 (CA) for striking down an area covenant against a reporter was that the uniqueness of the covenant tended to show its unreasonableness (in addition the employee was a minor at the time the contract was made and as a junior employee not exposed to any confidential information. The covenant was furthermore unlimited in time). Conversely, if the covenant is customary, that may help to show that it is reasonably necessary and hence be evidence that it is not unreasonably severe. See also *Marion White Ltd v Francis* [1972] 1 WLR 1423.

1(f)   Period of notice

10.10   The period of notice necessary to terminate the contract of employment may be a factor in determining the reasonableness of the covenant: *Mason v Provident Clothing Supply Co Ltd* [1913] AC 724, 732, 741: it is unreasonable that an employee whose employment may last only a couple of weeks should be limited in his activities for a lengthy period. See also *Gledhow Autoparts Ltd v Delaney* [1965] 1 WLR 1366, 1376 and 1377 (CA). Where the notice required to be given by employer and employee are different, what is significant is the length of notice required to be given by the employer to terminate. However, Hodson LJ expressed the view in *M & S Drapers (a firm) v Reynolds* [1956] 3 All ER 814 that the length of notice was not relevant. To take it into account was to enquire into the adequacy of the consideration for the covenant, which the court should not do. This is contrary to authority and indeed his own subsequent dictum in *Esso Petroleum Co Ltd v Harper's Garage (Stourport) Ltd* [1968] AC 269: see paragraphs 10.19 to 10.21. Whether the adequacy of consideration should be taken into account is a matter of some debate: see paragraphs 10.12 to 10.22.

10.11   In some modern contracts a 'ratchet system' is applied to notice periods: it is agreed that the notice period will be increased at stated intervals of time during the employee's service and the period of the covenants increased accordingly at the same time. This can be advantageous to the employer seeking to enforce the covenant in that in an appropriate case it may demonstrate to the court the logic of the period chosen for the restraint (ie that the more the employee becomes acquainted with the business and its customers, the more protection is required against potential competitive activity by him) and that careful consideration has been given to this aspect of the covenant.

1(g) Consideration for the covenants

10.12 An employer seeking to enforce a restrictive covenant must be able to show that he gave the employee consideration for it. This is so even if the covenant is contained in a deed: *Mitchel v Reynolds* (1711) 1 PWms 181; and *Gravely v Barnard* (1874) LR 18 Eq 518. To require consideration for a promise in a deed is a departure from the normal rule but arguably justifiable on grounds of public policy.

10.13 Where covenants are included as part of the offer of employment there is no difficulty. The consideration is the employer's promise to employ on the terms offered. Where, however, covenants are introduced after employment has begun and there is no obvious consideration for them, such as a pay rise or single bonus payment to which the employee is not otherwise entitled, the position is more difficult. In *Woodbridge & Sons v Bellamy* [1911] 1 Ch 326, the facts of which are set out at paragraph 12.5, and more recently in *Norbrook Laboratories Ltd v J Smyth* [1986] 15 NIJB 9, the courts were prepared to infer consideration from statements made by the employer at the hearing that they would have dismissed the employee had he not signed the restrictive covenant. In other words the consideration was the continuing employment of the employee. While these decisions may offer some comfort to an employer who did not offer any specific consideration for the covenants, in our view it would be unwise to place too much reliance on them. Both are first instance decisions on the point and in neither case does there appear to have been any evidence to contradict the employer's statement. If, for example, the employee could show that others who had refused to sign the covenant had not been dismissed that would cast considerable doubt on the veracity of the employer's statement. Furthermore, in *Woodbridge* the notice period was relatively short, three months, so that dismissal would not have been an unduly expensive option. (It is not clear what the notice period was in *Norbrook.*) It would be a less credible argument for an employer dealing with an employee on 12 or 24 months' notice to say that if the covenant had not been given he would have sacked the employee on the spot. It is clearly always advisable for an employer to provide specific consideration for the introduction of covenants.

10.14 Where covenants are introduced on termination of employment, again there is usually no problem in showing that consideration was given. For taxation reasons, however, it is strongly advisable for a particular (more than nominal) sum of money to be specifically attributed to the covenants: see paragraphs 12.20 to 12.21.

10.15 Perhaps the most vexed question that arises in relation to consideration and covenants is whether the courts are entitled to assess the value of the consideration given in deciding whether a covenant is reasonable. Under the law of contract the general rule is that the court need only be satisfied that consideration which is legal and of some value has been given. The courts do not enquire whether the consideration is adequate: *Haigh v Brooks* (1839) 10 Ad & El 309, 320; *Gravely v Barnard* (1874) LR 18 Eq 518. In other words the courts do not decide whether the parties have agreed a fair bargain or, in the words of Lord Denning MR in *Lloyds Bank Ltd v Bundy* [1975] QB 326, 336, 'no bargain will be upset which is the result of the ordinary interplay of forces.' Is there an exception where the court is considering the reasonableness or otherwise of restrictive covenants? Regrettably there is no clear answer; there are two diverging lines of judicial opinion which cannot be reconciled.

10.16 The authorities against the court considering adequacy begin with *Herbert Morris Ltd v Saxelby* [1916] 1 AC 688, 707 where Lord Parker said:

'It was at one time thought that, in order to ascertain whether a restraint were reasonable in the interests of the covenantor, the Court ought to weigh the advantages accruing to the covenantor under the contract against the disadvantages imposed upon him by the restraint, but any such process has long been rejected as impracticable. The court no longer considers the adequacy of the consideration in any particular case.'

This statement was cited as being the correct view in *Attwood v Lamont* [1920] 3 KB 571, 589 (CA) and was relied on by Hodson LJ in *M & S Drapers (a firm) v Reynolds* [1956] 3 All ER 814. Rejecting an argument that he should take into account the shortness of the employee's notice period under the contract, Hodson LJ said:

'... the court will not inquire into the adequacy of the consideration or weigh the advantages accruing to the covenantor under the contract against the disadvantages imposed on him by the restraint.'

10.17 More recently Lord Parker's statement was relied on by Millett J in *Allied Dunbar (Frank Weisinger) Ltd v Weisinger* [1988] IRLR 60, 65 paragraphs 30-32 in refusing to consider an argument by the defendant's counsel that a restrictive covenant in a practice buy-out agreement was invalid because the restraint was 'out of all proportion to the benefit obtained by the [claimants]'.

10.18 To be contrasted with the above are the authorities in favour of the court considering adequacy. Those authorities begin with *Nordenfelt v Maxim Nordenfelt Guns and Ammunition Company* [1894] AC 535, 565 HL. Lord Macnaghten dealt with the question of adequacy of consideration in the following way:

'It was laid down in *Mitchell v Reynolds* that the court was to see that the restriction was made upon a good and adequate consideration so as to be a proper and useful contract. But in time it was found that the parties themselves were better judges of that matter than the court, and it was held to be sufficient if there was legal consideration of value; though of course the quantum of consideration may enter into the question of the reasonableness of the contract.'

10.19 That opinion was endorsed by several members of the House of Lords in *Esso Petroleum Co Ltd v Harper's Garage (Stourport) Ltd* [1968] AC 269 which concerned the enforceability of restrictive covenants given as part of solus agreements; see Lord Reid at 300 A–B, Lord Hodson at 318 D–F and Lord Pearce at 323 E–F. The position of Lord Hodson is particularly interesting. In Esso after citing the above passage from *Nordenfelt* he says:

> 'Thus a restriction as to time may be reasonable or unreasonable according to whether sufficient compensation has been given to the person restrained.'

10.20 However, only three years before, he had rejected precisely that concept in *M&S Drapers* relying on the statement of Lord Parker in Herbert Morris. The adequacy of the consideration was also specifically considered in assessing the reasonableness of covenants in *A Schroeder Music Publishing Co Ltd v Macaulay* [1974] 3 All ER 616 HL; *Clifford Davis Management Ltd v W E A Records Ltd* [1975] 1 All ER 237 CA (both cases concerning agreements between music publishers and composers/performers); *Office Overload Ltd v Gunn* [1977] FSR 39 (CA) per Lawton J at 43-44 (a licensing agreement); and *Bridge v Deacons* [1984] AC 705 (a partnership agreement). Also in *Turner v Commonwealth & British Minerals Ltd* (CA) 13 October 1999 (unreported) the Court of Appeal regarded it as a legitimate factor to take into account that the employees had (in a severance agreement) been paid something extra for the covenants they signed. On the other hand in *J A Mont v Mills* [1993] IRLR 172 the Court of Appeal did not consider as relevant to the question of reasonableness of the covenant the fact that the ex-employee had received a substantial severance payment under the severance agreement containing that covenant. To similar effect was the decision of the deputy judge in *T S C Europe (UK) Ltd v Massey* [1999] IRLR 22 in which it was held that the fact that the claimants were obliged to make post-termination payments to the ex-employee for as long as the covenants remained in force did not render reasonable covenants which were more than necessary to protect the ex-employer's interests.

10.21 Since cases on both sides of the argument derive from the House of Lords it is only to be hoped that in the not too distant future the House will be afforded the opportunity to review the law on this point and to give definitive guidance. While (at least as far as employment contracts are concerned) the weight of authority favours not weighing up the adequacy of consideration, in practice the courts do appear to be influenced by the level of the consideration received for the covenant (if only subconsciously). In the words of Lord Pearce in *Esso* (at page 323):

> '... although the court may not be able to weigh the details of the advantages and disadvantages with great nicety it must appreciate the consideration at least in its more general aspects.'

10.22 Until such time as the matter is clarified, the only sensible course is for employers to provide adequate consideration in return for the covenants, so that if the Court is disposed to consider adequacy they can succeed on that ground, and for lawyers to adopt the approach which best suits their client's case and be prepared to cite all the relevant authorities.

2. Criteria relevant to reasonableness of area covenants

2(a) Extent of the area

10.23 The wider the area the more difficult it will be to justify it as no more than necessary to protect the ex-employer's legitimate interests. Area and duration are closely related – if the period is short a wider area may be tolerated: *Continental Tyre and Rubber (Great Britain) Company (Ltd) v Heath* (1913) 29 TLR 308. Conversely, if the area is small, a longer period may be permitted: *Fitch v Dewes* [1921] 2 AC 158, 168 (HL). Normally if no area is specified the area will be taken to be worldwide: *Dowden & Pook Ltd v Pook* [1904] 1 KB 45 and *Commercial Plastics Ltd v Vincent* [1964] 3 All ER 546, 550 (CA); but in *Littlewoods Organisation Ltd v Harris* [1977] 1 WLR 1472 (CA) the covenant was in these circumstances (surprisingly) interpreted as being limited to the United Kingdom. It is unusual for worldwide restrictions in employment contracts to be upheld: *Vandervell Products Ltd v McLeod* [1957] RPC 185, 191 and see also *Hinton & Higgs (UK) Ltd v Murphy and Valentine* [1989] IRLR 519 (Court of Session) but see paragraph 10.24 below. A wide area may be allowed where the ex-employer has the whole or a substantial part of the market share of the product: *Standex International Ltd v Blades* [1976] FSR 114.

2(b) The type of interest sought to be protected

10.24 The area must be no larger than is necessary to protect the legitimate interests of the ex-employer. An important factor in the determination of the appropriateness of the extent of the area will be the type of interest which the covenant serves to protect: covenants designed to protect business secrets will normally justify a wider area and indeed may justify a country-wide or even a world-wide restriction: *Nordenfelt v Maxim Nordenfelt Guns and Ammunition Company* [1894] AC 535; *Forster and Sons (Ltd) v Suggett* (1918) 35 TLR 87; *Kerchiss v Colora Printing Inks Ltd* [1960] RPC 235; *Caribonum Company Ltd v LeCouch* (1913) 109 LT 385 and 587. In *Scully UK Ltd v Lee* [1998] IRLR 259 the Court of Appeal specifically referred to the fact that business is becoming more international and the relevant covenant was to protect dissemination of confidential information. That was not constrained by national boundaries. Accordingly, in *Poly Lina Ltd v Finch* [1995] FSR 751 the claimant (a manufacturer of bin liners and other plastic goods) was able at trial to enforce against its former marketing controller, a worldwide covenant taken to protect both technical and commercial information. In the modern 'global village' a worldwide covenant may be the only way in which state-of-the-art technology or other trade secrets can be protected: in *Polymasc v Charles* [1999] FSR 711 (Laddie J) a worldwide interim injunction was obtained to protect highly sensitive bio-technological information. Contrast *F S S Travel & Leisure Systems Ltd v Johnson* [1998] IRLR 382 where a one year UK wide covenant failed for want of sufficient identification of a body of confidential information qualifying for protection.

2(c) Functional correspondence between restricted area and location of customers

10.25 Where the ex-employer relies on customer connection rather than business secrets to justify an area covenant (something which may in principle be hard to justify: see para 10.29), it will be for the ex-employer to demonstrate that the restricted area covered corresponds with the location of his clientele. In *Reed*

Executive v Somers (CA) (20 March 1986, unreported) the covenant failed when a recruitment agency was unable to show any 'functional correspondence' (in the words of Leggatt J) between the restricted area and the area in which the customers were situated – many being outside the area. This case was followed in *Office Angels Ltd v Rainer-Thomas and O'Connor* [1991] IRLR 214 (CA). It is not always necessary to show sales in relation to every part of the restricted area: *Kerchiss v Colora Printing Inks Ltd* [1960] RPC 235.

2(d) Nature of the area

10.26 When the area is a thinly populated rural area a greater area will be regarded as protectable than in a densely populated urban area: see *Scorer v Seymour-Johns* [1966] 3 All ER 347, 350 (CA). In some instances in a densely populated urban area only a very small radius will be tolerated, such as a quarter of a square mile – and indeed in some trades, eg that of employment agencies, an area covenant may not be upheld even where the area is very small. In *Office Angels Ltd v Rainer-Thomas and O'Connor* [1991] IRLR 214 a covenant in the contracts of employment of an employment agency precluded employment agents (for six months after the end of their employment) from undertaking the work of employment agents within a radius of 1000 metres of branches in the Greater London area in which they were employed in the last six months of their employment. This area (about 1.2 miles, including most of the City of London) was held to be too wide in view of the fact that there were some 400 employment agencies in the City of London and thousands of clients and jobseekers in the area. By contrast in *Spencer v Marchington* [1988] IRLR 392 the judge regarded as too wide an area restraint in favour of an employment agency covering a radius of 25 miles of their Banbury office, since all but one of their customers were within 20 miles. He would have allowed a radius of 20 miles.

2(e) Nature of business and the manner in which it is conducted

10.27 For example, in a credit betting business an area restraint as distinct from a non-solicitation covenant may be inappropriate: *S W Strange Ltd v Mann* [1965] 1 All ER 1069 (see above). If the business requires constant attention on customers this indicates a smaller area. In *Mason v Provident Clothing & Supply Co Ltd* [1913] AC 724 (HL) an area of 25 miles from London in relation to a travelling salesman was held to be excessive. In London alone about 1000 salesmen were employed. Conversely, if the business is conducted by a small number of people with customers widely distributed a wider area will be permissible.

2(f) Area of activities of the employee

10.28 Where the restraint is intended to protect trade connection there should be correspondence between the activities of the employee and the restricted area – a restricted area drawn with regard to an office in which the employee did not actually work will be unreasonable and unless severable will render the whole covenant unenforceable: *Scorer v Seymour-Johns* [1966] 3 All ER 347.

2(g) Whether an area covenant is appropriate

10.29 Where the interest which the employer seeks to protect is only customer connection, and there is no difficulty in identifying the customers, an area covenant may be difficult to justify. In *Office Angels Ltd v Rainer-Thomas and O'Connor* [1991] IRLR 214 (CA) the Court of Appeal struck down an area covenant in favour of an employment agency, since a suitably drafted non-solicitation/dealing covenant would have protected the employer adequately. See also the decision of Stamp J in *S W Strange Ltd v Mann* [1965] 1 All ER 1069 (credit betting business). On the other hand, the employer will more readily be able to justify an area covenant where he is seeking to protect:

● Trade connection in a cash business, where it may be difficult to identify the customers: *Strange v Mann*;
● Trade secrets or confidential information.

In *Turner v Commonwealth & British Minerals Ltd* (CA) 13 October 1999 (unreported) the Court of Appeal referred to the fact that it had been recognised in many cases that because there are serious difficulties in identifying precisely what is or is not confidential information, a properly drawn area covenant may be the most satatisfactory form of restraint. The same is true (it may be added) in relation to difficulties of 'policing' breaches of confidence. These cases should be contrasted with *Scorer v Seymour-Johns* [1966] 3 All ER 347, 352 where the Court of Appeal (perhaps too readily) accepted as justifying an area covenant given by an estate agent's negotiator/clerk an argument that it would be difficult to police a non-dealing covenant. In this case the clients were recurring clients and there was no evidence that it would be difficult to identify them. The interpretation of area covenants is dealt with in Ch 11.

3. Covenants against soliciting/dealing with customers/ prospective customers/suppliers

3(a) Meaning of 'solicitation' (by an ex-employee)

10.30 Solicitation may occur in many different ways, for example, face to face, by letter, circular or advertisement. An element of persuasion is required. It is often assumed that where it was the customer who first contacted the ex-employee, there is no solicitation. This is not necessarily the case. For example, where the customer telephones the ex-employee asking what the ex-employee will be doing after employment, there will normally be no solicitation if the ex-employee informs the customer that he will, for instance, be trading from a particular address in the same line of business as the ex-employer. However, if his response is, for instance, immediately to offer to make a sales presentation, it might be difficult to say that there has been no solicitation. Each case will turn on its own precise facts. If the gist of what the ex-employee says is responsive to the customer's enquiries there will be no solicitation. If there is significant use of persuasion by the ex-employee, this might be seen as soliciting. It is often difficult to draw the line. In *Austin Knight (UK) Ltd v Hinds* [1994] FSR 52 the ex-employee initially informed some customers of her redundancy (at a time following termination of her employment when she had no prospect of new employment and thus could not be said to be soliciting). Later, after she had found employment with a competitor some of her customers approached her to act for them. She accordingly submitted an offer or made a presentation to these clients, and to others who were required to put their work out to tender, but this was held not to be 'soliciting or endeavouring to entice away' because to hold otherwise would change the covenant into a non dealing covenant. In our view, this case was borderline but perhaps correct on the very particular facts of the initial contact having not been for the purposes of soliciting and thereafter the presentation being part of a statutory tender procedure. More questionable was the approach of the Court in another first instance decision: in *Taylor Stuart & Co v Croft* (7 May 1987, unreported Ch D) the deputy judge was of the view that a communication to the clients of the ex-employer by an ex-employee (an accountant) that he had left his employment and giving the address of the ex-employee, even if sent in the hope of attracting the client, would not have been a solicitation, but the use of the words 'I ... can be contacted as above' crossed the line and thus there was a solicitation. In our view, while a mere communication to clients of leaving employment is unlikely to amount to a solicitation, where this is coupled with the providing of an address where the ex-employee can be found, this is likely to amount to soliciting – particularly when done in the hope of attracting custom. Difficult questions may arise in relation to advertisements which come into the hands of customers. In these circumstances one would expect a *de minimis* principle to apply. If the advertisements are placed nationally, or locally in an area in which there are a substantial number of customers of the ex-employer, this might be solicitation. However, if the advertising is not done in this way, there will be no solicitation if some customers outside the area in which the customers are mainly situated come incidentally to see the advertisements. In *Sweeney v Astle* [1923] NZLR 1198 Hosking J said that solicitation:

> '... involves a selection of the persons appealed to ... In the cases put it is plain that the trader, by singling out the objects of his solicitation, evidences a specific purpose and intention to obtain orders from them.'

In order to avoid the difficulties of proving customer (or supplier) solicitation by the ex-employee, it is advisable for the employer to seek a non-dealing covenant from the employee.

10.31 In *Hanover Insurance Brokers v Schapiro* [1994] IRLR 82 (CA) the words 'endeavour to take way' were held not to be too vague – they prevented the ex-employees from actively seeking out the ex-employer's customers cf *Dentmaster (UK) Ltd v Kent* [1997] IRLR 636 (CA) where a prohibition against 'exerting influence' over customers (somewhat charitably) was taken as meaning making a sales pitch to customers.

3(b) The preferred type of covenant to protect customer connection

10.32 Non-solicitation/dealing covenants are the preferred type of covenant for the protection of the ex-employer's customer connection: *Office Angels Ltd v Rainer-Thomas* and *O'Connor and Strange Ltd v Mann* (see para 10.29). The employer is entitled by means of a properly drafted non-solicitation/dealing covenant to prevent his ex-employee from using his knowledge of and influence over customers (built up while he was on the employer's payroll) to entice them away from the ex-employer after the termination of employment.

3(c) Criteria relevant to reasonableness of non-solicitation/dealing covenants: generally

10.33 The validity of such covenants depends on:

- The nature of the business;
- The nature of the employment.

(per Romer LJ in *Gilford Motor Co v Horne* [1933] Ch 935, 966 (CA)).

10.34 As to the frst criteria (the nature of the business), the loyalty of the customers or clients to the ex-employer is an important factor. In *Stenhouse Australia Ltd v Phillips* [1974] 1 All ER 117 in concluding that in principle a covenant against solicitation of clients might be entirely reasonable Lord Wilberforce took into account the greater fragility of the relationship between insurance broker and client (as compared with that of solicitor and client!) and that a comparatively mild solicitation might deprive an insurance broker of valuable business.

10.35 As to the second (the nature of the employment), an important factor is whether the employment was such that the employee:

- Could gain influence over customers; and/or
- Had access to confidential information concerning customers.

10.36 A non-solicitation/dealing covenant should go no further than is necessary to protect the ex-employer's customer connection or confidential information. Accordingly, a non-solicitation/dealing clause should ordinarily be limited:

- To customers or potential customers with whom the ex-employee actually dealt during a specified period (for example, the last year) prior to termination of employment ; or
- To those customers or potential customers of whose identity or special requirements the ex-employee has knowledge by virtue of his access to confidential information or trade secrets of the ex-employer.

3(d) Who is a customer?

10.37 The cases referred to below suggest a tendency by the courts today to scrutinise more carefully non-solicitation/dealing covenants than in earlier cases and to strike such covenants down where the covenant is inappropriate because:

- Of difficulty in identifying customers, where dealings are infrequent; or
- The customers are not loyal only to the employer (or to a limited number of suppliers, including the employer).

3(d)(i) PROBLEM OF INFREQUENT DEALINGS

10.38 In *Gilford Motor Co v Horne* [1933] Ch 935, 966 (CA) Horne, the managing director of Gilford, had given a non-solicitation covenant (unlimited in time) in relation to those who had been at any time during the employment or were at the date of termination customers of Gilford or in the habit of dealing with it. Farwell J struck down the covenant on the basis that since the covenant covered even those who were cash customers (of one part) of the business with whom Horne as managing director would not come into contact or know their names and addresses, it was too wide. In his view it was necessary to define the customers by reference to some list or record of the employer or limit it in some other way.

10.39 The Court of Appeal overruled this decision. Lord Harnworth MR (at page 958) defined a customer as a 'person who frequents a place of business for the purpose of making purchases'. He also said that it was not necessary to limit the covenant in the manner prescribed by Farwell J, although he appeared to regard a 'casual purchaser' as falling outside the definition of customer (page 960). Romer LJ emphasised (at page 967) that it was necessary to look at the covenant as at the date it was entered into and that at that time it was not possible for the employer to furnish the employee with a list of customers: there was no way of limiting the target group otherwise than by calling them 'customers'.

10.40 However, in *Reed Executive v Somers* (CA) (20 March 1986, unreported) a carefully drafted non-solicitation covenant failed because of uncertainty as to the meaning of 'customer'. Somers, a branch manager, had given a one year covenant in relation to those who at the date of termination were customers of, or in the habit of dealing with, Reed (or its subsidiaries) and with whom any of the employees in any office in which Somers had been employed should have contracted or endeavoured to contract on behalf of Reed whilst Somers was employed at that office. Reed argued that 'customer' connoted a person who is on the books and has regularly and recently used the ex-employer's services. However, Leggatt J (cited with approval by Sir John Arnold in the Court of Appeal) stated that while in some trades such as that of milk roundsman there is no difficulty in identifying customers, there were more sporadic types of business such as employment agencies where different considerations applied. In the Court of Appeal Sir John Arnold referred to what he saw as an additional and possibly overriding difficulty, namely, that if one were to find a person who has resorted to the office to have been a customer at a time somewhat earlier than the date of the termination of the employment contract but who has not since then been back, it would be quite impossible to form any sensible conclusion as to whether after that interval of time the person concerned remained a customer, yet the essential qualification was that the person should have been a customer at the moment of termination. Surprisingly, no reference is made in the judgments to *Gilford Motor Co v Horne* and *Plowman v Ash* (both discussed in paras 10.45 to 10.46), Court of Appeal authority to the contrary. However, *Reed Executive* was followed in *Specialist Recruiters International Ltd v Taylor* (RCJ 4 July 1989, unreported) in which a non-solicitation covenant failed inter alia because it was not limited to firms with whom staff had been successfully placed. Vinelott J held that, on the face of it, it would cover a firm which had approached the employer at the inception of the ex-employee's employment and which had never been heard of again. See also *Spafax (1965) Ltd v Dommett* (1972) 116 Sol Jo 711 (CA) (per Phillimore LJ) where uncertainty of the meaning of 'customer' appears to have been one of the reasons for the failure of the covenant.

3(d)(ii) PROBLEM OF LOYALTY

10.41 Where the 'customer' is unaffiliated, for example, purchases from numerous 'suppliers' including the employer, the Court may decide that there is no personal influence wielded by the employee and no confidential information in relation to such customers who are on the books of many suppliers. In *Douglas LLambias Associates Ltd v Napier* (Lexis, 31 October 1990, unreported) LLambias was a recruitment agency specialising in recruiting legal staff. Napier, the employee, had given a 12-month non-solicitation/dealing covenant limited to those who were clients in the last two years of employment and for whom he had provided recruitment services. The clients were firms of Edinburgh solicitors who were accustomed to contacting all three legal recruitment agencies in the city. The covenant was struck down on the basis that there was no legitimate interest to protect. In particular there could, in the circumstances, be no confidential list of customers, nor apparently were other trade secrets alleged. Nor was there any possibility of clients being enticed away. (The position might have been different as far as candidates for recruitment were concerned but there was no evidence of solicitation of candidates). See also: *Bowler v Lovegrove* [1921] Ch 642, 654 (estate agents).

10.42 It should not be assumed in these circumstances that no non-solicitation/ dealing covenant could be effective. If, for example, there was evidence that the recruitment consultant had, in the course of his employment, built up strong personal connections with recruiting personnel at various firms of solicitors such that they tended to give him a greater share of their recruitment work (or to call him first) it is difficult to see why the employer ought not to be able to protect itself (by means of a properly drafted non-solicitation/dealing covenant) from the employee enticing away these clients to a new firm. The employer ought to be able to have a breathing space to enable another employee to build up a similar strong relationship with the clients.

3(e) Former customers

10.43 A non-solicitation covenant will be struck down if it covers those who were customers only before the commencement of employment: *Hinton & Higgs (UK) Ltd v Murphy and Valentine* [1989] IRLR 519 (Court of Session). However, the position is more difficult where the covenant prevents the ex-employee from soliciting or dealing with customers who were such at any time of the employment, and who may therefore not be customers at the time of termination of employment. This point is closely related to the question of 'who is a customer?' (see paras 10.37 to 10.42). The problem becomes more evident where, at the time when it is sought to enforce the covenant:

- The employee has been employed for a long time so that even those who were customers, say ten years ago, and have placed no business with the ex-employer since, are potentially within the ambit of the covenant. In relation to such 'former customers' the question is whether the ex-employer has any legitimate interest to protect;
- The customer's connection with the ex-employer was tenuous, for example, only one insignificant contract placed.

10.44 The courts initially upheld covenants covering those who were customers at any time during employment, but more recently a stricter view has prevailed. The position now is that covenants should be limited to those who were customers during a defined (short) period prior to termination of employment.

10.45 In *G W Plowman & Son Ltd v Ash* [1964] 2 All ER 10 (CA) Ash, a sales representative, had given to his employer, Plowman (a corn and agricultural merchant), a non-solicitation covenant in respect of anyone who had been a customer of Plowman at any time during his employment. Ash had been one of five sales representatives collectively covering an area to the west and south west of Spalding for a distance of about forty miles. The judge struck down the covenant on the basis that Ash did not know customers to the east or north of Spalding and Plowman was therefore not protecting a proprietary right in relation to such customers. One of the arguments put forward by Ash in the Court of Appeal was that the covenant did not exclude those who had ceased to be customers and were thus no longer part of the goodwill. However, the Court of Appeal held that if a man had been a customer at the beginning of the employment it was possible that he might become a customer again–and that people who had for the time being ceased to be customers accordingly did not fall outside the proprietary interest. See also *Gilford Motor Co v Horne* [1933] Ch 935, 966 (referred to above in paras 10.38 to 10.39) where a similar covenant to that in *Plowman* was upheld.

10.46 In *Specialist Recruiters International Ltd v Taylor* (RCJ 4 July 1989, unreported), referred to above, Taylor had given a six-month non-solicitation/dealing/supply of services covenant (in connection with the business of accountancy recruitment services) in respect of any person who was a customer of the employer at any time during the period of Taylor's employment with whom he dealt directly or in any supervisory capacity. One might have expected the covenant to be upheld since:

- The covenant was for a short period;
- The non-solicitation, and so on, was limited to customers over whom the ex-employee could reasonably have been expected to have personal influence;
- *Plowman v Ash* did not require that the customers should be limited to those who were customers at the time of termination of the employment.

10.47 However, Vinelott J referring to *Reed Executive v Somers* (20 March 1986, unreported) (CA) (see para 10.40) struck down the covenant as being too wide inter alia because it was not limited to those who were customers at the time of termination of employment. It is accordingly good practice to limit the non-solicitation/dealing to those who were customers during a specified period before termination of employment. In *Business Seating (Renovations) Ltd v Broad* [1989] ICR 729 Millett J (following *Plowman v Ash*) upheld a non-solicitation covenant effective for one year after termination of employment in relation to those who had been customers of the ex-employer during the last twelve months of employment – irrespective of whether or not Broad had had contact with such customers and whether or not they had discontinued their custom. See also *Spafax Ltd v Harrison* [1980] IRLR 442. It is also good practice to limit the scope of the embargo to customers with whom the employee dealt (or over whom he had supervisory control or with whom he had some other relevant connection) for a limited period before the end of employment, but in *Dentmaster (UK) Ltd v Kent* [1997] IRLR 636 the Court of Appeal upheld the covenant notwithstanding the absence of such limitation, in view, in particular, of the short period of restraint (six months) and the short customer backstop (defining the embargoed customer base).

10.48 The Court of Appeal was faced with a somewhat difficult situation in *John Michael Design plc v Cooke and another* [1987] 2 All ER 332 where a non-solicitation/dealing covenant was suitably drafted so as to be enforceable. There was, however, evidence that a particular client had no intention of placing any business with the ex-employer again. The judge below granted an injunction pending trial in general form but excluded the particular client from the scope of the injunction. The Court of Appeal allowed an appeal against the exclusion of that client saying that it did not matter that a particular client had no intention of dealing further with the ex-employer. It did not mean that there was no protectable interest in relation to that customer – for that was the very class of case against which the covenant is designed to give protection. It was only in respect of customers who might be coaxed by the ex-employees to transfer their allegiance that the ex-employer needed protection. While it is appreciated that there may be practical difficulties in allowing certain customers who are within the ambit of a properly drawn non-solicitation covenant to be exempted from the operation of the covenant, it is difficult to see how there can be a protectable interest in a former customer who has no intention of doing business in the future with the ex-employer. The effect of the judgment was to punish the ex-employee for breaches of contract rather than to protect the employer's legitimate interest. A similar question may arise where the covenant contains language to the effect that the employee may not solicit 'in competition with' or 'so as to compete with' the ex-employer. It may be argued that insofar as he is soliciting customers of the ex-employer who have no intention of placing further orders with the ex-employer, he is not competing with the ex-employer. Although the matter is one of interpretation of the particular language used, it is unlikely that the court will be any more sympathetic to the ex-employee than in *John Michael Design*.

3(f) Is customer contact a prerequisite?

10.49 Actual contact with customers during employment is not necessary for a covenant to be upheld as against those customers. It is sufficient that at the time of making the employment contract there was the possibility that the employee would get in touch with them. In *Gilford Motor Co v Horne* [1933] Ch 935 Farwell J struck down a non-solicitation covenant as being too broad inter alia because it extended to customers with whom Horne had had no contact and of whom he had no knowledge. The Court of Appeal reversed this decision. Lawrence LJ referred to the fact that the ex-employee had the fullest opportunity of getting to know all the customers. Likewise in *Plowman v Ash* one of the arguments by Ash was that the covenant in question did not confine itself to customers with whom Ash had had contact. Subsequently Ash confined his attention to only a part of the area. However, the Court of Appeal upheld the covenant because at the date of the contract the employer might have required the employee to work anywhere in the particular sales area, and he might thus obtain special influence over or knowledge of the customers throughout the whole area.

10.50 *Plowman* was distinguished and explained in *Marley Tile Co Ltd v Johnson* [1982] IRLR 75 (CA). Johnson, a manager, accepted (for a period of one year after termination of his employment) a non-solicitation and non-dealing covenant in relation to persons who in the area in which he had been employed in the 12 months prior to termination of his employment (almost the whole of Devon and Cornwall) were customers or in the habit of dealing with Marley. This clause was struck down since the number of customers who would have fallen within the scope of the covenant was 2,500 and Johnson could not have known of or come into contact with more than a small percentage of them. Lord Denning MR regarded the covenant as being too wide having regard to the size of the area, the number of customers and the class of products, although the period of 12 months was reasonable. Templeman LJ referred to the lack of evidence that Johnson had substantial influence over 2,500 customers (and the fact that enforcing the covenant would condemn Johnson to unemployment for (only) 12 months). Lord Denning stated that it was not necessary in order that the covenant should be upheld that the employee should know all the customers – it was sufficient that there was the possibility that he would get in touch with them. He referred to the basis of the decision of the Court of Appeal in *GWPlowman & Son v Ash* [1964] 1 WLR 568 as having been that the employer in that case was a local firm which carried on business with only five travellers such that in a small area the representatives might get to know all the customers.

10.51 Likewise in *Spafax (1965) Ltd v Dommett* (1972) 116 Sol Jo 711 (CA) a countrywide non-solicitation covenant in relation to a salesman who had only operated in West Cornwall and which was not limited to customers with whom he had had contact was struck down. See also *Office Angels Ltd v Rainer-Thomas and O'Connor* [1991] IRLR 214 where the judge below struck down a non-solicitation/dealing covenant because the employees knew only the clients of their branch (about 100 clients) whereas the covenant extended to the clients of all the branches (6,000 to 7,000 clients). In similar vein, in *Austin Knight (UK) Ltd v Hinds* [1994] FSR 52 the covenant was struck down for the same reason, on the basis that the employee had had dealings with about one-third of the customer base.

3(g) Is mere contact always enough?

10.52 The overriding question is whether the employee might obtain knowledge of or influence over the customers of his employer, as would enable him, if competition were allowed, to take advantage of his employer's trade connection: *Herbert Morris Ltd v Saxelby* [1916] AC 688. If the quality of contact is insufficient to give the employee the opportunity of gaining influence over customers, a covenant relying on contact alone would not be justifiable. In *Scorer v Seymour-Johns* [1966] 3 All ER 347 Salmon LJ (at page 351) referred to the customer relying on the employee to the extent that the customers regard him as the business rather than the employer. However, not in every case will it be necessary to go so far as to establish that the employee is the face of the business as far as the public are concerned. In *Gledhow Autoparts Ltd v Delaney*, although Sellers LJ (at page 1373) regarded the matter as questionable, he was apparently of the view that if a non-solicitation covenant extended to customers with whom there had been some sort of initial contact which might be expected to develop into something, it would be upheld. Diplock LJ thought (page 1377) that such a covenant might be enforceable but expressed no final view. On the other hand, there are many cases where the quality of the contact may be insufficient for there to be any real risk of the employee taking advantage of the employer's trade connection, for example, casual contact by receptionists and telephonists. A non-solicitation/dealing covenant in relation to employees of this sort would be difficult to justify.

3(h) Knowledge of customers short of contact

10.53 Where the employee is likely by virtue of his position to have access to confidential information regarding customers, the employer is entitled to protect that information by means of a properly drafted non-solicitation/dealing covenant. In *Spafax Ltd v Harrison* [1980] IRLR 442 the Court of Appeal upheld a non-solicitation covenant by a manager, Harrison, in relation to any person to whom, during the last 12 months of his employment, the manager or to his knowledge any member of his staff had sold Spafax's goods. (The covenant was limited to goods of the kind sold to such customers during the twelve-month period). The extension of the covenant outside Harrison's own territory (in which he acted as salesman four days a week) to other territories comprising the branch (apparently covering the whole of Cumbria) was justified on the basis of his:

- Access to reports whereby he had the means of acquisition of knowledge of the identity and buying patterns of all customers throughout the branch;
- The fact that his duties of training salesmen took him into the rest of the area outside his own (salesman's) territory – the training meant that he accompanied salesmen to the doors of customers throughout the branch territory.

10.54 The evidence of actual customer contact throughout the whole of Cumbria appears from the report of the decision somewhat unconvincing and the Court of Appeal appear to have placed at least equal reliance on the first factor. See also *Gilford Motor Co v Horne*, where the opportunity of the ex-managing director getting to know the names and addresses of customers was emphasised, and *Rex Stewart Jeffries Parker Ginsberg Ltd v Parker* [1988] IRLR 483 (CA).

3(i) Potential customers

10.55 As we have seen in paragraphs 10.43 to 10.48, a non-solicitation covenant can extend to former customers, who there is reason to believe, may place further business with the employer: *Plowman & Son v Ash* and *Gilford Motor Co v Horne*, and see *Gledhow Autoparts Ltd v Delaney* [1965] 1 WLR 1366 (CA). There seems to be no reason why a non-solicitation covenant cannot validly extend to those who have negotiations with the employer but who have not yet entered into a contract although they may do so.

10.56 This point is not contradicted by the decision in *Business Seating (Renovations) Ltd v Broad* [1989] ICR 729. Business Seating carried on a business renovating office furniture and commercial seating. They had an associated company which carried on the business of manufacturing and selling new office furniture and commercial seating and it appeared that attracting a customer to one business would be a step towards encouraging that customer to place its custom for other parts of its business with the other company. Broad's covenant extended to non-solicitation of customers of the associated company but Business Seating's only interest in the customers of the associated company was as potential customers of its own. Millett J held that it would be an unwarranted extension of *Plowman v Ash* to uphold the validity of a covenant which prohibited solicitation of potential customers even if they were defined as existing customers of another business. The part of the covenant relating to potential customers was struck down. The decision does not suggest that if the employer seeks to protect his interest in his potential customers this cannot be done by way of a properly drafted covenant. In *Business Seating* the means of defining those potential customers was deficient. It is fair to say, however, that there will often be difficulty in defining potential customers sufficiently narrowly to justify the covenant as reasonable.

3(j) Future customers

10.57 Plainly a non-solicitation covenant extending to those who become customers after termination of employment does not protect any legitimate interest of the employer and is invalid: *Konski v Peet* [1915] Ch 530. But an otherwise properly drawn non-solicitation covenant which extends to customers who become such after termination of employment may be cured by severance (see paras 11.18 to 11.23) of that part: *Rex Stewart Jeffries Parker Ginsberg Ltd v Parker* [1988] IRLR 483(CA).

3(k) Limitation of customers by area

10.58 It is not normally necessary to limit a non-solicitation clause to customers in a particular area. This is so because the limitation to customers of the ex-employer ought (properly drafted) to be a sufficient limitation in itself: *GW Plowman & Son v Ash* [1964] 2 All ER 10 (CA) (see para 10.45) and see *Gledhow Autoparts Ltd v Delaney* [1965] 1 WLR 1366, 1375 (CA). However, see *Hinton & Higgs (UK) Ltd v Murphy and Valentine* [1989] IRLR 519 (Court of Session) where a non-dealing clause was struck down inter alia because the employer's area of operations was Scotland whereas the covenant extended (at least) to customers in the whole of the United Kingdom. It is not clear from the report of the decision whether there were (a substantial number of) customers who were outside Scotland.

3(l) 'The employee's customers' – brought with him to the employer

10.59 A problem may arise in relation to the employee, who brings to his new employment customers from his previous employment or own business, and who accepts a non-solicitation/dealing covenant in favour of his new employer in which no distinction is made between 'his' customers and new customers whom he meets through his new employment. In *M & S Drapers (a firm) v Reynolds* [1956] 3 All ER 814 (CA) Reynolds (a collector and salesman) accepted a five-year non-solicitation covenant in relation to customers on whom he had called in the last three years of his employment. A large proportion of the customers covered by the covenant comprised persons with whom Reynolds had formed a connection before he entered into the service of M & S – when he was employed by someone else in the drapery trade (see page 817G of the report).

10.60 None of the Lord Justices in *M & S Drapers* regarded the fact that there were many customers who were the 'employee's' as meaning that the employer had no legitimate interest to protect in relation to such customers (although Denning LJ came close to such a finding (page 821). Indeed, the proprietary right of the employer in relation to such customers was expressly recognised by Hodson LJ at page 817 F–G and Morris LJ at page 820 F–G. The Court of Appeal, however, regarded the fact that a large proportion of customers had been known to the employee prior to his employment as being a factor relevant to the reasonableness of the covenant, that is, militating against a long restriction and that five years was in the circumstances far too long a period. The decision of the Court of Appeal appears to imply that in these circumstances both the (new) employer and the employee have some sort of proprietary interest in the customers whom the employee brings to the employment. No express consideration was given to the fact that the employee had presumably built up the connection with customers while employed by someone else and in that sense it might be argued that the customers were never 'his'. On the other hand, in *Hanover v Schapiro* [1994] IRLR 82 the Court of Appeal adopted a different approach where a more senior employee was concerned. A non-solicitation injunction was granted against a managing director in relation to several customers whom he had personally brought with him to the company. As a senior employee he was to be taken to be fully aware of the basis upon which he contracted with his employer and unlike in *M & S Drapers* his customers were not 'tools of his trade'.

10.61 It is suggested that what may be a reasonable period during which the new employer is entitled to protection must be determined by reference to the extent of his interest in these customers and what contribution he has made in relation to retaining and servicing them. Thus if a capital payment has been made in relation to the customers, the employer will be entitled to full protection: see *Allied Dunbar (Frank Weisinger) Ltd v Weisinger* [1988] IRLR 60. Usually, the employer may at least have incurred overheads to enable the new clients to be serviced such that if the employee leaves with those customers there will be wasted expenditure and the period of restraint should at least be sufficient to allow him to recover these.

10.62 Of course the covenant period will normally be geared to customers generally and the question arises whether the covenant falls to be struck down merely because, while reasonable in relation to the 'employer's' customers, it is unreasonable having regard to the 'employee's' customers. In these circumstances the answer must depend on the proportion of the 'employee's' customers to the whole. If the proportion is significant, the whole covenant may be struck down.

10.63 An additional complication may arise where the employer was complicit in the acceptance of customers 'brought' by the employee in breach of covenant with his ex-employer: apart from the question of the employer's own liability to the previous employer for inducing breach of the previous employment contract (see para 13.25), such an employer who seeks enforcement of the non-solicitation/dealing injunction is unlikely to be considered sympathetically when it comes to the exercise of (discretionary) injunctive relief. This may be seen as an application of the principle that those who seek equitable relief must come to the court with 'clean hands'.

3(m) Non-solicitation of persons who are not customers

10.64 On occasion a non-solicitation/dealing covenant may, because of its very wide scope, be similar in effect to an area covenant, and be struck down. In *Gledhow Autoparts Ltd v Delaney* [1965] 1 WLR 1366 (CA) a non-solicitation covenant by a salesman extended to any person in the area in which he had operated. The covenant was struck down because it was not limited to established customers or even potential customers in the sense of persons on whom the ex-employee had called but who had not given their custom to the ex-employer.

3(n) Period of non-solicitation covenant

10.65 We are aware of no reported cases where an otherwise suitably drafted non-solicitation covenant has been struck down only by reason of the period of the restraint. However, two years was held to be too long in *Dairy Crest v Wise,* (24 September 1993, unreported QBD, IDS Brief vol 515) in the light of evidence that the period had subsequently been reduced to 12 months for other roundsmen). For an illustration of the approach of the court to the question of the period of retraint. See also *Rex Stewart Jeffries Parker Ginsberg Ltd v Parker* [1988] IRLR 483 (CA) where a period of 18 months was held not to be excessive in relation to a managing director (of an advertising agency) who had by virtue of his senior position more opportunity to develop relationships with customers – as compared with a junior employee in relation to whom (in the view of the Judge below) a lesser period would have been appropriate. In *Stenhouse Australia Ltd v Phillips* [1974] 1 All ER 117 Lord Wilberforce stated (page 123h) that the relevant question was not how long the employee could be expected to enjoy, by virtue of his employment, a competitive edge over others seeking the clients' business. It was rather, what was a reasonable time during which the ex-employer was entitled to protection against the solicitation of clients with whom the employee had contact and influence during the employment and who were not bound to the employer by contract or stability of association. This could not conveniently be the subject of direct evidence – it was for the judge after informing himself of the facts and circumstances relating to the employer's business, the nature of the employer's interest to be protected, and the likely effect on this of solicitation to decide whether the contractual period was reasonable or not. The opinion could only be formed on a broad and common-sense view. A longer period of restraint may be justified in relation to a non-solicitation covenant than a non dealing covenant: see paragraph 10.66. Accordingly, in *Taylor Stuart & Co v Croft*, (7 May 1997, unreported Ch D) three years was held to be reasonable for a non-solicitation covenant in an employee-accountant's contract of employment but this period was held to be too long for a non-dealing covenant.

4. Non-dealing covenants

10.66 The employment contract will often include a covenant (usually by way of an addition to a non-solicitation covenant) which prevents not merely solicitation of customers but also dealing with those customers (by whomsoever initiated). The main advantage of such a covenant is that, in order to establish a breach of a non-dealing covenant, the ex-employer does not have to establish that it was the ex-employee who solicited the customer. It is all too easy for the ex-employee to assert that the customer approached the ex-employee (without solicitation by him). This is difficult for the ex-employer to disprove, particularly where the ex-employee and the customer are friendly. On the other hand, it may be argued that the customer should not be deprived of dealing with whom he pleases. The courts do not require the weapon of the restrictive covenant to be honed with complete precision and, bearing in mind that the courts will enforce properly drafted area covenants – which are almost always bound to affect at least some who were not customers of the ex-employer – it is to be expected that the courts will not be too quick to strike down properly drafted non-dealing covenants. In *John Michael Design plc v Cooke and another* [1987] 2 All ER

332 (CA) the Court of Appeal upheld in favour of ex-employers (shopfitters) against a former 'associate director' a two-year non-dealing/solicitation covenant in respect of those who had been customers in the last four years of employment. The court made no distinction between the non-dealing and the non-solicitation parts of the covenant (nor does there appear to have been any argument on the point). Also, in *Marley Tile Co Ltd v Johnson* [1982] IRLR 75 (CA), and in *T Lucas & Co Ltd v Mitchell* [1972] 3 All ER 689 (CA), there was a non-dealing covenant, but the distinction between non-solicitation and non-dealing covenants did not appear to play any part in the Court's decision in either case. See also *Hinton & Higgs (UK) Ltd v Murphy and Valentine* [1989] IRLR 519 (Court of Session) and *Specialist Recruiters International Ltd v Taylor* (RCJ 4 July 1989, unreported), both referred to above. In *London & Solent Ltd v Brooks* (IDS Brief 389 January 1989, unreported) the Court of Appeal upheld a non-dealing covenant in addition to a non-solicitation covenant given by an assistant director and head of a marine reinsurance broking team. In view of the intimate nature of the market in which movement of senior employees from one broker to another quickly became general knowledge, the company was entitled to the additional protection to prevent the natural gravitation of clients towards the ex-employee, who knew their personal requirements and in whom they had gained confidence. The present position is therefore favourable to non-dealing covenants. The same factors as are relevant to reasonableness of non-solicitation covenants apply in the case of non-dealing covenants.

5. Covenants against enticing/employing/arranging employment for fellow employees/consultants

10.67 As in the case of covenants prohibiting solicitation of customers, there may be difficulty in deciding what amounts to enticement or solicitation of colleagues or former colleagues. In many cases the position will be clear, but in some cases there may be difficulty in establishing breach. For example, does the providing of the names of former colleagues to the new employer amount to enticement or solicitation? Such activity may not in itself amount to a breach of covenant unless the employer acts on the information provided to him by the ex-employee and the covenant is drafted widely enough to cover procurement of enticement by the employer. As to advertisements in the general or trade press, similar considerations apply to those discussed in paragraph 10.30 in relation to solicitation of customers.

10.68 It is settled law (at least in the Court of Appeal) that an employer has a legitimate interest in maintaining the stability of his workforce sufficient to justify a non-poaching (of employees) covenant: *Dawnay Day & Co v de Braconier d'Alphen and others* [1997] IRLR 442 (CA) – settling the clash between *Hanover v Schapiro* [1994] IRLR 82 (CA) ('employees are not apples and pears') and *Ingham v A B C* (CA) Lexis, 12 November 1993) to the contrary see also *Alliance Paper Group plc v Prestwich* [1996] IRLR 25 in which the non-poaching covenant was upheld and *T S C Europe (UK) Ltd v Massey* [1999] IRLR 22 in which the covenant was regarded as enforceable in principle but struck down as being too widely drafted.

10.69 See also *Office Angels Ltd v Rainer-Thomas* [1991] IRLR 214 where the Court of Appeal held that a recruitment agency had a protectable interest in relation to its trade connection with its pool of temporary workers. The temporary workers were not employees of Office Angels, nor were they its clients since Office Angels was prohibited (by Section 6(1) of the Employment Agencies Act 1973) from taking a fee from them. The Court of Appeal, in upholding the covenant, distinguished its decision in *Kores Manufacturing Co Ltd v Kolok Manufacturing Co Ltd* [1959] Ch 108 (where a non-poaching agreement between employers was struck down).

10.70 The ex-employer will still need to show that the covenant goes no further than is necessary to protect his legitimate interest. In the case of employers who employ large numbers of staff it will be necessary to establish a connection between the employer and the colleagues whom the covenant prevents him from enticing (similar to the requirement of connection between employee and customer, often in the form of contact, discussed above in relation to non-solicitation of customer covenants). It is accordingly wise to limit the non-enticement to colleagues with whom the employee has had material contact for a limited period prior to the end of his employment or to limit it to staff of particular level over whom the employee might be expected to gain influence. *Hanover v Schapiro* was a case where this was not done. It is, accordingly, wise to limit such covenants to employees with whom the employee had material contact, in say the last 12 months of his employment or (where applicable) to staff of a particular level over whom the employee might be expected to gain influence. On the other hand the Courts have demonstrated a practical approach towards difficulties of definition. Thus in *Dawnay Day & Co v de Braconier d'Alphen and others* and also *Alliance Paper Group plc v Prestwich* criticisms of expressions in covenants such as 'senior employees' as too vague (without definition of the term) were regarded as unjustified.

10.71 In contradistinction to non-poaching covenants it is unlikely that the courts would favour 'non-employment' covenants, that is a covenant restraining an employee from employing or procuring the employment for his erstwhile colleagues (without the ingredient of solicitation): *Dawnay Day & Co v de Braconier d'Alphen and others* [1997] IRLR 285 obiter per Robert Walker J (para 77). The matter is arguable to the contrary since non-dealing (with customers) covenants have been upheld (see para 10.66) as an alternative to (or even additional to) non-solicitation covenants, in particular because of the difficulty of proving solicitation, a similar argument could be raised in relation to a non-employment covenant. However, it may have to be narrowly drafted to have any chance of success, to overcome a reluctance on the part of the courts or not to interfere unduly with the free movement of labour.

6. Covenants against the disclosure/use of trade secrets and confidential information

10.72 Since there is an implied duty of confidence imported into every employment contract the question is what (if any) advantage is gained by the incorporation into the employment contract of (often elaborate) express covenants relating to confidentiality. The advantages of incorporating an express confidentiality covenant are threefold:

- Since an employer who asserts confidentiality in relation to particular information is required to show that he treated the information as such and communicated to the employee the fact that the information was confidential, an express covenant may assist in identifying the categories of information which are to be treated as confidential;
- It may help to support an area covenant or non-solicitation/dealing covenant which is taken to protect confidential information of the employer, by supporting the case that such information does exist and that this was accepted by the parties;
- More fundamentally by obtaining protection for (mere) confidential information which would not otherwise be protected after employment. The view expressed by the Court of Appeal in *Faccenda Chicken Ltd v Fowler* [1986] 3 WLR 288 that information which is merely confidential but not trade secret cannot be protected by express covenant – and the subsequent decisions doubting that proposition – are discussed in Ch 5. If, as we believe, mere confidential information can be used to support an area restraint or non-solicitation covenant, logically the employer ought to be able to protect such information directly by means of a confidentiality covenant. On this analysis an express confidentiality covenant may go somewhat further than merely assisting the employee to demonstrate that specified information pertaining to the business of the employer is indeed confidential. On the other hand, a confidentiality covenant expressed in too wide terms may be struck down as being unreasonably in restraint of trade: *Intelsec Systems v Grech-Chini* [199] 4 All ER 11, 25j-26b.

6(a) Requirements of confidentiality covenants

10.73 There are two matters of particular significance:

- As we have seen (in Ch 5) there are considerable practical difficulties in distinguishing between proprietary information of the employer and information which is to be regarded as the general skill of the employee: see the judgment of Farwell LJ in *Sir W C Leng & Co Ltd v Andrews* [1909] 1 Ch 763, 773 (CA). The law will prevent the ex-employer from seeking (by way of a confidentiality covenant) or otherwise to expand the categories of confidential information so as to restrict the ex-employee's use of his skill or know-how: see *Triplex Safety Glass Co Ltd v Scorah* [1938] Ch 211, 216 (per Farwell J);
- In our view, an express confidentiality covenant will only assist the employer if it identifies with as much precision as possible the confidential information which the employer seeks to protect. In *Ixora Trading Inc v Jones* [1990] FSR 251 senior executives of a company operating bureaux de change agreed (inter alia) that any information to which they had access or knowledge which they acquired arising out of or in the course of their contracts of service should remain confidential and should not be used by them to obtain any gain or advantage for themselves or for their family. Mummery J (at page 259) said that these express covenants were far too wide in their unlimited terms to be enforceable for the protection of confidential information.

10.74 On the other side of the line to the cases referred to in paragraphs 10.72 to 10.73 is the decision in *Systems Reliability Holdings plc v Smith* [1990] IRLR 377, 384 in which Harman J held that an express covenant preventing the use or disclosure by the ex-employee of 'confidential information ... concerning the business or affairs or products of or services supplied by the company' lawfully prevented the ex-employee (for a limited period) from using or disclosing confidential knowledge or know-how in his head (as opposed to information), eg the various operations in reconfiguring certain computers (which he had been told not to disclose to anybody). This decision can be explained on the basis that this knowledge was in fact proprietary information of the employer rather than general skill or 'know-how', and in any event Harman J expressly applied the less stringent standard appropriate to vendor and purchaser covenants, saying that the covenant in question required to be judged by the tests appropriate to covenants between persons buying and persons selling a business which has information of which the purchaser hopes to get the benefit by his purchase.

10.75 Harman J also upheld those parts of the covenant which referred to confidential information:

- Of the subsidiaries, since there was evidence that the business of the subsidiaries was so closely linked with the business of the company that the defendant was likely to have confidential information affecting subsidiaries;
- Concerning persons having dealings with the company or its subsidiaries, for example, the layout of manufacturing plant, since it might be very damaging to the company's reputation if this sort of information was made public.

7. Combining different types of covenant

10.76 The effect of combining different covenants may often be to encourage the court to reject the more stringent clause and to uphold the less stringent. Thus, where there is an area covenant and a non-solicitation/dealing covenant the court may lean towards enforcement of the non-solicitation/dealing covenant and rejection of the area covenant (particularly where the interest sought or to be protected is that of business connection, since this type of interest will often be adequately protected by the non-solicitation covenant). In *Stenhouse Australia Ltd v Phillips* [1974] 1 All ER 117 the fact that there was a non-solicitation as well as a non-dealing covenant was one of the reasons for rejecting the latter:

> 'The presence of one restraint diminishes the need for the others, or at least increases the burden of those who must justify those others.'

(per Lord Wilberforce at page 124 f–g). In other cases the court has granted injunctions culmulatively, for example, *London & Solent v Brooks* (January 1989 unreported (CA)) (non-solicitation and non-dealing injunctions) and *Alliance Paper Group plc v Prestwich* [1996] IRLR 25 (area covenant, non-solicitation and non-dealing injunctions granted) and see *Turner v Commonwealth & British Minerals Ltd* (CA) 13 October 1999 (unreported).

7(a) Combining covenants with 'garden leave'

10.77 In *Credit Suisse Asset Management Ltd v Armstrong* [1996] IRLR 450 the Court of Appeal upheld six month non-competition and non-solicitation covenants, notwithstanding that the claimants had already had the benefit of six months' 'garden leave'. There was no basis for a set-off of the period of the covenant against the period of garden leave, nor could the court re-write the covenant so as to enforce it for a lesser period than that agreed.

10.78 However, the existence of a garden leave clause might be a factor to be taken into account in determining the validity of a restrictive covenant. Moreover in an exceptional case, where a long period of garden leave had elapsed, perhaps substantially in excess of a year, it was possible that the court would decline on the public policy ground to grant any further protection based on a restrictive covenant – the latter exception seems most unlikely to occur in practice. In our view, notwithstanding *Credit Suisse v Armstrong*, it is prudent when drafting covenants to provide that the length of the covenant will be reduced by any period spent on garden leave.

8. Indirect covenants

10.79 Covenants may be structured in such a way that they do not look like restrictive covenants. The court will look to the substance rather than to the form. Thus in *Stenhouse Australia Ltd v Phillips* [1974] 1 All ER 117 one of the covenants in a severance agreement provided that in the event of the ex-employee gaining financial benefit from the placing of any business by one of the customers of the employer, the employer would receive half the benefit. The court construed that covenant (in conjunction with a non-dealing covenant) not as a simple profit-sharing arrangement but as a restrictive covenant (which it struck down as being unreasonably wide). See also: *Wyatt v Kreglinger and Fernau* [1933] 1 KB 793 and *Bull v Pitney-Bowes Ltd* [1966] 3 AllER 384 (employee's pension scheme providing for forfeiture of pension in the event of competition struck down as being in restraint of trade) and also *Marshall v N M Financial Management* [1995] 1 WLR 1461 (self-employed sales agent to continue to receive commission in respect of introductions previously made by him, provided he did not compete after employment). Compare also *Sadler v Imperial Life Assurance Co of Canada Ltd* [1988] IRLR 388 and *Electronic Data Systems v Hubble* (Lexis 20 November 1987, unreported) discussed at paragraph 4.4.

9. Qualified covenants

10.80 Restrictive covenants are often qualified by a provision that they will not be enforced if written consent of the ex-employer is obtained to carry out the otherwise prohibited activity. This sort of qualification will not normally carry any weight. For example, the presence of such qualification does not appear to have affected the decision in *Stenhouse Australia Ltd v Phillips* [1974] 1 All ER 117. In *Kerchiss v Colora Printing Inks Ltd* [1960] RPC 235 the existence of such a provision (consent could not reasonably be withheld) was, however, one of the factors which persuaded the court to uphold the covenant, but in *Chafer Ltd v Lilley* (1947) 176 LT 22 a similar clause was regarded as a mere device.

10. Penalty clauses

10.81 It is not uncommon for restrictive covenants to be combined with clauses providing for payment of sums in the event of breach. These will very often amount to unenforceable penalty clauses and may contribute to the court forming a view that the restrictive covenant is unreasonable: cf *Taylor Stuart & Co v Croft* (7 May 1997, unreported Ch D). Further, such a clause (whether or not amounting to a penalty) may provide the ex-employee with an argument that damages will be an adequate remedy for breach, so as to preclude the grant of an injunction to enforce the covenant: see Ch 13. We do not recommend the use of such clauses, which in most cases are doomed to fail since in drafting employment covenants it will rarely be possible genuinely to pre-estimate the amount of loss likely to occur on breach of the contract of employment. That being said, such clauses are quite common in accountancy partnership deeds and employment contracts in the accountancy profession where the loss is sometimes expressed as a percentage of the fees which would have been generated over the period of the restriction, in relation to a client whom the ex-partner or ex-employee unlawfully solicits or deals with in the covenant period.

11. Termination 'howsoever caused'

10.82 During and after 1994 a number of decisions were handed down both in England and Scotland to the effect that covenants were unreasonably in restraint of trade if they were expressed to be applicable 'however [termination of the employment contract] comes about and whether lawful or not' for example, *Living Design v Davidson* [1994] IRLR 69 or 'if the agreement is terminated for any reason whatsoever' *D v M* [1996] IRLR 192 or using other such language designed to retain for the employer the benefit of covenants even where the employer had repudiated the contract of employment (thus seeking to circumvent the rule in *General Billposting Co v Atkinson* (1909) AC 118). This line of authority was decisively rejected by the Court of Appeal in *Rock Refrigeration v Seward* [1997] IRLR 675. It was held that where there is a repudiatory breach of the contract of employment by the employer, the principle in *General Billposting v Atkinson* applies. The employee is released from his obligations under the contract and restrictive covenants against him cannot be enforced. Therefore, the law applicable to covenants in restraint of trade is not relevant in such circumstances because it applies only where there exists an otherwise enforceable contract. The Court of Appeal held that if an otherwise reasonable covenant purports to remain binding in circumstances where the law will inevitably strike it down, there is no justification for holding that it is, on that account, an unlawful restraint of trade. Nor were there any grounds for holding that (despite the apparent sufficiency of the *General Billposting* principle to meet the justice of the case where the employer repudiates the contract) there remained a need for the restraint of trade doctrine to strike down in their entirety restrictive covenants which purport to apply in those circumstances because (so the employee argued) they have a detrimental effect on the mind of the employee in deciding whether or not to accept the employer's repudiation. In his judgment (concurring with the result) Phillips LJ surprisingly cast doubt on the rule in *General Billposting* stating that it accords neither with current legal principle nor with the requirements of business efficacy. Since there is no other principle of law which precludes the parties from validly agreeing to restraints that will subsist even if the employment is brought to an end by repudiation, it was (he stated) at least arguable that not every restrictive covenant will be discharged on a repudiatory termination of the contract of employment. See further paragraphs 8.19 to 8.22 in which the relationship between the *General Billposting* principle and that in *Photoproductions Ltd v Securicor Ltd* [1980] AC 827 (HL) is discussed. It is suggested that it would be wise on the part of those advising in this area to assume that the *General Billposting* principle continues to be applicable until revisited by the House of Lords.

Chapter 11

Drafting restrictive covenants

1. Why are express restrictive covenants important?

11.1 Express restrictive covenants are the ex-employer's primary source of protection against competition by a former employee. In the absence of such covenants the ex-employer's only protection, subject to one important exception, is to be found in the continuing implied duty of the ex-employee not to use or disclose his ex-employer's trade secrets. The exception is where the ex-employee's competitive activity involves use or disclosure of mere confidential information which is a continuation of a breach of confidence committed during employment. Common examples are the use of confidential information copied during employment in order to use it in a competitive business. Where the ex-employer can prove such a breach it will give him a remedy against the ex-employee and may enable him effectively to prevent the ex-employee competing (see Ch 14). Obtaining the necessary proof, however, can be very difficult. Often all the ex-employer has is a grave suspicion that a breach has occurred. As a result the exception, albeit important, will only provide protection for the ex-employer in a limited number of cases. It should never be treated by employers as a substitute for properly drafted covenants.

11.2 While restrictive covenants are notoriously difficult to draft and enforceability can never be guaranteed, an employer will never be worse off as a result of including restrictive covenants in his contracts of employment. He will often be in a significantly better position to prevent or limit competition as a result of their inclusion. References in this Chapter to restrictive covenants include confidentiality covenants that operate after termination of employment. The drafting of such covenants is considered at paragraph 4.30.

2. Drafting the covenants: preparatory steps

11.3 The draftsman of restrictive covenants has two aims to achieve. First, that the covenants drafted should have the best possible chance of being found to be enforceable and, second, that they prohibit or limit the competitive activities of the particular employee to the maximum extent consistent with their being enforceable. To achieve these aims the draftsman must understand:

- The basic criteria by which enforceability is judged;
- When the criterion of reasonableness is applied;

- The rules of construction applied to restrictive covenants; and
- The nature of the business in which the employee is/will be employed, the employee's role and the likely type of competitive activity.

2(a) Criteria for enforceability

11.4 In every case the employer must be able to show that the covenant protects a legitimate interest and that it goes no further than is reasonably necessary to protect that legitimate interest: *Mason v Provident Clothing & Supply Co Ltd* [1913] AC 724 (HL); *Herbert Morris Ltd v Saxelby* [1916] AC 688 (HL); *Stenhouse Australia Ltd v Phillips* [1974] 1 All ER 117 (PC). These two criteria are considered in detail in Chs 9 and 10. The draftsman should have them at the forefront of his mind at all times.

2(b) When must the covenant be reasonable?

11.5 The reasonableness of a covenant is judged at the time the contract is made, not at the time the ex-employer is seeking to enforce it: *Commercial Plastics Ltd v Vincent* [1965] 1 QB 623; see also *Gledhow Autoparts Ltd v Delaney* [1965] 1 WLR 1366 and *SW Strange Ltd v Mann* [1965] 1 WLR 629. The reasonable expectations of the parties at the time the contract was made can be taken into account: *Lyne-Pirkis v Jones* [1969] 1 WLR 1293. Reasonableness should not be judged on the facts applying when enforcement is sought: *NIS Fertilisers v Neville* [1986] 2 NIJB 70. In reality, however, to obtain an injunction the ex-employer needs to show that the covenant is reasonable at the time of enforcement. For this reason it is vital for the employer to ensure that restrictive covenants are always kept up to date although to do so can be problematic, see paragraphs 12.33 to 12.34 for the issues associated with variation of contract.

2(c) Rules of construction

11.6 The rules of construction which the courts can use in interpreting restrictive covenants are those available to interpret any contractual term. The difficulty in the case of restrictive covenants lies in predicting, with any degree of certainty, how those rules will be applied. A review of the cases reveals different trends. On the one hand are authorities which adopt a very strict or literal approach: *Commercial Plastics v Vincent* [1964] 3 All ER 546 (CA), *J A Mont (UK) v Mills* [1993] IRLR 172 (CA) in particular the comments of Simon Brown LJ) and see also *Greer v Sketchley Ltd* [1979] IRLR 445 (CA) and *Scully UK Ltd v Lee* [1998] IRLR 259 (CA). In the latter two cases the Court of Appeal refused to limit the scope of an area covenant to 'competing businesses' notwithstanding submissions on behalf of the former employer that this was the underlying purpose of the covenant. Cases on the other hand tending to what nowadays might be called a purposive approach include: *Marion White Ltd v Francis* [1972] 3 All ER 857; *Clarke v Newland* [1991] 1 All ER 397 (CA); *Hanover Insurance Brokers v Schapiro* [1994] IRLR 82 (CA) (in relation to a non-solicitation covenant) and, in its most extreme form, *Littlewoods Organisation Ltd v Harris* [1978] 1 All ER 1026 (CA). Most recently in *Turner v Commonwealth & British Minerals Ltd* (CA) 13 October 1999 (unreported) the Court of Appeal construed narrowly an area covenant in order to prevent it from failing (which it would have done on a broader interpretation). Discerning any logic in the courts' application of the rules is not easy.

11.7 The uncertainty over how the rules of construction will be applied makes it prudent for restrictive covenants to be drafted as clearly and precisely as possible to avoid the necessity of the courts having to invoke any rules of construction. However, it is appreciated that this may be asking the impossible of the draftsman and consequently it is essential for him to understand the various rules of construction. By doing so the draftsman can avoid at least some of the pitfalls. He is also best placed to know how to challenge the covenants of other draftsmen when acting for the ex-employee.

11.8 The following are the applicable rules of construction:

2(c)(i) THE COVENANT MUST BE CLEAR AND CERTAIN

11.9 Covenants which are expressed in vague terms or which use words or phrases that are unclear will not be upheld. In *Davies v Davies* (1837) 36 Ch D 359 a covenant to retire from business 'so far as the law allows' was held to be too vague to be enforced. Similarly, in both *Spafax (1965) Ltd v Dommett* (1972) 116 Sol Jo 711 and *Reed Executive v Somers* (CA) (20 March 1986, unreported) discussed at paragraph 10.40, the covenant failed because the term 'customer' was too uncertain and in *Gledhow Autoparts Ltd v Delaney* [1965] 3 All ER 288 Dankwerts LJ, in striking down a covenant, criticised the use of the phrase 'districts in which the traveller had operated' as too vague a definition of the geographic area of the covenant in circumstances where Delaney, a travelling salesman, was only ever given oral orders. In contrast, in two recent cases on non-enticement the covenants were upheld notwithstanding the use of somewhat vague phraseology to define the protected pool. In *Alliance Paper Group plc v Prestwich* [1996] IRLR 25 the prohibition applied in respect of those employed/engaged 'in a senior capacity'. In *Dawnay Day & Co Ltd v De Braconier D'Alphen* [1997] IRLR 442 (CA) it covered any 'senior employee'. For further discussion of defining the protected pool in non-enticement covenants see paragraphs 10.67 to 10.70 and 11.51 to 11.52.

2(c)(ii) WORDS USED ARE GIVEN THEIR ORDINARY MEANING

11.10 The basic rule is that words are to be given their ordinary and natural meaning subject to some limited exceptions. In *Mallan v May* (1844) 13 M&W 511 the rule was stated in the following way (at page 517):

'Words are to be construed according to their strict and primary acceptation, unless from the content of the instrument and the intention of the parties to be collected from it, they appear to be used in a different sense, or unless in their strict sense, they are incapable of being carried into effect.'

However, if it is plain from the background to the contract that something has gone wrong with the language so that the words given their ordinary meaning do not reflect the parties' intentions, the words will be interpreted in the context of the parties' intentions: *Investors Compensation Scheme v West Bromwich Building Society* [1998] 1 All ER 98 (HL). In the words of Lord Hoffmann at 115d ' the law does not require judges to attribute to the parties an intention which they plainly could not have had'. See also Lord Hoffmann's comments generally on interpretation of contracts at 114h to 115e.

11.11 Technical words will normally be given their technical meaning unless the contract excludes that meaning: *Laird v Briggs* (1881) 19 Ch D 22. So, for example, if it is clear from the contract in what sense the words are used that sense will be used instead of the technical meaning: *Graham v Ewart* [1856] 1 H & N 550.

2(c)(iii) THE COVENANT MUST BE INTERPRETED IN THE CONTEXT OF THE AGREEMENT AS A WHOLE AND TO GIVE EFFECT TO THE INTENTION OF THE PARTIES

11.12 In practice this rule of construction gives the court considerable latitude to save a covenant that might otherwise be too wide. In *GW Plowman & Son Ltd v Ash* [1964] 3 All ER 10 Ash had been employed as a sales representative in Plowman's business of corn and agricultural merchants and animal feeding stuff manufacturers. He had covenanted that he would not, for two years after his employment terminated, canvass or solicit business from farmers or market gardeners who had been Plowman's customers during his employment. The clause did not, however, define the type of goods Ash was prohibited from selling. When Plowman sought to enforce the covenant Ash argued, inter alia, that the covenant was too wide to be enforced because its effect was to prohibit him selling goods of any description to those who had been customers of Plowman during his employment. The Court of Appeal unanimously rejected this argument. They held that looking at the agreement as a whole the covenant was confined to those goods which were the subject of Ash's employment, notwithstanding that there was no such express limitation in the covenant itself. In reaching this conclusion two members of the Court of Appeal specifically referred to the fact that the nature of Plowman's business was set out in the same clause of Ash's Service Agreement. Similarly, in *Business Seating (Renovations) Ltd v Broad* [1989] ICR 729 the Court interpreted a covenant which prohibited the ex-employee, Broad, from canvassing, soliciting or endeavouring to take away from the employer 'the business of any customers or clients of the employer' as only prohibiting Broad from seeking to obtain orders to repair or renovate office furniture. The Court found this interpretation could be inferred from an earlier clause in the contract which described Business Seating's business. In *Home Counties Dairies Ltd v Skilton* [1970] 1 All ER 1227 a covenant in the contract of employment of a milk roundsman not to 'serve or sell milk or dairy produce' or to 'solicit orders for milk or dairy produce' was construed only to prohibit the ex-employee, Skilton, doing those things as a milk roundsman and not in any other capacity. Finally, in *Hanover Insurance Brokers Ltd v Schapiro* [1994] IRLR 85(CA) a covenant prohibited the canvassing of the 'business' of the ex-employer's customers but did not define the nature of the business the ex-employees were prohibited from canvassing. The ex-employees had all been engaged in the insurance broking business for Hanover and it was held that the covenant prohibited only the canvassing of that type of business and was therefore enforceable.

11.13 The most extreme example of the purposive approach is to be found in the majority decision of Lord Denning MR and Megaw LJ in *Littlewoods Organisation Ltd v Harris* [1978] 1 All ER 1026. Harris had been employed by Littlewoods as a divisional director of ladies' fashions in their mail order business. The covenant prevented Harris for twelve months after the termination of his employment from entering into 'a Contract of Service or other Agreement of like nature with GUS Limited or any company subsidiary thereto' or being 'directly or indirectly engaged concerned or interested in the trading or business of GUS Ltd or any such company aforesaid.' Harris argued that the covenant was unreasonable on three grounds:

- It included subsidiaries of GUS Ltd which had nothing to do with the mail order business;
- There was no geographic limit although the business of Littlewoods was limited to the UK; and
- The covenant was not limited to the mail order business which was the only legitimate interest Littlewoods had to protect vis-à-vis Harris.

The court rejected all three arguments. They found that it was legitimate for the covenant to include subsidiaries in order to prevent Harris being employed by another company in the GUS Ltd group and passing confidential information back to the mail order business. In reaching this view the majority relied on the fact that because of the control structure in the GUS group it was appropriate to look at the group as a single entity. They construed the clause as only applying to those parts of the GUS Group that operated in the UK on the basis that, to do so reflected the perceived intention of the parties. Finally, the business in which Harris was prohibited from being involved was limited to the mail order business on the ground that it was that business in which Harris had been employed by Littlewoods. The lengths to which the Court of Appeal went to enforce the covenant against Harris are very surprising. Of the three findings, the second is the most unjustifiable and directly contradicts the normal rule that where there is no geographical limit expressed in the covenant it will be construed as imposing a worldwide ban: *Dowden & Pook Ltd v Pook* [1904] 1 KB 45 and *Commercial Plastics Ltd v Vincent* [1964] 3 All ER 546.

11.14 For a recent case, in which the court arguably declined to save an area covenant by applying the rule of construction that the covenant must be interpreted in the context of the agreement and to reflect the intention of the parties, see *Scully UK Ltd v Lee* [1998] IRLR 259 (CA). Scully was involved in supplying overfill prevention systems, liquid level detection systems and fuel handling systems to the petrochemical industry. Lee's contract forbade him for one year after employment from being involved in any business which carried out activities in relation to 'overspill prevention or tank gauging'. The restriction was not expressly limited to businesses competing with Scully and the Court of Appeal refused to imply such a limitation. In the Court's view the phraseology used 'was intended to extend the ambit of the covenant to any business which dealt in such equipment'.

2(c)(iv) EXTRAVAGANT INTERPRETATIONS OF THE COVENANT CAN BE IGNORED

11.15 This is really a part of the previous rule but it is sufficiently important to consider separately. In *Haynes v Doman* [1899] 2 Ch 13 (CA) at pages 24 and 25 Lindley LJ expressed the rule in the following way:

'Another matter which requires attention is whether a restriction on trade must be treated as wholly void because it is so worded as to cover cases which may possibly arise, and to which it cannot be reasonably applied ... Agreements in restraint of trade, like other agreements, must be construed with reference to the object sought to be obtained by them. In cases such as the one before us, the object is the protection of one of the parties against rivalry in trade. Such agreements cannot be properly held to apply to cases which, although covered by the words of the agreement, cannot reasonably be supposed ever to have been contemplated by the parties, and which on a rational view of the agreement are excluded from its operation by falling, in truth, outside and not within its real scope.'

11.16   In *Haynes v Doman* the covenant was a mixed confidentiality and area covenant designed to protect Haynes' confidential information and business methods. The court found that the possibility of Doman leaving employment before having acquired any knowledge of Haynes' confidential information or business methods, which had not in the event happened, fell outside the scope of the covenant and could be ignored. In *Home Counties Dairies* the possibility that could be ignored was that of a customer of Home Counties and the ex-employee both moving to the same distant place and the non dealing/non solicitation covenant thereby preventing the ex-employee serving milk or dairy produce to that customer.

2(c)(v)   THE COURT HAS NO POWER TO RE-WRITE THE COVENANT

11.17   A distinction must always be drawn between a court using the rules of construction to interpret a covenant in a way that it may be upheld, which is permissible, and re-writing the covenant, which is not permissible. At times that distinction has become somewhat blurred: *Littlewoods Organisation Ltd v Harris* [1978] 1 All ER 1026, but it is a fundamental tenet of contract law that the courts have no power to re-write the bargain struck by the parties and that rule applies as much to restrictive covenants as to any other contractual term: *Mason v Provident Clothing and Supply Company Ltd* [1913] AC 724 at page 745 (HL), applied in *J A Mont (UK) Ltd v Mills* [1993] IRLR 172. It follows that the Court has no power to extend a covenant to prohibit an activity which the draftsman omitted to cover. So in *WAC Ltd v Whillock* [1990] IRLR 23 (Court of Session) a covenant prohibiting Whillock carrying on any business in competition with the company did not preclude him from being either a director or employee of a competing company. The prohibition was only against Whillock personally carrying on a competitive business and the court could not extend that. However, query whether nowadays a party can be penalised in costs for refusing to accept a rewritten covenant proposed as a CPR Part 36 offer: see paragraph 13.66.

2(c)(vi)   SEVERANCE

11.18   Severance is the process whereby the court deletes an unenforceable provision from a contract leaving a valid and enforceable provision. Requests to the court to exercise its power of severance are commonplace in the litigation of restrictive covenants. Since the nineteenth century there have been a considerable number of reported cases in which severance has been an issue. Although the approach of the courts has not always been entirely consistent, the conditions which must exist for the court to exercise the power of severance are now fairly well settled. Anomalies which arise do so from the court's application of those conditions rather than from any fundamental change in the conditions themselves. The conditions are as follows:

- It must be possible to remove the unenforceable provision without the need to add to or modify the wording of what remains: *Attwood v Lamont* [1920] 3 KB 571 (CA). If as a result of severance it would be necessary to amend the remaining provision in any way in order that it makes sense, severance is not possible. For this reason it is never possible to validate by severance a covenant stated to cover a single area which the court has ruled is too wide or otherwise inappropriate. The only gloss on this condition is that the severed words continue to be available to explain the remaining words: *British Reinforced Concrete Engineering Co Ltd v Scheff* [1921] 2 Ch 563 (Ch D). So in *T Lucas & Co Ltd v Mitchell* [1974] Ch 129 (CA) the court was able to sever an invalid covenant not to 'deal in' particular goods from a valid covenant not to solicit orders for or supply those type of goods to customers of the former employer, notwithstanding that the definition of the type of goods covered was contained in the severed covenant. The definition remained available for the purpose of construing the remaining words. This condition, often referred to as the 'blue pencil test', is not, however, alone sufficient to justify severance: *Attwood v Lamont* and *Business Seating (Renovations) Ltd v Broad* [1989] ICR 729, per Millett J at 734.

- The words to be severed must constitute a separate and independent promise and be capable of being severed without the severance affecting the meaning of the part remaining: *Attwood v Lamont* [1920] 3 KB 571 (CA). In *Attwood v Lamont* the court found that the covenant constituted a single covenant and therefore could not be severed. Attwood carried on business in Kidderminster as a draper, tailor and general outfitter. Lamont had been employed as an Assistant in Attwood's tailoring department. Lamont's contract of employment included a covenant that after leaving Attwood's employ he would not at any time be involved in 'the trade or business of a tailor, dressmaker, general draper, milliner, hatter, haberdasher, gentlemens', ladies' or childrens' outfitters' within a ten-mile radius of Kidderminster. The court ruled that this was a single promise to protect Attwood's entire business and not severable. Similarly in *N I S Fertilisers v Neville* [1986] 2 NIJB 70 the court regarded as a single promise a covenant not to do certain things 'in an area which covers the territory within which you represented the company and any area outside this territory which stands at a distance of 20 miles from the boundary of it.' The court acknowledged that it was grammatically possible to limit the covenant to the area in which Neville had operated but refused to do so on the ground that the covenant was a single promise. Compare *Scorer v Seymour-Johns* [1966] 3 All ER 347 where a provision not to do certain prohibited activities within a radius of five miles of Scorer's Kingsbridge or Dartmouth offices was held to amount to two separate promises. The promise in connection with the Dartmouth office was unenforceable, since Seymour-Johns had never worked there, but it could properly be regarded as a separate concern, and the court held it was severable and granted an injunction to enforce the covenant in connection with the Kingsbridge office. Similarly, in *Rex Stewart Jeffries Parker Ginsberg Ltd v Parker* [1988] IRLR 483 (CA) the court found that a clause prohibiting the solicitation of customers amounted to three separate covenants, namely: a covenant not to solicit (1) those who had been customers during the employment, (2) those who became customers subsequently, and (3) customers of associated companies for whom Parker had never worked. The Court found that the second and third covenants were unenforceable but as they constituted separate covenants, they could be severed leaving the first covenant enforceable. See also *Business Seating (Renovations) Ltd v Broad* [1989] ICR 729 where the court permitted severance of references to 'associated employers' of Business Seating (Renovations) Limited in a clause prohibiting the solicitation of customers or clients.

11.19 The conditions for severance were put in the following way in *Sadler v Imperial Life Assurance Co of Canada Ltd* [1988] IRLR 388:

- The unenforceable provision is capable of being removed without the necessity of adding to or modifying the wording of what remains.
- The remaining terms continue to be supported by adequate consideration.
- The removal of the unenforceable provision does not so change the character of the contract that it becomes 'not the sort of contract that the parties entered into at all'.

11.20 In *Sadler* the question was whether an invalid restraint of trade provision, the effect of which was to prevent Sadler indefinitely from working for any other insurance company, could be severed from a clause dealing with Sadler's entitlement to commission after the termination of employment. The High Court found that it could, the three conditions being satisfied.

11.21 In *Marshall v N M Financial Management Ltd* [1996] IRLR 20, upheld on appeal [1997] IRLR 449 (CA), Jonathan Sumption QC sitting as a deputy High Court Judge suggested a fourth condition should be added to those in *Sadler* which is that severance must be consistent with the public policy underlying the avoidance of the offending part. It is, however, unclear to us what the proposed fourth condition added to the other three and the position is not illuminated in the judgment. On its facts, *Marshall* was very similar to *Sadler*. The case turned on whether an unenforceable restrictive covenant could be severed leaving intact an entitlement to renewal commission. N M Financial Management argued it could not, primarily because the right to commission was, it argued, conditional on the restrictive covenant. Converting a conditional right into an unconditional one would be a substantial change in the balance of the parties' agreement. This argument was rejected both at first instance and by the Court of Appeal. Those courts acknowledged that severance would entail an alteration in the character of the contract. However, they concluded that alteration was not objectionable because the restrictive covenant did not represent the 'whole or substantially the whole consideration' given by Marshall in return for the promise to pay renewal commission (Court of Appeal applying *Bennett v Bennett* [1952] 1 KB 249). The consideration Marshall had given for the covenants was procuring the business for his then employer prior to termination of employment, not the acceptance of the covenant. Both courts stressed the importance of looking at the substance of the consideration, not the form of the agreement, and Millet LJ warned against 'attempts by parties to disguise their true intentions by artificial stratagems': see paragraph 20.

11.22 For other recent cases in which severance has been considered see *Client Entertainment Services Ltd v Cowley* (unreported 19 December 1997 Lexis). In that case a non solicitation clause defined the protected pool of customers as not only those with whom Cowley had had dealings but also those whom Cowley had 'knowledge of'. The effect of including within the protected pool those customers of whom Cowley had knowledge would have rendered the covenant unenforceable. However, the court was prepared to sever the reference to those customers thereby leaving an enforceable covenant. Compare *Scully UK Ltd v Lee* [1998] IRLR 259 where the Court of Appeal found that an invalid area covenant could not be cured by severing the offending words.

11.23 Severance is applied more readily in the case of vendor/purchaser covenants: *Ronbar Enterprises Ltd v Green* [1954] 1 WLR 815, distinguishing *Attwood v Lamont*. However, even in the case of employer/employee covenants the Court of Appeal has now confirmed that once the two conditions set out in paragraph 11.18 are satisfied it is not then a matter for the court's discretion to decide whether to treat the covenants as separate: *T Lucas & Co Ltd v Mitchell* [1974] Ch 129.

11.24 Express severance clauses – Often the employer will include an express provision seeking to permit him to rely on the good parts of a restrictive covenant in the event that parts are found to be bad. Such clauses merely express what is the common law in any event; see for example: *Hinton & Higgs (UK) Ltd v Murphy and Valentine* [1989] IRLR 519 (Court of Session) – although the clause in that case also included a provision for reducing the period of the covenant, which is not permissible. The more elaborate severance clauses sometimes found in employment contracts, which purport to confer on the court the power to rewrite the contract by substituting such reasonable periods of time (or area) as the court thinks appropriate, are ineffective *Living Design (Home Improvement) Ltd v Davidson* [1994] IRLR 69 (Court of Session Outer House). Arguably such clauses might even render all the restrictive covenants the subject of such an elaborate clause void for uncertainty, but this seems too extravagant a view.

2(c)(vii) MISCELLANEOUS RULES

11.25 Contra proferentem – This rule applies only in cases of ambiguity where other rules of construction do not assist. The substance of the rule is that where the ambiguity can be removed by construing the contract against the originator (or proferens) that will be done *Doe d Davies v Williams* (1788) 1 Hy Bl 25. Sometimes the rule is said to be that the ambiguity will be resolved against the party seeking to rely on the contractual term but strictly speaking that is incorrect unless that person is also the 'originator' of the term. In the context of this book difficult issues can arise where, although the requirement for the covenants in dispute originates from the ex-employer, the actual wording was subject to detailed negotiations and the final version was drafted by the ex-employee's solicitor. Does the contra proferentem rule apply in those circumstances? In our view the answer should be yes because it will be the employer's interests that have driven the inclusion of the covenants in the contract. Indeed there is some support for that view: see *Paperlight Ltd and Others v Swinton Group Ltd* [1998] CLC 1667 at 1673B, although somewhat surprisingly there is no other authority on the point.

11.26 Rectification of mistakes – In limited circumstances where, as a result of a mistake, a written contract does not accurately reflect the intention of the parties, a court has the power to cure that mistake by amending, or rectifying, the wording of the contract, thereby ensuring that the parties' intentions are implemented. Rectification is available where:

● By reason of a mistake common to both parties the written contract does not represent their previous oral understanding: *Burroughes v Abbott* [1922] 1 Ch 86; *Joscelyne v Nissen* [1970] 2 QB 86;

● Only one party (A) is mistaken about the written agreement but the other party (B) knows of the mistake and fails to draw it to the attention of (A) and it would be inequitable to allow (B) to insist on the agreement as written being enforced: *Thomas Bates & Son Ltd v Wyndham's (Lingerie) Ltd* [1981] 1 WLR 505;

● A purely clerical error has been made.

Rectification is not available to deal with points which the parties have simply failed to address and on which they have no common intention: *Harlow Development Corporation v Kingsgate (Clothing Productions)* (1973) 226 Estates Gazette 1960.

11.27   Only mistakes of fact, not law, can be rectified: *Jervis v Howle* and *Talke Colliery Co Ltd* [1937] Ch 67, and the burden of proving the mistake is on the party seeking rectification: *Tucker v Bennett* (1888) 38 Ch D 1. Where rectification is sought in the case of a unilateral mistake it is necessary to show actual knowledge of the mistake; suspicion alone is insufficient: *Agip SpA v Navigazione Alta Italia SpA* [1984] 1 Lloyds Rep 353.

11.28   To obtain rectification it is not necessary to show that there was a concluded contract prior to the written contract of which rectification is being sought. However, there must have been a continuing common intention regarding the particular provision to the moment of execution manifested by an 'outward expression of accord': *Joscelyne v Nissen* [1970] 2 QB 86. The parole evidence rule does not apply in an application to rectify a document: *Lovell and Christmas Ltd v Wall* (1911) 104 LT 85. In an application to rectify, the burden of proof is on the party seeking rectification and he must produce convincing proof (*Joscelyne v Nissen* [1970]) of the inaccuracy of the initial document and the accuracy of the proposed rectified document: *Fowler v Fowler* (1859) 4 De G & J 250.

11.29   It is a ground for refusing rectification that the parties cannot be restored to the position they were in before the contract of which rectification is sought, but restoration to substantially the same position is probably adequate: *Beauchamp (Earl) v Winn* (1873) LR 6 HL 223.

11.30   With the exception of clerical errors the instances of rectification being an available option in the case of restrictive covenants are likely to be rare. However, it is a power which the court has and which should in appropriate cases be given proper consideration rather than being dismissed out of hand.

11.31   Business sale agreements – Covenants in Business Sale Agreements are traditionally easier to enforce: see paragraph 9.8.

2(d)   Nature of business/role of the employee/likely competitive activity

11.32   It is imperative to have a full understanding of each of these factors before any drafting is undertaken. One of the most common problems encountered by those seeking to enforce restrictive covenants is that the covenants simply do not reflect the facts accurately and consequently provide only limited protection or, worse still, none at all. For example, if the ex-employee was a senior employee in possession of a considerable amount of confidential information concerning clients but had direct contact with only a very few of them, a covenant prohibiting him from dealing with customers with whom he had direct contact whilst employed would achieve little. Similarly, a covenant which prohibited an ex-employee from competing within a radius of five miles of an address of his employer at which he had never worked would not provide any protection at all for the employer. To avoid these types of pitfalls it is critical that the draftsmen of the covenant undertake a fully comprehensive fact-gathering exercise at the outset. To assist in that exercise, set out in paragraphs 11.33 to 11.36, is an Information Checklist which identifies the types of information which will be needed. One word of caution, the Checklist is not, and cannot be, exhaustive and should be used intelligently rather than slavishly followed. If a draftsman of covenants thinks he needs more information he should ask for it. It is better to err on the side of caution at the drafting stage rather than draft defective covenants.

Information checklist

2(d)(i) NATURE OF BUSINESS

11.33 The key facts which must be established in relation to each company/organisation for which the employee is to perform services are:

(a) The nature of the business and whether it includes types of activity different from those in which the employee will be involved;
(b) Who the relevant customers will be, the regularity with which they place orders/require services, whether they also use other suppliers/providers of services for their requirements; the approximate number of customers and whether they are readily identifiable;
(c) Who the relevant suppliers will be, and any relevant information relating to them, for example whether there is any scarcity of any particular item supplied to the employer;
(d) Where (geographically) the business in which the employee will be involved is carried on;
(e) Whether in future there is likely to be any material change in the type of business, relevant customers or suppliers, or in the area where the business in which the employee is involved will be carried on;
(f) How the employer's employment structure works in terms of grading and salary arrangements.

2(d)(ii) ROLE OF THE EMPLOYEE

11.34 The key facts that must be established are:

(a) The identity of the employer;
(b) The employee's job title, status and basic remuneration package;
(c) What the employee's duties will be: if he is to have a job description then a copy, in final form, should be obtained;
(d) Whether the employee's skills are very specialised or of general application, and the employee's career history;
(e) Where (geographically) the employee will perform his duties;
(f) Whether the employee will be required to perform duties for any other company or organisation connected with the employer, for example a subsidiary or associated company.

(g) Whether the employee will have direct contact with customers, actual or prospective. If he will have direct contact, with what types and numbers of customer, how regularly and for what reason;

(h) Whether the employee will have direct contact with suppliers. If he will have direct contact, with what types and numbers of suppliers, how regularly and for what reason;

(i) Whether the employee will be responsible for supervising other employees: if he will, the same information which is needed for the employee will be required for each employee he supervises. In addition, where those employees already have contracts of employment copies of those contracts will be needed to see how the various restrictive covenants might mesh together;

(j) The identity of other key employees/personnel with whom the employee will work. As in (i) the same information which is needed for the employees together with their contracts of employment will be required;

(k) What trade secrets or confidential information the employee will be privy to and, where relevant, the 'shelf life' of that information;

(l) Whether the employee will be a director under the Companies Act 1985;

(m) The length of notice required to terminate the contract and whether there is to be a garden leave clause in the contract;

(n) How long the employee is likely to stay with the employer and whether there is likely to be any change in his role during that period.

2(d)(iii) LIKELY COMPETITIVE ACTIVITY

11.35 To draft restrictive covenants which will protect the employer it is essential to understand from where the real potential for competition is likely to come. The employer will be the person best placed to judge this and in every case he must be required to give clear and specific instructions. In addition he must be asked to justify those instructions by explaining why a particular competitive activity is likely to cause him real harm. If the employer is unable to justify his concerns when the covenant is being drafted, that will normally be a strong indication that there is no sound basis for the covenant.

11.36 In some instances the competitive activity which the employer anticipates may be very specific. For example, in *Littlewoods Organisation Ltd v Harris* [1978] 1 All ER 1026 Littlewoods perceived the real threat as Harris joining their arch-rival Great Universal Stores, hence the area covenant prohibiting Harris joining any part of that group of companies. In other cases the likely competitive activity may be more general, for example the possibility that the employee builds up a customer following from the employer's existing customers so that were he to join another organisation, those customers would transfer their business with him.

3. Drafting the covenants

11.37 This is a two-stage process. First the draftsman must decide what types of covenant he is going to include, and secondly he must determine the ambit of each covenant (see the case studies in the Appendix to this Chapter).

3(a) Types of covenant

11.38 The different types of key covenant are listed at paragraph 9.22; in summary they are:

- Area covenants;
- Non-dealing covenants;
- Non-solicitation covenants;
- Non-enticement covenants;
- Confidentiality covenants.

The drafting of trade secrets and confidentiality covenants is dealt with in paragraph 4.30. Usually the only key decision the draftsman will have to make is whether there is sufficient justification to include an area covenant. That question is considered at paragraphs 9.23 to 9.26 and 10.29.

11.39 Ambit of each covenant – This is a far more difficult question and one to which the draftsman needs to give very careful thought, taking into account the rules on enforceability set out in Chapter 9. Employers almost invariably want to have very wide covenants to catch every eventuality. While ultimately the employer's wishes must prevail, the draftsman should endeavour to curb what have been described as the wilder extravagances of the employer and to draft the covenants as narrowly as is consistent with providing the employer with protection while remaining within the bounds of probable enforceability. Where the employer rejects this approach the likelihood is that the covenants will not be enforceable and the draftsman should advise the employer of this in writing. This is important for two reasons: first, so that there can be no question of any misunderstanding, and secondly to avoid any negligence actions as and when the courts refuse to uphold the covenant.

3(b) Ambit of the specific covenants

3(b)(i) AREA COVENANTS

11.40 There are three key factors: geographic area, duration and prohibited activity.

11.41 Area – The factors to be taken into account in fixing the geographical area are considered in paragraphs 10.23 to 10.28. As those paragraphs illustrate, because there are an increasing number of businesses that are genuinely international, if not global, the definition of area is a less significant topic than hitherto. Where the business is international or global the courts accept the 'area' should reflect that state of affairs. However, many purely domestic businesses remain, which draw their customers from a more local base. For those businesses the definition of area is critically important and the factors referred to in paragraphs 10.23 to 10.28 as well as the following issues need to be taken into account. Care should always be taken to include a degree of flexibility within the definition of the area to avoid the covenant being rendered obsolete by, for example, the employer moving premises, or expanding into new geographical areas. In addition, the area should be defined with precision, for example where a radius of say five miles is used there should be a stated point from which the radius is measured. The covenant should not say 'within five miles of Leeds'.

11.42 Duration – Enforcing area covenants is notoriously difficult and the draftsman should always choose the shortest period possible. General points on duration are discussed at paragraphs 10.5 to 10.8.

11.43 Prohibited activity – In all cases the prohibited activity should be clearly set out and should be no more than is absolutely necessary. Whilst the courts have used the rules of construction to cut down an apparently excessive prohibition in order to give effect to an area covenant: *Marion White Ltd v Francis* [1972] 3 All ER 857 and *Clarke v Newland* [1991] 1 All ER 397, the draftsman should never rely on the court to do so.

11.44 Two particular ways in which the prohibited activity may be sensibly limited are by avoiding blanket bans and by the use of provisos. So, for example, instead of saying that the employee is prohibited from working for Competitor A, the clause should provide that the employee is prohibited from working for Competitor A in the capacity in which he is currently employed. (However, this may not be an acceptable solution where the interest to be protected is confidential information and the justification for the covenant is that it would be impossible to protect that information other than by an area covenant.) Similarly, particular activities can be expressly carved out from an otherwise wide prohibition by provisos. For example, common provisos are that the employee is not prohibited from working in the public sector or not prohibited from working for certain named organisations. In addition, where the employer has several different types of businesses and the employee was not engaged in all of them the covenant should only prohibit the employee from working in a business which competes with the employer's business in which the employee has been involved.

3(b)(ii) Non-solicitation/non-dealing covenants

11.45 The key factors are duration, the definition of the customer/supplier and prohibited activity.

11.46 Duration – In practice the period of these types of covenants is scrutinised less than the period of an area covenant. However, the court has no power to reduce the period the parties agree and therefore the period should be selected carefully taking into account matters such as the regularity with which customers place orders/require services. Duration is considered in more detail in paragraphs 10.5 to 10.8 and 10.65.

11.47 Defintion of the customer/supplier – Which customers can legitimately be the subject of restrictive covenants and the basis on which they can constitute a legitimate interest of the employer are discussed in Chapter 10. While it is not easy to draw clear conclusions from the authorities the following are our suggested guidelines:

- It must be clear what is meant by the term 'customer'. In many cases it is, but there are instances where it is not, for example, who is the 'customer' of a recruitment consultant: the individual whom the consultant places with a new employer or the new employer? If there is any doubt the term should be defined to avoid subsequent dispute.
- The covenant should not include anyone who becomes a customer after the employment terminates – the only exception to this is where there is

a separate covenant dealing with prospective customers.

- Customers should be defined as such within a specified period prior to termination (or, where a garden leave provision is included prior to the date any such provision is exercised) the period being fixed by reference to the 'customer cycle', that is the intervals at which the customer normally requires goods or services, for example, in the case of an insurance contract it will be annual.
- If prospective customers are to be included the term should be carefully defined to catch only those persons on whom the employer has expended time and effort and consequently money in an attempt to secure their custom. The covenant should also appear in a separate sub-clause to facilitate severance if needs be.
- The link between the employee and the customer, either through direct dealings or indirectly through, for example, supervision of other employees with whom the customer had direct dealings or through access to confidential information about the customer, should be apparent from the covenant.

Where the covenant is against solicitation or dealing with suppliers the same basic points apply, modified to take account of the different relationship.

11.48 Prohibited activity – Where a covenant does not expressly define the type of business the employee is prohibited from soliciting/transacting with the customer, the court may nonetheless interpret the covenant to be limited to that part of the employer's business in which the employee is engaged: *G W Plowman v Ash* [1964] 3 All ER 10 and *Business Seating (Renovations) Ltd v Broad* [1989] ICR 729, see paragraph 11.12. However, the draftsman should never rely on the court taking this approach; it did not do so, for example, in *Greer v Sketchley Ltd* [1979] IRLR 445 (CA) nor in *Scully UK Ltd v Lee* [1998] IRLR 259 (CA). The draftsman should always define the precise activity which is to be prohibited.

3(b)(iii) Non-enticement covenants

11.49 The key factors are duration, defining the staff, and the prohibited activity.

11.50 Duration – The difficulty is that there is no real yardstick by which to set a period in this type of covenant. Effectively what the employer is seeking to do is to prevent the ex-employee using the knowledge he has acquired of the skills and aptitudes of other members of staff and capitalising on the working relationship he has built up with them. Since the latter relationship will obviously weaken as time passes, lengthy periods are unlikely to be reasonable and normally the absolute maximum should be twelve months. In practice, the enticement of staff is something which tends to take place either before employment has ended or shortly thereafter. It is most common in occupations where staff work in teams and consequently where other members of the team are necessary to support the key member of the team.

11.51 Defining the staff – In this section we have deliberately used the word 'staff' rather than employees. The reason is that the employer may have one or more independent contractors working for him who are significant in the context of the employer's business and whom he may therefore want to try to retain for himself by the covenant. Where the poaching of independent contractors is to be precluded by covenant it is prudent either to include a separate covenant dealing only with independent contractors or, at the very least, prefix the reference to independent contractors in the covenant with a disjunctive 'or'.

11.52   In the case of both employees and independent contractors the definition should cover only those who were employed/engaged at the same time as the ex-employee (that is, not individuals who were employed/engaged after the ex-employee left). The covenant should be limited to only those employees/ independent contractors the employer really needs to protect. Precisely who that will be will depend on the particular facts but usually it will not extend to the entire workforce and often junior and support staff can, and should, be excluded from the scope of the covenant. In defining the protected pool we do not advocate the use of general descriptions such as 'senior employees'. While this and a similar formulation have been accepted by the courts: *Dawnay Day & Co Ltd v De Braconier D'Alphen* [1997] IRLR 422 (CA) and *Alliance Paper Group plc v Prestwich* [1996] IRLR 25 are both cases where the employees had behaved reprehensibly and the courts were keen to show their disapproval by upholding the covenant. Against a different factual background it is possible that these types of general phrase could be found insufficiently certain. Consequently, in our opinion the description should be as specific as possible. Often it will be, for example, the more senior employees/independent contractors the employer wishes to protect and definitions linked to grading or salary structure may be appropriate, subject to allowing some degree of flexibility to cover the possibility of change. In addition, the covenant should normally require there to be a particular link between the ex-employee and those he is to be prohibited from poaching. The most common basis for the link is material contract or dealings during the course of the ex-employee's employment or perhaps during the final 12 months of his employment or where the employee may be sent on garden leave the 12 months immediately before his garden leave starts. However, other formulae may be considered, for example defining the protected pool by reference to direct/indirect reports to the ex-employee or the business unit for which the ex-employee was responsible.

11.53   Prohibited activity – There are various degrees of prohibition the employer can select. In a similar way to covenants taken to protect customers, the primary distinction is between a prohibition on enticement and one preventing dealing in the sense of not employing/engaging or arranging employment for the services of the ex-employer's staff. The employer needs to decide whether he wants to attempt to prohibit both types of activity and then define them with precision. As a note of caution, we remain unconvinced that the 'non-dealing' formulation will find favour with the courts. That view is supported by obiter comments in the first instance decision of Walker J in *Dawnay Day & Co Ltd v De Braconier D'Alphen* [1997] IRLR 285. In that case the service agreements of the defendants included a 'non-employment' covenant. Although *Dawnay Day* did not seek to rely on the covenant Walker J said that, had they done so, he would have declined to uphold the clause as an unreasonable restraint of trade (paragraph 81). When *Dawnay Day* reached the Court of Appeal one of the factors that Evans LJ took into account in upholding the reasonableness of the non-enticement covenant was the impact it would have on the protected pool. On the negative side he concluded that it would restrict their opportunities 'to learn about future employment possibilities for themselves' but that was outweighed by the fact that their ability to make their own enquiries through 'advertisements and other channels of communication in the normal way was not restricted at all': see paragraph 47. Clearly where the prohibition would affect a member of the protected pool being employed by another employer the balance changes somewhat. The problem becomes particularly acute where, because of the field in which the employee works, there are only a limited number of potential employers.

3(c) General drafting points

11.54 Preambles – Preambles to covenants should be used only with caution. Whilst they may serve as a useful aide-memoire to what was in the mind of the employer, and possibly also the employee, at the time the covenants were entered into, the covenants must be construed in the light of any preamble, which may prove to be unduly limiting: see *Office Angels Ltd v Rainer Thomas and O'Connor* [1991] IRLR 214 (CA) at paragraphs 39 to 43, where the preamble was one of the reasons why an area covenant was held to be unenforceable.

11.55 Definitions – Definitions of particular terms such as 'customer' and 'prohibited activity' may make the covenants more readable but again should be used with caution, particularly where the defined term appears in more than one covenant. The court's powers of severance would not, in our view, permit the severance of part of the definition for one covenant but not another although there may be arguments to the contrary based on *British Reinforced Concrete Co Ltd v Schelff* [1921] 2 Ch 563: see paragraph 11.18.

11.56 Flexibility – As a general rule covenants should be drafted to include some flexibility, allowing for changes in the facts. Although very specific covenants are the best if they are kept up to date, invariably they are not, and in addition there is the problem that the employee's consent is required for any change.

11.57 No covenants during employment – Covenants should not be expressed to run during as well as after employment. The interests the employer is entitled to protect in these two periods are quite different.

11.58 Garden leave offset – The period of the covenants should arguably be reduced by the period for which the employee is sent on garden leave but see *Credit Suisse Asset Management Ltd v Armstrong & Others* [1996] IRLR 450. For a full discussion on this point see paragraph 4.84.

11.59 Indirect activities – The ex-employee should always be prevented from carrying out the prohibited activities not only directly but also indirectly. In the absence of such a provision the ex-employee will simply ensure that any activities he is banned from taking part in are carried out by a third party not caught by the covenant, for example the new employer.

11.60 Repudiatory breach – Attempts to provide that the covenants survive a repudiatory breach of contract are ineffective: *Rock Refrigeration Ltd v Jones & Seward Refrigeration Ltd* [1996] IRLR 675 (CA). In the words of Simon Brown LJ at paragraph 26 to the extent such provisions are included 'they are merely writ in water' and unenforceable under the *General Billposting* principle. For an explanation of the *General Billposting* principle see paragraphs 8.19 to 8.24. However, the mere inclusion of such a provision will not of itself render restrictive covenants unreasonable and unenforceable: *Rock*. The line of authorities beginning with *Briggs v Oates* [1990] IRLR 472 and including *Living Design (Home Improvements) Ltd v Davidson* [1994] IRLR 69; *PR Consultants Ltd v Mann* [1996] IRLR 188 and *D v M* [1996] IRLR 192 had, according to the Court of Appeal in *Rock*, proceeded on the erroneous assumption that the ex-employee remains bound by restrictive covenants after an accepted repudiatory breach. In fact the ex-employee is not so bound and therefore there is nothing to which to apply the reasonableness principle. Consequently, while there is now no practical advantage in including this type of provision in restrictive covenants, those seeking to enforce covenants which purport to survive a repudiatory breach may breath a sigh of relief that all the covenants will not fail on that ground alone. These comments are subject to only one caveat which is whether the *General Billposting* principle holds good. In our view it does, but for a discussion on the issue see paragraphs 8.20 to 8.22.

11.61 Protection for 'Group Companies' – Where the covenants are designed to protect the interests of the employing company and other companies, for example subsidiaries, thought must be given to how the covenants will be enforced on behalf of the subsidiary. Two basic options are available which may be used separately or together. The contract can provide that the benefit of the covenants is held on trust for the subsidiaries by the parent employing company and/or includes an obligation on the part of the employee that, if requested to do so, he will enter into separate covenants with each subsidiary in the terms of the covenants he has given to his employer. The difficulty with the latter formulation is that covenants in the same terms may not be wholly appropriate. However, in our view any attempt to retain flexibility, for example by framing the obligation as one to enter into covenants in substantially the same form, or worse still 'an appropriate form' is unlikely to be legally enforceable. It may nonetheless be a commercial lever to achieve the employer's goals. For further discussion on this subject see paragraphs 9.17 to 9.19.

11.62 Acknowledgement of reasonableness – There is no practical purpose in including within the covenants an acknowledgement by the parties that they are reasonable. Such a provision was considered by the Court of Session (Outer House) in *Hinton & Higgs v Murphy and Valentine* [1989] IRLR 519 where it was regarded as 'probably an illegitimate attempt to oust the jurisdiction of the court' Lord Dervaird at paragraph 4. In contrast, where the employee has had separate legal advice in connection with entering into the covenants that is worth recording in the contract. Strictly, this fact should not affect enforceability of the covenants. However, in practice, it can assist an employer in obtaining an injunction where the ex-employee is attempting to run highly questionable arguments on the interpretation of the covenant. In those types of cases, the courts often take the view that the ex-employee knew full well the import of the covenants at the time he entered into them. By running disingenuous arguments on interpretation at a later stage that simply reinforces the courts' resolve to hold the ex-employee to his bargain. Consequently, including a reference to the fact that the ex-employee had separate legal advice is a useful reminder of a potential argument that could otherwise be overlooked.

11.63 Note of rationale – Once the covenants are drafted, the draftsman (who is a solicitor) should prepare an aide-memoire for his file setting out the rationale for each covenant and, where he is of the view that any covenant is unenforceable or borderline, he should give that advice in writing to avoid any subsequent negligence action.

3(d) Indemnities

11.64 Where an individual terminates his employment with his existing employer to join a competitor and anticipates that his (then) previous employer may threaten/institute proceedings against him, seeking either to prevent him joining the competitor or limiting his activities for that competitor, it is not unusual for the employee to seek an indemnity from his new employer against the risk he is taking. The indemnity sought may be limited to the costs and expenses the employee incurs in defence of any threatened or actual proceedings instituted by the former employer or may extend to cover any costs and/or damages which the employee agrees to pay or is ordered to pay to the former employer.

11.65 Despite the increasing frequency of such indemnities there is a paucity of authority on their validity. From such authorities as there are the principles that can be extracted are as follows:

- An indemnity will not be invalid on grounds of maintenance even where it contemplates the instituting or defence of an action, provided it is given in the legitimate defence of a business, commercial or other common interest: *British Cash and Parcel Conveyors Ltd v Lamson Store Service Co Ltd* [1908] 1 KB 1006. In *British Cash* the indemnity was given to customers of a manufacturer and indemnified them against any action by a rival manufacturer for using apparatus by the giver of the indemnity.
- An indemnity against civil or criminal liability resulting from commission of a crime is unenforceable: *Haseldine v Hosken* [1933] 1 KB 822; *Colburn v Patmore* (1834) 1 CrM & R 73.
- An indemnity given against liability resulting from the commission of a tort may be unenforceable, depending on the nature of the act and the circumstances of its commission: *Lister v Romford Ice and Cold Storage Co Ltd* [1957] AC 555.
- There is no authority as to the position of the validity of an indemnity against a liability resulting from a commission of a breach of contract. However, where the giving of the indemnity itself amounts to or is connected with a deliberate commission of a tort (in the context of the sort of indemnities we are here considering that is highly likely), for example the tort of inducing a breach of contract or of conspiracy to injure, then in our view it is arguable the indemnity is therefore unenforceable on the principle above.

11.66 It should be noted that in *British Cash*, although the claimant's action included a claim that the defendant had induced a breach of contract, that matter was disposed of at first instance where the judge ruled there was no evidence on which the allegation could be put to the jury. Due to the uncertainty of the enforceability of indemnities in the context in which we are here considering them, an employee should exercise considerable caution in the taking of such an indemnity, and should always bear in mind the possibility that the indemnity may subsequently be ruled to be unenforceable. Both the seeker and giver of any indemnity should also give careful thought as to whether the indemnity should be included in any document (on paper or otherwise) bearing in mind that such a document would become subject to disclosure in any subsequent proceedings.

Case studies

Case study 1: Excel Copiers Limited and Brian Thomas

(a) Facts

The lettering used below follows the numbering in the information checklist in paragraphs 11.33 to 11.36.

(a)(i) NATURE OF BUSINESS

(a) Excel Copiers Limited is a company engaged in the sale and servicing of photocopiers. It has a wholly owned subsidiary, Office Supplies & Sales Limited, which sells office stationery. In practice Excel Copiers Limited and Office Supplies & Sales Limited are run as though they are a single company using the same regional and national management teams.

(b) The relevant customers will be the customers of Excel Copiers Limited and of Office Supplies & Sales Limited who have any business premises in the South East of England (comprising Kent, Surrey and Sussex). The relevant customers of Excel Copiers Limited fall into two categories: occasional customers who simply buy a photocopier and continuing customers who, having bought a machine, enter into an annual service contract. The position is much the same for Office Supplies & Sales Limited: some customers are occasional, others have annual supply contracts. The majority of customers of both Excel Copiers Limited and Office Supplies & Sales Limited use primarily those companies for their relevant requirements.

(c) Excel Copiers Limited sell three different makes of photocopier. Of these one, manufactured by Easy Copy Inc, is sold (but not serviced) by them in the UK under an exclusive distribution agreement. Over the last ten years revenue deriving from the sale and servicing of Easy Copy's machines has consistently accounted for 50% or more of Excel Copier Limited's turnover. The other two makes of photocopier are sold under non-exclusive distribution agreements. Office Supplies & Sales Limited has a multitude of different suppliers.

(d) Excel Copiers Limited and Office Supplies & Sales Limited operate throughout the UK. Both companies are run on the same regional basis.

(e) There is a possibility that Excel Copiers Limited will extend their operations into Europe although it is unlikely that they will open offices outside the UK.

(f) Neither Excel Copiers nor Office Sales and Supplies Ltd have a formal grading structure. They do however have very distinct salary bands. The most senior employees are in Band A and the most junior in Band J. The majority of support staff will be in Bands E to J. Bands C and D apply exclusively to Salesmen and Service Engineers. Brian Thomas and other Regional Directors are in Band B. Basic annual salaries for salary Bands A to D are as follows:

Band A: £50,001 +;
Band B: £42,001 - £50,000;
Band C: £38,001 - £42,000;
Band D: £32,001 - £38,000.

(a)(ii) ROLE OF THE EMPLOYEE

(a) The employer will be Excel Copiers Limited.
(b) Brian Thomas' job title will be Regional Director – South East England – reporting to the Managing Director. His remuneration package will be £45,000 with a car, private health insurance, pension scheme and the right to participate in a profit-share scheme.
(c) Brian Thomas' duties will be the co-ordination of the businesses of Excel Copiers Limited and Office Supplies & Sales Limited in the South East of England with particular emphasis on acquiring significant new business. He is not to have a job description.
(d) Brian Thomas' skills are essentially those of a salesman and a manager. He has previously held similar positions in the motor trade, in retail clothing and most recently with a company which sells and services facsimile machines.
(e) Brian Thomas will be based at offices in Guildford but required to travel throughout the South East of England.
(f) Brian Thomas will be required to perform services for Excel Copiers Limited and Office Supplies & Sales Limited.
(g) Brian Thomas' direct contact with customers will be limited, his role being more a co-ordinating and strategy role. Whilst having overall responsibility for sales and servicing he will only have regular contact with around the twenty most important customers in the South East Region. He will, however, have prime responsibility for significant prospective customers being those whose potential initial business is worth £20,000 in the case of Excel Copiers Limited or £10,000 in the case of Office Supplies & Sales Limited.
(h) Brian Thomas's only expected contact with suppliers will be with the suppliers of the photocopiers to Excel Copiers Limited. Because the Chief Executive of Easy Copy Inc is Brian Thomas's uncle, with whom he has a good relationship, it is proposed to put him in charge of liaison with Easy Copy Inc and the negotiation from time to time of any variations to the exclusive distribution agreement.
(i) Brian Thomas will be responsible for supervising the sales and servicing staff of Excel Copiers Limited in the South East Region and the sales staff of Office Supplies & Sales Limited in the South East Region. Each of those members of staff will have direct contact with customers but not suppliers, all ordering being dealt with through the central supplies department. The regularity of contact with customers will depend on the type of customer, but customers other than occasional ones would normally be visited once per month. The employment documentation for the sales and servicing staff is minimal and is limited to a statement under Section 1 Employment Rights Act 1996.
(j) The key personnel Brian Thomas will work with are the sales and servicing staff of Excel Copiers Limited in the South East Region; the sales staff of

Office Supplies & Sales Limited in the South East Region and, on a much less regular basis, the other Regional Directors. There are no relevant independent contractors. The Regional Directors do have contracts of employment but they do not include restrictive covenants.

(k) There are no trade secrets. Excel Copiers Limited regard the following information as confidential: the terms of the distribution agreement with Easy Copy Inc; details of the new product lines from Easy Copy Inc and the two other manufacturing companies whose photocopiers Excel Copiers Limited sell; the identity, contact names and requirements of the South East Region customers, including prospective customers. Thomas has no access to information relating to the other regions' customers (other than financial information about volume of business which does not identify the customer), pricing policy generally and special deals negotiated with particular South East Region customers.

(l) Brian Thomas will not be a director under the Companies Act 1985.

(m) To terminate the contract either party must give not less than three months' notice. Excel Copiers Limited have expressly reserved the right to send Brian Thomas on garden leave and they have not reserved the right to make a payment in lieu of notice.

(n) Excel Copiers Limited have no firm idea how long Brian Thomas may stay with them or whether his role may change. If the European expansion goes ahead there is a possibility that Brian Thomas could be promoted, join the Board and take responsibility for Germany since he is a fluent German speaker and has previously worked in Germany.

(a)(iii) LIKELY COMPETITIVE ACTIVITY

Excel have two key concerns, firstly that Brian Thomas may seek to obtain for himself or a competitor the exclusive distribution agreement with Easy Copy Inc. Secondly, the possibility of Brian Thomas setting up in competition or joining an existing competitor and concentrating on the sale and servicing of photocopiers and/or the supply of office stationery. Excel are keen to have an area covenant to discourage this possibility.

(b) Drafting

In the covenants Excel Copiers Limited is referred to as 'the Company' and Brian Thomas as 'the Executive'.

1.1 Within this Clause 1 the following words shall have the following meanings:

'Employee' shall mean any employee of the Company or Office Supplies & Sales Ltd remunerated on Salary Band D or above or on such equivalent salary bands as the Company may adopt from time to time.

'Relevant Period' shall mean the twelve month period ending with the Termination Date or if the Company exercises its right under Clause **[insert clause number of garden leave provision]** the twelve month period ending with the date on which the Company first exercises those rights.

'Restricted Customer' shall mean any person, firm, company or other organisation who was at any time in the Relevant Period a customer of the Company or of Office Supplies & Sales Limited.

'Prohibited Business' shall mean any business or activity carried on by the Company or Office Supplies & Sales Limited at the Termination Date or at any time in the Relevant Period in which the Executive shall have been directly concerned in the course of his employment at any time in the Relevant Period.

'Prospective Customer' shall mean any person, firm, company or other organisation who was at the Termination Date negotiating with the Company or with Office Supplies & Sales Limited with a view to dealing with the Company or Office Supplies & Sales Limited as a customer.

'Protected Supplier' shall mean any supplier of the Company with whom the Executive shall have had material dealings in the course of his employment during the Relevant Period including, but not limited to, Easy Copy Inc.

'Termination Date' shall mean the date of termination of the Executive's employment with the Company.

1.2   The Executive shall not so as to compete with the Company or Office Supplies & Sales Limited during the period of twelve months after the Termination Date directly or indirectly on his own account or on behalf of or in conjunction with any person, firm or company or other organisation canvass or solicit or by any other means seek to conduct Prohibited Business with or conduct Prohibited Business with any Restricted Customer with whom the Executive shall have had material dealings in the course of his duties hereunder at any time in the Relevant Period or with whom and to the knowledge of the Executive any employee of the Company or Office Supplies & Sales Limited under the Executive's control shall have had material dealings in the course of their duties to the Company or Office Supplies & Sales Limited in the Relevant Period.

1.3   The Executive shall not so as to compete with the Company or Office Supplies & Sales Ltd during the period of twelve months after the Termination Date directly or indirectly on his own account or on behalf of or in conjunction with any person, firm, company or other organisation canvass or solicit or by any other means seek to conduct Prohibited Business with or conduct Prohibited Business with any Prospective Customer with whom the Executive shall have had material dealings in the course of his duties hereunder at any time in the Relevant Period or with whom and to the knowledge of the Executive any employee of the Company or Office Supplies & Sales Limited under the Executive's control shall have had material dealings in the course of their duties to the Company or Office Supplies & Sales Limited in the Relevant Period.

1.4   The Executive shall not during the period of twelve months after the Termination Date directly or indirectly induce or seek to induce any Employee of the Company or Office Supplies & Sales Limited engaged in the Prohibited Business who was such an Employee at the Termination Date and with whom the Executive shall during the Relevant Period have had material dealings in the course of his duties hereunder to leave the employment of the Company or Office Supplies & Sales Limited whether or not this would be a breach of contract on the part of the Employee.

1.5   The Executive shall not during the period of twelve months after the Termination Date directly or indirectly seek to entice away from the Company or otherwise solicit or interfere with the relationship between the Company and any Protected Supplier.

1.6   The period of each of the above restrictions shall be reduced by the period, if any, during which the Company exercises its rights under Clause **[insert clause number of garden leave provision].**

1.7   The restrictions in this Clause are held by the Company for itself and on trust for Office Supplies & Sales Limited and shall be enforceable by the Company on behalf of Office Supplies & Sales Limited as though it were a party to this Agreement. The Executive shall at the request and cost of the Company enter into a direct agreement with Office Supplies & Sales Limited whereby he will accept restrictions in the same form as those included in this Clause 1.

1.8   These restrictions are entered into by the Company and the Executive after having been separately legally advised.

1.9   Each of the restrictions contained in this Clause 1 is intended to be separate and severable. In the event that any of the restrictions shall be held void but would be valid if part of the wording thereof were deleted such restriction shall apply with such deletion as may be necessary to make it valid and effective.

(For a precedent of a confidentiality covenant see para 4.30.)

(c) Rationale for the covenants

1.   The covenants do not include an area covenant because this is a classic case where the employer's interests are adequately protected by a non-solicitation/dealing covenant. The likelihood of an area covenant being upheld is extremely remote. If, notwithstanding this, Excel Copiers Limited were to insist on such a covenant, a suitable draft would be as follows:

> The Executive shall not so as to compete with the Company or Office Supplies & Sales Limited during the period of twelve months after the Termination Date within the Territory carry on or be directly or indirectly engaged or concerned or interested whether as principal, agent, shareholder, investor, director, employee or otherwise howsoever in any business [or the setting up of any business] engaged in [or which it is intended to be engaged in] any Prohibited Business. For the purpose of this sub-clause acts done by the Executive outside the Territory shall nonetheless be deemed to be done within the Territory where their primary purpose is the obtaining of any Prohibited Business from any person, firm, company or other organisation with business premises within the Territory.

In addition the following definition would be necessary:

Territory: the counties of Kent, Surrey and Sussex.

The covenant is drawn narrowly but would still not in our view be enforceable.

2. The covenants are designed to protect only Excel and Office Supplies & Sales Limited on the basis that there are no plans for new companies in the group. To increase the flexibility of the covenants the words 'or other company in the Group' could be added but a definition of 'Group' would then also be required. As to the question of whether a company may protect the legitimate interests of an associated company see paragraphs 9.17 to 9.20.

3. In the non-solicitation/enticement covenants the period of twelve months has been chosen to ensure that there is adequate protection vis-a-vis customers with annual service agreements or prospective customers about to enter into such an agreement. In some cases an extra month should be added to allow for a grace period during which a customer may effectively be given the benefit of continued services under the original contract; the new contract being backdated to the expiry of the original contract provided the new contract is entered into within one month of the expiry of the original one.

4. In the non-enticement covenant the protected pool of employees has been drawn to exclude the more junior and support staff and to allow a degree of flexibility in the event of change of salary structure. The provision also requires a material link between Thomas and the employees he is not able to poach.

5. 'Prospective Customers' have been separately defined and a separate covenant included in respect of them to ensure that if a Court were to find the covenant in respect of them void there would be no problems with severance.

6. 'Prohibited Business' is limited to activities in which Brian Thomas has been directly concerned, to ensure that the covenant does not become too wide if Excel or Office Supplies & Sales Limited expand into other areas in which Brian Thomas is not involved.

7. 'Protected Supplier' is designed to allow for flexibility but still to highlight the importance of Easy Copy Inc.

8. The covenants provide that credit is given for any period of time spent on garden leave. This prevents any argument that the combined duration of garden leave and the covenants makes the covenants unenforceable.

9. The fact that the covenants are held on behalf of Office Supplies & Sales Limited is recognised and an option is included under which Thomas can be required to enter into direct covenants with that Company. These provisions are included to cover the possibility that instead of focusing on the copying business, Thomas decides to compete with Office Supplies' business and circumvent any potential problems of enforceability, ie that Thomas argues Excel has no interest to protect in Office Supplies' business.

10. The acknowledgement in Clause 1.8 that both parties have been separately legally advised is a useful aide-memoire but little more.

11. The severability provision in Clause 1.7 is limited to severance and is of the sort found to be useful in *Hinton & Higgs (UK) Limited v Murphy and Valentine* [1989] IRLR 519. It does not purport to allow re-writing and therefore avoids any argument that it renders the covenants void for uncertainty.

Case study 2: Smith & Jones HR Services Limited and Ian Simpson

(a) Facts:

The lettering used below follows the numbering in the information checklist in paragraphs 11.33 to 11.36.

(a)(i) NATURE OF BUSINESS

(a) Smith & Jones HR Services Limited is a small company engaged in the business of providing advice on all human resource issues such as the recruitment of staff, career development, disciplinary matters, the termination of employment including redundancy programmes, and Trade Union/ collective issues. The Company has no parent, subsidiary or associated companies.

(b) The customers relevant to the prospective employee, Ian Simpson, will be those allocated to him by the Managing Director. Some will simply require one-off or occasional advice while others will have annual contracts with Smith & Jones HR Services Limited under which the minimum service will be monthly reviews of their human resource position. The majority of customers use only Smith & Jones HR Services Limited for their human resource advice, except where they obtain legal advice from their respective solicitors.

(c) There are no suppliers relevant to the business.

(d) The business is carried on throughout England and Wales.

(e) There are not likely to be any material changes to the information given in points (a) to (d) (inclusive).

(f) As a small company Smith & Jones HR Services Limited has no formal grading or salary structure. The employees essentially divide into HR consultants and support staff.

(a)(ii) ROLE OF THE EMPLOYEE

(a) The employer will be Smith & Jones HR Services Limited.

(b) The employee's job title will be HR Consultant. He will be one of ten HR Consultants reporting directly to the Managing Director. His remuneration package will be a basic salary of £35,000; a commission arrangement under which he could earn up to an additional £35,000, giving potential earnings of £70,000, a car and private health insurance.

(c) Ian Simpson's duties will be providing advice on all human resource issues to the clients of Smith & Jones HR Services Limited allocated to him.

(d) Ian Simpson's skills are specialised to the extent that he has never done anything other than human resource work. He has previously worked as a personnel officer in a multinational company and in the legal department of a major Trade Union.

(e) Ian Simpson will be based in the City of London but required to travel and work at customer's premises throughout England and Wales; work is not allocated on any sort of regional basis.

(f) Ian Simpson will work for only Smith & Jones HR Services Limited.

(g) Ian Simpson will have direct contact with customers. The regularity of contact will vary, depending on the type of customer. In the case of one-off or occasional customers, contact will be as and when advice is requested.

For customers who have annual contracts, the contact will be at least once per month. Ian Simpson will have no contact with prospective customers.

(h) There will be no contact with suppliers.

(i) Ian Simpson will not supervise other employees.

(j) Ian Simpson will work together with various of the other HR consultants of Smith & Jones HR Services Limited, none of whom have any employment documentation other than a very basic offer letter – a typical case of cobblers' children! With regard to job title, Smith & Jones HR Services Limited say that there is no possibility of their altering the job title 'HR Consultant'.

(k) The company has no trade secrets. It does, however, regard as confidential the following information to which Ian Simpson will have access: the identity of customers, the contact names at those customers, details of the customers' requirements, confidential information of the customer provided to Smith & Jones HR Services Limited by the customer, pricing information (including details of special arrangements) and marketing strategy, in particular plans to open new offices.

(l) Ian Simpson will not be a director under the Companies Act 1985.

(m) To terminate the contract either side must give not less than three months notice. There is no payment in lieu of notice provision nor any right to send Ian Simpson on garden leave.

(n) It is unlikely that Ian Simpson will stay with Smith & Jones HR Services Limited for more than three years because there is no prospect of promotion. It is not anticipated that his job will change in any material way.

(a)(iii) Likely competitive activity

The principal competitive threat which Smith & Jones HR Services Limited perceive is that Simpson will establish a competitive business possibly taking two or three of their other HR consultants with him. Alternatively, they think Simpson may join a competitor, of which there are several, again with possibly two or three other HR consultants.

(b) Drafting

In the covenants Smith & Jones HR Services Limited is referred to as 'the Company' and Ian Simpson as 'the Executive'.

1.1 The Executive shall not so as to compete with the Company during the period of twelve months after the termination of his employment directly or indirectly on his own account or on behalf of or in conjunction with any person, firm, company or other organisation provide or canvass or solicit or by any other means seek to provide services of a type provided by the Company, which the Executive shall at any time during the twelve months immediately preceding the termination of his employment have been employed by the Company to provide, to any customer of the Company to whom the Executive provided services on behalf of the Company in the twelve months immediately preceding the termination of his employment.

1.2 The Executive shall not during the period of twelve months after the termination of his employment directly or indirectly induce or seek to induce to leave the Company any employee employed by the Company as an HR Consultant and with whom the Executive had during the last twelve months of his employment with the Company material contact in the course of that employment.

1.3 [As in 1.8 in Case study 1].
1.4 [As in 1.9 in Case study 1].

(For a precedent of a confidentiality covenant see para 4.30.)

RATIONALE FOR THE COVENANTS

1. The covenants do not include an area covenant since Smith & Jones HR Services Limited's interests can be adequately protected by a non-solicitation/ dealing covenant. An area covenant would in effect mean that Ian Simpson would be precluded from working as an HR consultant throughout the UK. If an area covenant were to be included, its range could be cut down by the use of provisos eg that Ian Simpson was not prohibited from being employed by anyone other than clients of Smith & Jones HR Services Limited for whom he had performed services.
2. Throughout the covenants the period of twelve months has been chosen to ensure that there is adequate protection vis-a-vis customers with annual contracts. The justification for the period is the same as in Case Study 1: see point 3 under Rationale for the Covenants (page 162).
3. The non-enticement covenant, Clause 1.2, has been drafted to catch only HR consultants of Smith & Jones HR Services Limited with whom Ian Simpson has had material contact. The protected pool has deliberately been drawn extremely narrowly to maximise the chances of enforceability.

Of the two sets of covenants in this Appendix the first is undoubtedly the better, not least because it is included in a contract which also expressly allows for the employee to be sent on garden leave. However, the two sets have been included to illustrate alternative styles of drafting and different considerations which apply depending on the facts. Both companies would be well advised to put in place fuller contracts for other key personnel.

Chapter 12

Introducing/varying restrictive covenants

Introduction

12.1 This Chapter looks at the various issues that arise when an employer or prospective employer seeks to introduce restrictive covenants or vary the terms of existing restrictive covenants, often with a view to narrowing their scope and thereby increasing their prospects of enforceability. Special and complex considerations apply when the exercise is being undertaken against the background of an actual or contemplated transfer of a business to which the Transfer of Undertaking (Protection of Employment) Regulations 1981 apply. For that reason TUPE transfers are considered separately in paragraphs 12.35 to 12.44.

1. Introducing the covenants

12.2 There are three distinct stages at which restrictive covenants can be introduced:

- As part of the offer of employment;
- During the currency of employment; and
- On termination of employment.

Different factors are relevant depending on when the covenants are to be introduced and it is therefore essential to look at each stage separately.

1(a) Introduction as part of the offer of employment

12.3 From a legal point of view, this is by far the easiest stage at which to introduce covenants, since neither party is under any obligation to the other. The prospective employee can evaluate the offer, aware that if he accepts it, his activities will be subject to restrictions after the employment ends. The prospective employer is under no obligation to employ the prospective employee without the benefit of the covenants.

12.4 A prospective employer who includes covenants as part of the offer does, however, need to take care. Before making the offer, the prospective employer needs to have decided what the role of the prospective employee is to be and to have had the covenants drafted so as to be reasonable bearing in mind that role.

Prospective employers should never use covenants drafted for other employees without first checking that they are appropriate. If they are not appropriate, the effect of including them may be to leave the employer with no protection at all, even though the prospective employee would have been willing to enter into reasonable covenants. It is not advisable to agree in principle to the inclusion of covenants on the understanding that the precise wording will be dealt with later. Invariably the matter is forgotten until the employer wants to enforce the covenant or the parties find they cannot reach agreement on the wording. Once the employment has commenced, the incentive to agree the wording, especially for the employee, will usually have been lost. The prospective employer who is unable to finalise the restrictive covenants at the time of making the offer should at the very least make the offer subject to contract and, where commercially possible, in the event of actual employment commencing before finalisation of the covenants, ensure that he is able to terminate by giving a short period of notice.

12.5 Prospective employers should also ensure that the covenants form part of the offer of employment in order to avoid arguments that the covenants amount to a variation of the contract for which the employee's consent and consideration are needed. An illustration of the problems that may arise can be seen in *Woodbridge & Sons v Bellamy* [1911] 2 Ch 326. Woodbridge, a firm of solicitors, advertised for a clerk. Bellamy, who was a qualified solicitor, was interviewed on 29 March and at the interview an oral offer of employment was made to him, subject to satisfactory references. Although the report is not entirely clear, Bellamy appears to have accepted the offer by letter on 1 April. The references were satisfactory and on 4 April Woodbridge wrote to Bellamy confirming that they wished to employ him from 17 April. However, on 16 April Bellamy saw Woodbridge's junior partner who asked him to sign an agreement which was stated to be 'In consideration of your agreeing to employ me ...' and which contained a restrictive covenant. Bellamy signed the document and commenced employment but was subsequently dismissed. In an action to enforce the covenant Bellamy argued that as a concluded agreement was already in existence when he signed the agreement of 16 April the new agreement was ineffective, there being no consideration for it. Woodbridge argued in response that until 16 April the agreement to employ was inchoate. Although the case went to the Court of Appeal the point was only dealt with at first instance. Eve J held that the agreement of 16 April did form part of the contract of service. His grounds for so finding appear to have been (1) that Bellamy was a solicitor who was capable of negotiating on his own behalf and fully aware of the nature of the document that he was signing, and (2) that the agreement was expressed to be in consideration of Woodbridge's agreeing to employ him. Neither of these grounds seem to meet Bellamy's point, but Eve J felt 'bound to infer' that the consideration for the agreement of 16 April would have been Woodbridge's retention of Bellamy's services when they would otherwise have terminated the employment relationship at the earliest opportunity.

1(b) Introduction during the currency of the employment

12.6 To introduce covenants after employment has begun the employer must obtain the employee's consent and show that there is consideration to support the covenants. Consideration is dealt with at paragraphs 10.12 to 10.22 and 12.5.

12.7 The employee's consent is required because the introduction of the covenants constitutes a variation of the contract and contracts cannot be unilaterally varied. Comparatively recently it has become common to insert provisions in contracts of employment, frequently 'buried' in the depths of the Staff Handbook, which purport to give the employer power to vary the contract of employment unilaterally simply by informing the employee of the change the employer has decided to make. Such a provision was considered by the EAT in United Association for the Protection of Trade Ltd v Kilburn (17 September 1985, EAT 787/84 unreported). The clause read as follows:

'This handbook constitutes your contract of employment. The Association reserves the right to make alterations to the contract of employment. Such changes will be notified to you ...'

The EAT held that the clause only empowered the employer to make minor changes of a non-fundamental nature. Clearly, the introduction of restrictive covenants would not be permitted by such a clause.

12.8 The employee's consent may be express or implied. Express consent may be written or oral. Express written consent is clearly desirable in order to minimise the scope for arguments. An employer who fails to obtain express consent may be able to argue that the employee impliedly consented by his conduct. However, this is by no means a straightforward argument for the employer. Consent will never be implied where there is evidence that the employee has objected to the variation and, even where he has not, the courts have at least until recently shown a considerable reluctance to imply consent where the variation is adverse to the employee's interests: *Sheet Metal Components v Plumridge* [1974] ICR 86. The courts have also distinguished variations which have no immediate practical impact: *Jones v Associated Tunnelling Co Ltd* [1981] IRLR 477 where the EAT expressed the obiter view that it was 'unrealistic' to expect an employee to raise an objection to something which would have no immediate effect. In *Jones* the EAT was considering the case of an erroneous statement in written particulars under what was then Section 1 Employment Protection (Consolidation) Act 1978, (now Section 1 Employment Rights Act 1996) but in principle the point is the same for restrictive covenants.

12.9 The obiter view in *Jones* was applied by the EAT in *Aparau v Iceland Frozen Foods plc* [1996] IRLR 119 in rejecting an argument that a mobility clause had become part of Mrs Aparau's contract by implied consent. Contrast, however, the interim decision of the Court of Appeal in *Credit Suisse Asset Management Ltd v Armstrong & Others* [1996] IRLR 450 where revised restrictive covenants contained in an updated Staff Handbook were found to be incorporated into the employee's contracts notwithstanding that there had been no express acceptance of the terms contained in the Handbook.

12.10 It is worth focusing on the *Credit Suisse* decision because the introduction of the new Handbook followed a pattern commonly used, particularly in larger companies. The new Handbook was issued under cover of an internal memorandum. The memorandum referred to the Handbook as 'largely an update of existing terms and policies'. It said that in some areas changes had been introduced to reflect 'recent legislation' or rule changes. A new death in service widows/widowers pension benefit was also mentioned but no express reference was made to any change in the existing covenants. Employees were asked to acknowledge receipt and were asked to 'try to find the time to read the book' which they were told contained 'important contractual rights and obligations'. The memorandum also asked employees to raise queries or concerns within one month, failing which they were 'to be treated as having fully accepted the rights and obligations as written'. In the Court of Appeal it was accepted that each of the defendant employees acknowledged receipt of the Handbook. It also seems to be the case that none of the defendant employees had raised any issues on the Handbook. The Court was referred to *Jones* (above) and to the judgment of Lightman J in *Re Leyland Daf* [1995] ICR 1100 but not apparently to *Aparau* (above) which had been decided seven months previously. While stressing their decision was not a final one, applying the test in *Lansing Linde Ltd v Kerr* [1991] IRLR 80 (CA) (for which see para 13.32) the Court concluded that there was sufficient likelihood that *Credit Suisse* would succeed in showing that the revised covenants formed part of the defendant employees' contracts of employment. In our view, this conclusion is somewhat surprising. The judgment gives virtually no detail as to why the Court reached this decision. The only clue given is in a comment of Lord Justice Neill that the defendants were 'men of experience and sophistication who are used to looking at complex documents': see paragraph 27. For the future, there is therefore a clear suggestion that the courts are likely to have less sympathy with senior employees who fail to raise issues on new contractual obligations suggested by their employers than more junior employees. However, in our view it is unwise for employers to place too great a reliance on the *Credit Suisse* decision. It may be of considerable assistance in those cases where the changes have already been proposed without consent being sought. However, best practice remains to seek and obtain the employee's consent for all changes.

12.11 Difficult questions on implied consent arise where the covenants form part of a new package and where the employee takes the benefit of the package but seeks to avoid its burdens. Such a situation commonly arises where a company issues new service agreements introducing covenants at the time of a salary increase. The employee fails to sign and return the new agreement but accepts, without protest, the increased salary which is paid by the employer. Sometimes the increased salary is paid under the mistaken belief that the employee has signified his consent to the variation. More often it is paid quite deliberately in order to allow the employer to contend that the employee has consented to the variation by his conduct. Ultimately, the question is one of fact, but the employee's conduct will be evidence on which the employer can rely. An employee, and particularly a senior employee, who wishes to continue in employment but avoid any risk of the covenants binding him should reject the covenants in writing and should refuse the salary increase, unless he can show that he is otherwise entitled to it, for example, because of a clause linking his salary to the Retail Price Index. To avoid misunderstandings the employee should always make it clear that he will continue to be bound by his existing contract of employment and will perform all his obligations under that contract.

12.12 Where the new service agreement entails changes in addition to the introduction of the covenants and the salary increase the position becomes more complex, but in our view the same principle applies. The employee cannot unilaterally pick and choose which revisions he will accept. He must accept the revisions as a whole or put forward proposals as to which revisions are acceptable.

In the latter case he should reject the covenants in writing and should not accept any improved benefits until he has agreement from the employer to revised terms. Employees often find this advice unpalatable since making their position clear may jeopardise their employment. However, the only alternative is to take the risk that the court may find implied consent, a risk which is now rather greater for employees following the *Credit Suisse* decision.

12.13 An employee whose job involves settling terms of employment for other employees should take care that his conduct does not give rise to an argument of implied consent. For example, it has been argued that directors who vote in favour of the introduction of a new Service Agreement for senior employees including directors may be said to be impliedly, or indeed even expressly, consenting to an agreement for themselves in those terms. Whilst such an argument in our view has little merit it is sensible for an employee in this position to make clear his own stance to avoid the point being argued against him.

12.14 Employers seeking to introduce restrictive covenants need to approach the issue carefully. Where the introduction of new terms is coupled with a threat to give notice under the existing contract if the employee does not accept, this has been held to amount to an anticipatory breach giving rise to a constructive dismissal under Section 95(1)(c) Employment Rights Act 1996: *Greenaway Harrison Ltd v Wiles* [1994] IRLR 350 EAT. In *Greenaway* the new terms were changes to shift patterns which Mrs Wiles could not accept because of family commitments. The correctness of this decision is, in the authors' view, very doubtful. It is difficult to see how a threat of lawful performance of a contractual term can be a breach of anything. However, because of the constructive dismissal risk, when dealing with employees eligible to present unfair dismissal claims, it is unwise for the employer to mention the possibility of dismissal at the initial stages unless the covenants are absolutely necessary for the protection of the business and the employer could cope without the employee immediately. It goes almost without saying that under no circumstances should an employer threaten to dismiss without proper notice – to do so would, in appropriate cases, invite not only a wrongful dismissal claim but also an unfair dismissal claim.

12.15 Where the employee refuses to give consent to the introduction of covenants but remains in employment, the employer has four courses of action open to him: (i) to abandon the proposed covenants and continue to employ on the existing terms; (ii) to continue the employment as before but to enter into negotiations with the employee in the hope that he will ultimately agree; (iii) to dismiss the employee, or (iv) to dismiss but offer the employee continued employment on the revised terms, that is including the covenants, from the expiry of the notice period. To avoid claims of wrongful dismissal the employer who chooses to dismiss should give the employee whichever is the longer of his contractual notice or statutory minimum notice in accordance with Section 86 Employment Rights Act 1996. An employer taking this route needs to do so unequivocally to avoid having to pay the notice period twice: *Rigby v Ferodo Ltd* [1987] IRLR 516. A lump sum payment in lieu of notice may be made where expressly permitted by the contract or where agreed by the parties. Employees with the necessary continuity of service to present a claim of unfair dismissal may allege that the dismissal was unfair. Special rules apply where there has been a transfer to which the Transfer of Undertakings (Protection of Employment) Regulations 1981 apply and these are set out at paragraphs 12.35

to 12.44. In other cases the only ground on which the employer can defend such a claim is 'some other substantial reason' under Section 98(2) Employment Rights Act 1996.

12.16   The defence of 'some other substantial reason' succeeded in *RS Components Ltd v Irwin* [1974] 1 All ER 41 (NIRC). RS Components were distributors of electrical components in England and Northern Ireland. They operated through a team of 92 salesmen, each of whom worked in an allocated territory and visited customers in accordance with a schedule provided by RS Components. In the two years preceding the dismissal of Irwin, RS Components had lost a number of orders to ex-salesmen. Those ex-salesmen, using knowledge gained in their employment of the names and addresses of customers and the times of calls by RS Components staff, set up their own businesses and called upon the customers to solicit orders shortly before the customer was due a visit by the RS Components representative. This resulted in a loss of business and complaints being received from RS Components salesmen, who were paid partly by salary and partly by commission. RS Components took advice and concluded that the appropriate way forward would be to introduce a reasonable non-solicitation of customers covenant. RS Components issued new service agreements to its salesmen on 1 February 1973 containing a 12-month non-solicitation covenant. The service agreements contained other alterations but none were relevant to the unfair dismissal claim. The covering memorandum required the employee to consider the new agreement carefully and to sign and return it by 23 February. Although the memorandum sought the employee's views it also made it clear that the revised terms were the only terms on which the company could continue to employ and that the new terms would come into effect from 1 March. On 21 February Irwin wrote to the company saying he would not sign the covenants. Subsequent attempts to persuade him to change his mind, including a personal interview with the Chairman, failed and consequently at the beginning of March his employment was terminated by a payment in lieu of notice. Of the 92 salesmen Irwin was one of only four who refused to sign. The employment tribunal held that the covenant was reasonable and would probably have been enforceable and that the effect on the future interests of RS Components of Irwin's refusal to agree to the covenant was so substantial as to justify dismissal. However, by a majority the employment tribunal found Irwin had been unfairly dismissed since on the proper construction of the phrase 'some other substantial reason' it had to be read ejusdem generis (that is, be restricted to the same class of reasons) with the other reasons for dismissal contained in what was then the Industrial Relations Act 1971, now Section 98(2) Employment Rights Act 1996. On appeal the NIRC allowed RS Components' appeal, holding that the phrase 'some other substantial reason' was not to be construed ejusdem generis and that Irwin's dismissal was a fair dismissal for 'some other substantial reason'. Two further points are worth noting. The first, referred to in the industrial tribunal's decision, was that they recognised a need for uniformity amongst the terms of employment of the sales staff and they placed some reliance on the fact that as there had been an opportunity for 'consultation and explanation' it could not be said that Irwin had been treated unfairly. The second is the recognition, as part of the justification of the NIRC's decision, that cases could clearly arise where it would be essential for an employer to introduce restrictive covenants The two examples referred to are where covenants are necessary to limit the use of knowledge acquired in employment of a new technical process or where a licensing agreement imposed on the licensee an obligation to extract restrictive covenants from its employees. As Brightman J put it, 'It would be unfortunate for the development of industry if an employer were unable to meet such a situation without infringing or risking infringement of rights conferred by the 1971 Act' (page 45).

12.17   As is apparent from what is said above, the introduction of covenants during the currency of employment can be difficult. Since it is something upon which advice is frequently sought by employers, set out in the Appendix to this Chapter is a practical note of the approach that should be adopted.

1(c) Introduction on termination of employment

12.18   Introduction at this stage normally only occurs as part of a negotiated agreement for the termination of employment of a senior employee. The covenants are necessary either because there are no covenants in the contract of employment (this is particularly common in the case of long-serving employees who have 'risen through the ranks'), or because there is doubt about the enforceability of the existing covenants. For example, the covenants may be too widely drawn or it may be unclear whether the employee has consented to them.

12.19   Covenants given on termination of employment are subject to the same basic requirements as covenants given at any other time. The covenantor must agree to them, he must receive consideration for them, and they must be reasonable. Covenants given on termination of employment are not contrary to public policy and therefore void simply because they are given at that stage rather than at the beginning of the employment. This was one of the contentions of the Defendant, Spink, in *Spink (Bournemouth) Ltd v Spink* [1936] Ch 544. Spink had been an employee, director and shareholder of the company. Disputes had arisen with his fellow directors and, as a result, in consideration of a payment of £100 Spink had agreed to resign his positions and enter into a restrictive covenant. For a separate consideration he agreed to sell his shares. In an action to enforce the restrictive covenant the company succeeded. In particular, Luxmoore J rejected Spink's argument that the covenant was void simply because it was given on termination of employment. He said:

> 'I cannot appreciate the view that public policy requires that a person who is seeking to be released from his employment should not be able to obtain the release and a payment to himself as consideration for his giving up his service and entering into a proper restrictive covenant as part of the bargain. Such a covenant cannot affect adversely any member of the public or the person who, with his eyes open, takes the consideration and gives the covenant.' (Page 548)

Nowadays covenants given on termination of employment are regularly before the courts, see for example *Stenhouse Australia Ltd v Phillips* [1974] AC 391, *J A Mont (UK) Ltd v Mills* [1993] IRLR 172 and *Turner v Commonwealth & British Minerals Ltd* (CA) 13 October 1999 (unreported): see further paragraph 12.22.

12.20   The taxation of consideration given for covenants entered into at this stage is something to which careful attention needs to be paid. Under Section 313 Income and Corporation Taxes Act 1988 income tax is charged on any payment by an employer to an employee for entering into a covenant restricting him from competing. That provision applies whenever consideration is paid but normally it raises no problems since the employer is deducting tax at source from the employee's income. Where, however, the employment is being terminated problems can arise because of the special tax treatment of payments made to employees to compensate them for the loss of their employment. Under Section 188 Income and Corporation Taxes Act 1988 the first £30,000 of such payments (excluding payments made in accordance with contractual pay in lieu of notice clauses: *EMI Group Electronics Ltd v Coldicott (Inspector of Taxes)* [1999] STC 803 (CA) see paragraps 4.66 to 4.76 for further details) are generally free of tax. So the employer who pays £30,000 or less deducts no tax, whereas the employer paying more than £30,000 deducts tax only on the excess.

12.21   As Section 188 Income and Coporation Taxes Act does not override Section 313 of the same Act, an employer who merely pays a global consideration to the employee will have failed to deduct the necessary tax pursuant to Section 313 and the whole payment made to the employee is at risk of being charged to tax by the Inland Revenue. To avoid this risk what the employer should do is expressly attribute a sum as consideration for the covenants and account for tax on that sum in the ordinary way. There is currently some debate amongst Revenue practitioners, whether the sum attributed can simply be a nominal figure of, for example, £1 or whether the Inland Revenue could legitimately go behind such a figure and attribute a more realistic value to the covenants for the purpose of assessing the tax charge. Another question is whether an employer could go behind a stated nominal consideration to demonstrate that the consideration was otherwise than stated. It would not be safe to assume that the court would permit this. It follows that the only safe course is to attribute adequate consideration to the covenants taken: see paragraphs 10.12 to 10.22 on the question of consideration for covenants generally.

2.   Renewal of covenants in severance agreements

12.22   Often as part and parcel of severance arrangements the restrictive covenants in the contract of employment are repeated in the same or a modified form. (Such covenants are valid even though entered into as part of the consideration for the release from employment: *Spink (Bournemouth) Ltd v Spink* [1936] Ch 544.) The question arises whether in principle these covenants afford the employer any stronger protection than those in the original employment contract. It might be argued that sometimes in these circumstances the bargaining position of the employee is stronger than when he is seeking employment. His position may seem a little closer to that of the vendor of the business. In *Stenhouse Australia Ltd v Phillips* [1974] 1 All ER 117 (PC) the court did take into account the fact the covenants were being entered into on termination in assessing whether the lengthy period of the covenant was justifiable. The court commented that whereas at the inception of the contract of employment the period of the covenants is necessarily a pre-estimation, at the date of termination the ex-employee (in this case a managing director) was in as good a position as any to appraise the nature and quality of the interest which the employer wished to protect and what was accordingly a suitable period for the covenant to run. Consequently, '... unless the period fixed was clearly excessive they [the parties] may be thought to have agreed on a realistic limitation' (pages 401 and 402). Accordingly in *Stenhouse* the court upheld a five-year prohibition on solicitation of clients as defined.

12.23 Where covenants in a contract of employment are affirmed in a severance agreement no charge to tax should arise under Section 313 Income and Corporation Taxes Act 1988. One possible exception to this arises where there has been a repudiatory breach by the employer accepted by the employee so that it is arguable the 'affirmation' in fact constitutes a fresh restriction. This risk needs to be borne in mind by those drafting severance agreements. In practice, taking the risk of a tax liability may well be preferable to alerting the employer to the fact that his covenants may be unenforceable. However, as always it will be a matter of balancing the comparative risks.

3. Covenants in collateral contracts

12.24 In certain circumstances, the courts will treat statements made in the course of negotiations for a contract (which are intended to have contractual effect) as a collateral contract or warranty, distinct from the main contract. The consideration for the collateral contract is provided by entering into the main contract: see *De Lassalle v Guildford* [1901] 2 KB 215; *Hill v Harris* [1965] 2 QB 601. A feature of a collateral contract is that it may be actionable even if the main contract is unenforceable: *Strongman (1945) Ltd v Sincock* [1955] 2 QB 525. But compare *Quickmaid Rental Services Ltd v Reece* (CA), Times 22 April 1970 and [1970] 114 SJ 372 which suggest that the connection between a contract and a collateral contract may be such that a repudiatory breach of one contract (in that case the collateral contral) would entitle the innocent party to treat himself as discharged from the other contract.

12.25 Is it possible, by use of a collateral contract, to overcome the difficulty posed by the principle enunciated in *General Billposting Co Ltd v Atkinson* [1908] 1 Ch 537? In other words, if, as a result of a repudiatory breach by his employer, an employee would not be bound by the terms of his contract of employment, might the court nonetheless be persuaded to give effect to restrictive covenants if they formed part of a collateral contract?

12.26 In the case of very important employees the practice of putting covenants in a separate document in the form of a collateral contract between the employer and the employee is not unusual. As far as is known there is no authority as to whether such a practice will be effective but in our view, for the following reasons the court would be unlikely to give effect to restrictive covenants in such a document where there had been a repudiatory breach by the employer which was accepted by the employee.

• The claim that there is a collateral contract would arouse suspicion that it was nothing more than a 'device'. If such a 'device' were effective, an employer could persuade a prospective employee to agree to restrictive covenants in a collateral contract and then quite deliberately flout the provisions of the main contract, knowing that the employee would remain bound by the restrictive covenants. Such conduct on the part of the employer would in our view be regarded as unconscionable and the court would be unlikely to exercise its discretion to grant equitable relief by way of injunction. See, however, the obiter comments of Philips LJ in *Rock*

Refrigeration Ltd v Jones and Seward Refrigeration Ltd [1996] IRLR 675 which are considered in paragraphs 8.21 to 8.22.

- Restrictive covenants would not normally form the kind of statements which typify a collateral warranty or contract. Nor would they constitute representations which could afford the employee a right to bring a claim based on misrepresentation in the event that they were false. Looking at all the factual circumstances, the court is likely to conclude that the restrictive covenants form an integral part of a larger, single agreement.

- Even if the court were to conclude that a genuine collateral contract had come into existence, the likelihood is that the employee would be able to show that there were implied terms of the collateral contract to the effect that the employer could not derogate from the rights granted to the employee under the main contract, or terminate it unlawfully. In other words, the position of the employee would be no worse under the collateral contract than it would have been if there had been a single agreement embracing all relevant contractual terms. In this event, the employer's reliance on a collateral contract would achieve nothing.

12.27 Contrast with the use of a collateral contract as a device the situation where there is a good and genuine reason for the covenants being contained in a separate agreement. In *Emersub XXXVI Inc and Control Techniques plc v Wheatley* 18 July 1998 (unreported) the covenants were in a deed entered into in connection with the sale of Wheatley's shares in his employing company Control Techniques plc. The deed was in favour of the purchaser of the shares, Emersub and was to protect the goodwill being bought. After the sale Control Techniques plc dismissed Wheatley, allegedly wrongfully. Emersub sought an injunction to enforce the covenants. Granting the injunction Wright J rejected an argument that the covenants did not survive the alleged repudiatory breach. As he pointed out, the covenants were not given to Wheatley's employer, the alleged repudiator, in connection with his employment. Rather they were given in favour of Emersub in connection with the purchase of Wheatley's shares for which he received around £11 million. In such circumstances Wright J felt that:

> 'I, for my part do not see how what happened to his [Wheatley's] employment with Control Techniques PLC has any impact upon or relevance to that contractual undertaking' (Transcript, page 14).

4. Reviewing the covenants

12.28 It is essential that the wording of restrictive covenants is reviewed regularly and, in any event, where there is a material change in the facts upon which the covenants were prepared. The more specific the wording of the covenants the greater the need to review. Often a review will reveal the need for a variation of the covenants. How variation can be achieved is considered at paragraphs 12.6 to 12.17 and the Appendix to this Chapter.

12.29 Review is necessary primarily to ensure that the covenants accurately reflect the current facts, thereby providing the best chance of appropriate protection for the employer. Common is the case where the ex-employer, faced with competition from a key ex-employee, turns to the restrictive covenants only to find that they will afford him limited protection or, even worse, none, because they were drafted when the ex-employee was a much more junior employee and regarded as relatively insignificant.

12.30 Two situations where review of the restrictive covenants is of vital importance are:

- The role of the employee, including his location and/or responsibilities, is altered;
- A business is acquired.

4(a) Role of employee altered

12.31 This will occur most commonly where the employee is promoted or there is a change in his responsibilities or location not involving a change in status. Whatever the cause of the alteration in the employee's role, his restrictive covenants should be looked at carefully to see whether they remain appropriate. For example, on promotion an employee may become entitled to a longer notice period from his employer and to receive significantly more confidential information, factors potentially justifying a change in his existing covenants. Similarly, if an employee moves to another location, that may necessitate revision of an area covenant either because the area is defined by reference to the previous location or the area is too narrow or too wide in the context of the new location. For example, the area may be too narrow because the original location of the employee was in a city or town whereas the new location is in a rural setting, where a much wider area is necessary to afford protection and can be justified.

4(b) Acquisition of a business

12.32 Where a business is acquired in circumstances in which any of its employees will be part of what is acquired (whether by operation of law or by agreement), the acquirer should review the restrictive covenants of those employees *and* of any of his existing employees whose roles or status will be affected by the acquisition. For the special rules that apply in connection with a TUPE transfer see paragraphs 12.35 to 12.44.

5. Variation of covenants

12.33 The employer cannot unilaterally vary an existing restrictive covenant; he must obtain the employee's express or implied consent. In effect the employer is in the same position as an employer seeking to introduce covenants after employment has commenced, see paragraphs 12.6 to 12.17 and the Appendix to this Chapter.

12.34 Whether in practice the employer suffers the same disadvantages will depend on whether the existing covenants are enforceable and the degree of variation he proposes. If, for example, the existing covenants are unenforceable, unless the employee agrees to the variation, there is no real distinction between the employer seeking to introduce enforceable covenants by variation and the employer introducing them as new terms.

6. TUPE transfers – special problems

12.35 The Transfer of Undertakings (Protection of Employment) Regulations 1981 (the 'Regulations'), designed to implement the Acquired Rights Directive (EEC) 77/187, apply where there is a transfer of a business. The transfer of part of a business will also be caught by the Regulations where the part is a separate identifiable portion of the whole. The Regulations do not currently apply where the ownership of a business alters because of the sale of shares in a company. However, there is a distinct possibility that the current position will change. Section 38(2) of the Employment Relations Act 1999 (yet to be brought into force) gives the Secretary of State power by regulations to apply the TUPE principles to, among other things, share transfers. At the moment the Department of Trade and Industry says that there are no plans to extend the TUPE principles to share transfers. However, Section 38(2) clearly envisages that possibility and it remains to be seen whether the change will be introduced at a later date. The rationale for the current position is simple. Because there is no change in the identity of their employer the employees neither need nor, arguably, should they be entitled to, any special protection. Consequently, from an employment law perspective, where commercially practical, there are currently distinct advantages to the purchaser for the acquisition to be achieved by a share acquisition rather than a TUPE transfer. One note of caution, prospective purchasers should not assume that an acquisition by share purchase will avoid the Regulations entirely. Often, following an acquisition the purchaser carries out a reorganisation to integrate the acquired business into the purchaser's group of companies. Frequently these types of reorganisations involve TUPE transfers and the possibility should always be addressed before any irreversible steps are taken.

12.36 What do the Regulations do? The main effect of the Regulations is that employees, employed by the transferor in the business which is being transferred, immediately before the transfer automatically become employees of the transferee; their contracts are regarded as though originally made with the transferee (Regulation 5). In other words, the transferee acquires the employees on their existing terms and conditions. Additionally, subject to one exception, any dismissal by reason of the transfer or for a reason connected with it will be automatically unfair (Regulation 8). This is so whenever the dismissal takes place and whether the dismissed employee is an employee of the transferor or the transferee, as long as he has sufficient continuity of service to present a claim. The exception to the automatically unfair rule is where the dismissal is for an economic, technical or organisational reason, entailing changes in the workforce (Regulation 8). To secure the protection afforded to employees by Regulations 5 and 8, agreements to exclude or limit this operation are automatically void (Regulation 12).

12.37 In the context of restrictive covenants three specific questions commonly arise:

- What is the correct interpretation of pre-transfer covenants post transfer?
- Can restrictive covenants be introduced or existing covenants varied in connection with a transfer?
- What are the implications of dismissing an employee who refuses to agree to new/varied covenants in connection with a transfer?

In considering these questions it is important to bear in mind that the provision which makes dismissal automatically unfair in Regulation 8 applies, not only to the employees who transfer to the transferee, but also to his existing employees and the employees of the transferor. This is a point often overlooked by advisers.

6(a) Interpretation of covenants

12.38 Perhaps a little surprisingly there have been very few cases in which the question of the correct interpretation of pre-transfer covenants have been argued before the courts. The starting point is Regulation 5 which provides that the contract of employment has effect post-transfer as if originally made between the employee and the transferee. In *McCall v Initial Supplies Ltd* (2 May 1990, unreported) IDS Employment Law Cases, Employment Protection 8.4.5 the Court of Session in refusing an application by Initial Supplies Ltd for an interim interdict (interim injunction) doubted whether Regulation 5 transferred the benefit of the restrictive covenants. Lord Coulsfield said that in many situations the effect of substitution of the new employer for the former employer would be to make a radical alteration in the rights and obligations of the parties. For example, the practical scope and effect of a restrictive covenant may be altered if regard has to be had to the customers of the new employer instead of or as well as the former employer. However, more recently in *Morris Angel & Son Ltd v Hollande* [1993] ICR 71 (in which *McCall* was not referred to) the Court of Appeal granted an interim injunction to the transferee of a business to enforce a restrictive covenant contained in the contract of employment of Hollande. Hollande was the managing director of a company called Altolight Ltd which transferred its business to Morris Angel. Immediately after the transfer Morris Angel dismissed Hollande. Subsequently Hollande sought to compete with Morris Angel in breach of a restrictive covenant in the contract he had signed with Altolight Ltd. The relevant covenant prohibited Hollande for one year after the termination of his employment from soliciting or doing business with anyone who had been a customer of the 'group' within the year preceding that termination. The term 'group' was defined as Altolight Ltd and its subsidiaries. Morris Angel sought an interim injunction to restrain further breaches of the covenant. At the initial hearing, ex parte on notice, Turner J held that the effect of Regulation 5 was that Hollande's contract was to be read as if originally made with Morris Angel. Consequently, since it was not customers of Morris Angel which Hollande was seeking to do business with but customers of Altolight Ltd, there was no covenant under which injunctive relief could be granted. That decision was followed by Judge Laurie QC at the inter partes hearing. The Court of Appeal, however, rejected Turner J's interpretation of Regulation 5, Dillon LJ explaining their reason for doing so as follows:

'The difficulty about that approach to my mind is that it turns the obligation on the employee under clause 15(1) into a quite different and possibly much wider obligation than the obligation which bound him before the transfer, that is to say an obligation not to do business etc with the persons who had done business in the relevant year with the [claimants], not the company. Such an obligation was not remotely in contemplation when the service agreement was entered into and I can see no reason why the regulation should have sought to change the burden on the employee.' (Page 78D.)

Dillon LJ found that the correct construction of Regulation 5 was:

'... the words '[the contract] shall have effect' are to be read as referring to the transferee as the owner of the undertaking transferred or in respect of the undertaking transferred. The effect therefore is that clause 15(1) can be enforced by the [claimants] if Mr Hollande within the year after 29 April 1992 does business with persons who in the previous year had done business with the undertaking transferred of which the [claimants] are deemed as a result of the transfer retrospectively to have been the owner. The [claimants] are thus given locus standi to enforce the restriction.'

Where termination of employment takes place shortly after the transfer, and the undertaking transferred continues after the transfer to be run as a separate business, the approach of the Court of Appeal will probably present no problems. In other cases, the outcome may well not be so simple and the transferee will have to consider alternative means of protecting his newly acquired business.

6(b) Changing terms and conditions

12.39 After a period of considerable uncertainty, during which a number of cases have been considered by the courts, the current position can be summarised as follows:

- A transferee and transferring employee cannot validly agree changes to the transferring employees terms and conditions of employment where the reason for the change is the transfer: *Foreningen af Arbejdsledere v Daddy's Dance Hall* [1988] IRLR 315 ECJ applied in *Credit Suisse First Boston (Europe) Ltd v Padiachy and Others* [1998] IRLR 504 [QB] and *Credit Suisse First Boston (Europe) Ltd v Lister* CA [1998] IRLR 700 (CA). This is so even where the disadvantages for the employee of such an agreement are 'offset by advantages so that overall, he is left in no worse a position', (*Daddy's Dance Hall* paragraph 19) or it would seem, although this comment was obiter, a better position (*Padiachy*). Interestingly, the two *Credit Suisse* cases concerned new restrictive covenants introduced in connection with Credit Suisse's acquisition of the business of Barclays de Zoete Wedd Services Ltd. In both cases consideration was given for the new covenants and in particular Mr Lister stood to benefit by an amount exceeding £625,000. Notwithstanding this the Court of Appeal rejected the idea of any sort of balancing exercise.
- In contrast to the first proposition, where there has been a pre-transfer dismissal the transferee is free to negotiate and agree new terms with the dismissed employee: *British Fuels Ltd v Meade and Baxendale* and *Wilson and Others v St Helens Borough Council* [1998] IRLR 706 (HL). The dismissal is effective in law and while liability for the dismissal passes to the transferee he is under no obligation to honour the pre-dismissal terms and conditions of employment.

12.40 The combined effect of the cases referred to in paragraph 12.39 is that, unless there is a clear and obvious reason for the variation which is not the transfer or a reason connected with it, the only truly safe course for a transferee is to insist that the employees whose terms he wants to change are dismissed by the transferor and he obtains financial cover, for example either through a reduction in or deferral of part of the purchase price or an indemnity against the risk of statutory claims. It has to be said that this is a result that can hardly have been contemplated by the draftsmen of the Directive, nor is it an option likely to promote good industrial relations or staff morale.

12.41 Deciding when the necessary causal link between transfer and variation exists was acknowledged by Lord Slynn in *Wilson* to be 'difficult' (page 716 para 93). In *Wilson* the cases were disposed of by the finding that the pre transfer dismissals were effective, consequently it was not necessary for the House to rule on the variation question. However, it might have been hoped that some indication of the type of approach favoured could have been given. The only assistance in fact offered, which is, of course obiter, is to be found at page 15 paragraph 90. In those paragraphs Lord Slynn rejects the proposition that the variation is 'only invalid if it is agreed on or as part of the transfer itself' and comments that in his view 'there must, or at least may, come a time when the link with the transfer is broken or can be treated as no longer effective'. Lord Slynn then added that if the appeal had turned on this question then he would have found it necessary to refer the matter, as far as Meade and Baxendale were concerned, to the ECJ. In short, the guidance from Lord Slynn is hardly of great assistance. In practical terms, however, there is unlikely to be any greater certainty until the ECJ rule on the issue and an early reference of the question would undoubtedly be helpful.

12.42 Pending clarification from the ECJ, employment lawyers are being called on to be creative and to find methods to effect variations not involving the draconian measure of dismissal. In the context of restrictive covenants it will often be impractical to argue that the necessary causal link between transfer and variation is absent. On the contrary, the transfer is usually precisely the reason for the variation and the two Credit Suisse cases (para 12.39) are good examples. Where the employer is a company the only alternative route which in our view has any possible chance of succeeding is what might be described as the 'shareholder route'. Under this option the relevant employees are made shareholders post sale and enter into new covenants in their capacity as shareholders. The number of shares owned by the employees needs to be more than nominal to support the argument that there are genuine shareholder covenants and not simply a device to circumvent the Regulations. However, if the employees are sufficiently important to the business being acquired the employer's investment will be justified. While this approach is by no means watertight it may well be the only option available, at least until we have a ruling from the ECJ.

12.43 Finally, on the issue of variation, it remains unclear precisely what effect an invalid variation has on the contract of employment as a whole. Tantalisingly in *Credit Suisse v Lister* (para 12.39) the Court of Appeal recognised that difficult questions arose but then gave no assistance on possible answers. In *Padiachy*, albeit a first instance decision, the judge simply indicated that he could see no basis on which *Padiachy* could retain the consideration received for the covenants. For the moment that is all the guidance available. Advisers will have to think carefully how to marshal arguments to deal with this issue until some clearer assistance is available. Where the employer is simply seeking to recover monies paid for ineffective variations it may be that in appropriate cases he can benefit from the recent change in the law relating to monies paid as a result of a mistake, see *Kleinwort Benson Ltd v Lincoln City Council* [1998] 3 WLR 1095 (HL). In that case, the House of Lords swept away the rule that money paid under a mistake of law (as opposed to fact) cannot be recovered, so that arcane arguments as to whether or not the mistakes fall to be classified as ones of fact or law need no longer be entered into.

6(c) Dismissal

12.44 Where the introduction of the covenants is connected with the transfer, which is often the case, the combined effect of Regulations 5, 8 and 12 is to make the dismissal of an employee with sufficient service to bring an unfair dismissal claim an extremely risky option. It will soon be a much more expensive option in view of the imminent raising of the cap on the compensatory award for unfair dismissal to £50,000 (Section 30(4) Employment Relations Act 1999). There is no reported case in which the question of whether the introduction of restrictive covenants can fall within the exception in Regulation 8 so that the dismissal is not automatically unfair. In our view, however, it is unlikely to do so because the introduction of restrictive covenants would not involve a change in the workforce even on the interpretations of that phrase in *Delabole Slate Ltd v Berriman* [1985] ICR 546 and in *Crawford v Swinton Insurance Brokers Ltd* [1990] ICR 85 (EAT).

Guidelines on introducing covenants during employment

Employers contemplating introducing covenants during the currency of employment frequently seek advice as to how to do so. The purpose of these Guidelines is to assist the adviser and the employer in formulating a strategy. Because of the specific problems associated with introducing covenants in the context of a transfer of a business to which the Transfer of Undertaking (Protection of Employment) Regulations 1981 apply these Guidelines do not cover such a situation. For the purpose of the Guidelines it is assumed that a 'TUPE Transfer' has neither happened nor is contemplated.

Deciding whether to introduce covenants

The first step the adviser should take is to assist the employer in deciding whether the potential benefits to be gained justify the cost and disruption of the exercise. Reaching this decision involves weighing up a number of factors and seeing where the balance falls. The following points need to be considered:

- What is the employer seeking protection against?
- Why is the employer seeking protection and what are the likely consequences of not obtaining it in terms of impact on the employer's business?
- The grades and number of employees from whom covenants would be required.
- The likelihood of covenants which will achieve the employer's aims being enforceable.
- What incentive, if any, the employer is willing/likely to need to offer to obtain consent and the likely level of consents.
- Whether any employees, and particularly key ones, are likely to treat the introduction of the covenants as a repudiation of the contract and leave.
- How practical it will be to continue to employ employees who refuse to give their consent.
- The cost of any dismissals that may become necessary; costs include direct costs, namely notice payments and possible compensation in the employment tribunal, and indirect costs such as the likely cost of the employee doing exactly what the employer is seeking to prevent, namely competing with the employer.

With these answers the employer will be able to decide whether the exercise is likely to be worthwhile.

Formulating a strategy for drafting covenants

Where the employer decides to go ahead with the introduction of covenants the next step is for the adviser to draft appropriate covenants and to help the employer determine his strategy. The more employees involved in the exercise, the greater the degree of precision required, but in every case the strategy will need to cover the following points:

- When the matter is to be put to the employees.
- How the matter is to be put to the employees.
- What arrangements there are to be for consultation/discussion between the employees and management.
- The timescale for acceptance.
- How employees who do not accept are to be dealt with.
- How employees who do not respond are to be dealt with.

The following points should be borne in mind in settling the strategy:

(a) TIMING

Unless the introduction is to be linked to the salary review date or bonus payment date, timing is not usually of crucial importance. However, employers should avoid popular holiday periods and should ensure that dates specified as the deadline for acceptances do not fall on public holidays.

(b) METHOD

Presentation is often all important. Meetings with the employee or small groups of employees in appropriate cases to explain what is proposed and, where commercially practical, why it is being proposed should always be considered. In addition, to avoid arguments of whether the employee consented to the variation, the best course is usually for the employer to write to the employee setting out the terms of the covenants and seeking his written consent. Provided there are cogent reasons for the introduction of the covenants (and if there are not, why is the employer seeking to introduce them?) the employer is well advised to set out those reasons in detail. It is those reasons he will have to rely on before the employment tribunal if any unfair dismissal claims are presented. Indications, including veiled indications, that dismissal will result if the employee does not accept should be avoided save in exceptional cases.

(c) CONSULTATION/DISCUSSION

The employer should discuss the restrictive covenants with the employee and listen, with an open mind, to any representations the employee may make. To do so will indicate that the employer has acted fairly and reasonably. In *RS Components Ltd v Irwin* [1974] 1 All ER 41 the fact that such an opportunity was afforded to Irwin was a point which in the opinion of the tribunal was evidence that Irwin had been treated fairly. For a fuller discussion of *RS Components* see paragraph 12.16.

(d) TIMESCALE FOR ACCEPTANCE

This will be dictated by the degree of urgency the employer attaches to the exercise and whether he is proposing to dismiss employees who refuse to consent but offer them the opportunity of continued employment on revised terms. An employer who is proposing this course, and wishes to do so immediately, will be unable to introduce the revised terms until the expiry, in each case, of that employee's notice period. In all other cases, that is, where there is no intention to dismiss or the employer is undecided, the employer can set whatever period he likes. The optimum is usually around two to three weeks which is sufficient time to allow the employee to consider the proposal, take advice if he chooses, and discuss the position with the employer, but not so long that the matter is forgotten about.

(e) DEALING WITH OBJECTORS

The employer will already have decided in principle whether or not he is to dismiss. If he is not to dismiss, the employment simply continues on the existing terms, that is, without the covenants and any incentive offered for them. In this instance there is probably no real gain to the employer providing the incentive offered. In the face of a clear objection the likelihood of the court implying consent is remote. If the employer is to dismiss, it is only a matter of when and whether a further opportunity to accept the covenants is to be offered.

In some cases the employee may make the employer's decision for him by treating the employer's conduct as a repudiation of the contract. In such circumstances the employer has to evaluate the strength of the employee's claim and respond appropriately. That response may either be rejecting the employee's claim and seeking to keep the contract alive or, whilst denying that the proposed introduction of the covenants amounted to a repudiatory breach, accepting the employee's wish to bring the contract to an end as itself a repudiatory breach but this time by the employee.

(f) DEALING WITH THOSE WHO DO NOT RESPOND

Here the employer has two choices: to press the employee for an answer or not to do so but to provide the incentive, hope the employee accepts it and then argue implied consent at a later date. Following the decision in *Credit Suisse Asset Management Ltd v Armstrong* [1996] IRLR 450 (see paras 12.9 and 12.10) the prospects of such an argument are at least reasonable.

Chapter 13

Interim remedies: general

1. Interim remedies: introduction

13.1 In the usual course of events the elaborate pre-trial procedures and the length of the lists of cases awaiting trial mean that litigants cannot expect (except in exceptional circumstances) to have their cases heard for some considerable time after proceedings have been started. Typically, an employment dispute in the High Court (our principal focus in this Chapter) may take two years (or even more) to come on for trial. It is to be expected that the changes brought in by the Civil Procedure Rules 1998 ('CPR 1998') which commenced on 26 April 1999 will result in considerably earlier trial dates being achieved. Evidence at trial will nearly always be by way of 'live' oral testimony and follow disclosure (exchange of all relevant documents in the possession of the parties relevant to the dispute), exchange of experts' reports (if any), the answering of interrogatories, (or since 26 April 1999, new requests for information, instead) (if any) and (usually) exchange of witness statements setting out the evidence which the witnesses intend to give at trial.

13.2 The parties will often need immediate assistance from the court which cannot await trial and the courts have developed procedures to enable relief to be granted pending trial. The range of these intermediate or interlocutory remedies, since 26 April 1999 called interim remedies, is discussed below but they are normally in the form of orders (injunctions) to perform or, more usually, not to perform certain specified acts on pain of being committed to prison for contempt of court.

13.3 In these interim applications evidence is almost always by way of written statements, without the court having the benefit of seeing the evidence tested by cross-examination. The court is required to 'hold the ring' as best it can on the basis of this less satisfactory form of testimony. In order to obtain an interim injunction the person seeking it must pay a price. He must give to the court an undertaking, known as a 'cross-undertaking in damages', that in the event of the court later, on hearing all of the evidence at trial, concluding that the relief ought not to have been granted, he will compensate the party against whom the relief was obtained for any losses he has suffered by the grant of the injunction.

13.4 As cumbrous as full trial procedure may appear to litigants, so the speed with which interim proceedings are dealt with by the courts often takes litigants by surprise, all the more when the decisions of the court taken at the interim stage are often so significant as to dispose of the issues between the parties for all practical purposes. This may be because the parties do not wish to incur the substantial costs of a full trial and so are prepared to abide by a preliminary determination by the court, or because the grant of interim relief may render the decision at trial largely academic. For example, if an ex-employee is restrained by interim injunction from soliciting customers of the ex-employer for, say twelve months, unless a speedy trial is ordered (see below), that decision will govern the position in the twelve-month period and full trial of the question of whether the ex-employer was entitled to that relief will be academic (but not as to questions of damages and legal costs).

2. Jurisdiction

13.5 The jurisdiction of the High Court to grant interim injunctions is set out in Section 37(1) of the Supreme Court Act 1981 which gives the High Court power to grant injunctions (whether interim or final) in all cases in which it appears to the court to be just and convenient to do so.

13.6 Section 37(1) is supplemented by CPR r 25.1 which refers specifically to the grant of interim injunctions. For the county court, see Section 38 of the County Courts Act 1984: search orders (formerly known as Anton Piller orders) may be granted in the county court by any 'Judge duly authorised' (PD 25 paragraph 1.1); litigants should not have to enquire whether a judge in the county court has the necessary 'ticket'; however it would be prudent in seeking a search order in the county court to draw to the attention of the Court Service to the need for a 'duly authorised judge' to entertain the application: *Civil Procedure* (White Book Supplement) paragraph 25.1.2.

3. Exercise of discretion

13.7 The grant of an interim injunction is a matter of the exercise of the court's discretion. It is not granted as of right. Factors which may preclude the grant of a permanent injunction are dealt with in paragraph 15.31. The same factors apply to the grant of interim injunctions. Further, the courts have developed particular principles to be applied in applications for interim injunctions. These were stated by Lord Diplock in *American Cyanamid Co v Ethicon Ltd* [1975] AC 396, 407 (HL) in the following way:

- The applicant must establish that he has a good arguable claim to the right which he seeks to protect, that there is a 'serious issue to be tried'. Accordingly the court must not try to decide the claim on the basis of the affidavits (or evidence in other written format permitted under the CPR). The threshold is not high – it is sufficient that the claim is not frivolous or vexatious.
- If the applicant succeeds in showing a good arguable claim the court will have regard to the balance of convenience.

3(a) Balance of convenience

13.8 The factors relevant to the balance of convenience are various:

● The first question is whether damages would be a sufficient remedy – this will not be so where the respondent is unlikely to be able to pay them (or they will be difficult to quantify). If damages would be an adequate remedy then an interim injunction will not ordinarily be granted. Where it is sought to enforce non-solicitation or area covenants or to restrain the misuse of confidential information, damages will rarely be an adequate remedy.

● If the applicant is unlikely to be able to pay damages under the cross-undertaking (or they would be difficult to quantify) this points towards not granting an interim injunctions.

● It will generally be material to consider whether more harm will be done by the granting or refusal of an interim injunction: *Cayne v Global Natural Resources plc* [1984] 1 All ER 225, 237H (CA). An injunction may be refused if it would be oppressive: *Ocular Sciences Ltd v Aspect Vision Care Ltd* [1997] FSR 289.

● Where the balance of convenience is unclear the court will favour maintenance of the status quo: *Graham v Delderfield* [1992] FSR 313; cf *Garden Cottage Foods Ltd v Milk Marketing Board* [1985] AC 130, 140 (where Lord Diplock refers to meaning of this phrase).

● The court may examine the respective strengths of the evidence but only as a last resort.

● There may be special factors. For example, delay may contra-indicate the grant of relief as in *CMI-Centers for Medical Innovation GmbH v Phytopharm plc* [1999] FSR 235.

3(b) The position under the CPR

13.9 In the Appendix to this Chapter are set out CPR Part 25 (Interim Remedies) and the related Practice Direction ('PD'). It is an open question whether and to what extent the position set out in paragraph 13.8 will be any different under the CPR. While the *Cyanamid* approach is not expressly adopted by the CPR, it would be surprising if the case law as to how the statutory jurisdiction to grant interim injunctions should be exercised, were jettisoned or substantially changed. That said, in exercising the power to grant an interim injunction (given under CPR r 25.1(1)(a)) the Court must seek to give effect to the overriding objective (set out in CPR r 1.1, which is included in the Appendix to this Chapter). The *Cynamid* principles are consistent with the overriding objective of enabling the court to deal with cases justly. These principles are consistent with many (if not all) of the specified elements of the overriding objective:

● **Ensuring that the parties are on an equal footing** – An interim injunction is aimed at preventing harm to the applicant which cannot be compensated in damages but is counterbalanced by the cross undertaking in damages to protect the respondent.

● **Saving expense** – Often interim injunctions involve the outlay of substantial legal costs over a short period - but the grant of relief may save the costs of a full trial, which may be pointless if irremediable damage has been suffered in the meantime.

● **Dealing with cases in ways which are proportionate to the amount of money involved, the importance of the case, the complexity of the issues**

and the financial position of each party – In most restraint of trade, breach of confidence or garden leave injunction cases (see Chapter 14) the applicant should have no difficulty in satisfying this objective. In general terms the courts already have regard to the concept of proportionality: see, for example, *Lock v Beswick* [1989] 1 WLR 1268 in which Hoffmann J stressed that the form of relief should be proportionate to the harm (reasonably) apprehended. As to the last element (financial position of each party) it will usually be the case that the employee or ex-employee (unless supported by a new employer) will have poor financial resources in comparison with the (ex-)employer. This fact will often under *Cyanamid* favour the grant of an injunction. It is difficult to see that this will be any different under the CPR.

- **Ensuring that the case is dealt with expeditiously and fairly** – Expedition and fairness is of the essence to the way the discretion to grant such relief has historically been granted; the notion of balance of convenience is founded on notions of a fair 'holding of the ring' until trial.
- **Allotting to the case an appropriate share of the court's resources, while taking into account the need to allot resources to other cases** – This should not affect cases properly presented. This objective can be seen to confirm the existing practice of the court in the case of long covenants which are arguably enforceable (see para 13.30) of encouraging the respondent to offer up undertakings until speedy trial, so as to avoid unnecessary interim wrangles. The low threshold of proof (triable issue) under *Cyanamid*, is of course also designed to prevent long debates on the merits at the interim stage. On the other hand it may be that in certain cases (as presaged by the much questioned decision of Laddie J in *Series 5 Software v Clarke* [1996] 1 All ER 853) the court may feel more able to have regard to the merits of the dispute, where it is able relatively easily to do so.

13.10 Accordingly, we think that in general terms the CPR is unlikely substantially to affect the way in which discretion in relation to interim injunctions has previously been exercised. However, in particular cases it may be that regard to the overriding objective could produce a different interim result than hitherto. The court may also now be prepared more freely to use the occasion of an interim injunction hearing to adjudicate summarily on certain issues (CPR r 1.4: 'Court's duty to manage cases') and to take other case management decisions.

4. The range of remedies

13.11 Where there have been breaches of the employment contract by the (ex-)employee the principal interim remedies which may be available to the employer are:

- Prohibitory injunctions to restrain breaches of specific restrictive covenants of the employment contract, in particular:
  - non-solicitation/dealing (of or with customers or suppliers) or non-enticement (of employees) covenants;
  - area covenants;
- Injunctions to enforce 'garden leave' provisions of the contract of employment: relief aimed at keeping the contract alive;
- Prohibitory injunctions to enforce covenants (express or implied) relating to

confidential information, and in particular 'springboard injunctions';
- Delivery-up orders in relation to documents (or other property) belonging to the employer;
- Search orders (previously known as Anton Piller orders).

In addition, the CPR offers new opportunities for both claimant and defendant:

- Interim declarations (Rule 25.1(b));
- Pre-action disclosure (Rule 31.16);
- Summary judgment – by claimant and now also by defendant (Part 24).

These remedies are considered in Ch 14.

5. Preliminary considerations

5(a) Notice to the respondent?

13.12 An important initial consideration is whether the application for interim relief should be made on notice to the respondent. There are three possibilities:

- Without notice to the respondent (previously known as ex parte);
- With notice being given to the respondent (previously known as inter partes);
- On short informal notice, where the respondent is given a limited amount of notice, which does not normally allow him enough time to put witness statements or affidavit evidence before the court, although he can be present and make representations (previously known as 'ex parte on notice'). Although this hybrid form of proceeding is not specifically referred to in the CPR it appears to be sanctioned, even favoured above applications without notice (PD 15 paragraph 4.3(3)) which provides that except in cases where secrecy is essential, the applicant should take steps to notify the respondent informally of the application.

5(a)(i) WITHOUT NOTICE

13.13 CPR r 25.3(1) provides in relation to interim remedies that the court may grant an interim remedy on an application made without notice if it appears to the court that there are 'good reasons for not giving notice'. Where an application is made without notice, the applicant should take steps to notify the respondent informally of the application, except in cases where secrecy is essential (PD 25 paragraph 4.3(3)).

13.14 Applications without notice are for cases of real urgency where there has been a true impossibility of giving notice or where (as in applications for search orders) it is essential to maintain secrecy. It is thought that the wide language of CPR r 25.3(1) will in no way relax the approach of the court in this regard. It seems almost certain that the rule will be preserved whereby an application without notice may be refused if there has been delay in bringing the application which has not been properly explained: *Bates v Lord Hailsham of St Marylebone* [1972] 1 WLR 1373, 1380.

13.15 Against the advantage of obtaining relief with maximum speed must be weighed the corresponding responsibility on the part of the applicant and his legal advisers to ensure that full and frank disclosure is made of all relevant matters. Although the duty is not expressly referred to in the CPR, it plainly survives, being a matter of substantive law and is certainly inherent in the overriding objective. PD 25 paragraph 3.3 provides that the applicant's evidence must include 'all material facts of which the court should be aware', which is clearly intended to include adverse evidence. The duty is not limited to matters actually within the knowledge of the applicant but includes also a duty to make reasonable investigation. Failure in this duty can result in disastrous consequences with the injunction being set aside and the applicant being made responsible for damages in respect of loss suffered by the respondent as a result of the (initial) grant of the injunction as well as the legal costs (of both sides).

13.16 Normally the fact that the respondent is represented by solicitors, and the fact that there has been correspondence between the solicitors for the parties, is an indication that an injunction should not be sought without notice.

13.17 Where proper notice has been given for the hearing of an application with notice, the court could nevertheless grant an interim injunction without notice if the application could not, because of pressure of business in the court, be brought on: *Beese v Woodhouse* [1970] 1 WLR 586. If the application has to be adjourned to enable a party to file further evidence, and the respondent will not give an undertaking, the court may grant an interim injunction provided urgency can be demonstrated.

13.18 Parties should now give particularly careful consideration to the potential effects of the requirements of disclosure of evidence before proceeding without notice. Under the CPR, even an unsuccessful applicant (previously only a successful applicant) must, following an application without notice, serve on the previously un-notified respondent a copy of the application notice and any evidence in support (CPR r 23.9(2)). It may be possible to avoid such service by application to the court, which retains a power to order that there need be no service, perhaps in circumstances where such service would involve the disclosure of confidential information. However, the tactical disadvantage of being required in ordinary circumstances to disclose even just the fact of an application might be sufficient in many cases to dissuade potential applicants from making an application without notice, or to delay the making of such applications until the applicant is completely confident of success. Disclosure of evidence which (by virtue of the duty to make full and frank disclosure) contains indications of arguments favourable to the respondent may place the respondent in a much stronger position than previously on the return date.

5(a)(ii) With Notice

13.19 An application with notice for an injunction will normally involve the giving of three clear days' notice together with any evidence in support to the respondent (see below). The rule that evidence should also include all material evidence of which the court should be made aware applies equally to applications with notice (PD 25 paragraph 3.3).

5(a)(iii)   WITH INFORMAL NOTICE

13.20 In view of the amount of notice required for inter partes hearings, there developed the peculiar 'hybrid' of proceeding 'ex parte on notice' (seemingly a contradiction in terms). In practice this meant that the respondent would be present by solicitor or counsel but would not have been given sufficient (or any) time to consider the applicant's evidence in order to enable him to present evidence in reply, although if he managed to do so, he would normally be allowed to rely on it. The application remained technically ex parte and thus the applicant remained under a duty to make full disclosure – although it was not unknown for the applicant to enjoy the unexpected benefit of having non-disclosure 'cured' by matters put before the court by the respondent's representatives at the hearing. Given the direction in PD 25 paragraph 4.3(3) to applicants to give informal notice where possible, it is likely that a similar form of hybrid hearing will continue to exist under the CPR.

An alternative way of dealing with lack of time for service of notice would be to apply at the hearing to abridge time under CPR r 23.7(4) and/or r 3.1(2)(a), the practical effect of which would be to remove the need for a return day.

5(b) The return date

13.21 The return date is the day on which the court considers with notice to all parties whether the relief granted without notice should be continued. The return date will usually be a date a few days after the first hearing. The former distinction in practice between Queen's Bench and Chancery Divisions (no automatic return date in the Queen's Bench Division) has been abrogated. All interim injunctions must contain a return date (PD 25 paragraph 5.1(3)).

5(c) Which court: Chancery Division/Queen's Bench/county court?

13.22 An application for an injunction in the context of the contract of employment may be made in either the Queen's Bench Division or the Chancery Division of the High Court. The decision whether to proceed in one or the other division of the High Court depends on a range of factors. For instance, other relief sought in the action may make proceeding in one division mandatory, for example, if breaches of copyright (or patent, trade marks or registered design) are alleged, the proceedings must be brought in the Chancery Division: Schedule 1 to the Supreme Court Act 1981. Another consideration will be the state of the list in the different divisions and hence the speed with which one can obtain a with notice hearing. In the Chancery Division a hearing of up to two hours may be obtained relatively quickly – it is only if the hearing is estimated as being in excess of two hours that an application by order (special appointment) is required. In the Queen's Bench Division if the hearing is estimated as longer than one hour a special appointment is necessary. Thus, if it is thought that the likely length of the hearing is between one hour and two hours (all other things being equal), this might make proceedings in the Chancery Division desirable. All hearings are now ordinarily held in public (CPR r 39.2(1)) and there is no longer a distinction between Queen's Bench Division and Chancery Division practice in this regard.

13.23 Now that there is no monetary limit on the jurisdiction of the county court to award damages in relation to actions in contract and tort (Section 15 of the County Courts Act 1984, Section 1 of the Courts and Legal Services Act 1990, and Article 7 of the High Court and County Courts Jurisdiction Order 1991), and following the unification of procedures under the CPR, it may be that more injunction cases will be brought in the county court. Although, as mentioned in paragraph 13.6 the county court has only limited power (depending on authorisation of judges) to grant search orders (or freezing injunctions).

5(d) Cross-undertaking as to damages

13.24 The price for being granted an injunction without a full dress trial is that the party seeking the injunction must undertake to the court that if it later be found (on fuller consideration) that the injunction ought not to have been granted, he will compensate the other party for any damage which he has suffered as a result of the injunction having been (wrongly) granted. This is a preliminary consideration of great importance. It will of course depend entirely on the facts of the particular case what the extent of 'exposure' under the cross-undertaking may be. For instance where the employer seeks merely the return of documents which belong to him, the potential liability under the cross-undertaking may be nil (indeed, where there is no dispute as to ownership he may be required to give no cross-undertaking: cf *Fenner v Wilson* [1893] 2 Ch 656 where it was held that if the order is in the nature of a final order no undertaking will be required). However, in the case of a non-dealing or springboard injunction the respondent may be restrained from concluding lucrative contracts or indeed be put out of business altogether – in which case the liability under the cross-undertaking may be very substantial. The party seeking an interim injunction will normally be required to provide evidence of his financial position so as to demonstrate that he will be good for any damages which he may be required to pay under the cross-undertaking. If the financial position of the applicant is inadequate, he may be required to fortify the cross-undertaking, for example, by a bank guarantee or the undertaking of a third party such as a director or associated company of the applicant.

5(e) Which defendants? Ex-employees/third parties who induce breach of contract or conspire to cause economic loss

13.25 The (ex-)employer will need to decide whether he wishes only to proceed against the ex-employee or employees or also against others who have procured the breaches of contract by the ex-employee, typically the new employer. The basis of the claim against the new employer is usually the tort of wrongfully procuring or inducing a breach by the ex-employee of his contract of employment. The gist of the action is the knowing violation of the rights of the ex-employer by the interference with his contractual relations without justification: *Lumley v Gye* [1843-1860] All ER Rep 208; *Quinn v Leathem* [1901] AC 495, 510. An action will, of course, not lie for inducing an employee to leave his employment by giving proper notice to terminate, but will lie if the new employer knowingly induces the employee to leave without proper notice, or to breach the post-employment restraints in the contract of employment, or to use or divulge trade secrets (see *Bents Brewery Co Ltd v Hogan* [1945] 2 All ER 570). The tort of inducing a breach of contract does not require the inducer to know of the 'relevant terms' of the contract. Knowledge of the existence of the contract is sufficient: *Stratford (JT) & Son Ltd v Lindley* [1965] AC 269 (HL). If the inducer is in 'honest doubt' about the contract, he may avoid liability, but only where that doubt goes to the existence of the contract, not as to 'the legal result of known facts': *Solihull MBC v NUT* [1985] IRLR 211. Assuming knowledge of the existence of the contract, the test of intention is objective: *Greig v Insole* [1978] 1 WLR 302, 337–378 (but ignorance of the precise terms may in particular circumstances enable a defendant to satisfy the court that he did not have such intent. Ignorance of this nature, however, does not alone suffice to show absence of intent to procure a breach (per Slade J at page 336)). We do not think that a court would readily assume knowledge on the part of a new employer of restrictive covenants operating post employment, unless there are particular facts to suggest that he is 'turning a blind eye', for example, where they are standard in the particular industry or the ex-employee had a senior position with the previous employer. It has become common in certain sectors for the new employer to extract a warranty from the employee to the effect that he is not, by joining the new employer, acting in breach of obligations owed to the ex-employer. Such a clause is extremely dangerous if the new employee knows of facts which contradict the warranty (because this is likely to lead to charges of 'window dressing') and would, in any event, be unlikely to absolve the new employee where circumstances exist which ought to put him on enquiry. On the other hand, it is not uncommon for contracts of employment in certain sectors to provide that restrictive covenants in the contract of employment should be disclosed to any prospective employee. This may help to undermine the ex-employee where the new employer contends that he did not know of restrictions in the earlier contract of employment. An employer who innocently employs an employee and thereafter discovers that the employment is in breach of the employee's previous contract of employment procures a breach of that contract by continuing the employment: *Jones Brothers (Hunstanton) Ltd v Stevens* [1954] 3 All ER 677 (CA); cf *De Francesco v Barnum* (1890) 45 Ch D 430.

13.26 It is necessary to consider with particular care the evidence that the new employer knew of the term allegedly breached, for example, a post-employment restrictive covenant, and of the breaches. There are also other tactical considerations, for example, by drawing the new employer into the fray, the ex-employer may be inviting the new employer to support the ex-employee in his defence. Unless the ex-employer expects to be able to recover at trial substantial damages which the ex-employee will not be able to pay but which the new employer would be able to pay, there may be little point in joining the new employer as a party to the action. These strategic considerations are dealt with further in Ch 16. Actions for procurement of breach of contract may lie against persons other than the new employer, for example against the ex-employee for inducing a breach of a contract between the ex-employer and a customer (for example, an exclusive long-term supply agreement) or even against customers for inducing a breach by the ex-employee of his contract of employment (for example, a post-termination non-dealing covenant).

13.27 Third parties may be joined as parties to the action on the basis of their being in receipt of confidential information of the claimant (see paras 5.47 to 5.51). They may also be joined on the basis of torts other than procuring breach of contract. Foremost is the tort of conspiracy to injure. Conspiracy is the agreement of two or more parties to do an unlawful act, or to do a lawful act by unlawful means: *Mulcahy v R* (1868) LR 3 HL 306. There are two kinds of conspiracy:

- Where acts which the conspirators agree to do or the means involved are unlawful, involve commission of a crime or civil wrong (for instance, tort or breach of contract);
- Where the conspiracy does not involve the commission of an unlawful act, but where its sole or predominant purpose is to injure another party. In this case conduct which would not be wrongful if carried out by one person becomes tortious because of the combination with the purpose to injure: *Crofter Hand Woven Harris Tweed Co Ltd v Veitch* [1942] AC 435; *Lonrho Ltd v Shell Petroleum Co Ltd (No 2)* [1982] AC 173.

After long debate it has now been established by the House of Lords in *Lonrho plc v Fayed* [1991] 3 WLR 188 that in the case of conspiracy a 'predominant intention to injure' is irrelevant. Accordingly, where a proposed new employer agrees with employees of another employer that they will remove confidential information belonging to the employer or commit other breaches of their contracts of employment, it is not necessary for that employer to show that it was the predominant intention of the proposed employer to injure the employer (rather than merely to advance his own interests). For a detailed discussion of the torts of inducement to breach contract, conspiracy to injure, and other related 'economic torts' see Clerk and Lindsell on *Torts* (16th edn) Chapter 15. Often activities of the ex-employee and/or the new employer may give rise to claims of malicious falsehood by the ex-employer. The essentials of this cause of action are the making of a statement which is untrue, which is made without just cause or excuse and that the ex-employer has suffered special damage thereby: *Royal Baking Powder Co v Wright, Crossley & Co* (1900) 18 RPC 95, 99 (HL).

6. The evidence: the strength of the case

6(a) Summary

13.28 The principles to be applied in applications for interim injunctions were explained by Lord Diplock in *American Cyanamid Co v Ethicon Ltd* [1975] AC 396 (HL) are referred to in paragraph 13.7. Once the applicant has established a serious issue to be tried, the court will not (save as a matter of last resort) ordinarily consider the respective strengths of the witness statement evidence. The *Cyanamid* principles apply to cases of breach of confidence: the (ex-) employer who seeks to restrain the use of confidential information must merely establish an arguable case that the information is confidential or a trade secret as the case may be; see for instance: *Johnson & Bloy (Holdings) Ltd v Wostenholme Rink plc* [1987] IRLR 499; *Lock International plc v Beswick* [1989] 3 All ER 373 and *PSM International Limited plc v Whitehouse* [1992] IRLR 279. These principles survive the CPR: see paragraph 13.9.

13.29 However, the courts will consider the applicant's chances of succeeding at trial where the grant or refusal of an interim injunction would effectively dispose of the whole action: *NWL Ltd v Woods* [1979] 1 WLR 1294 (HL): see also *Cayne v Global Natural Resources plc* [1984] 1 All ER 225 (CA). This is particularly significant in relation to applications for injunctions to enforce covenants in restraint of trade which are of short duration, for example, six- or twelve-month area or non-solicitation/dealing covenants. In the case of short covenants (up to six months and even up to twelve months) it will not usually be possible for there to be a trial until after all or a substantial proportion of the period has elapsed. Accordingly, since the interim proceedings will for practical purposes be decisive as to the position of the parties during the whole or substantially all of the covenant period, the court will take the strength of the case of the respective parties into account. In particular, this means that the court may need to be persuaded that more likely than not the covenant will be regarded at trial as being enforceable (rather than simply being satisfied that it is arguably enforceable). If the covenant is longer than a year, normally (depending on when the alleged breaches were discovered) it will be possible to arrange a speedy trial, well before expiry of the covenants, in which case ordinary *Cyanamid* principles will apply. It should, however, be noted that where breaches of covenant are discovered early, it is sometimes possible to arrange a very early trial indeed (where the legal advisers are energetic, and subject to court listing and, presumably increasingly frequently, following the introduction of the CPR): see paragraph 13.54. This may result in ordinary *Cyanamid* principles applying even to short covenants. This summary of the position appears from the cases discussed below.

6(b)   Discussion

6(b)(i)   Long covenants: *Lawrence David Ltd v Ashton*

13.30   After some doubt (see for example: *Fellowes & Son v Fisher* [1976] 1 QB 122 and *Office Overload v Gunn* [1977] FSR 39) the Court of Appeal has in three recent decisions unequivocally stated that the *Cyanamid* principles are applicable to injunctions to enforce restrictive covenants in employment contracts. In *Dairy Crest Ltd v Piggot* [1989] ICR 92 (a case involving a two-year non-solicitation/dealing covenant) Balcombe LJ stated that since the grant or refusal of the injunction would not effectively dispose of the action (there was clearly going to be a trial), *Cyanamid* principles were applicable. Likewise in *Lawrence David Ltd v Ashton* [1989] IRLR 22 (a case involving a two-year area covenant) the Court of Appeal held that *Cyanamid* principles, governing the grant of interim injunctions, are applicable where either there is an unresolved dispute on the affidavit evidence or a question of law to be decided, and also apply in cases of interim injunctions in restraint of trade cases just as in other cases. Balcombe LJ stated that covenants in restraint of trade are not a special category and the legal profession should be disabused of the widely-held view that the *Cyanamid* approach is not relevant where an interim injunction is sought to enforce a contractual obligation in restraint of trade. He went on to express the view that cases in which an employer seeks to enforce a restrictive covenant in a contract of employment are singularly appropriate for speedy trial. Further, a respondent who has entered into a contractual restraint should seriously consider offering an appropriate undertaking (see para 13.50) until the hearing of the action, provided that a speedy hearing of the action can then be fixed and the applicant is likely to be able pay damages on his cross-undertaking. It is only if a speedy trial is not possible and the action cannot be tried before the period of restraint has expired or has run a large part of its course, that it will be necessary to have a contest on the interim application, because the grant of the interim injunction will effectively dispose of the action, thus bringing the case within the exception to the rule in *Cyanamid*, such as was considered in *NWL v Woods*. It is then that the judge may appropriately go on to consider the prospects of the applicant succeeding in the action. Balcombe LJ continued that another way of reaching the same conclusion is to say that the longer the period of the interim injunction, the more likely it is that the respondent may suffer damage (if the injunction is wrongly granted) which is uncompensatable by the applicants on their cross-undertaking, and therefore it becomes necessary to consider the relative strengths of each party's case under the last stage of *Cyanamid*. This latter comment is inconsistent with practice because the ordering of a speedy trial (to which the court will readily accede) undermines the argument.

13.31 Applying the *Cyanamid* approach the court in *Lawrence David* allowed the appeal (in part) and granted an injunction in terms of the area covenant (which had most of the period of two years still to run) since:

- There were serious questions to be tried as to:
  - Whether the employers had acted in repudiatory breach of contract so as to destroy the covenant relied on by them;
  - The validity of the covenant, which was not 'obviously bad';
  - Issues of fact such as the nature of the trade secrets and confidential information, and the area of restraint.
- Damages would not be an adequate remedy for the employers.
- The employers were good for damages on their cross-undertaking.
- The long-term damage to the employee through being kept out of the employment market could be minimised by ensuring a speedy trial.

It was accordingly not necessary to compare the relative strengths of the respective cases. The injunction was granted for a period of about three and a half months by when it was expected the matter would be ready for trial.

6(b)(ii) Short covenants: *Lansing Linde Ltd v Kerr*

13.32 In *Lansing Linde Ltd v Kerr* [1991] 1 All ER 418 (a case of a 12-month area covenant), in which the trial would not take place until the period of restraint had expired or nearly expired, the Court of Appeal (applying Balcombe LJ's dictum in *Lawrence David*) held that the judge below was right to require the employer to satisfy him that not only was there a serious issue to be tried, but also that it was more likely than not that he would succeed at trial. Since the delay in obtaining a trial date meant that the likely effect of the grant of an injunction would be finally to decide the dispute against the employee, some assessment of the merits, more than merely that there was a serious issue to be tried, was required. It should, however, be noted that the Court of Appeal were of the view that it would have been wrong to regard the likelihood of success as the sole consideration (even though it had apparently been the determinative factor in that particular case). Staughton LJ (at page 424 a–b) emphasised that there should in such cases be only 'some assessment' of the merits because the courts constantly seek to discourage prolonged interlocutory battles on witness statement evidence – it was for the judge to control the extent of this assessment.

6(c) Conclusions

13.33 Despite recent emphasis by the Court of Appeal that *Cyanamid* principles apply to restrictive covenant injunctions, the applicant in his witness statement should not merely set up an arguable case on the merits but (within reasonable limits) show the strength of his case.

This is because:

- There is a tendency in modern practice for the period of covenants not to be long, and it is relatively unlikely that the parties and the court will be ready for trial before the expiry of the covenant. In many cases the grant or refusal of the injunction may effectively dispose of the action, therefore the court will often have regard to the merits.

- Conversely, where the covenants are long and a trial cannot be held within a short time, damages may not adequately compensate the respondent and this may result in the court referring to the merits (see statement of Lord Justice Balcombe in *Lawrence David* referred to in para 13.30).

- The court may conclude that the issues are simple or do not require further investigation and therefore decide the matter on the merits: see *Business Seating (Renovations) Ltd v Broad* [1989] ICR 729; *Mainmet Holdings plc v Austin* [1991] FSR 538. Under its case management powers the court may strike out a statement of case if it concludes that it discloses no reasonable grounds for bringing or defending the claim or is an abuse of the court's process or is shown to be likely to obstruct the just disposal of the proceedings (CPR r 3.4) or it may give summary judgment where a party has no real prospect of succeeding in his claim or defence (CPR r 24.2).

- In a breach of confidence case the applicant must identify properly the confidential information on which he relies. In a restrictive covenant case it should be borne in mind that the court (even when applying *Cyanamid*) will not hesitate to strike out covenants which are plainly bad.

- In relation to mandatory injunctions there is authority to the effect that *Cyanamid* rules do not apply: *Leisure Data v Bell* [1988] FSR 367 (CA); cf *Locabail International Finance Ltd v Agroexport, The Sea Hawk* [1986] 1 All ER 901 (CA) and *Films Rover International Ltd v Cannon Film Sales Ltd* [1987] 1 WLR 670; *Nottingham Building Society v Eurodynamics Systems plc* [1993] FSR 468, 474 approved by the Court of Appeal in *Zocknoll Group Ltd v Mercury Communications Ltd* [1998] FSR 354.

7. Obtaining the evidence

13.34 Usually the witness statements necessary to support an application for an injunction are provided by the employer and his present employees. Sometimes witness statements are provided by customers, although for obvious reasons there is often a reluctance on the part of employers to draw their customers into the fray.

7(a) The use of enquiry agents

13.35 Sometimes the evidence of enquiry agents is required to bolster a case in which the evidence of breach of covenant or confidence is too sketchy or anecdotal. There is no objection in principle to using enquiry agents for this purpose. Trap orders by an agent provocateur are permissible but the applicant must make full disclosure in his application: *Walt Disney Productions Ltd v Gurvitz* [1982] FSR 446. The court may, however, look askance at such evidence – it should be used judiciously. Where the identity of informants cannot be revealed, the judge must be told that this information cannot be given to him. It will be for the judge to decide to what extent he is prepared to rely on information coming from anonymous and unidentifiable sources: *WEA Records Ltd v Vision's Channel 4 Ltd* [1983] 1 WLR 721, 724. The duty to make full and frank disclosure will require the applicant to disclose the fact that he has used enquiry agents, and probably also the means whereby they have obtained their information.

8. Witness statements or other evidence in writing

8(a) Form

13.36 The rules relating to the form and content of witness statements are set out in PD 32 paragraphs 17 to 22. Statements of information and belief (that is, information not within the personal knowledge of the person signing the witness statement) are admissible, but PD 32 paragraph 18.2 requires that the witness statement indicate which statements are from the witness's own knowledge and which are matters of information or belief and that the source of such information or belief be identified. If the source of the information is not identified, the court may refuse to admit it as evidence and may refuse to allow the costs arising from its preparation (PD 32 paragraph 25.1).

8(b) General contents checklist

13.37 The witness statements will need to cover:

- Each of the elements of the particular cause of action in order to show a serious issue to be tried; in cases based on contract this involves identification of the contract, particular terms relied on, the facts constituting breach, and reference to the loss or expected loss flowing from the breach. Where the injunction sought is to enforce a non-solicitation/dealing covenant or area covenant, all the facts relevant to show the reasonableness of the covenant must be covered, including the particular interest which the covenant is intended to protect. In breach of confidence cases (see para 13.38) it is necessary to set out all the facts relied on as proving that the information is a trade secret or confidential (see Ch 5).
- The facts generating a claim for injunctive relief, in particular:
  - Where the injunction is on the basis of threatened (not actual) breach (quia timet), the grounds for such apprehension must be set out;
  - The elements relevant to the balance of convenience, for example:
    - (i) the nature of the potential harm to the applicant, if the injunction is not granted, and the reasons why such harm is not compensatable in damages: what is known about the financial position of the respondent and (where appropriate) that the harm which the applicant might suffer is not easily quantifiable;
    - (ii) the reasons why the cross-undertaking in damages will provide adequate protection to the respondent: the financial position of the applicant and (where appropriate) that any loss to the respondent is easily quantifiable.
- All other facts which are required to be disclosed by virtue of the duty to make full and frank disclosure.
- If the application is made without notice – the facts justifying this course.

For an example of a witness statement, see Ch 16, Appendix 3.

8(c) Special case: witness statements in breach of confidence cases

13.38 Particular difficulties may be experienced in the preparation of witness statements in confidential information cases. The employer will need sufficiently to identify the secrets or confidential information to persuade the court that there are genuine trade secrets or items of confidential information and the reasons therefor (see Ch 5). Against this is the need not to refresh the (ex-)employee's knowledge of the trade secrets in question – or indeed (in cases of uncertainty as to precisely which of a range of secrets the (ex-)employee has learnt) not to disclose the full range of secrets to him. Normally in the case of commercial secrets it is easy enough to describe the class of documents (eg customer list) without revealing its contents. In cases of technical secrets it is usually also possible to describe the class of secrets and the reasons why the information or particular elements of it are secret or confidential without divulging the detailed contents–but not always. The dilemma is described by Graham J in *Diamond Stylus Co Ltd v Bauden Precision Diamonds Ltd* [1973] RPC 675:

> '[The applicant's] difficulty is that if he does disclose in detail what his process is, he thereby gives away secrets, which is the one thing he does not want to do, though he may in such a case be able to make out his prima facie case by showing that the defendant has used part or the whole of that process. If on the other hand he is not prepared to disclose his secret then he is in obvious difficulty in showing that what the defendant has done is to take that secret, because there is not ex hypothesi sufficient identification of the latter to enable a satisfactory conclusion to be drawn.'

13.39 In *Under Water Welders & Repairers v Street and Longthorne* [1968] RPC 498 Buckley J said that:

> 'It is not to be expected that a [claimant] who is seeking to protect some commercial secret will disclose the nature of that secret, particularly in interlocutory proceedings ...'

Buckley J (somewhat surprisingly) granted an injunction despite finding that the applicants had not in their evidence condescended to any details as to precisely which characteristic of the process gave it a confidential character.

13.40 However, in *Diamond Stylus* Graham J distinguished *Under Water Welders* saying:

> '... each case must be judged in the light of its own particular facts and the governing principle in each case is that the [claimant] must make out a prima facie case if he is to be entitled to an interlocutory injunction. It may be in some cases that a [claimant] process in which he claims secrecy or confidence. On the other hand there are other cases where it seems to me, depending on the surrounding circumstances and the state of knowledge generally in the art, that he may have to go further and disclose at any rate the essential features of his process which he says have been taken.'

13.41 Although since the decision of the House of Lords in *American Cyanamid Co v Ethicon Ltd* [1975] AC 396 the applicant need only show a serious question to be tried as to the existence of a trade secret, it is suggested that post *Cyanamid* there has been no real change in the standard of proof in this regard. In *Lock International plc v Beswick* [1989] 3 All ER 373, 378 h–j Hoffmann J said:

'It is of course tempting in an action such as this, concerned with the technicalities of electronics, to say that the questions at issue can only be investigated at the trial and that for *Cyanamid* purposes the plaintiff must be treated as having an arguable case ... It would however, be unjust to the defendants simply to allow the [claimant] to blind the court with scientific banalities.'

In *CMI-Centers for Medical Innovation GmbH v Phytopharm plc* [1999] FSR 235 Laddie J reiterated the importance even at the interim stage of the claimant identifying precisely the information he relies on.

13.42 Indeed, in accordance with the decision of the Court of Appeal in *Faccenda Chicken Limited v Fowler* [1986] 3 WLR 288 it is necessary, in the absence of an express non-solicitation/dealing or area covenant, to show an arguable case that the information is a trade secret and not merely confidential (unless there has been a breach of confidence during employment, for example, removal of confidential documents): see *Johnson & Bloy (Holdings) Ltd v Wostenholme Rink plc* [1987] IRLR 499; it is essentially a question of degree: *PSM International plc v Whitehouse* [1992] IRLR 279, 282 (see Ch 5).

13.43 As in cases where it is necessary to reveal secrets to the court in order to discharge the duty to make full and frank disclosure (referred to above), a practical solution in many cases may be to include the details of the secret information in a separate witness statement to the main witness statement or by way of an exhibit – which will be disclosed to the respondent's solicitors and counsel (and where necessary, any expert witnesses) but not to the respondent. Again, each such document should be marked as confidential and numbered, and a specific undertaking extracted from the respondent's solicitor not to 'read' such documents onto its computer system, not to disclose the contents except, for example, to legal advisers and expert witnesses, not to copy the document (or not to make more than a fixed number of copies), and at the end of the proceedings to return to the applicant all the documents (and any copies): see *Warner-Lambert Co v Glaxo Laboratories* [1975] RPC 354.

13.44 Even without such express safeguards, the applicant will be protected by the rule that a party who obtains disclosure may use the documents disclosed to him only for the purpose of conducting his own case (except where the document has been read or referred to in a public hearing (save where the court otherwise orders), or the court gives permission, or the parties agree): CPR r 31.22. Particular consideration should be given to the fact that once documents are read in open court they are considered to be in the public domain. Further, documents read by the court as part of pre-trial preparation are likely to be treated as if they had been read out in open court: *SmithKline Beecham Biological SA v Connaught Laboratories Inc*: (1999) Times 13 July. See also *Robert Bunn v BBC* [1997] FSR 70. Accordingly, if it is sought to maintain confidentiality in particular documents, those documents should be placed in a separate confidential file and it may be that references to those documents should be contained in a separate confidential skeleton argument. The court should then be asked to deal with all matters relating to those documents in private.

13.45 A different aspect of the same problem is shown by *Amber Size & Chemical Co Ltd v Menzel* [1913] 2 Ch 239. In that case Astbury J held that where the court is satisfied that there is a secret process and that the employee has learnt it in the course of his employment, but the court does not know the full nature and extent of the secret process, it can still grant an injunction – despite the normal rule that the court will not make an order the performance of which it cannot enforce. In the event of alleged breach of the order the applicant could supply to the court details of the process, subject to proper safeguards against disclosure.

9. Documentation: generally

13.46 For the purpose of obtaining an interim injunction it is necessary to produce the following documents:

- **A claim form** – Application may be made before issue of proceedings (CPR r 25.2(a)), but the court will require an undertaking to issue a claim form immediately (PD 25 paragraph 4.4(1) or direct that proceedings be commenced pursuant to its power under CPR r 25.2(3). Where possible, the claim form should be served with any order obtained. Because of the requirements of urgency and, often, lack of knowledge of the full details of the claimant's case, it will often be wise not to serve Particulars of Claim with the claim form at the outset (as had become the practice with writs which were commonly generally endorsed) – but then the Particulars of Claim must be served in accordance with CPR r 7.4(1)(b), within 14 days of service of the claim form, unless an extension of time is obtained from the defendant or the court. In *Hytrac Conveyors Limited v Conveyors International Limited* [1983] 1 WLR 44 the claimant's claim was struck out through failure to serve the Statement of Claim (as it was then known) within the time limits, despite having executed a Search Order.
- **An application notice** – (Form N244) – although the court may in cases of real urgency dispense with the need for a notice (CPR r 23.3(2)(b)) and instead accept an undertaking to file an application notice (and any evidence in support) and pay the appropriate fee on the same or next working day (PD 25 paragraph 5.1(4)). The notice must set out, briefly, the grounds relied on (CPR r 23.6(b)) and must be verified by a statement of truth pursuant to CPR Part 22.
- **A witness statement or witness statements** – Signed or in draft, unless the applicant proposes to rely on the contents of his application notice or particulars of claim (provided that such notice or particulars are verified by a statement of truth in accordance with CPR Part 22);
- **Draft minutes of order** – Which should also be made available to the court on disk in WordPerfect 5.1 format. Standard form precedents for interim injunctions were set down in *Practice Direction (Interlocutory Injunctions: Forms)* [1996] 1 WLR 1551, and should continue to be used with modification to reflect the CPR. Standard forms for search and freezing orders are annexed to PD 25.

10. Obtaining interim injunctions

10(a) Without notice

13.47 The procedure for making urgent applications (including applications by telephone) and applications without notice is set out in CPR rule 25 and PD 25 paragraph 4 (set out in the Appendix to this Chapter).

10(b) On notice

13.48 Not later than three days before the hearing, the application notice and evidence in support must be served on the respondent (PD 25 paragraph 2.2). If the court is to serve the application notice on the respondent, the applicant must file evidence in support at the same time as he files the application notice (CPR r 23.7(1)(2)), because an application notice, when served, must be accompanied by a copy of any evidence in support. The applicant must file sufficient copies of the application notice and evidence for the court and each respondent.

13.49 There is no specific requirement that counsel provide time estimates for the hearing. It is the sort of good practice which is encompassed by the overriding objective and will therefore continue.

11. Undertakings

11(a) Undertakings to the court

13.50 Frequently, a defendant faced with an application for injunctive relief will offer to the court undertakings pending trial at least in relation to some of the relief claimed (or he may consent to all or part of the interim order sought by the applicant). This may be convenient where:

- The respondent believes that the chances of defending the interim application are poor (for example, where an express covenant in restraint is not obviously bad), and the period of the covenant is long enough for there to be trial well before the expiry of the restrictions; or
- There is no inconvenience in offering the undertaking, for example, the respondent has no intention of using the applicant's trade secrets.

13.51 It should be noted that the consent by the respondent to an interim order does not prejudice the respondent's entitlement to claim damages under the cross-undertaking, if at trial it is found that the order ought not to have been granted (at all or in such wide terms): *Universal Thermosensors Ltd v Hibben* [1992] 1 WLR 840, 857. Presumably the same will apply where the respondent gives an undertaking in the form sought by the applicant.

13.52 An undertaking is as good as an injunction: breach of either may amount to contempt of court. The party giving such an undertaking may not apply to vary or discharge it without a change of circumstances: *Chanel Ltd v FW Woolworth & Co Ltd* [1981] 1 WLR 485. The respondent who is prepared to give interim undertakings but wishes to reserve to himself the possibility (for example, once he has gathered his evidence) to apply to vary or discharge the undertakings should insist on the inclusion in the order of a 'liberty to apply without showing change of circumstances'.

11(b) Contractual undertakings

13.53 Frequently, instead of offering an undertaking to the court, a respondent will offer a so-called contractual undertaking, that is, an undertaking offered to the applicant. This happens frequently where proceedings are threatened but have not yet been issued. It is unclear what the precise status and effect of this sort of undertaking may be, in particular whether an ex-employee who gave such an undertaking (for example, not to carry on business in a certain area defined in an area covenant) would thereafter still be able to argue that the covenant was too broad. In our view, at least where the ex-employee is legally advised, the courts would be likely to enforce the undertaking. Otherwise it would mean that in all cases, it would be necessary to go through the formality of issuing proceedings and making application to the court, a matter which is hardly in the public interest. In other cases (at least where it is clear that no undue pressure has been brought to bear on the employee), similar arguments might be said to apply. If we are wrong as to the enforceability of contractual undertakings, at the very least the ex-employer may be able successfully to argue that the fact that the ex-employee has confirmed the covenants after employment (and on advice, if that be the case) is further evidence of the reasonableness of the covenants.

12. Order for speedy trial

13.54 RSC Order 29 r 5 provided:

> 'Where on the hearing of an application, made before the trial of a cause or matter, for an injunction it appears to the court that the matter in dispute can be better dealt with by an early trial than by considering the whole merits thereof for the purposes of the application, the court may make an order accordingly and may also make such orders as respects the period before trial as the justice of the case requires.
>
> Where the court makes an order for early trial it shall by the order determine the place and mode of trial.
>
> While the CPR do not include specific reference to such a power it is almost certainly subsumed within the court's general powers of case management.'

13.55 In *Lawrence David Ltd v Ashton* [1989] IRLR 22, 27 Balcombe LJ said that cases where it is sought to enforce restrictive covenants in employment contracts are singularly appropriate for speedy trial and that a defendant who has entered into a contractual restraint should seriously consider, when the matter first comes before the court, offering an appropriate undertaking until the hearing of the action, provided that a speedy hearing of the action can then be fixed, and the claimant is likely to be able to pay any damages on his cross- undertaking. In this case (heard in the Court of Appeal on 4 July), directions were given for the action to be tried in October. Directions may include that the witness statements stand as pleadings (usually where a party is unrepresented).

13. Interim declarations

13.56 Interim declarations were, until the introduction of the CPR, unknown to English law. However, CPR r 25.1(1)(b) provides that a court may grant such a remedy. It remains to be seen how the provision will be implemented in practice. Interim declarations may be useful for example to an (ex-)employee who cannot find alternative employment because others will not risk litigation against the ex-employer who makes it known that he will enforce restrictive covenants of the contract of employment, which the ex-employee believes are unenforceable). It may be quicker and cheaper to go down the route of an interim declaration than to head for speedy trial. An interim declaration may be sufficient reassurance to third parties until trial. If matters are thrashed out in detail in the interim proceedings, it may be that the parties will not want to spend further money on going to trial on the same matters. Until more is known about the operation of interim declarations, however, it is not possible precisely to gauge the usefulness of this remedy in the context of this book.

14. Summary judgment

13.57 Under the CPR it is now possible for a defendant (as well as a claimant) to obtain summary judgment, where there is no real prospect of the claimant succeeding in his claim: CPR r 24.2. This provides a defendant with a greater prospect of terminating hopeless proceedings at an early stage. In *TSC (Europe) v Massey* [1999] IRLR 22 the defendant obtained the dismissal of an action under RSC Order 14A on the basis that the covenant was unenforceable. However, it is important to note that the court reached its conclusion on the suitability of RSC Order 14A on the basis that the defendant accepted as accurate the evidence of the claimant such that there was a comprehensive factual basis for the issue to be determined under Order 14A, and the evidence so elicited put the matter in a way which was as favourable to the claimant as it could reasonably have hoped. Accordingly, although the enforceability of the covenant was an issue 'sensitive to the facts' and issues of fact were 'interwoven' with the legal issue of enforceability, the court felt able to decide the issue. If (as has been suggested) the test for summary judgment is less stringent than under the old rules, more adventurous use may be made by both claimants and defendants of the summary procedure.

15. Pre-action disclosure orders

13.58 Since April 1999 pre-action disclosure (previously limited in application) is now available in all kinds of proceedings: Civil Procedure (Modifications of Enactments) Order 1998 (SI 1998/2940). An application for pre-action disclosure may only be made:

- Where the applicant and the respondent are likely to be parties to the proceedings; and
- If proceedings had been started, the respondent's duty by way of standard

disclosure would extend to the document or class of document of which the applicant now seeks disclosure: (CPR r 31.16(a), (b)(and (c)); and

- If disclosure before proceedings have been started is 'desirable in order to dispose fairly of the anticipated proceedings, assist the dispute to be resolved without proceedings or save costs' (r 31.16(3)(d)).

Accordingly, an applicant may now use this procedure to demonstrate whether or not he may have a cause of action at all. On the other hand, it is to be expected that the courts will continue to be wary to ensure that these new provisions are not used as 'fishing expeditions'. Three methods of control may be used. First, an order for pre-action disclosure must specify the documents or class of documents to be disclosed: (r 31.16(4)(a)) so that a general application for 'standard disclosure' will be likely to fail. Second, the court is likely to insist on an appropriate level of evidence being before it, to ensure that the application is not being used oppressively, speculatively or simply to advance normal time limits for disclosure. Third, by imposing costs on the applicant (cf CPR r 48.1(2)) the general rule is that costs are awarded to the party ordered to make disclosure but see r 48.1(3) for circumstances in which the prima facie rule may be displaced). Pre-action disclosure may also be made against non-parties (CPR r 3.17(2)). The application must be supported by evidence and may only lead to an order where the documents which are sought are likely to support the case of the applicant or adversely affect the case of another party and disclosure is necessary to dispose fairly of the claim or to save costs r 3.17(3)). This procedure is in addition to the existing procedures for obtaining documents from third parties notably:

- Norwich Pharmacal orders (*Norwich Pharmacal Co v Commissioners of Customs and Excise* [1974] AC 133) – in which it is necessary to show that the party against whom disclosure is sought is (through no fault of his own) 'mixed up' in the tortious conduct of a party to the proceedings. For a recent generous grant of such an order see *The Coca Cola Co v British Telecommunications plc* [1997] FSR 518 in which BT was ordered to provide the address of an intended defendant in respect of which it was the mobile telephone service provider. The mobile phone was likely to have been used by the intended defendant in committing the torts alleged against him of breach of trade marks/passing off.
- The device used in *Khanna v Lovell White Durrant* [1995] 1 WLR 121– where the court invented the idea of notional early trial dates for witnesses to attend to bring under subpoena documents required for trial, so that they could be examined and copied before the 'real' trial date.

It is to be expected that the new pre-action disclosure procedure will now become the usual procedure and that only rarely will it be necessary to resort to the pre-existing methods. There are certain kinds of cases in which the new pre-action disclosure procedure may be expected to be of considerable benefit in particular to (ex-)employers. For instance an (ex-)employer may believe that its data has been removed by an (ex-)employee and/or has transferred to a competitor which employs or is about to employ the (ex-)employee. There may not be evidence sufficient to justify a search order or it may not wish to incur the costs of executing such an order. Further, it may not wish to commence full scale proceedings until it has verified its suspicions. An application for pre-action disclosure against the (ex-)employee and/or the competitor may be a viable proposition. Quite apart from pre-action disclosure, there lies the possibility of early disclosure in the action. For example, *Intelsec Systems Ltd v Ogrechie-Cini* [1999] 4 All ER 11 the deputy judge ordered disclosure by ex-employees of the names and addresses of business contacts, irrespective of whether the contacts had been made before or after termination of employment. Where such contacts had been made during employment on behalf of the employer, he was entitled to make use of them and the employee had to disclose the names and addresses, even if he was allowed to approach such contacts after his employment ceased. Similarly, if the employee had approached the contact on his own account during his employment, there would be a prima facie breach of the duty of fidelity and the employee was entitled to claim the contact as his own. In respect of persons approached after the termination of employment, the position was more difficult, but such disclosure could be justified if needed to rectify misrepresentations arising out of passing off. The disclosure ordered in respect of persons approached after termination of employment was accordingly more limited. Also in *SBJ Stevenson Ltd v Mandy* (unreported) 30 July 1999 (RCJ) the court had, at the interim stage, ordered the defendant to disclose on affidavit any soliciting of the clients of SBJ Stevenson (and disclosure of certain of its confidential information).

16. Stay in favour of mediation

13.59 The CPR now makes provision for the court of its own motion at any stage of the proceedings to stay proceedings for the purposes of mediation of the dispute CPR r 26.4. This is in addition to the existing procedure under Section 9 of the Arbitration Act 1996 for compulsory stay in favour of arbitration where there is a binding agreement in writing to arbitrate (satisfying Section 1 of that Act). In the case of mediation, however, there is no necessity for any pre-existing agreement. It is to be expected that in appropriate cases a defendant facing an application for an interim injunction may seek to persuade the court not to grant such relief pending mediation. However, it is to be expected in cases where urgent relief is required by the claimant, an application to stay would not succeed unless the defendant was prepared to give appropriate undertakings pending the mediation. No doubt the court would be wary of this procedure being used to frustrate the legitimate needs of those seeking to enforce restrictive covenants or obligations of confidentiality. Equally, there may be occasions on which a claimant may wish to use this procedure.

17. Serving interim orders

13.60 The order should be endorsed with a penal notice warning of the consequences of breach of the order: RSC Order 45 r 7(4); CCR Order 29(1)(3) (preserved under CPR). The order must be served personally on the respondent: RSC 45 r 7(2). If the respondent is a company, it must be served on the officer against whom it is sought to enforce the order: RSC Order 45 r 7(3); CCR Order 29(1)(2)(a). This is essential in the case of a mandatory injunction (that is, an order requiring the respondent to undertake positive action). However, in order to enforce a negative injunction (that is, an order that the respondent refrain from doing something) it is not strictly necessary that the order containing the order should be drawn, endorsed with a penal notice and served in accordance with RSC Order 45 r 7, provided the respondent knew of the terms of the order: RSC Order 45 r (6). Likewise, in the case of an undertaking given by the respondent to the court, it is sufficient that the respondent understood the effect of the undertaking, but the practice is still to serve the order containing the undertaking with a suitably worded penal notice: *Hussain v Hussain* [1986] 1 All ER 961 (CA); CCR Order 29 r 1A.

18. Committal proceedings

13.61 Breach of an injunction or an undertaking given to court is punishable as a contempt of court by committal: RSC Order 52 (for the county court see Order 29) – both preserved under the CPR Schedule 1. Apart from the power to imprison for contempt, there is power to impose a fine or occasionally to order sequestration of assets (see RSC Order 45 r 5). An application may be made against a third party who aids and abets the commission of a contempt. For example, where an ex-employer has obtained an injunction against an ex-employee, for example, restraining him from working in a particular area, he should inform the new employer employing the ex-employee of the injunction, so that the ex-employer can enforce the injunction against both ex-employee and new employer. Where the order is against a body corporate, a director or other officer may be committed: RSC Order 45 r 5(1) (iii). Committal proceedings are brought by Notice of Motion supported by witness statement. It is vital that the Notice of Motion should state precisely the acts which constitute the alleged contempt.

19. Trial or settlement

13.62 Usually disputes involving breaches of covenants in restraint of trade or confidence do not proceed to trial. Because of the urgency which usually attends such cases, it is usual for there to be an application for an interim injunction. Where such an application is made, the decision of the court at the interim stage is often treated by the parties for practical purposes as determinative of the issues between them, with the question of liability for legal costs being left to be negotiated between the parties. The reasons for the parties adopting this pragmatic approach are:

- That often the real issue, namely whether the (ex-)employee may or may not carry out certain activities for a limited period, is effectively decided by the grant or refusal of the interim injunction;
- The financial cost of proceeding to trial (both legal and administrative). There will nearly always be an irrecoverable costs element, even for the winning party who wins all the points in issue, because he will normally be awarded his costs only on a 'standard basis' (see para 13.65);
- The difficulty for the applicant of proving that damage has resulted from the alleged breaches and the amount of such loss;
- The unlikelihood of recovering substantial damages and legal costs from the (ex-)employee, having regard to what is known of his financial position. The position may be different where the new employer is included as a defendant.

For these reasons the parties may decide to treat the application for interim relief as the trial of the action. This may be agreed before the interim hearing and may be appropriate where the whole case depends on whether or not a restrictive covenant is enforceable. The parties may feel that the judge has as good an opportunity of deciding the matter on witness statement as on oral evidence at trial, and that therefore a trial will be a waste of expense: see for instance *Greer v Sketchley Ltd* [1979] FSR 197. Alternatively, the parties may, after the interim decision of the judge, decide to treat the matter as final, again to save costs. As either claimant or defendant may now make an offer to settle, an increasing number of actions may settle following the interim decision, with the view of the judge at the interim stage shaping the parties' approach to Part 36 offers (see further para 13.66).

20. Costs orders

13.63 Legal costs are dealt with under CPR Part 44 ff. Some of the various types of costs orders which may be made by the court are defined in CPR r 44.3(6). The award of legal costs is always a matter for the discretion of the court, but that discretion in relation to the costs of interim applications has hitherto normally be exercised as follows:

- On an application without notice costs will be reserved for later decision.
- After an interim hearing on notice:
  - In the Queen's Bench Division: costs in the case (formerly known as costs in the cause, that is, costs are awarded to the party who ultimately wins at trial);
  - In the Chancery Division: if the applicant wins the interim application: applicant's costs in the case (the applicant will recover his costs of the interim proceedings if he wins at trial, but even if he loses at trial he will not have to pay the respondent's costs of the interim application). If the respondent wins: respondent's costs in the case. However, in the Chancery Division the order may be as in the Queen's Bench Division, that is, costs in cause irrespective of who wins the interim application: see the discussion in *Steepleglade Limited v Stratford Investments Ltd* [1976] FSR 3. The Queen's Bench Division approach appears preferable because it would be quite wrong that, for instance, where an applicant has obtained an injunction by means of evidence which at trial is shown to be false, or even in cases such as *Universal Thermosensors Ltd v Hibben* [1992] 1 WLR 840 where at trial it is found that the interim injunction was too wide in its scope, the successful respondent (at trial) should be deprived of his costs of the interim hearing. At least in cases where there is a substantial (and material) conflict of evidence at the interim stage, the proper order ought to be costs in the cause, all the more where the court applying the *Cyanamid* guidelines refuses to consider the merits in any detail.
- At trial, the costs will usually follow the event, that is, the costs of the winner are to be paid by the loser who thus has to bear two sets of costs, his own and that of his opponent.

13.64 Perhaps the most dramatic change to interim applications has been brought about by the rules relating to summary assessment of costs (CPR r 44.7 and PD48 paragraph 4). The effect is that in cases lasting a day or less (and many interim injunction cases fall into this category) the court will often immediately assess costs and these will be ordered to be paid within fourteen days. This prospect is having, and is likely to continue to have, a dramatic impact on the advice given to clients whether to pursue or resist interim applications. Gone are the days in which advice could be given that no costs would have to be paid until well into the future, by which time they might well be subsumed in the overall negotiations between the parties. Where it is sought to obtain a summary assessment of costs, a written statement of costs in the form required by PD48 paragraph 4 must be filed at court and copies served against the intended paying party not less than 24 hours before the date fixed for the hearing.

13.65 Costs are normally awarded on a 'standard basis' which in practice used to mean that the party awarded costs would only recover about two-thirds of the costs actually expended by him. The basis of assessment has now changed and costs assessed on the standard basis will only be allowed where they are proportionate to the matters in issue (CPR r 44.4(2)). It is only (fairly rarely) that in order to mark its disapproval of the conduct of a party, in particular as to the mode of conduct of the proceedings, the court will award indemnity costs, in which case it is presumed, unless the contrary is shown, that costs have been incurred reasonably. In committal proceedings it is usual for costs to be awarded on an indemnity basis.

13.66 Under CPR Part 36, either party may now make an offer, with attendant costs consequences, to settle the claim. The costs consequences, in the context of an action for an injunction, are as follows:

- If the offer is accepted (either the defendant accepts the claimant's offer or the claimant accepts the defendant's offer) then the claimant will be entitled to costs up to the date of that acceptance;
- Where a defendant's offer is not accepted but the claimant fails to 'obtain a judgment which is more advantageous' than that offer, the claimant will usually be ordered to pay the defendant's costs from the latest date on which the claimant could have accepted the offer;
- Where a claimant's offer is not accepted and the claimant obtains a judgment which is 'more advantageous' to the claimant, he may obtain costs on the indemnity basis from the latest date on which the offer could have been accepted and interest on those costs at up to 10% over base rate.

Now that a claimant may make an offer, for example restricting an (ex-)employee's activities to a more limited extent than set out in the relevant post termination covenants (for example, by not seeking to enforce particular covenants or 'blue pencilling' others), there is considerably greater scope and incentive to settle actions for an injunction. Where the period of restraint may lead to a covenant being unenforceable, for example, an offer by the claimant to restrain the defendant for what is unarguably a reasonable period may avoid the need for an interim injunction hearing with the attendant litigation risk. The possibility of paying costs on the indemnity basis, with interest at a penal rate, may lead more defendants to settle in cases concerning covenants at the borderlines of enforceability. The effect on costs of an offer in terms which the court could not itself order is problematic, particularly in the post-Woolf era, where the courts are likely to take a much broader view on who should be awarded what proportion of its costs. Further, the courts may now be far more interventionist in suggesting that the parties give undertakings to resolve disputes – and in view of the broad discretion of the judge regarding costs, parties may feel diffident about resisting strong 'hints' from the judge in this regard. In many more complex cases it may not always be so easy in these circumstances (or in any event) to see who has 'won' the hearing or case. In such circumstances, it may be helpful for a party on the question of costs to show the court that it had made an earlier offer in similar or even less favourable terms than those eventually achieved at court. On the other hand, it may be argued that the court should not take into account the question of cost order, which were in terms which the court could not itself offer but the safer course may well be to assume that such an offer could be taken into account.

21. Appeals

13.67 There is now a new Practice Direction dealing with appeals (Practice Direction for the Court of Appeal Civil Division of 19 April 1999). An appeal against the grant or refusal of an interim injunction by a judge to the Court of Appeal can only be made with the permission of the court who made the order or, failing such permission, with the permission of the Court of Appeal. The decision to grant or refuse an interim injunction is a matter of the discretion of the judge and the Court of Appeal will not interfere with the exercise of that discretion unless the judge:

- Exercised that discretion under a mistake of law;
- Acted in disregard of principle; or
- Acted under a misapprehension of facts;
- Took into account irrelevant matters;
- Failed to exercise his discretion; or
- His order would result in injustice.

It is apparent from the terms of the Practice Direction that it will now be harder than ever to persuade the Court of Appeal to overturn the exercise of discretion by the judge. An appeal may be made to the Court of Appeal against the refusal of the judge to award an interim injunction on an application without notice. The Notice of Appeal must usually be served not later than four weeks after the date on which the judgment or order of the court below was sealed or otherwise perfected. Where permission to appeal is granted by the Court of Appeal or the court below, on an application made within the time limited for service of the notice of appeal, a notice of appeal may instead of being served within that time, be served within seven days after the date when permission is granted.

Part 25 Civil Procedure Rules 1998

PART 1

1.1 THE OVERRIDING OBJECTIVE

(1)   These Rules are a new procedural code with the overriding objective of enabling the court to deal with cases justly.

(2)   Dealing with a case justly includes, so far as is practicable:
    (a) ensuring that the parties are on an equal footing;
    (b) saving expense;
    (c) dealing with the case in ways which are proportionate:
        (i)   to the amount of money involved;
        (ii)   to the importance of the case;
        (iii) to the complexity of the issues; and
        (iv)   to the financial position of each party;
    (d) ensuring that it is dealt with expeditiously and fairly; and
    (e) allotting it to an appropriate share of the court's resources, while taking into account the need to allot resources to other cases.

PART 25

INTERIM REMEDIES

CONTENTS OF THIS PART

ORDERS FOR INTERIM REMEDIES

25.1 (1) The court may grant the following interim remedies –
    (a)   an interim injunction ;
    (b)   an interim declaration;
    (c)   an order –
        (i)   for the detention, custody or preservation of relevant property;
        (ii)   for the inspection of relevant property;

       (iii) for the taking of a sample of relevant property;

       (iv) for the carrying out of an experiment on or with relevant property;

       (v) for the sale of relevant property which is of a perishable nature or which for any other good reason it is desirable to sell quickly; and

       (vi) for the payment of income from relevant property until a claim is decided;

(d)   an order authorising a person to enter any land or building in the possession of a party to the proceedings for the purposes of carrying out an order under sub-paragraph (c);

(e)   an order under section 4 of the Torts (Interference with Goods) Act 1977 to deliver up goods;

(f)   an order (referred to as a 'freezing injunction') –

       (i) restraining a party from removing from the jurisdiction assets located there; or

       (ii) restraining a party from dealing with any assets whether located within the jurisdiction or not;

(g)   an order directing a party to provide information about the location of relevant property or assets or to provide information about relevant property or assets which are or may be the subject of an application for a freezing injunction ;

(h)   an order (referred to as a 'search order') under section 7 of the Civil Procedure Act 1997 (order requiring a party to admit another party to premises for the purpose of preserving evidence etc.);

(i)   an order under section 33 of the Supreme Court Act 1981 or section 52 of the County Courts Act 1984 (order for disclosure of documents or inspection of property before a claim has been made);

(j)   an order under section 34 of the Supreme Court Act 1981 or section 53 of the County Courts Act 1984 (order in certain proceedings for disclosure of documents or inspection of property against a non-party);

(k)   an order (referred to as an order for interim payment) under rule 25.6 for payment by a defendant on account of any damages, debt or other sum (except costs) which the court may hold the defendant liable to pay;

(l)   an order for a specified fund to be paid into court or otherwise secured, where there is a dispute over a party's right to the fund;

(m)   an order permitting a party seeking to recover personal property to pay money into court pending the outcome of the proceedings and directing that, if he does so, the property shall be given up to him; and

(n)   an order directing a party to prepare and file accounts relating to the dispute.

(Rule 34.2 provides for the court to issue a witness summons requiring a witness to produce documents to the court at the hearing or on such date as the court may direct)

(2) In paragraph (1)(c) and (g), 'relevant property' means property (including land) which is the subject of a claim or as to which any question may arise on a claim.

(3) The fact that a particular kind of interim remedy is not listed in paragraph (1) does not affect any power that the court may have to grant that remedy.

(4) The court may grant an interim remedy whether or not there has been a claim for a final remedy of that kind.

TIME WHEN AN ORDER FOR AN INTERIM REMEDY MAY BE MADE

25.2 (1) An order for an interim remedy may be made at any time, including –
    (a) before proceedings are started; and
    (b) after judgment has been given.

(Rule 7.2 provides that proceedings are started when the court issues a claim form)

(2) However –
    (a) paragraph (1) is subject to any rule, practice direction or other enactment which provides otherwise;
    (b) the court may grant an interim remedy before a claim has been made only if –
        (i) the matter is urgent; or
        (ii) it is otherwise desirable to do so in the interests of justice; and
    (c) unless the court otherwise orders, a defendant may not apply for any of the orders listed in rule 25.1(1) before he has filed either an acknowledgment of service or a defence.

(Part 10 provides for filing an acknowledgment of service and Part 15 for filing a defence)

(3) Where the court grants an interim remedy before a claim has been commenced, it may give directions requiring a claim to be commenced.

(4) In particular, the court need not direct that a claim be commenced where the application is made under section 33 of the Supreme Court Act 1981 or section 52 of the County Courts Act 1984 (order for disclosure, inspection etc before commencement of a claim).

HOW TO APPLY FOR AN INTERIM REMEDY

25.3 (1) The court may grant an interim remedy on an application made without notice if it appears to the court that there are good reasons for not giving notice.

(2) An application for an interim remedy must be supported by evidence, unless the court orders otherwise.

(3) If the applicant makes an application without giving notice, the evidence in support of the application must state the reasons why notice has not been given.

(Part 3 lists general powers of the court)
(Part 23 contains general rules about making an application)

APPLICATION FOR AN INTERIM REMEDY WHERE THERE IS NO RELATED CLAIM

25.4 (1) This rule applies where a party wishes to apply for an interim remedy but –
   (a) the remedy is sought in relation to proceedings which are taking place, or will take place, outside the jurisdiction; or
   (b) the application is made under section 33 of the Supreme Court Act 1981 or section 52 of the County Courts Act 1984 (order for disclosure, inspection etc. before commencement) before a claim has been commenced.
   (2) An application under this rule must be made in accordance with the general rules about applications contained in Part 23.

(The following provisions are also relevant –
- Rule 25.5 (inspection of property before commencement or against a non-party)
- Rule 31.16 (orders for disclosure of documents before proceedings start)
- Rule 31.17 (orders for disclosure of documents against a person not a party))

INSPECTION OF PROPERTY BEFORE COMMENCEMENT OR AGAINST A NON-PARTY

25.5 (1) This rule applies where a person makes an application under –
   (a) section 33(1) of the Supreme Court Act 1981 or section 52(1) of the County Courts Act 1984 (inspection etc. of property before commencement);
   (b) section 34(3) of the Supreme Court Act 1981 or section 53(3) of the County Courts Act 1984 (inspection etc. of property against a non-party).
   (2) The evidence in support of such an application must show, if practicable by reference to any statement of case prepared in relation to the proceedings or anticipated proceedings, that the property –
   (a) is or may become the subject matter of such proceedings; or
   (b) is relevant to the issues that will arise in relation to such proceedings.
   (3) A copy of the application notice and a copy of the evidence in support must be served on –
   (a) the person against whom the order is sought; and
   (b) in relation to an application under section 34(3) of the Supreme Court Act 1981 or section 53(3) of the County Courts Act 1984, every party to the proceedings other than the applicant.

INTERIM PAYMENTS – GENERAL PROCEDURE

25.6 (1) The claimant may not apply for an order for an interim payment before the end of the period for filing an acknowledgment of service applicable to the defendant against whom the application is made.

(Rule 10.3 sets out the period for filing an acknowledgment of service)
(Rule 25.1(1)(k) defines an interim payment)

(2) The claimant may make more than one application for an order for an interim payment.

(3) A copy of an application notice for an order for an interim payment must –
   (a) be served at least 14 days before the hearing of the application; and
   (b) be supported by evidence.

(4) If the respondent to an application for an order for an interim payment wishes to rely on written evidence at the hearing, he must –
   (a) file the written evidence; and
   (b) serve copies on every other party to the application,
   at least 7 days before the hearing of the application.

(5) If the applicant wishes to rely on written evidence in reply, hemust –
   (a) file the written evidence; and
   (b) serve a copy on the respondent,
   at least 3 days before the hearing of the application.

(6) This rule does not require written evidence –
   (a) to be filed if it has already been filed; or
   (b) to be served on a party on whom it has already been served.

(7) The court may order an interim payment in one sum or in instalments.

(Part 23 contains general rules about applications)

INTERIM PAYMENTS – CONDITIONS TO BE SATISFIED AND MATTERS TO BE TAKEN INTO ACCOUNT

25.7 (1) The court may make an order for an interim payment only if –
   (a) the defendant against whom the order is sought has admitted liability to pay damages or some other sum of money to the claimant;
   (b) the claimant has obtained judgment against that defendant for damages to be assessed or for a sum of money (other than costs) to be assessed;
   (c) except where paragraph (3) applies, it is satisfied that, if the claim went to trial, the claimant would obtain judgment for a substantial amount of money (other than costs) against the defendant from whom he is seeking an order for an interim payment; or
   (d) the following conditions are satisfied –
      (i) the claimant is seeking an order for possession of land (whether or not any other order is also sought);and
      (ii) the court is satisfied that, if the case went to trial, the defendant would be held liable (even if the claim for

possession fails) to pay the claimant a sum of money
for the defendant's occupation and use of the land
while the claim for possession was pending.

(2) In addition, in a claim for personal injuries the court may make an
order for an interim payment of damages only if –

    (a)   the defendant is insured in respect of the claim;

    (b)   the defendant's liability will be met by –

        (i)   an insurer under section 151 of the Road Traffic Act 1988;
or

        (ii)   an insurer acting under the Motor Insurers Bureau
Agreement, or the Motor Insurers Bureau where it is
acting itself; or

    (c)   the defendant is a public body.

(3) In a claim for personal injuries where there are two or more
defendants, the court may make an order for the interim payment of
damages against any defendant if –

    (a)   it is satisfied that, if the claim went to trial, the claimant
would obtain judgment for substantial damages against at least
one of the defendants (even if the court has not yet determined
which of them is liable); and

    (b)   paragraph (2) is satisfied in relation to each of the
defendants.

(4) The court must not order an interim payment of more than a
reasonable proportion of the likely amount of the final judgment.

(5) The court must take into account –

    (a)   contributory negligence; and

    (b)   any relevant set-off or counterclaim.

POWERS OF COURT WHERE IT HAS MADE AN ORDER FOR INTERIM PAYMENT

25.8 (1) Where a defendant has been ordered to make an interim payment,
or has in fact made an interim payment (whether voluntarily or under
an order), the court may make an order to adjust the interim payment.

(2) The court may in particular –

    (a)   order all or part of the interim payment to be repaid;

    (b)   vary or discharge the order for the interim payment;

    (c)   order a defendant to reimburse, either wholly or partly,
another defendant who has made an interim payment.

(3) The court may make an order under paragraph (2)(c) only if –

    (a)   the defendant to be reimbursed made the interim payment
in relation to a claim in respect of which he has made a claim
against the other defendant for a contribution , indemnity
or other remedy; and

    (b)   where the claim or part to which the interim payment relates
has not been discontinued or disposed of, the circumstances are
such that the court could make an order for interim payment under
rule 25.7.

(4) The court may make an order under this rule without an application
by any party if it makes the order when it disposes of the claim or any
part of it.

(5) Where –
  (a) a defendant has made an interim payment; and
  (b) the amount of the payment is more than his total liability
       under the final judgment or order,

the court may award him interest on the overpaid amount from the date
when he made the interim payment.

RESTRICTION ON DISCLOSURE OF AN INTERIM PAYMENT

25.9 The fact that a defendant has made an interim payment, whether voluntarily
      or by court order, shall not be disclosed to the trial judge until all questions
      of liability and the amount of money to be awarded have been decided
      unless the defendant agrees.

INTERIM INJUNCTION TO CEASE IF CLAIM IS STAYED

25.10   If –
  (a) the court has granted an interim injunction; and
  (b) the claim is stayed other than by agreement between the
       parties,

the interim injunction shall be set aside unless the court orders
that it should continue to have effect even though the claim is
stayed.

INTERIM INJUNCTION TO CEASE AFTER 14 DAYS IF CLAIM STRUCK OUT

25.11 (1) If–
  (a) the court has granted an interim injunction; and
  (b) the claim is struck out under rule 3.7 (sanctions for non-
       payment of certain fees),

the interim injunction shall cease to have effect 14 days after the
date that the claim is struck out unless paragraph (2) applies.

(2) If the claimant applies to reinstate the claim before the interim
     injunction ceases to have effect under paragraph (1), the injunction
     shall continue until the hearing of the application unless the court orders
     otherwise.

Practice Direction – Interim Injunctions

THIS PRACTICE DIRECTION SUPPLEMENTS CPR PART 25

JURISDICTION

1.1 High Court Judges and any other Judge duly authorised may grant 'search orders' and 'freezing injunctions'.

1.2 In a case in the High Court, Masters and district judges have the power to grant injunctions:
(1) by consent,
(2) in connection with charging orders and appointments of receivers,
(3) in aid of execution of judgments.

1.3 In any other case any judge who has jurisdiction to conduct the trial of the action has the power to grant an injunction in that action.

1.4 A Master or district judge has the power to vary or discharge an injunction granted by any Judge with the consent of all the parties.

MAKING AN APPLICATION

2.1 The application notice must state:
(1) the order sought, and
(2) the date, time and place of the hearing.

2.2 The application notice and evidence in support must be served as soon as practicable after issue and in any event not less than 3 days before the court is due to hear the application.

2.3 Where the court is to serve, sufficient copies of the application notice and evidence in support for the court and for each respondent should be filed for issue and service.

2.4 Whenever possible a draft of the order sought should be filed with the application notice and a disk containing the draft should also be available to the court. This will enable the court officer to arrange for any amendments to be incorporated and for the speedy preparation and sealing of the order. The current word processing system to be used is WordPerfect 5.1.

EVIDENCE

3.1 Applications for search orders and freezing injunctions must be supported by affidavit evidence.

3.2 Applications for other interim injunctions must be supported by evidence set out in either:
(1) a witness statement, or
(2) a statement of case provided that it is verified by a statement of truth, or
(3) the application provided that it is verified by a statement of truth, unless the court, an Act, a rule or a practice direction requires evidence by affidavit.

3.3 The evidence must set out the facts on which the applicant relies for the claim being made against the respondent, including all material facts of which the court should be made aware.

3.4   Where an application is made without notice to the respondent, the evidence must also set out why notice was not given.

(See Part 32 and the practice direction that supplements it for information about evidence.)

URGENT APPLICATIONS AND APPLICATIONS WITHOUT NOTICE

4.1   These fall into two categories:
   (1)   applications where a claim form has already been issued, and
   (2)   applications where a claim form has not yet been issued, and, in both cases, where notice of the application has not been given to the respondent.

4.2   These applications are normally dealt with at a court hearing but cases of extreme urgency may be dealt with by telephone.

4.3   Applications dealt with at a court hearing after issue of a claim form:
   (1)   the application notice, evidence in support and a draft order (as in 2.4 above) should be filed with the court two hours before the hearing wherever possible,
   (2)   if an application is made before the application notice has been issued, a draft order (as in 2.4 above) should be provided at the hearing, and the application notice and evidence in support must be filed with the court on the same or next working day or as ordered by the court, and
   (3)   except in cases where secrecy is essential, the applicant should take steps to notify the respondent informally of the application.

4.4   Applications made before the issue of a claim form:
   (1)   in addition to the provisions set out at 4.3 above, unless the court orders otherwise, either the applicant must undertake to the court to issue a claim form immediately or the court will give directions for the commencement of the claim,
   (2)   where possible the claim form should be served with the order for the injunction,
   (3)   an order made before the issue of a claim form should state in the title after the names of the applicant and respondent 'the Claimant and Defendant in an Intended Action'.

4.5   Applications made by telephone:
   (1)   where it is not possible to arrange a hearing, application can be made between 10.00 am and 5.00 pm weekdays by telephoning the Royal Courts of Justice on 0171 936 6000 and asking to be put in contact with a High Court Judge of the appropriate Division available to deal with an emergency application in a High Court matter. The appropriate district registry may also be contacted by telephone. In county court proceedings, the appropriate county court should be contacted,
   (2)   where an application is made outside those hours the applicant should either –
      (a) telephone the Royal Courts of Justice on 0171 936 6000 where he will be put in contact with the clerk

            to the appropriate duty judge in the High Court (or the appropriate area Circuit Judge where known), or

  (b) the Urgent Court Business Officer of the appropriate Circuit who will contact the local duty judge.

(3) where the facility is available it is likely that the judge will require a draft order to be faxed to him,

(4) the application notice and evidence in support must be filed with the court on the same or next working day or as ordered, together with two copies of the order for sealing,

(5) injunctions will be heard by telephone only where the applicant is acting by counsel or solicitors.

ORDERS FOR INJUNCTIONS

5.1 Any order for an injunction, unless the court orders otherwise, must contain:

(1) an undertaking by the applicant to the court to pay any damages which the respondent(s) (or any other party served with or notified of the order) sustain which the court considers the applicant should pay,

(2) if made without notice to any other party, an undertaking by the applicant to the court to serve on the respondent the application notice, evidence in support and any order made as soon as practicable,

(3) if made without notice to any other party, a return date for a further hearing at which the other party can be present,

(4) if made before filing the application notice, an undertaking to file and pay the appropriate fee on the same or next working day, and

(5) if made before issue of a claim form –

  (a) an undertaking to issue and pay the appropriate fee on the same or next working day, or

  (b) directions for the commencement of the claim.

5.2 An order for an injunction made in the presence of all parties to be bound by it or made at a hearing of which they have had notice, may state that it is effective until trial or further order.

5.3 Any order for an injunction must set out clearly what the respondent must do or not do.

FREEZING INJUNCTIONS

ORDERS TO RESTRAIN DISPOSAL OF ASSETS WORLDWIDE AND WITHIN ENGLAND AND WALES

6 Examples of Freezing Injunctions are annexed to this practice direction.

SEARCH ORDERS

ORDERS FOR THE PRESERVATION OF EVIDENCE AND PROPERTY

7.1 The following provisions apply to search orders in addition to those listed above.

The Supervising Solicitor:

7.2   The Supervising Solicitor must be experienced in the operation of search orders. A Supervising Solicitor may be contacted either through the Law Society or, for the London area, through the London Solicitors Litigation Association.

7.3   Evidence:

(1)   the affidavit must state the name, firm and its address, and experience of the Supervising Solicitor, also the address of the premises and whether it is a private or business address, and

(2)   the affidavit must disclose very fully the reason the order is sought, including the probability that relevant material would disappear if the order were not made.

7.4   Service:

(1)   the order must be served personally by the Supervising Solicitor, unless the court otherwise orders, and must be accompanied by the evidence in support and any documents capable of being copied,

(2)   confidential exhibits need not be served but they must be made available for inspection by the respondent in the presence of the applicant's solicitors while the order is carried out and afterwards be retained by the respondent's solicitors on their undertaking not to permit the respondent –

(a)   to see them or copies of them except in their presence, and

(b)   to make or take away any note or record of them,

(3)   the Supervising Solicitor may be accompanied only by the persons mentioned in the order,

(4)   the Supervising Solicitor must explain the terms and effect of the order to the respondent in every day language and advise him of his right to –

(a)   legal advice, and

(b)   apply to vary or discharge the order,

(5)   where the Supervising Solicitor is a man and the respondent is likely to be an unaccompanied woman, at least one other person named in the order must be a woman and must accompany the Supervising Solicitor, and

(6)   the order may only be served between 9.30 am and 5.30 pm Monday to Friday unless the court otherwise orders.

7.5   Search and custody of materials:

(1)   no material shall be removed unless clearly covered by the terms of the order,

(2)   the premises must not be searched and no items shall be removed from them except in the presence of the respondent or a person who appears to be a responsible employee of the respondent,

(3)   where copies of documents are sought, the documents should be retained for no more than 2 days before return to the owner,

(4)   where material in dispute is removed pending trial, the applicant's solicitors should place it in the custody of the

respondent's solicitors on their undertaking to retain it in safekeeping and to produce it to the court when required,

(5)   in appropriate cases the applicant should insure the material retained in the respondent's solicitors' custody,

(6)   the Supervising Solicitor must make a list of all material removed from the premises and supply a copy of the list to the respondent,

(7)   no material shall be removed from the premises until the respondent has had reasonable time to check the list,

(8)   if any of the listed items exists only in computer readable form, the respondent must immediately give the applicant's solicitors effective access to the computers, with all necessary passwords, to enable them to be searched, and cause the listed items to be printed out,

(9)   the applicant must take all reasonable steps to ensure that no damage is done to any computer or data,

(10)   the applicant and his representatives may not themselves search the respondent's computers unless they have sufficient expertise to do so without damaging the respondent's system,

(11)   the Supervising Solicitor shall provide a report on the carrying out of the order to the applicant's solicitors,

(12)   as soon as the report is received the applicant's solicitors shall –

(a) serve a copy of it on the respondent, and

(b) file a copy of it with the court, and

(13)   where the Supervising Solicitor is satisfied that full compliance with paragraph 7.5(7) and (8) above is impracticable, he may permit the search to proceed and items to be removed without compliance with the impracticable requirements.

GENERAL

8.1   The Supervising Solicitor must not be an employee or member of the applicant's firm of solicitors.

8.2   If the court orders that the order need not be served by the Supervising Solicitor, the reason for so ordering must be set out in the order.

8.3   The search order must not be carried out at the same time as a police search warrant.

8.4   There is no privilege against self incrimination in Intellectual Property cases (see the Supreme Court Act 1981, section 72) therefore in those cases, paragraph (4) of the Respondent's Entitlements and any other references to incrimination in the Search Order, should be removed.

8.5   Applications in intellectual property cases should be made in the Chancery Division.

8.6   An example of a Search Order is annexed to this Practice Direction.

Annex

Freezing Injunction	IN THE [HIGH COURT OF JUSTICE]
Order to restrain assets in	[CHANCERY DIVISION]
England and Wales	[Strand, London WC2A 2LL]
Before The Honourable Mr Justice	[ ]

Claim No

Dated

Applicant

Seal

Respondent

Name, address and reference of Respondent

PENAL NOTICE

IF YOU THE WITHIN NAMED [   ] DISOBEY THIS
ORDER YOU MAY BE HELD TO BE IN CONTEMPT OF COURT AND
LIABLE TO
IMPRISONMENT OR FINED OR YOUR ASSETS SEIZED

IMPORTANT

NOTICE TO THE RESPONDENT

You should read the terms of the Order and the Guidance Notes very carefully. You are advised to consult a Solicitor as soon as possible.

This Order prohibits you, the Respondent, from dealing with your assets up to the amount stated in the Order, but subject to any exceptions set out at the end of the Order. You have a right to ask the Court to vary or discharge this Order.

If you disobey this Order you may be found guilty of Contempt of Court and may be sent to prison or fined. In the case of a Corporate Respondent, it may be fined, its Directors may be sent to prison or fined or its assets may be seized.

THE ORDER

An application was made today [*date*] by [Counsel][Solicitors][*or as may be*] for the Applicant to Mr Justice [   ] who heard the application. The Judge read the affidavits listed in Schedule A and accepted the undertakings set out in Schedule B at the end of this Order. As a result of the application **IT IS ORDERED** that until [[   ] ('the return date')] [or further Order of the Court]:

1   The Respondent must not remove from England and Wales or in any way dispose of or deal with or diminish the value of any of his assets which are in England and Wales whether in his own name or not and whether solely or jointly owned up to the value of £   .

    This prohibition includes the following assets in particular:—
    (a)   the property known as [*title/address*] or the net sale money after payment of any mortgages if it has been sold;
    (b)   the property and assets of the Respondent's business known as (or carried on at [*address*]) or the sale money if any of them have been sold; and
    (c)   any money in the account numbered [*a/c number*] at [*title/address*].

2   If the total unincumbered value of the Respondent's assets in England and Wales exceeds £   , the Respondent may remove any of those assets from England and Wales or may dispose of or deal with them so long as the total unincumbered value of his assets still in England and Wales remains above £   .

3   Exceptions to this Order:-
    (1)   This Order does not prohibit the Respondent from spending £   a week towards his ordinary living expenses [and £   a week towards his ordinary and proper business expenses] and also £   a week [*or a reasonable sum*] on legal advice and representation. But before spending any money the Respondent must tell the Applicant's legal

representatives where the money is to come from.

[(2) This Order does not prohibit the Respondent from dealing with or disposing of any of his assets in the ordinary and proper course of business.]

(3) The Respondent may agree with the Applicant's legal representatives that the above spending limits should be increased or that this Order should be varied in any other respect, but any agreement must be in writing.

(4) The Respondent may cause this Order to cease to have effect if the Respondent provides security by paying the sum of £   into Court or makes provision for security in that sum by another method agreed with the Applicant's legal representatives.

4   The Respondent must:

(1) Inform the Applicant in writing at once of all his assets in England and Wales and whether in his own name or not and whether solely or jointly owned, giving the value, location and details of all such assets. [The Respondent may be entitled to refuse to provide some or all of this information on the grounds that it may incriminate him.

This sentence may be inserted in cases not covered by the Theft Act 1968, s 31.]

(2) Confirm the information in an affidavit which must be served on the Applicant's legal representatives within [   ] days after this Order has been served on the Respondent.

[5   *Where an Order for service by an alternative means or service out of the jurisdiction has been made –*

(1) The Applicant may issue and serve a Claim Form on the Respondent at [*address*] by [*method of service*].

(2) If the Respondent wishes to defend the Claim where the Claim Form states that Particulars of Claim are to follow he must complete and return the Acknowledgement of Service within [   ] days of being served with the Claim Form. Where the Particulars of Claim are served with the Claim Form, and the Respondent wishes to defend part or all of the Claim he must complete and return an Acknowledgement of Service within [   ] days of being served with the Claim Form or a Defence within [   ] days.

GUIDANCE NOTES

EFFECT OF THIS ORDER

(1) A respondent who is an individual who is ordered not to do something must not do it himself or in any other way. He must not do it through others acting on his behalf or on his instructions or with his encouragement.

(2) A respondent which is a corporation and which is ordered

not to do something must not do it itself or by its directors, officers, employees or agents or in any other way.

VARIATION OR DISCHARGE OF THIS ORDER

The Respondent (or anyone notified of this Order) may apply to the court at any time to vary or discharge this Order (or so much of it as affects that person), but anyone wishing to do so must first inform the Applicant's legal representatives.

PARTIES OTHER THAN THE APPLICANT AND RESPONDENT

(1) Effect of this Order:
It is a Contempt of Court for any person notified of this Order knowingly to assist in or permit a breach of this Order. Any person doing so may be sent to prison, fined or have his assets seized.

(2) Set off by banks:
This injunction does not prevent any bank from exercising any right of set off it may have in respect of any facility which it gave to the respondent before it was notified of this Order.

(3) Withdrawals by the Respondent:
No bank need enquire as to the application or proposed application of any money withdrawn by the Respondent if the withdrawal appears to be permitted by this Order.

INTERPRETATION OF THIS ORDER

(1) In this Order, where there is more than one Respondent, (unless otherwise stated), references to 'the Respondent' means both or all of them.

(2) A requirement to serve on 'the Respondent' means on each of them. However, the Order is effective against any Respondent on whom it is served.

(3) An Order requiring 'the Respondent' to do or not to do anything applies to all Respondents.

COMMUNICATIONS WITH THE COURT

All communications to the Court about this Order should be sent, where the Order is made in the Chancery Division, to [Room TM 510], Royal Courts of Justice, Strand, London WC2A 2LL quoting the case number. The telephone number is 0171 936 [6827]; and where the order is made in the Queen's Bench Division, to Room W11 (0171 936 6009). The offices are open between 10 am and 4.30 pm Monday to Friday.

SCHEDULE A

AFFIDAVITS

The Applicant relied on the following affidavits:
[*name*]   [*number of affidavit*]   [*date sworn*]   [*filed on behalf of*]

(1)
(2)

SCHEDULE B

UNDERTAKINGS GIVEN TO THE COURT BY THE APPLICANT

(1) If the Court later finds that this Order has caused loss to the Respondent, and decides that the Respondent should be compensated for that loss, the Applicant will comply with any Order the Court may make.

(2) The Applicant will on or before [*date*] cause a written guarantee in the sum of £   to be issued from a bank having a place of business within England or Wales, such guarantee being in respect of any Order the Court may make pursuant to paragraph (1) above. The Applicant will further, forthwith upon issue of the guarantee, cause a copy of it to be served on the Respondent.

(3) As soon as practicable the Applicant will [issue and serve on the Respondent a Claim Form in the form of the draft produced to the Court] [serve on the Respondent the Claim Form] claiming the appropriate relief, together with this Order.

(4) The Applicant will cause an affidavit to be sworn and filed [substantially in the terms of the draft affidavit produced to the Court] [confirming the substance of what was said to the Court by the Applicant's Counsel/Solicitors].

[(5) *Where a return date has been given* – As soon as practicable the Applicant will serve on the Respondent an Application for the return date together with a copy of the affidavits and exhibits containing the evidence relied on by the Applicant.]

(6) Anyone notified of this Order will be given a copy of it by the Applicant's legal representatives.

(7) The Applicant will pay the reasonable costs of anyone other than the Respondent which have been incurred as a result of this Order including the costs of ascertaining whether that person holds any of the Respondent's assets and if the Court later finds that this Order has caused such person loss, and decides that such person should be compensated for that loss, the Applicant will comply with any Order the Court may make.

(8) If for any reason this Order ceases to have effect (including in particular where the Respondent provides security as provided for above or the Applicant does not provide a bank guarantee as provided for above), the Applicant will forthwith take all reasonable steps to inform, in writing, any person or company to whom he has given notice of this Order, or who he has reasonable grounds for supposing may act upon this Order, that it has ceased to have effect.

NAME AND ADDRESS OF APPLICANT'S LEGAL REPRESENTATIVES

The Applicant's Legal Representatives are:

[Name, address, reference, fax and telephone numbers both in and out of office hours.]

Annex

Freezing Injunction

IN THE [HIGH COURT OF JUSTICE]

Order to restrain assets worldwide

[CHANCERY DIVISION]
[Strand, London WC2A 2LL]

Before The Honourable Mr Justice

[   ]

Claim No

Dated

Applicant

Seal

Respondent

Name, address and reference of Respondent

PENAL NOTICE

IF YOU THE WITHIN NAMED [   ] DISOBEY THIS

ORDER YOU MAY BE HELD TO BE IN CONTEMPT OF COURT AND
LIABLE TO

IMPRISONMENT OR FINED OR YOUR ASSETS SEIZED

IMPORTANT

NOTICE TO THE RESPONDENT

You should read the terms of the Order and the Guidance Notes very carefully. You are advised to consult a Solicitor as soon as possible.

This Order prohibits you, the Respondent, from dealing with your assets up to the amount stated in the Order, but subject to any exceptions set out at the end of the Order. You have a right to ask the Court to vary or discharge this Order.

If you disobey this Order you may be found guilty of Contempt of Court and may be sent to prison or fined. In the case of a Corporate Respondent, it may be fined, its Directors may be sent to prison or fined or its assets may be seized.

THE ORDER

An application was made today [*date*] by [Counsel][Solicitors][*or as may be*] for the Applicant to Mr Justice [   ] who heard the application. The Judge read the affidavits listed in Schedule A and accepted the undertakings set out in Schedule B at the end of this Order. As a result of the application IT IS ORDERED that until [[   ] ('the return date')] [further Order of the Court]:-1 The Respondent must not:

(1) remove from England and Wales or in any way dispose of or deal with or diminish the value of any of his assets which are in England and Wales whether in his own name or not and whether solely or jointly owned up to the value of £ ,or

(2) in any way dispose of or deal with or diminish the value of any of his assets whether they are in or outside England or Wales whether in his own name or not and whether solely or jointly owned up to the same value. This prohibition includes the following assets in particular:-

(a) the property known as [*title/address*] or the net sale money after payment of any mortgages if it has been sold;

(b) the property and assets of the Respondent's business known as (or carried on at [*address*]) or the sale money if any of them have been sold; and

(c) any money in the account numbered [*a/c number*] at [*title/address*].

2 (1) If the total unincumbered value of the Respondent's assets in England and Wales exceeds £   , the Respondent may remove any of those assets from England and Wales or may dispose of or deal with them so long as the total unincumbered value of his assets still in England and Wales remains above £   .

(2) If the total unincumbered value of the Respondent's assets in England and Wales does not exceed £   , the Respondent must not remove any of those assets from

England and Wales and must not dispose of or deal with any of them, but if he has other assets outside England and Wales the Respondent may dispose of or deal with those assets so long as the total unincumbered value of all his assets whether in or outside England and Wales remains above £   .

3   Exceptions to this Order:-
   (1)   This Order does not prohibit the Respondent from spending £   a week towards his ordinary living expenses [and £   a week towards his ordinary and proper business expenses] and also £   a week [*or a reasonable sum*] on legal advice and representation. But before spending any money the Respondent must tell the Applicant's legal representatives where the money is to come from.
   [(2)   This Order does not prohibit the Respondent from dealing with or disposing of any of his assets in the ordinary and proper course of business.]
   (3)   The Respondent may agree with the Applicant's legal representatives that the above spending limits should be increased or that this Order should be varied in any other respect, but any agreement must be in writing.
   (4)   The Respondent may cause this Order to cease to have effect if the Respondent provides security by paying the sum of £   into Court or makes provision for security in that sum by another method agreed with the Applicant's legal representatives.

4   The Respondent must:-
   (1)   Inform the Applicant in writing at once of all his assets whether in or outside England and Wales and whether in his own name or not and whether solely or jointly owned, giving the value, location and details of all such assets. [The Respondent may be entitled to refuse to provide some or all of this information on the grounds that it may incriminate him. *This sentence may be inserted in cases not covered by the Theft Act 1968, s 31.*]
   (2)   Confirm the information in an affidavit which must be served on the Applicant's legal representatives within [   ] days after this Order has been served on the Respondent.

[5   *Where an Order for service by an alternative means or service out of the jurisdiction has been made –*
   (1)   The Applicant may issue and serve a Claim Form on the Respondent at [*address*] by [*method of service*]
   (2)   If the Respondent wishes to defend the Claim he must complete and return the Notice of Intention to Defend within [   ] days of being served with the Claim Form.]

GUIDANCE NOTES

EFFECT OF THIS ORDER

(1)   A Respondent who is an individual who is ordered not to do something must not do it himself or in any other way. He must not do it through others acting on his behalf or on his instructions or with his encouragement.

(2)   A Respondent which is a corporation and which is ordered not to do something must not do it itself or by its directors, officers, employees or agents or in any other way.

VARIATION OR DISCHARGE OF THIS ORDER

The Respondent (or anyone notified of this Order) may apply to the Court at any time to vary or discharge this Order (or so much of it as affects that person), but anyone wishing to do so must first inform the Applicant's legal representatives.

PARTIES OTHER THAN THE APPLICANT AND RESPONDENT

(1)   Effect of this Order:-
It is a Contempt of Court for any person notified of this Order knowingly to assist in or permit a breach of this Order. Any person doing so may be sent to prison, fined or have his assets seized.

(2)   Effect of this Order outside England and Wales:-
The terms of this Order do not affect or concern anyone outside the jurisdiction of this Court until it is declared enforceable by or is enforced by a Court in the relevant country and then they are to affect him only to the extent they have been declared enforceable or have been enforced **UNLESS** the person is:
(i)   a person to whom this Order is addressed or an officer or an agent appointed by power of attorney of that person; or
(ii)   a person who is subject to the jurisdiction of this Court and (a) has been given written notice of this Order at his residence or place of business within the jurisdiction of this Court and (b) is able to prevent acts or omissions outside the jurisdiction of this Court which constitute or assist in a breach of the terms of this Order.

(3)   Set off by Banks:-
This injunction does not prevent any bank from exercising any right of set off it may have in respect of any facility which it gave to the Respondent before it was notified of this Order.

(4)   Withdrawals by the Respondent:-
No bank need enquire as to the application or proposed application of any money withdrawn by the Respondent if the withdrawal appears to be permitted by this Order.

INTERPRETATION OF THIS ORDER

    (1)   In this Order, where there is more than one Respondent, (unless otherwise stated) references to 'the Respondent' means both or all of them.

    (2)   A requirement to serve on 'the Respondent' means on each of them. However, the Order is effective against any Respondent on whom it is served.

    (3)   An Order requiring 'the Respondent' to do or not to do anything applies to all Respondents.

COMMUNICATIONS WITH THE COURT

All communications to the Court about this Order should be sent, where the Order is made in the Chancery Division, to [Room TM 510], Royal Courts of Justice, Strand, London WC2A 2LL quoting the case number. The telephone number is 0171 936 [6827]; and where the order is made in the Queen's Bench Division, to Room W11 (0171 936 6009). The offices are open between 10 am and 4.30 pm Monday to Friday.

SCHEDULE A

AFFIDAVITS

The Applicant relied on the following affidavits:

[*name*]   [*number of affidavit*]   [*date sworn*]   [*filed on behalf of*]

(1)
(2)

SCHEDULE B

UNDERTAKINGS GIVEN TO THE COURT BY THE APPLICANT

    (1)   If the Court later finds that this Order has caused loss to the Respondent, and decides that the Respondent should be compensated for that loss, the Applicant will comply with any Order the Court may make.

    (2)   The Applicant will on or before [*date*] cause a written guarantee in the sum of £   to be issued from a bank having a place of business within England or Wales, such guarantee being in respect of any Order the Court may make pursuant to paragraph (1) above. The Applicant will further, forthwith upon issue of the guarantee, cause a copy of it to be served on the Respondent.

    [(3)   As soon as practicable the Applicant will [issue and serve on the Respondent a Claim Form in the form of the draft produced to the Court] [serve on the Respondent the Claim Form] claiming the appropriate relief, together with this Order.]

    (4)   The Applicant will cause an affidavit to be sworn and filed [substantially in the terms of the draft affidavit produced to the Court] [confirming the substance of what was said to the Court by the Applicant's Counsel/Solicitors].

[(5)   Where a return date has been given- As soon as practicable the Applicant will serve on the Respondent an application for the return date together with a copy of the affidavits and exhibits containing the evidence relied on by the Applicant.]

(6)   Anyone notified of this Order will be given a copy of it by the Applicant's legal representatives.

(7)   The Applicant will pay the reasonable costs of anyone other than the Respondent which have been incurred as a result of this Order including the costs of ascertaining whether that person holds any of the Respondent's assets and if the Court later finds that this Order has caused such person loss, and decides that such person should be compensated for that loss, the Applicant will comply with any Order the Court may make.

(8)   If for any reason this Order ceases to have effect (including in particular where the Respondent provides security as provided for above or the Applicant does not provide a bank guarantee as provided for above), the Applicant will forthwith take all reasonable steps to inform, in writing, any person or company to whom he has given notice of this Order, or who he has reasonable grounds for supposing may act upon this Order, that it has ceased to have effect.

[(9)   The Applicant will not without the leave of the Court begin proceedings against the Respondent in any other jurisdiction or use information obtained as a result of an Order of the Court in this jurisdiction for the purpose of civil or criminal proceedings in any other jurisdiction.]

[(10)   The Applicant will not without the leave of the Court seek to enforce this Order in any country outside England and Wales [or seek an Order of a similar nature including Orders conferring a charge or other security against the Respondent or the Respondent's assets].]

NAME AND ADDRESS OF APPLICANT'S LEGAL REPRESENTATIVES

The Applicant's Legal Representatives are:

[Name, address, reference, fax and telephone numbers both in and out of office hours.]

Annex

Search Order	IN THE [HIGH COURT OF JUSTICE]
Order to preserve evidence	[CHANCERY DIVISION]
and property	[Strand, London WC2A 2LL]
Before The Honourable Mr Justice	[ ]

Claim No

Dated

Applicant

Seal

Respondent

Name, address and reference of Respondent

PENAL NOTICE

IF YOU THE WITHIN NAMED [   ] DISOBEY THIS
ORDER YOU MAY BE HELD TO BE IN CONTEMPT OF COURT AND
LIABLE TO
IMPRISONMENT OR FINED OR YOUR ASSETS SEIZED

IMPORTANT

NOTICE TO THE RESPONDENT

You should read the terms of the Order and the Guidance Notes very carefully. You are advised to consult a Solicitor as soon as possible.

This Order orders you, the Respondent, to allow the persons mentioned in the Order to enter the premises described in the Order and to search for, examine and remove or copy the articles specified in the Order. The persons so named will have no right to enter the premises or, having entered, to remain at the premises, unless you give your consent to their doing so. If, however, you withhold your consent you will be in breach of this Order and may be held to be in Contempt of Court.

The Order also requires you to hand over any of such articles which are under your control and to provide information to the Applicant's Solicitors, and prohibits you from doing certain acts.

If you, the Respondent, disobey this Order you may be found guilty of contempt of Court and may be sent to prison or fined. In the case of a Corporate Respondent, it may be fined, its Directors may be sent to prison or fined or its assets may be seized.

THE ORDER

AN APPLICATION was made today [*date*] by [Counsel] [Solicitors] for the Applicant to Mr Justice [   ]hw heard the application. The Judge read the affidavits listed in Schedule F at the end of this Order and accepted the undertakings by the Applicant, the Applicant's Solicitors and the Supervising Solicitor set forth in the Schedules at the end of this Order. As a result of the application IT IS ORDERED that until [[   ] ('the return date')] [or further Order of the Court]:

1. (1) The Respondent must allow Mr/Mrs/Miss [   ] ('the Supervising Solicitor'), together with Mr [   ] a Solicitor of the Supreme Court, and a partner in the firm of [   ] the Applicant's Solicitors and up to [   ] other persons being [*their capacity*] accompanying them, to enter the premises mentioned in Schedule A to this Order and any other premises of the Respondent disclosed under paragraph 4(1) below and any vehicles under the Respondent's control on or around the premises so that they can search for, inspect, photograph or photocopy, and deliver into the safekeeping of the Applicant's Solicitors all the documents and articles which are listed in Schedule B to this Order ('the listed items') or which Mr [   ] believes to be listed items.

   (2) The Respondent must allow those persons to remain on the premises until the search is complete, and to re-enter the premises on the same or the following day in order to complete the search.

2. (1) No item may be removed from the premises until a list of

the items to be removed has been prepared, and a copy of the list has been supplied to the person served with the Order, and he has been given a reasonable opportunity to check the list.

(2) The premises must not be searched, and items must not be removed from them, except in the presence of the Respondent or a person appearing to be a responsible employee of the Respondent or in control of the premises.

(3) If the Supervising Solicitor is satisfied that full compliance with paragraph 2(1) or (2) above is impracticable, he may permit the search to proceed and items to be removed without compliance with the impracticable requirements.

3. (1) The Respondent must immediately hand over to the Applicant's Solicitors any of the listed items which are in his possession or under his control save for any computer or hard disk integral to any computer.

(2) If any of the listed items exists only in computer readable form, the Respondent must immediately give the Applicant's Solicitors effective access to the computers, with all necessary passwords, to enable them to be searched, and cause the listed items to be printed out. A print-out of the items must be given to the Applicant's Solicitors or displayed on the computer screen so that they can be read and copied. All reasonable steps shall be taken by the Applicant to ensure that no damage is done to any computer or data. The Applicant and his representatives may not themselves search the Respondent's computers unless they have sufficient expertise to do so without damaging the Respondent's system.

4. (1) The Respondent must immediately inform the Applicant's Solicitors:-

(a) where all the listed items are; and

(b) so far as he is aware –

(i) the name and address of everyone who has supplied him, or offered to supply him, with listed items,

(ii) the name and address of everyone to whom he has supplied, or offered to supply, listed items, and

(iii) full details of the dates and quantities of every such supply and offer.

(2) Within [ ] days after being served with this Order the Respondent must swear an affidavit setting out the above information.

5. (1) Except for the purpose of obtaining legal advice, the Respondent or anyone else with knowledge of this Order must not directly or indirectly inform anyone of these proceedings or of the contents of this Order, or warn anyone that proceedings have been or may be brought against him by the Applicant until [[ ] the return date] [or further Order of the Court].

(2) The Respondent must not destroy, tamper with, cancel or

part with possession, power, custody or control of the listed items otherwise than in accordance with the terms of this Order.

(3)   [*Insert any negative injunctions.*]

[6   *Insert any further order.*]

GUIDANCE NOTES

EFFECT OF THIS ORDER

(1)   A Respondent who is an individual who is ordered not to do something must not do it himself or in any other way. He must not do it through others acting on his behalf or on his instructions or with his encouragement.

(2)   A Respondent which is a corporation and which is ordered not to do something must not do it itself or by its directors officers employees or agents or in any other way.

(3)   This Order must be complied with either by the Respondent himself or by an employee of the Respondent or other person appearing to be in control of the premises and having authority to permit the premises to be entered and the search to proceed.

(4)   This Order requires the Respondent or his employee or other person appearing to be in control of the premises and having that authority to permit entry to the premises immediately the Order is served upon him, except as stated in paragraph 6 below.

RESPONDENT'S ENTITLEMENTS

(1)   Before you the Respondent or the person appearing to be in control of the premises allow anybody onto the premises to carry out this Order you are entitled to have the solicitor who serves you with this Order explain to you what it means in everyday language.

(2)   You are entitled to insist that there is nobody [or nobody except Mr] present who could gain commercially from anything he might read or see on your premises.

(3)   You are entitled to refuse to permit entry before 9:30 am. or after 5:30 pm or at all on Saturday and Sunday unless the Court has ordered otherwise.

(4)   Except in certain cases, you may be entitled to refuse to permit disclosure of any documents which may incriminate you ('incriminating documents') or to answer any questions if to do so may incriminate you. It may be prudent to take advice, because if you so refuse, your refusal may be taken into account by the Court at a later stage.

(5)   You are entitled to refuse to permit disclosure of any documents passing between you and your Solicitors or Patent or Trade Mark Agents for the purpose of obtaining advice ('privileged documents').

(6)   You are entitled to seek legal advice, and to ask the Court

to vary or discharge this Order, provided you do so at once, and provided you do not disturb or move anything in the interim and that meanwhile you permit the Supervising Solicitor (who is a Solicitor acting independently of the Applicant) to enter, but not start to search.

(7)   Before permitting entry to the premises by any person other than the Supervising Solicitor, you (or any other person appearing to be in control of the premises) may gather together any documents you believe may be [incriminating or] privileged and hand them to the Supervising Solicitor for the Supervising Solicitor to assess whether they are [incriminating or] privileged as claimed. If the Supervising Solicitor concludes that any of the documents may be [incriminating or] privileged documents or if there is any doubt as to their status the Supervising Solicitor shall exclude them from the search and shall retain the documents of doubtful status in his possession pending further order of the Court. While this is being done, you may refuse entry to the premises by any other person, and may refuse to permit the search to begin, for a short time (not to exceed two hours, unless the Supervising Solicitor agrees to a longer period). If you wish to take legal advice and gather documents as permitted, you must first inform the Supervising Solicitor and keep him informed of the steps being taken.

RESTRICTIONS ON SERVICE

Paragraph 1 of the Order is subject to the following restrictions:–

(1)   This Order may only be served between 9:30 am and 5:30 pm on a weekday unless the Court has ordered otherwise.

(2)   This Order may not be carried out at the same time as a police search warrant.

(3)   This Order must be served by the Supervising Solicitor, and paragraph 1 of the Order must be carried out in his presence and under his supervision. Where the premises are likely to be occupied by an unaccompanied woman and the Supervising Solicitor is a man, at least one of the persons accompanying him as provided by paragraph 1 of the Order shall be a woman.

(4)   This Order does not require the person served with the Order to allow anyone [or anyone except Mr] to enter the premises who in the view of the Supervising Solicitor could gain commercially from anything he might read or see on the premises if the person served with the Order objects.

VARIATION OR DISCHARGE OF THIS ORDER

The Respondent (or anyone notified of this Order) may apply to the Court at any time to vary or discharge this Order (or so much of it as affects that person), but anyone wishing to do so must first inform the Applicant's Solicitors.

INTERPRETATION OF THIS ORDER

(1)   In this Order, where there is more than one Respondent, references to 'the Respondent' means both or all of them.

(2)   A requirement to serve on 'the Respondent' means on each of them. However, the Order is effective against any Respondent on whom it is served.

(3)   An Order requiring 'the Respondent' to do or not to do anything applies to all Respondents.

(4)   Any other requirement that something shall be done to or in the presence of 'the Respondent' means to or in the presence of any one of them or in the case of a firm or company a director or a person appearing to the Supervising Solicitor to be a responsible employee.

COMMUNICATIONS WITH THE COURT

All communications to the Court about this Order should be sent, where the Order is made in the Chancery Division, to [Room TM 510], Royal Courts of Justice, Strand, London, WC2A 2LL quoting the case number. The telephone number is 0171 936 [6827]; and where the order is made in the Queen's Bench Division, to Room W11 (0171 936 6009). The offices are open between 10 am and 4.30 pm Monday to Friday.

SCHEDULE A

The premises

SCHEDULE B

The listed items

SCHEDULE C

UNDERTAKINGS GIVEN TO THE COURT BY THE APPLICANT

(1)   If the Court later finds that this Order or carrying it out has caused loss to the Respondent, and decides that the Respondent should be compensated for that loss, the Applicant will comply with any Order the Court may make. Further, if the carrying out of this Order has been in breach of the terms of this Order or otherwise in a manner inconsistent with the Applicant's Solicitors' duties as Officers of the Court the Applicant will comply with any order for damages the Court may make.

[(2)   As soon as practicable to issue a Claim Form [in the form of the draft produced to the Court] [claiming appropriate relief.]]

[(3)   To [swear and file an affidavit] [cause an affidavit to be sworn and filed] [substantially in the terms of the draft produced to the Court] [confirming the substance of what was said to the Court by the Applicant's Counsel/ Solicitors].]

(4)   To serve on the Respondent at the same time as this Order is served upon him:

(i)   the Claim Form, or if not issued, the draft produced to the Court,

(ii)   an Application for hearing on [*date*],

(iii)   copies of the affidavits [or draft affidavits] and exhibits capable of being copied containing the evidence relied on by the Applicant [Copies of the confidential exhibits need not be served, but they must be made available for inspection by or on behalf of the Respondent in the presence of the Applicant's Solicitors while the Order is carried out. Afterwards they must be provided to a Solicitor representing the Respondent who gives a written undertaking not to permit the Respondent to see them or copies of them except in his presence and not to permit the Respondent to make or take away any note or record of the exhibits.], and

(iv)   a note of any allegation of fact made orally to the Judge where such allegation is not contained in the affidavits or draft affidavits read by the Judge.

(5)   To serve on the Respondent a copy of the Supervising Solicitor's report on the carrying out of this Order as soon as it is received.

(6)   Not, without the leave of the Court, to use any information or documents obtained as a result of carrying out this Order nor to inform anyone else of these proceedings except for the purposes of these proceedings (including adding further Respondents) or commencing civil proceedings in relation to the same or related subject matter to these proceedings until after the return date.

[(7)   To maintain pending further order the sum of £   in an account controlled by the Applicant's Solicitors.]

[(8)   To insure the items removed from the premises.]

SCHEDULE D

UNDERTAKINGS GIVEN BY THE APPLICANT'S SOLICITORS

(1)   To answer at once to the best of their ability any question whether a particular item is a listed item.

(2)   To return the originals of all documents obtained as a result of this Order (except original documents which belong to the Applicant) as soon as possible and in any event within two working days of their removal.

(3)   While ownership of any item obtained as a result of this Order is in dispute, to deliver the article into the keeping of Solicitors acting for the Respondent within two working days from receiving a written undertaking by them to retain the article in safe keeping and to produce it to the Court when required.

(4)   To retain in their own safe keeping all other items obtained as a result of this Order until the Court directs otherwise.

SCHEDULE E

UNDERTAKINGS GIVEN BY THE SUPERVISING SOLICITOR

(1)   To offer to explain to the person served with the Order its meaning and effect fairly and in everyday language, and to inform him of his right to seek legal advice (such advice to include an explanation that the Respondent may be entitled to avail himself of [the privilege against self-incrimination or] [legal professional privilege]) and apply to vary or discharge the Order as mentioned in the Respondent's Entitlements above.

(2)   To make and provide to the Applicant's Solicitors and to the Judge who made this Order (for the purposes of the Court file) a written report on the carrying out of the Order.

SCHEDULE F

AFFIDAVITS

The Applicant relied on the following affidavits:-
[*name*] [*number of affidavit*] [*date sworn*] [*filed on behalf of*]

NAME AND ADDRESS OF APPLICANT'S SOLICITORS

The Applicant's Solicitors are:-
[Name, address, reference, fax and telephone numbers both in and out of office hours.]

Chapter 14

Specific interim remedies

1. Prohibitory injunctions to restrain breaches of area covenants and non-solicitation/dealing covenants

14.1 Points which require particular consideration when considering interim relief are:

- The interest of the (ex-)employer which the covenant is intended to protect, for example, confidential information or business connection or stability of the workforce: see paragraphs 9.10 to 9.14;
- Whether the covenants go no further than is reasonably necessary to protect that interest: see paragraphs 9.21 to 9.26. Consideration should be given to the extent to which the ability of the ex-employee to earn a living is affected by the enforcement of the covenant – a properly drafted covenant will seek to ensure that while the ex-employer's interests are protected, the ex-employee is left with adequate scope to earn a living: see paragraph 10.3 and cf paragraph 14.3;
- If the covenants are too wide, whether they can be saved by severance ('blue-penciling'): see paragraphs 11.18 to 11.23. If the covenants are too wide because of an obvious error in drafting (which is not too uncommon!) and cannot be rescued by severance, whether they can be saved by a rule of construction or rectification: see paragraphs 11.6 to 11.16 and 11.25 to 11.30.

2. Garden leave injunctions

2(a) Keeping the contract alive

14.2 Garden leave injunctions are dealt with in paragraphs 14.4 to 14.5; see also paragraphs 4.79 to 4.87 and 8.32 to 8.34. Whereas injunctions to enforce restrictive covenants of the employment contract normally (but not always) arise in the context of the contract of employment having terminated, so-called 'garden leave' injunctions arise in the context of the employer seeking to keep the contract of employment alive. The basis for this type of relief is the modern view that (like other contracts) the contract of employment cannot be brought to an end by the unilateral wrongful act of one of the parties. A repudiatory breach of contract is of no effect (as far as the continued existence of the contract is concerned) unless and until it is accepted by the innocent party as bringing the contract to an end: *Gunton v Richmond-upon-Thames London Borough Council* [1980] ICR 755 (CA). See also *Rigby v Ferodo Ltd* [1988] ICR 29 (HL) and *Boyo v Lambeth*

Borough Council [1994] ICR 727 (CA) and the discussion at paragraph 8.18. There are many contrary dicta in other cases, notably *Vine v National Dock Labour Board* [1956] QB 658 [1957] AC 488, 500, 504, 506; *Denmark Productions Ltd v Boscobel Productions* [1969] 1 QB 699 (CA); *Sanders v Ernest A Neale Ltd* [1974] ICR 565; and in *Powell v London Borough of Brent* [1987] IRLR 466, 470 (CA) the question was regarded as open. In *Thomas Marshall (Exports) Ltd v Guinle* [1979] 1 Ch 227 Sir Robert Megarry VC held that although the court could not force the employee to work in accordance with his contract, it could restrain him from committing other breaches of his obligations during the period of his contract. He awarded the employer interim non-solicitation/dealing injunctions against a managing director who had purported to resign from his employment well before the expiry of a fixed term but whose resignation the employer refused to accept. However, the court will readily infer acceptance of breach by the innocent party (per Buckley LJ in *Gunton* at page 772 E–F); see also *Dietman v London Borough of Brent* [1987] IRLR 259 (Hodgson J).

2(b) Specific enforcement of an employment contract

14.3 It has long been accepted that an employment contract cannot generally be specifically enforced by either party: *Ridge v Baldwin* [1964] AC 40 (HL) per Lord Reid at page 65. An employer may not by way of decree of specific performance or injunction force an employee to work: *De Francesco v Barnum* (1890) 45 Ch D 430, 438. Further, by Section 236 of the Trade Union and Labour Relations (Consolidation) Act 1992 the courts are precluded (whether by way of an order of specific performance of an employment contract or an injunction restraining a breach or threatened breach of such a contract) from compelling an employee to work. However, an injunction may be granted which indirectly puts pressure on the employee to stay in employment: *Lumley v Wagner* (1852) 1 De GM & G 604 (injunction enforcing a covenant not to sing at another theatre) and cf *William Robinson & Co Ltd v Heuer* [1898] 2 Ch 451. In *Warner Brothers Pictures Inc v Nelson* [1937] 1 KB 209 Branson J granted an injunction against the actress Bette Davis preventing her, during the currency of her contract with Warner, from acting for third parties. She could still work otherwise than as a film artiste even though this would mean a substantial drop in earnings. However, the court will not enforce a covenant which requires the employee to choose between performing his contract or remaining idle, for example, an injunction preventing the employee from working for anyone else in any trade or profession at all: *Ehrman v Bartholomew* [1898] 1 Ch 671 and *Warner Brothers* (at page 217). However, a likelihood of idleness is not a decisive factor but may be a factor in determining whether an injunction is appropriate: *Euro Brokers Ltd v Rabey* [1995] IRLR 206. The employee ought to be left with some reasonable means of earning a living: *Page One Records Ltd v Britton (trading as The Troggs)* [1968] 1 WLR 157 (Stamp J) in which the manager of a pop group 'The Troggs' failed to obtain an injunction restraining them from employing another manager since they were 'simple persons' who could not survive without a manager (and also because of lack of mutuality – the group could not have specifically enforced the obligations of the manager involving personal services and being obligations of trust and confidence). It is accordingly doubtful whether the injunction obtained in *Warner Brothers* would be granted today: see *Evening Standard Co Ltd v Henderson* [1987] ICR 588 and *Provident Financial Group plc v Hayward* [1989] ICR 160 (discussed in para 14.4). See also the decision of the Court of Appeal in *Warren v Mendy* [1989] 1 WLR 853 (an action between two boxing promoters) in which the Court of Appeal refused indirectly to enforce an exclusive management contract between a boxer and his promoter since it was a contract for the performance of personal services involving the continuing exercise of special skill and talent and a high degree of trust between the parties. Compulsion was a question of fact and might be inferred where the employer sought relief against the new employer and was likely to seek relief against any other employer. The Court of Appeal expressed a clear preference for the approach of Stamp J in *Page One* to that of Branson J in *Warner Brothers* and reaffirmed the principle applied in *Whitwood Chemical Co v Hardman* [1891] 2 Ch 416 (CA) that the court will not by the back door grant specific performance of an employment contract.

2(c) Garden leave

14.4 One way in which the employer may seek to enforce the contract of employment is by way of seeking to enforce garden leave provisions on the contract: see paragraphs 4.79 to 4.88. Although the employee is not forced to work, provided the employer (who has not accepted the employee's repudiation of the contract) continues to make available to the employee the full benefits to which he is entitled under the contract of employment, he may be able to ensure that during the notice period the employee does not provide his services to a rival. The circumstances in which the court will grant 'garden leave' injunctions are considered in paragraphs 4.79 to 4.88 in which the decisions of the Court of Appeal in the case of *Evening Standard Co Ltd v Henderson* [1987] ICR 588 and *Provident Financial Group plc v Hayward* [1989] ICR 160 are considered. These decisions emphasise that such injunctions can only be obtained if the employee does not have a contractual right to work. Although garden leave injunctions were initially granted simply relying on the notice period (that is, without any express garden leave provisions in the contract of employment) following the decision of the Court of Appeal in *William Hill v Tucker* [1998] IRLR 313 (CA) – discussed at paragraph 4.82 to 4.83 in many cases it will be necessary to have express provisions in particular excluding the right to work. Prudent advice must now be that in all cases the right to put the employee on garden leave should be expressly retained. Furthermore in that case Morritt LJ expressed the view that the court should be careful not to grant interlocutory relief to enforce a garden leave clause to any greater extent than would be covered by a justifiable covenant in restraint of trade previously entered into by an employee. It is not clear exactly what Morritt LJ had in mind with this comment.

Garden leave clauses have the best chance of being upheld where:

- The period of potential garden leave is not too long (although in contrast with typical restrictive covenants the court may where appropriate reduce the duration of garden leave: *GFI Group Inc v Eaglestone* [1994] IRLR 119) and see *Credit Suisse Asset Management Ltd v Armstrong* [1996] IRLR 450 (CA) referred to in paragraph 14.7 below;
- The skill of the employee is not one which is subject to rapid atrophication; and
- The employee has been exposed to confidential information of the business of the employer or the employer can show that some other detriment will result from the employee working for a rival. In strict theory, since by maintaining the contract the employer prolongs the duty of fidelity (or at

least the duty not to compete with the employer) it should not be necessary for the employer to identify a protectable interest such as confidential information or client connection, as in the case of covenants operating after termination of employment. However, it should be borne in mind that in *William Hill v Tucker* [1998] IRLR 313, the Court of Appeal appeared keen to assimilate garden leave with post-termination covenants: see discussion of this case at paragraphs 4.82 to 4.83.

14.5 In many cases where there are both garden leave provisions as well as post-employment restrictive covenants in the contract of employment, the employer may (in particular where there are any doubts regarding the effectiveness of the post-employment restrictions), be best advised to keep the contract alive and rely on the garden leave provisions. The advantages of so doing arise from the fact that the courts are more amenable to granting relief to the employer during the subsistence of the employment contract than thereafter (see paras 3.2 to 3.3 and 9.1). More specifically the courts will during employment:

- Protect confidential information which does not amount to trade secrets;
- More readily restrain competitive activity.

14.6 Conversely, where employment is at an end the courts will:

- Very carefully scrutinise covenants restraining competitive activity, including confidentiality covenants;
- Protect only trade secrets.

14.7 Furthermore, an employee is not entitled to 'credit' as against the period of the (post employment) restrictive covenant for time spent on garden leave: *Credit Suisse Asset Management Ltd v Armstrong* [1996] IRLR 450 (CA). In that case it was held that the judge had not erred in concluding that the claimants were entitled to the protection of restrictive covenants prohibiting the defendants from competing with or soliciting the claimant's business for a period of six months after their employment terminated, notwithstanding that the claimants had already had six months of complete protection by placing the defendants on 'garden leave' throughout their notice periods. If a restrictive covenant is valid, the employer is entitled to have it enforced, subject to the usual grounds on which an injunction can be withheld. The Court of Appeal went on to say that although the court can exercise its discretion in deciding the permissible length of garden leave, the courts have not rewritten a restrictive covenant so as to enforce it for a lesser period than that which the parties have purported to agree. The existence of a garden leave clause, however, may be a factor to be taken into account in determining the validity of a restrictive covenant. Moreover, in an exceptional case where a long period of garden leave had already elapsed, perhaps substantially in excess of a year, without any curtailment by the court, it is possible that the court would decline on public policy grounds to grant any further protection based on a restrictive covenant. The latter comment, insofar as it points to garden leave substantially in excess of a year, is out of kilter with the periods of garden leave normally granted by the court. We know of no reported case in which six months has been exceeded. The safer course would be to assume that garden leave in excess of six months would be very difficult to justify.

2(d) Enforcement of employment contracts by employees

14.8 The recognition in recent cases of the employer's right to enforce contracts of employment by garden leave injunctions (see paras 14.4 to 14.7) is mirrored in recent cases in which employees have been allowed to obtain interim orders of reinstatement (or orders restraining implementation of instructions to cease normal work and carry out other work). These are rare cases, usually involving a large employer such as a local authority employing numerous employees where, despite the dispute between employer and employee, there has been no breakdown in the mutual confidence between them. In these circumstances if an injunction is granted, the situation will still be 'workable': see *Irani v Southampton and South West Hampshire Area Health Authority* [1985] IRLR 203; *Powell v London Borough of Brent* [1987] IRLR 466 (CA); *Hughes v London Borough of Southwark* [1988] IRLR 55; *Wadcock v London Borough of Brent* [1990] IRLR 223; *Robb v London Borough of Hammersmith and Fulham* [1991] IRLR 72; *Jones v Gwent County Council* [1992] IRLR 521, *Anderson v Pringle of Scotland Ltd* [1998] IRLR 64 and *Peace v City of Edinburgh Council* [1999] IRLR 417. On the other hand, see *Alexander v Standard Telephones & Cables Ltd* [1990] IRLR 55 and *Wishart v National Association of Citizens' Advice Bureaux Ltd* [1990] IRLR 393 in which trust and confidence had broken down.

3. Confidentiality injunctions

14.9 The subject of confidential information is dealt with in Chapter 5.

14.10 When considering injunctions to restrain the unauthorised use or disclosure of trade secrets or confidential information, points which require particular consideration are:

- The identification of the specific items of information which it is sought to protect as being confidential or a trade secret: *P A Thomas & Co v Mould* [1964] 2 QB 913, *FSS Travel & Leisure Systems Ltd v Johnson* [1998] IRLR 352 and *CMI-Centers v Phytopharm plc* [1999] FSR 235;
- The basis on which it is alleged that the information is confidential or a trade secret (for example, that it is specified as such in the contract of employment and/or the steps which were taken during employment to maintain confidentiality);
- That the claimant (and not someone else) is beneficially entitled to the information: *Fraser v Evans* [1969] 1 QB 349, 361-362;
- The extent (if any) to which it will be open to the defendant to raise the just cause (or iniquity) defence:see paragraphs 6.6 to 6.21.

14.11 Even if a confidentiality injunction is refused, the claimant may be able to obtain an undertaking by the defendant to keep an account of royalties received and payment of the same (or part) into a joint account (of the claimant's and the defendant's solicitors) and to supply regular statements to the claimant: cf *Coco v Clark (A N) (Engineers) Ltd* [1969] RPC 41. This 'halfway house' may be appropriate where the claimant has established an arguable case of breach of confidence by the defendant but the balance of convenience militates against the grant of an interim injunction. In these circumstances the claimant is at least given security for his claim in the event of his succeeding at trial.

3(a) Confidential information: springboard injunctions

3(a)(i) Use of springboard injunctions

14.12 Injunctions to restrain the misuse of confidential information often include what is known as a springboard injunction. This type of injunction often constitutes the most important part of the relief sought. It is designed to put the confidant (in the context of employment, the ex-employee) who has (during employment) misused confidential information to gain a head start over the confider (the ex-employer) under a special disability which cancels the head start. Typically the misuse is in the form of the copying of confidential documentation of the employer (whether by photocopying or downloading onto computer disc) for use after employment in competition with the ex-employer.

14.13 This type of injunction is sought when an ordinary confidential information injunction will not provide adequate protection because the information is no longer confidential (often because of the very activities of the ex-employee). The disability is special because the ex-employee will be prevented for a limited period from using the information in question, while everyone else may use it.

14.14 An ex-employer will sometimes seek a springboard injunction to attempt to protect (mere) confidential information (as opposed to trade secrets) when there are no enforceable express covenants in the contract of employment. A springboard injunction will not, however, be granted merely as substitute relief to assist an ex-employer who has not troubled to take an express covenant to protect his confidential information.

3(a)(ii) Statement of springboard doctrine

14.15 The classic statement of the 'springboard' doctrine is found in the judgment of Roxburgh J in *Terrapin Ltd v Builders' Supply Co (Hayes) Ltd, Taylor Woodrow Ltd and Swiftplan Ltd* [1960] RPC 128, 130:

> '... the essence of this branch of the law, whatever the origin of it may be, is that a person who has obtained information in confidence is not allowed to use it as a springboard for activities detrimental to the person who made the confidential communication, and springboard it remains even when all the features have been published or can be ascertained by actual inspection by any member of the public ... The possessor of the confidential information still has a long start over any member of the public ... It is, in my view, inherent in the principle on which *Saltman Engineering Co Ltd v Campbell Engineering Co Ltd* (1963) 65 RPC 203 (noted at [1963] 3 All ER 413) rests that the possessor of such information must be placed under a special disability in the field of competition to ensure that he does not get an unfair start.'

14.16 In this case a set of drawings and tools had been made from original drawings containing confidential information of Terrapin. Taylor had dispensed with the necessity of themselves going through the process which Terrapin had gone through in compiling these drawings and thereby saved a great deal of labour and careful draughtsmanship.

3(a)(iii) Is some other breach of fidelity, not being a breach of confidence, enough?

14.17 In our view the answer is probably no. All the reported springboard cases involved an initial breach of confidence. Some other breach of the employee's duty of fidelity (not amounting to a breach of confidence) is unlikely to be sufficient. In *Balston Ltd v Headline Filters Ltd* [1987] FSR 330 the employee, during garden leave, had set up a competitive company which was to commence business on expiry of the notice. During employment he had breached his duty of fidelity by encouraging the diversion of business. The employers argued that the ex-employee should not be allowed to reap the benefit of the preparation for competition. In refusing to grant an interim springboard injunction Scott J held (at page 340) that springboard injunctions ought only to be granted in cases of (continuing) misuse of confidential information. In *CBT Systems UK Ltd v Campopiano* 24 July 1995 (unreported) Carnwath J expressed caution about extending springboard injunctions to breaches of the duty of fidelity. On the other hand in *Renton Inspection and Technical Engineering (Training Division) Ltd v Renton* 25 October 1991 (unreported) the Court of Appeal appeared to treat the remedy of a springboard injunction as being available if there had been breaches by a director/employee of his fiduciary duty and/or duty of fidelity (although on the facts it was held that no such injunction should have been granted). Since the fiduciary duty – like the duty of confidence – arises in equity it is perhaps not surprising that the Court was prepared to go that far.

3(a)(iv) Must the breach of confidence be continuing?

14.18 In *Balston* Scott J held that past breaches of duty could not sustain an interim injunction on their own account. He doubted (without deciding the point) whether an injunction (whether interim or otherwise) could ever be justified on the grounds that its grant was necessary to deprive the contract-breaker of the fruits of breach of contract. This would be an important limitation in the tendency to expand the ambit of these injunctions. However, without further explanation, this statement would seem to deprive the springboard doctrine of any meaning. If breaches of confidence are continuing, the claimant will simply claim injunctive relief to prevent these further breaches of confidence – there is no need for the springboard doctrine. The whole purpose of the springboard injunction is to cancel the head start obtained by past breaches of confidence. Plainly if there is no continuation of conduct whereby the defendant continues to enjoy and build on the head start which he has obtained, the case would be one for damages only and not for an injunction. Accordingly, the true area of application of this type of injunction is where the defendant has committed an initial breach of confidence and continues activities (not amounting in themselves to breaches of confidence) whereby he builds on and gains further benefit from the initial breaches of confidence. In the words of May LJ in *Roger Bullivant Ltd v Ellis* [1987] IRLR 491, 497 (see para 39):

'The principal purpose of the injunction now appealed against therefore was not so much directly to protect the respondents [the employers] as to prevent the appellants [the ex-employees] from taking unfair advantage of their breach of duty.'

3(a)(v) Criticisms of the springboard doctrine

14.19 The doctrine has been subject to criticism. In *Cranleigh Precision Engineering Ltd v Bryant* [1964] 3 All ER 289 Roskill J defended the authority of *Terrapin* referring to it as a logical consequence of the decision in Saltman (at page 302 E). Roskill J distinguished the decision of the House of Lords in *Mustad & Son v Allcock & Co Ltd and Dosen* (reported 36 years after the event at [1963] 3 All ER 416), in which the claimant was held to have destroyed the confidentiality of the subject matter of the action by publishing the complete specification relating to the confidential information, on the basis that publication in *Cranleigh* was by a third party and not the employer himself. In *Speed Seal Products Ltd v Paddington* [1986] 1 All ER 91 it was held, on the basis of *Cranleigh*, that if the confidant is not released from his duty of confidence when publication is by a third party, he cannot be released when it is he himself who has published the information.

14.20 However, in *Attorney General v Guardian Newspapers Ltd (No 2)* (the *Spycatcher* case) [1988] 3 All ER 545 (HL) Lord Goff (at pages 661J to 662C) in a penetrating analysis pointed to the illogicality of artificially prolonging the duty of confidence. (See to similar effect Laddie J in *Ocular Sciences Ltd v Aspect Vision Care Ltd* [1997] RPC 395, 401). Lord Goff disapproved of the *Cranleigh* case (and hence the *Speed Seal* case) insofar as it might support the proposition that if it is a third party who puts the confidential information in question into the public domain, as opposed to the confider, the confidant will not be released from his duty of confidence. If the confidentiality of the information has been destroyed so must the duty of confidence be destroyed. On this analysis the principal (if not the only) area of operation of the springboard doctrine is against the confidant who in breach of confidence has destroyed the confidential nature of the information entrusted to him: a springboard injunction places him under a special disability as to the use of this information.

14.21 This approach also provides a possible explanation of the difficult (majority) decision of the Court of Appeal in *Schering Chemicals Ltd v Falkman Ltd* [1981] 2 All ER 321. In this case the claimant drug company, Schering, employed the first defendant, Falkman, a company which specialised in television training. Falkman's task was to counter adverse publicity regarding a certain drug by training Schering's employees to put its case across effectively in television interviews. Falkman gave an express confidentiality covenant. Falkman in turn hired the second defendant, Elstein, a television broadcaster, to carry out part of the training. A large amount of information on the drug was supplied to the two defendants. Thereafter Elstein, prompted by what he had learnt on the training course, made together with Falkman for their own gain a documentary film about the drug. The majority of the Court of Appeal unsurprisingly upheld the grant of an injunction to restrain publication of the film. The difficulty with the decision lies in the fact that all (or substantially all) of the information given to the defendants was in the public domain – although Falkman acknowledged that the information was received 'in confidence'. On the other hand it was conceded by Elstein that if he had promised not to make use of the information, whether confidential or not, he would be bound by that promise. Templeman LJ held (at page 345) that even if Elstein did not know about Falkman's covenant (a matter which was in dispute), Elstein impliedly promised Schering that the information which he received, public or private, would be used by him only for the purpose of the training programme. In those circumstances it would seem that the case did not really concern the law of confidence at all and it was unnecessary for Templeman LJ to hold (at page 346) that although the information would not have been confidential in the hands of Elstein if he had obtained it from other sources, it was confidential as between himself and Schering because of the manner in which he received it (see also judgment of Shaw LJ at page 339). The true position would appear to be that the information was never confidential but that Elstein was under a contractual obligation not to disclose it. This restraint was supported by a legitimate interest in not having the information re-published and recycled (page 345 j) thereby causing the very damage he had been paid to prevent.

3(a)(vi) SUMMARY OF THE REQUIREMENTS FOR A SPRINGBOARD INJUNCTION

14.22 From the above decisions the springboard doctrine is applicable where:

- There has been an initial breach of confidence;
- The confidential information has been published but:
  - Not with the authority of the claimant (*Cranleigh*); alternatively
  - Not too widely: thus in *Terrapin* Roxburgh J rejected the defendant's argument that the claimant had destroyed the confidentiality of the designs in question when they placed on the market their own building embodying the designs and published descriptions of those buildings; likewise in *Ackroyds (London) Ltd v Islington Plastics Ltd* [1962] RPC 97 Havers J stated (at page 104) that the mere publication of an article by manufacturing and placing it on the market is not necessarily enough to make such information available to the public; see also *Cranleigh*;
  - The defendant has obtained an unfair advantage or head start by the use of the information (while it was still confidential);
  - The defendant is continuing to derive advantage from the head start.

3(a)(vii) *BULLIVANT V ELLIS:* GOOD AUTHORITY?

14.23 The decision in Bullivant – The highwater mark of the springboard doctrine is the decision of the Court of Appeal in *Roger Bullivant Ltd v Ellis* [1987] IRLR 491. This decision is often of great practical significance in cases involving competition between ex-employer and ex-employee. However, there are reasons to question this decision – at least its full extent. In this case the defendant, Ellis, was the ex-managing director of the claimant, Bullivant. While still employed by Bullivant, Ellis acquired a company which subsequently became the vehicle of a rival business. When he left Bullivant, Ellis took with him a vast number of documents of Bullivant, including a card index listing Bullivant's contacts.

14.24 What is significant about this decision is that Ellis was restrained by injunction from dealing with customers whose names appeared on the card index and whom he contacted while the index was in his possession:

- Using the card index – but whom he could have contacted without using it;
- Without using the card index at all (paragraph 15 of the decision) although Ellis probably used the index to contact all the names on it: see paragraph 13.

Nourse LJ stated (at paragraph 24):

'While I recognise that it would have been possible for [Ellis] to contact some, perhaps many, of the people concerned without using the card index, I am far from convinced that he would have been able to contact anywhere near all of those whom he did contact between February and April 1985. Having made deliberate and unlawful use of the [claimant's] property, he cannot complain if he finds that the eye of the law is unable to distinguish between those whom he could, had he chose, have contacted lawfully and those whom he could not. In my judgment it is of the highest importance that the principle of *Robb v Green* [1895] 2 QB 1 (upheld by the Court of Appeal at [1895] 2 QB 315) which, let it be said, is one of no more than fair and honourable dealing, should be steadfastly maintained.'

In *Bullivant* Nourse LJ said (at paragraph 28) that in *Robb v Green* the defendant was not precluded from contracting with any of the claimant's customers if he was able to do so without using the information which he had unlawfully acquired. He was, however, of the view that in *Bullivant* it would be difficult for either party to know whether that sort of injunction would be or had been breached and it was accordingly difficult to enforce. He therefore preferred the wider form of order. Nourse LJ did not expressly consider the fact that the injunction granted was something which the employer would not have been entitled to at trial: *Evans Marshall & Co Ltd v Bertola SA* [1973] 1 WLR 349 (CA). However, the Court of Appeal has subsequently held that there is nothing to prevent the court under Section 37(1) of the Supreme Court Act 1981 from making orders at the interim stage which would not be appropriate at trial: *Fresh Fruit Wales Ltd v Halbert* (1991) Times, 29 January (CA) and *Khorasandjian v Bush* [1993] QB 727. Now, CPR r 25.1(4) makes it clear that an interim remedy may be granted whether or not there is a claim for a similar final remedy.

3(a)(viii)   OTHER CASES

14.25 This latter point (in *Evans Marshall,* ie, that an interim remedy should not be granted where a final order in those terms would not be appropriate) was one of the reasons that such a wide injunction was not granted in the case of *Rapid Fixings v Northwest Fixings and others* [1993] FSR 281 which was not cited in *Bullivant*. In *Rapid Fixings* the defendant employees left that company, secretly removing lists of Rapid Fixings' customers. Kilner Brown J granted an ex parte injunction inter alia to restrain the ex-employees from contacting or attempting to contact or do business with any customers named in the lists – which Rapid Fixings had recovered in the course of the execution of a search order. Lawton LJ, with whom Brandon and Templeman LJJ agreed, rejected a springboard argument and refused to continue this injunction on grounds that:

● There was no express restrictive covenant;
● The court would not restrain the ex-employees from using their memory of the customers;
● Rapid Fixings could not obtain such a wide injunction at trial.

The Court of Appeal accordingly ordered a specific proviso to the effect that the ex-employees would not be enjoined from calling on customers remembered by them or whose names were acquired from other sources. This was consistent with the decision of Hawkins J in *Robb v Green* where the form of the injunction granted (at trial) against a former employee who had during his employment copied a list of customers and their addresses from the employer's order book for the purpose of using the information for his own use after termination of his employment was that he be restrained from making use of the information obtained by him by copying or extracting such names and addresses.

14.26 Likewise in *Louis v Smellie* (1895) 73 LT 226 (also not cited in *Bullivant*) the Court of Appeal would go no further than grant a (final) injunction restraining the ex-employee, a process server, who had during his employment secretly copied extracts of the employer's register of agents, from making use of any copies or extracts made during his employment and would not restrain him from dealing after employment with agents whose names he could remember and whose addresses he could find from public directories (per Lindley LJ at page 228).

14.27 See also *Baker v Gibbons* [1972] 1 WLR 693, where Pennycuick VC held (at page 700F–H) that the name and address of a particular employee of the employer or the names of the employer's selling agents were not (apart from the case where a list was taken or memorised) confidential. At page 702 B–D he followed Lord Lindley's dictum in *Smellie* that the court would not restrain the use of names and addresses which the employee could remember and regarded *Seager v Copydex* [1967] 1 WLR 923 as authority for the proposition that even where there is a list, one cannot regard every name and address on it in isolation as being confidential in itself.

14.28 However, in *Johnson & Bloy (Holdings) v Wolstenholme Rink plc* [1987] IRLR 499 (CA) the Court of Appeal supported the approach in *Bullivant*: both Fox and Parker LJJ were prepared to hold that an initial wrongdoing by the employee could in effect disentitle an employee from using his 'know-how' (provided it fell within the second category of *Faccenda*, that is, information which was confidential during employment) where the documents removed by the employee in breach of his duty of fidelity contained both know-how and confidential information of the employer. Again in *PSM International plc v Whitehouse* [1992] IRLR 279 (decided on 23 January 1992) the Court of Appeal followed *Bullivant*.

14.29 Universal Thermosensors Ltd v Hibben – To be contrasted with *Bullivant* is the recent decision in *Universal Thermosensors Ltd v Hibben* [1992] 1 WLR 840 (decided on 5 February 1992 before the decision in *PSM International plc v Whitehouse* had been reported) in which Sir Donald Nicholls VC was far more cautious. The facts of the case were strikingly similar to those in *Bullivant*. The individual defendants were ex-employees of the claimant, Thermosensors. The ex-employees (who had given no express area or non-solicitation covenants) had dishonestly taken customer lists and pricing matrices of Thermosensors and after terminating their employment with Thermosensors set up a competing business. The timing of events is significant The first defendant, Hibben, left her employ in September 1988. During the first nine months of 1989 the two other individual defendants (who were still employed by Thermosensors) engaged (with the encouragement of Hibben) in the systematic theft of Thermosensors' confidential documents. The defendants' new business began trading in September 1989. The defendants approached and obtained orders from several customers whose names were contained in Thermosensors' lists although they also compiled their own customer lists partly by legitimate means. On 3 April 1990 a search order was awarded ex parte and an injunction obtained restraining the defendants from soliciting or entering into or fulfilling any contracts with any customer whose name was contained in any confidential document of Thermosensors. In the course of the execution of a search order Thermosensors found and removed components and documents including the customer lists. In July 1990 an interim injunction was obtained by consent restraining the defendants from soliciting or entering into or fulfilling any contract for the manufacture or supply of their product with any person whose name appeared in Thermosensors' customer lists with whom the defendants (or any of them) had contact while those lists (or their own list) were in their possession. The width of this order caused the collapse of the defendants' business. At trial (a significant fact differentiating this case from many of the other decisions on the point, which were interim) the defendants sought damages on Thermosensors' cross-undertakings given to the court on the grant of the interim injunction (see para 13.24) on the grounds that (on the facts as established at trial) the injunctions which had caused the downfall of their business had been too widely drawn.

14.30   Sir Donald Nicholls VC found in favour of the defendants on this point. In July 1990 Thermosensors were entitled to be protected by means of an injunction against any *further* misuse by the defendants of Thermosensors' confidential information, for example, the use of their lists. As regards misuse which had already occurred the clock could not be set back, Thermosensors could only claim damages or an account of profits. In particular, if by misuse of confidential information the defendants had already made contact with a customer and received an order from him, an injunction to restrain the defendants' company from fulfilling that order or any future order would go too far. An injunction in such a form would not be aimed at preventing further misuse of confidential information since the misuse occurred when the claimant's customers were approached. Fulfilling outstanding or future orders would not be a further misuse of confidential information. (This part of the decision is contrary to that of the subsequently reported decision of the Court of Appeal in *PSM International plc v Whitehouse*: see para 14.33.) Nor could the injunction be justified even for a short period of time in order to cancel the springboard advantage gained by the defendants. It is to be noted that this part of the decision is based on the timing of the injunction. The Vice Chancellor said that had there been no use by the defendants of the confidential information, the individual defendants would in the autumn of 1989 have run up a large telephone bill locating suitable contacts; and, given their knowledge of the claimant's customers and contacts, they would by July 1990 have been in substantially the same position as to customers and contacts as in fact was the case at that date. Thus in July 1990 to prevent the defendants from dealing with customers whom they had already approached was to put the claimant in a better position for the future than if there had been no misuse of confidential information.

14.31   The Vice Chancellor derived support for his view in *Universal Thermosensors* from *Robb v Green* and *Louis v Smellie* and relied on certain dicta in *Bullivant*. However, it is difficult to reconcile his approach with that of the Court of Appeal in *Bullivant* and *Johnson & Bloy*. On one level it may be said that *Bullivant* and *Johnson & Bloy* were cases of interim injunctions granted before the facts have been ascertained and that (in the words of Nourse LJ) having made deliberate and unlawful use of the claimant's property, the defendant cannot complain if he finds that the eye of the law is unable to distinguish between those customers whom he could, had he chose, have contacted lawfully and those whom he could not. However, the same difficulties of policing injunctions, which are couched in the more limited form favoured by *Louis v Smellie* and *Robb v Green*, exist in relation to final injunctions as in relation to interim injunctions. The full effect of the *Universal Thermosensors* case is still not clear, but claimants would be well advised to think twice before seeking to obtain orders as wide as that in *Bullivant*.

14.32 Practical considerations post Universal Thermosensors – Where interim injunctions are sought against former employees who have taken customer lists (and other confidential documents) for the purpose of contacting customers of the claimant it is wise before seeking any springboard injunctions to consider carefully whether any springboard advantage still exists, that is, whether, even without using confidential information, the defendants would not be in the position in which they are at the date of the interim application – this is only likely to be the case where (unusually) there has been a considerable lapse of time between the taking of the documents and the hearing. Where there is no continuing springboard advantage the injunction ought to be limited to restraining the defendant from using the claimant's confidential documents and information. Where there is a continuing springboard advantage in the sense that the claimant is enjoying a head start, that is, continuing to exploit a position at which he would not have arrived but for his use of the claimant's confidential information, the claimant will need to consider limiting the springboard injunction to those customers whom the defendant contacted using the claimant's documents but whom he would not otherwise have been able to contact – the disadvantage of the difficulty of policing such an injunction has to be weighed against the possibility that at trial it may be found that the injunction was too wide, with potential liability to the defendants on the cross-undertaking. In a genuine springboard case, where the injunction is limited to restraining contact with customers whom the defendant has contacted using the list, the danger may not be great. As the Vice Chancellor pointed out in *Universal Thermosensors* (at page 851) the court may view with scepticism the contention of a defendant who has chosen to use a list, that he already carried some of the information in his own head and that looking at the list for any particular name or names was unnecessary. Moreover, any doubts and obscurities arising from the evidence would be likely to be resolved against the defendant.

14.33 Prevention of the fulfilment of existing orders – In *PSM International plc v Whitehouse* [1992] IRLR 279 (CA) it was submitted that there had never been a case in which a claimant had been granted an injunction against an ex-employee restraining him from fulfilling a contract already made with a third party. Such an injunction had been granted in *Bullivant* at first instance but was abandoned on appeal. Lloyd LJ (with whom Neill LJ agreed) accepted that the court should be chary of granting an equitable remedy which would have the effect of interfering with the contractual rights of third parties, but he did not doubt that equity has the power to do so in appropriate cases. Although a court would no doubt be more ready to restrain the ex-employee from entering into future contracts in breach of the ex-employer's right to its trade secrets, Lloyd LJ did not think that the equitable jurisdiction was confined to future contracts. The Court of Appeal accordingly upheld the injunction preventing fulfilment of existing contracts made in breach of confidence. The view of the Court of Appeal is preferable to that of the Vice Chancellor (referred to in para 14.29) since the defendant by the fulfilment of the orders is continuing the breaches already committed, and therefore the injunction is not being granted merely to deprive the defendant of the fruits of past breaches of contract (*Balston Ltd v Headline Filters Ltd* [1987] FSR 330, 341).

3(a)(ix) PERIOD OF THE SPRINGBOARD INJUNCTION

14.34 Having regard to the nature of the springboard injunction, which is to nullify an illegitimately obtained head start, it is normally inappropriate to grant an injunction until trial or further order (which may be appropriate in the case of true trade secrets: *Bullivant* paragraph 46). The parties and the judge should consider the proper length of the injunction: *Bullivant* paragraphs 46 and 47. In that case the duration of the injunction was, on appeal, limited to one year from termination of employment, in view of the fact that the names and addresses of potential customers were available in public directories. A one year period was also applied in *Fisher-Karpark Industries Ltd v Nichols* [1982] FSR 351). In *Prout v British Gas plc* [1992] FSR 478 (a Patents County Court trial) an employee had disclosed to his employer an invention under an employees' suggestion scheme but the employer had waived its rights in relation to it. However, the employer later used the idea, gaining a time advantage from using the employee's suggestion after it had waived its rights until the time of filing of a patent application by the claimant. It was held that the scheme gave rise to a contractually enforceable duty of confidence, alternatively a fiduciary relationship binding in equity, protecting suggestions which were of a potentially patentable nature. In answer to the question of how long the duty of confidence lasted, it was held that in a situation in which there could be no question of long-term trade or commercial secrecy or of applications for patent protection, the duty would come to an end when the defendant used the suggestion publicly for its own purposes without objection from the employee. However, if (as in this case) the employee gave notice of his intention to apply for a patent, the employee must be under a duty in principle which might be a fresh wholly equitable duty to continue to respect the confidence thereafter, at least until such time as the rights of the employee had been safeguarded by the filing of the patent application on his behalf. That would be the appropriate date for ending the springboard period. Since it was conceded at trial that it was too late for an injunction or delivery up of the confidential information, the employee was awarded an enquiry as to damages or at his option an account of profits for the period until the filing of his patent application. For an amusing attempt by a defendant to invoke the 'springboard' doctrine see *Electro Cad Australia Pty Ltd v Mejati* [1999] FSR 219 (High Court of Malaysia). The Court refused to restrict the period of the injunction for a limited time because, on the evidence, it was not possible to 'reverse engineer' the claimant's product.

4. Orders to recover property of the employer

4(a) Different classes of documents of interest to the ex-employer

14.35 Where the ex-employer brings interim proceedings against the ex-employee there are four different classes of document which the ex-employer may be seeking to recover or at least to see:

- Documents belonging to the ex-employer which have been removed by the ex-employee.
- Documents which, although not physically belonging to the ex-employer, contain confidential information belonging to him; these are normally treated on the same basis as the first class.

- Documents which infringe the ex-employer's copyright and are subject to the discretionary power of the court to order delivery up to the ex-employer (Section 99 of the Copyright, Designs and Patents Act 1988) or destruction (Section 114); see also right of seizure (Section 100).
- Documents belonging to the defendant which contain evidence of breaches of the contract of employment, for example, letters and invoices showing solicitation of or dealing with customers in breach of a non-solicitation/dealing covenant. The right to obtain copies of documents, which do not belong to the ex-employer, arises from the obligation of litigants under the CPR (Part 31) to make full disclosure to each other (with certain exceptions) of (broadly) all relevant documents in their control, including documents which help to advance their opponent's case.

Under this heading (recovery of property of the ex-employer) we are concerned with the first class of documents (and indirectly with the second class).

4(b) Property of the ex-employer

14.36 Section 4 of the Torts (Interference with Goods) Act 1977 empowers the High Court on an application in accordance with the rules of court:

> '... to make an order providing for the delivery up of any goods which are or may become the subject-matter of subsequent proceedings in the court or as to which any question may arise in the proceedings.'

CPR r 25.1(1)(e) provides that the court may grant:

> 'an order under section 4 of the Torts (Interference with Goods) Act 1977 to deliver up goods'.

14.37 Although the wording of CPR r 25.1(1)(e) covers cases even where the claimant does not assert a right of property, most frequently the ex-employer in invoking this jurisdiction will be relying on his property in the documents. Application may be made without notice to the defendant: CPR r 25.3. The power to order delivery up of goods is sufficiently broad to cover an order providing for the claimant himself to collect the goods.

14.38 In *CBS UK Ltd v Lambert* [1983] Ch 37 (where the court made a combined search order and freezing injunction – see paras 14.47ff for search orders) the Court of Appeal said (at page 44) that when making an interim order for the delivery up of goods pending trial the court should apply the following guidelines:

- There should be clear evidence that the defendant is likely, unless restrained by order, to dispose of or otherwise deal with his goods in order to deprive the claimant of the fruits of any judgment obtained, but the court should be slow to order the interim delivery up of the defendant's property unless there is some evidence or inference that the property has been obtained by the defendant as a result of his alleged wrongdoing;
- Certain items are excluded (for example, clothes, furniture, tools, stock-in-trade);
- The order should specify as clearly as possible what goods or classes of goods are to be delivered up – the inability of the claimant to identify what he wants delivered up and why is an indication that no order should be made;

- The order should not authorise the claimant to enter the defendant's premises or to seize the defendant's property without his consent;
- No order should be made for delivery up to anyone except the claimant's solicitor (or a receiver appointed by the court);
- The court should follow the appropriate guidelines for the grant of a freezing injunction laid down in *Z Ltd v A-Z and AA-LL* [1982] QB 558 insofar as they are applicable to goods in the possession, custody or control of third parties;
- Provision should always be made for liberty to apply to stay, vary or discharge the order.

14.39 These guidelines (referred to in the context of the court exercising its jurisdiction under Section 37 of the Supreme Court Act 1981 to award a freezing injunction, and in relation to a case where there was strong evidence to suggest that the defendant had put the profits he had made from infringing the claimant's copyright into easily removable and disposable assets, such as motor cars) are, in our view, applicable to cases where the goods in question belong to the defendant and not to the more usual case which arises in employment-related disputes where the ex-employer seeks to recover documents or other property belonging to him. In these cases there is often no real dispute as to ownership of the documents or other goods and the court will order delivery up without detailed consideration of other matters. The difficulty as regards the implementation of these orders lies more often in the proof of whether the documents or other goods are in fact in the control of the ex-employee. Often the ex-employee will file an affidavit or witness statement to the effect that he does not have in his control the documents in question – and there is little (at the interim stage) which the ex-employer can do about that. Hence, where one is dealing with an unscrupulous ex-employee, there is sometimes the need for the more drastic remedy of the search order : see paragraphs 14.47 to 14.101.

14.40 Applications under CPR r 25.1(1)(e) should be made to a Master of the Supreme Court or District Judge in the county court in accordance with CPR Part 23. However, since these applications are often bound up with other injunctive relief sought by the ex-employer, the application under CPR r 25.1(1)(e) will normally be made to the Judge to whom it is necessary to make application for the injunctions. The Master or District Judge does not have general power to grant injunctions otherwise than by consent: PD25 paragraph 1.2. In case of urgency the application may be made without notice to the respondent (CPR r 25.3).

5. Detention, preservation and inspection orders

14.41 CPR r 25.1(1)(c) provides that the court may make an order:

'(i) for the detention custody or preservation of [property which is the subject of a claim or as to which any question may arise on a claim]' and/or

'(ii) for the inspection of such property.'

And r 25.1(1)(d) provides for:

'an order authorising a person to enter any land or building in the possession of a party to the proceedings for the purposes of carrying out an order under sub-paragraph (c)' Applications under CPR r 25.1(1)(c) are of limited relevance to interim proceedings between ex-employer and ex-employee. However, such an application may occasionally be of assistance to the ex-employer. For instance, in the light of the increasing reluctance of the courts to grant search orders and the expensive safeguards now built into them (see below), cases may arise where the less drastic relief within this rule will be appropriate, eg an order for preservation of certain documents without a search order.'

14.42 Before the court will make an interim preservation order it must normally be shown that the defendant has the property in his possession or control: *Wilder v Wilder and Charters (No 2)* (1912) 56 Sol Jo 571 (but see *Penfold v Pearlberg* [1955] 1 WLR 1068 where an order was made against a party not in possession, but subject to the consent of a requisitioning local authority, on the basis that the authority would in all probability not object).

14.43 A document the authenticity of which was a vital question in the action is included within the meaning of 'property': *Re Saxton (decd)* [1962] 1 WLR 859 (in which Lord Wilberforce ordered the document to be delivered up for inspection by an expert); but in *Huddleston v Control Risks Information Services Ltd* [1987] 1 WLR 701 – in an application under Sections 33(1) and (2) of the Supreme Court Act 1981 and RSC Order 29 r 7A for pre-action inspection of property and disclosure of documents (see now CPR rr 25.2 to 25.5) – Hoffmann J (at page 703F–H) drew a distinction between the 'medium' and the 'message'. If the question which arises in the proceedings is concerned with the medium, the actual physical object which carries the information, the application would be for inspection of property under Section 33(1). If the question is concerned with the message, the information which the object conveys, the application is for discovery. In the context of an interim preservation application, if the significance of the document is its contents, seemingly it would not be regarded as property and would thus fall outside the ambit of this rule.

14.44 The court has power to allow a party to photocopy documents (or other property) in the possession of the opposing party: *Lewis v Earl of Londesborough* [1893] 2 QB 191. Usually inspection is by an expert (as in *Re Saxton*) but sometimes inspection may be permitted by an employee of a party instead: *Centri-Spray Corpn v CERA International Ltd* [1979] FSR 175.

14.45 Applications under CPR r 25.1(1)(c) should be made in accordance with CPR Part 23 to a Master of the Supreme Court or a District Judge in the county court, but if bound up with other relief being sought, application should be made to the Judge. The application may be made at any time, including before the issue of proceedings. Where an application is issued before the commencement of proceedings, special rules apply (see CPR rr 25.4 and 25.5). The defendant may only make an application under this rule once he has acknowledged service or filed a defence, unless the court otherwise directs. In cases of urgency the application may be made without notice to the respondent.

14.46 Claimants should also note the possibility of obtaining an interim injunction for delivery up where, for example, they have a contractual right to possession, as for example in *Nottingham Building Society v Eurodynamics*

Systems plc [1993] FSR 468. Such applications will be determined in accordance with the usual principles applicable to interim injunctions.

6. Search orders (formerly 'Anton Piller orders')

14.47 The search order is a powerful weapon in the hands of the ex-employer where he has good reason to believe that the ex-employee has documents which show wrongdoing on his part, such as the conversion of documents or misuse of confidential information, and that the conduct of the ex-employee shows that there is a real possibility that he might destroy them before a hearing at which both parties will be present, and that the damage, potential or actual, will be very serious for the ex-employer. For a fuller exposition reference should be made to Steven Gee QC *Mareva Injunctions and Anton Piller Relief* (4th edn) .

6(a) Nature of the order

14.48 This type of order, first sanctioned by the Court of Appeal in the case of *Anton Piller KG v Manufacturing Processes Ltd* [1976] Ch 55, is now on a statutory footing set out in Section 7 of the Civil Procedure Act 1997. The power of the court to make such an order is expressly referred to at CPR r 25.1(1)(h). The order:

- Empowers the claimant to enter the defendant's premises and search for and seize documents and other articles. While it is not a search warrant (per Lord Denning MR in *Anton Piller* at page 60) in the sense that it does not permit the use of force, nonetheless, since the defendant risks punishment for contempt if he does not submit to the order, its effect is often similar: *Thermax Ltd v Schott Industrial Glass Ltd* [1981] FSR 289, 291 per Browne-Wilkinson J (see, however, Gee pages 246 to 247);
- Is essentially mandatory, requiring the defendant immediately to disclose the whereabouts of and to deliver up documents and other goods, and typically includes a number of different orders including other mandatory orders;
- Will almost always be made in the absence of the defendant.

6(b) Usual relief

14.49 The standard form for a search order is set out in CPR PD25 at page 323 of the *Civil Practice* (2nd edn) and is reproduced as an appendix at the end of Ch 13. A typical order may include the following:

- Prohibitory injunctions restraining unlawful acts such as breaches of contract (for example, breaches of restrictive covenants in employment contracts) and confidence (including springboard injunctions); breaches of copyright and torts (for example, passing off and procurement of breaches of contract).
- A prohibitory injunction (included in the standard form order) restraining the defendant from warning third parties of the grant of the search order; this is important where it is intended to search different premises, to prevent persons at other premises still to be searched from being tipped off – although it is often wise to search as many as possible of the premises simultaneously.
- An order (included in the standard form order) directing the defendants to permit the search of their premises and to reveal the whereabouts of items

listed in the order (whether at the premises named in the order or other premises) and authorising the claimant to remove or copy these items; in relation to information on computer the order provides that the material be printed out and the print-out be removed.

- An order (formerly known as a 'Norwich Pharmacal' order: *Norwich Pharmacal Co v Customs and Excise Commissioners* [1974] AC 133) requiring immediate disclosure of the names and addresses of third parties 'mixed up' in the alleged wrongful activities of the defendants (for example, as customers or suppliers) in order to establish causes of action against third parties: *EMI Ltd v Sarwar and Haidar* [1977] FSR 146 (order for immediate disclosure of names and addresses of suppliers of infringing articles and information, and forthwith to deliver up all relevant documents relating thereto) and *Gates v Swift* [1981] FSR 57 (disclosure of names and addresses of those to whom the defendant has supplied infringing articles or information). The standard form order includes provision for the disclosure of names and addresses of customers and suppliers, but in view of the potential danger to a defendant's business, this should not be automatically granted: see Gee pages 259 to 261.

14.50 In rare cases the court will order delivery up by the defendant of his passport in order to ensure compliance with a search order: *Bayer AG v Winter* [1986] 1 WLR 497 (CA).

6(c) Requirements

14.51 The search order is an exceptional remedy (described by Donaldson LJ in *Bank Mellat v Nikpour* [1985] FSR 87 as a 'nuclear weapon of the law') such that the claimant is required (see judgment of Ormrod LJ in *Anton Piller* at page 62) to show:

- An extremely strong prima facie case;
- That the damage, potential or actual, will be very serious for the claimant;
- By clear evidence that the defendant has in his possession incriminating documents or things; and
- That there is a real possibility that he might destroy them before a hearing at which both parties will be present. The fact that the defendant is operating openly or is a respectable company may be a reason for refusing an order: *Booker McConnell plc v Plascow* [1985] RPC 425; *Systematica Ltd v London Computer Centre Ltd* [1983] FSR 313; but in *Yousif v Salama* [1980] 3 All ER 405 evidence of a forgery of a cheque was held to be enough: see *EMI Ltd v Pandit* [1975] 1 WLR 302.

In view of the exceptional nature of this relief evidence must be provided by the claimant on affidavit, not merely by witness statement (PD25 paragraph 3.1).

6(d) Limits on the use of search orders

6(d)(i) PROPORTIONALITY

14.52 One of the principal aspects of the overriding objective in litigation is that cases be dealt with proportionately (CPR r 1.1). Search orders constitute a severe inroad into the privacy of the individual and the courts have become increasingly unwilling to grant them. Thus, while these orders could once be obtained with relative ease (particularly in the Queen's Bench Division), because of abuses which have occurred in the obtaining and service of these orders, there is now a judicial reluctance to grant them at all. The court will normally require to be persuaded that some lesser order, such as a mandatory order for delivery up, is not likely to provide the claimant with sufficient protection – without the concomitant invasion of the privacy of the defendant. While this may be easy to demonstrate in a large-scale commercial fraud or video piracy case, the position may be different where the claimant is an ex-employer seeking to recover documents from an ex-employee: the fact that there is evidence to suggest that the ex-employee has acted dishonestly may be insufficient to persuade a judge that the defendant is the type of person who, if served with a mandatory order for immediate delivery up, will destroy the documents or other articles, the subject-matter of the order.

14.53 This judicial reticence is illustrated by the decision in *Lock International plc v Beswick* [1989] 3 All ER 373. Lock obtained a search order against eight former employees who commenced a rival business manufacturing and marketing metal detectors. It is worthwhile quoting at some length from the judgment of Hoffmann J (from page 383 h):

> 'Anton Piller orders are frequently sought in actions against former employees who have joined competitors or started competing businesses of their own. I have learnt to approach such applications with a certain initial scepticism. There is a strong incentive for employers to launch a pre-emptive strike to crush the unhatched competition in the egg by causing severe strains on the financial and management resources of the defendants or even a withdrawal of their financial support. Whether the claimant has a good case or not, the execution of the Anton Piller order may leave the defendants without the will or the money to pursue the action to trial in order to enforce the cross-undertaking as to damages.

> Some employers regard competition from former employees as presumptive evidence of dishonesty. Many have great difficulty in understanding the distinction between genuine trade secrets and skill and knowledge which the employee may take away with him.

> Even in cases in which the claimant has strong evidence that an employee has taken what is undoubtedly specific confidential information, such as a list of customers, the court must employ a graduated response. To borrow a useful concept from the jurisprudence of the European Community, there must be proportionality between the perceived threat to the claimant's rights and the remedy granted. The fact that there is overwhelming evidence that the defendant has behaved wrongfully in his commercial relationships does not necessarily justify an Anton Piller order. People whose commercial morality allows them to take a list of customers with whom they were in contact while employed will not necessarily disobey an order of the court requiring them to deliver it up. Not everyone who is misusing confidential information will destroy documents in the face of a court order requiring him to preserve them.

> In many cases it will therefore be sufficient to make an order for delivery up of the claimant's documents to his solicitor or, in cases in which the documents belong to the defendant but may provide evidence against him, an order that he preserve the documents pending further order, or allow the claimant's solicitor to make copies. The more intrusive orders allowing searches of premises or vehicles require a careful balancing of, on the one hand the claimant's right to recover his property or to preserve important evidence against, on the other hand, violation of the privacy of a defendant who has had no opportunity to put his side of the case. It is not merely

that the defendant may be innocent. The making of an intrusive order ex parte even against a guilty defendant is contrary to normal principles of justice and can only be done when there is a paramount need to prevent a denial of justice to the claimant. The absolute extremity of the court's powers is to permit a search of a defendant's dwelling house, with the humiliation and family distress which that frequently involves.'

In this case, because the evidence disclosed did not satisfy the requirements stated by Ormrod LJ (see para 14.51) and because of material non-disclosure in the supporting affidavits of the claimant the search order was discharged.

14.54 Also in *Columbia Picture Industries Inc v Robinson* [1987] Ch 38 (a case in which items were seized which were not covered by the order) Scott J said that search orders were being granted too readily.

14.55 In *Universal Thermosensors Ltd v Hibben* [1992] 1 WLR 840 Nicholls VC said that it was his impression that the warning signals regarding abuses of the search order had been heeded and that they were, rightly, being used much more sparingly than previously. However, because of continuing abuse further safeguards were required to protect defendants. The novel safeguard (referred to below) introduced was that of an independent solicitor to supervise the execution of the search order. Nicholls VC said that while this procedure would add considerably to the costs of executing a search order, since in suitable and strictly limited cases search orders furnished courts with a valuable aid in their efforts to do justice between parties, especially in cases of blatant fraud, it was important that the order should not be allowed to fall into disrepute. Where the ex-employer decides that a search order is excessive, there is always the alternative of some lesser remedy such as a delivery-up or inspection order under CPR r 25.1(1)(c) referred to above.

14.56 In view of the new express requirement of proportionality, referred to above, it seems likely that the courts' reticence to grant search orders will continue and, if anything, increase in the future.

6(e) Safeguards where the search order is granted

6(e)(i) FULL AND FRANK DISCLOSURE

14.57 The duty – The duty on the part of the claimant applying for a search order without notice to the defendant to make full and frank disclosure is an important safeguard for the defendant. This duty includes an obligation to make sufficient enquiry: *Jeffrey Rogers Knitwear Productions Ltd v Vinola (Knitwear) Manufacturing Co* [1985] FSR 184; *Brink's MAT Ltd v Elcombe* [1988] 1 WLR 1350; *Sal Oppenheim J R & Cie Kgaa v Rotherwood (UK) Ltd* (CA, 19 April 1996, unreported) and cf *Bank Mellat v Nikpour* [1985] FSR 87 (CA). Failure to comply with this duty will, if material, normally result in discharge of the order and an enquiry as to damages on the cross-undertaking. The court may order discharge even though the failure was inadvertent: *Wardle Fabrics v GMyristis Ltd* [1984] FSR 263 and *Thermax Ltd v Schott Industrial Glass Ltd* [1981] FSR 289 (in both cases the mandatory part of the order was discharged). These cases should be compared with *Yardley & Co v Higson* [1984] FSR 304 and *Brink's MAT Ltd v Elcombe* [1988] 1 WLR 1350 in which the court, having discharged the original order on the grounds of material (but innocent) non-disclosure, granted a further application for an injunction. The matter is essentially one for the court's discretion, but the fact that the non-disclosure was innocent and that an injunction could properly have been granted even had the facts been disclosed are important factors: *Lloyds Bowmaker Ltd v Britannia Arrow Holdings plc* [1988] 1 WLR 1337 (CA); *Behbehani v Salem* [1989] 1 WLR 723 (CA). The duty relates to disclosure of facts only. A breach of the general duty on advocates to draw attention to particular points of law will not ordinarily result in discharge of a search order: *Memory Corporation plc v Sidue* (1999) Times, 31 May. In our view the duty to make full and frank disclosure is not affected by the advent of the CPR.

14.58 The claimant should not use the search order application as part of a 'fishing expedition' to ascertain what causes of action he may have against the defendant: *Hytrac Conveyors Ltd v Conveyors International Ltd* [1983] 1 WLR 44 – and the duty of full and frank disclosure helps to ensure that this does not happen.

14.59 Examples of non-disclosure – Examples of cases where the search order was set aside for non-disclosure (together with the matters not disclosed) are:

- *Lock International plc v Beswick* [1989] 3 All ER 373 (true financial position of claimant and therefore value to the defendant of cross-undertaking);
- *Thermax Ltd v Schott Industrial Glass Ltd* [1981] FSR 289 (inter alia that the defendant was not simply a creature of other defendants (former directors of the claimant) and the existence of secrets of the defendants at their premises);
- *Manor Electronics Ltd v Dickson* [1988] RPC 618 (true financial position of the claimant: cross-undertaking worthless);
- *Columbia Picture Industries Inc v Robinson* [1987] Ch 38 (inter alia misleading impression that the defendant's business was being carried out clandestinely).

14.60 Trade secret cases – special problem of disclosure – In a case involving trade secrets there may be a conflict between the duty of disclosure and the need not to divulge (on affidavit) the secrets to the defendant. In *WEA Records Ltd v Vision's Channel 4 Ltd* [1983] 1 WLR 721 the judge had on the application without notice been given information which the claimants alleged was confidential and which was not incorporated into the affidavits in support of the motion. Sir John Donaldson MR said at page 724D–E:

> '... I cannot at the moment visualise any circumstances in which it would be right to give a judge information in an ... application [made without notice] which cannot at a later stage be revealed to the party affected by the result of the application.'

and at page 726G:

> '... there was no possible justification for this information being revealed to the defendants' counsel but not to their solicitors. Solicitors are officers of the court and are to be trusted to the same extent as counsel.'

14.61 This view was reiterated in *Helitune Ltd v Stewart Hughes Ltd* [1994] FSR 422, where it was held that disclosure of confidential exhibits to parties could be prevented. Note also that the court has power to grant an injunction restraining the use of confidential affidavits: *Lubrizol Corpn v Esso Petroleum Co Ltd (No 2)* [1993] FSR 53.

14.62 A practical solution is provided by CPR PD 25 paragraph 7.4 which provides that confidential exhibits to an affidavit need not be served but must be made available for inspection by the respondent in the presence of the claimant's solicitors during the search. Confidential exhibits may be retained by the respondent's solicitors on their undertaking not to permit the respondent to see the exhibits, save in their presence, or to make or take away any note or record of them. It is suggested that each such document should be marked as confidential and numbered.

6(e)(ii) SUPERVISING SOLICITOR

14.63 CPR PD 25 paragraphs 7.1 ff requires:

(a) that the order and evidence in support should be served, and its execution should be supervised by a solicitor other than a member of the firm of solicitors acting for the claimant in the action;
(b) that he should be a solicitor experienced in the operation of search orders;
(c) that the supervising solicitor should prepare a written report on what happened when the order was executed;
(d) that a copy of the report should be served on the defendant; and
(e) that a copy of the report be filed with the court – it will be considered at the 'return date' hearing when both parties are present.

As to (b), the claimant must include in his evidence, to put to the judge in support of the application for the search order, details of the name of the supervising solicitor and of his experience.

14.64 The claimant is responsible for paying the costs of the supervising solicitor without prejudice to a decision by the court on whether ultimately those costs should be borne in whole or in part by the defendant.

6(e)(iii) EXPLANATION OF THE ORDER

14.65 The order requires the supervising solicitor to explain the terms of the order fairly and in everyday language to the defendant or other persons served with the order and to inform the defendant of his right to seek immediate legal advice: *Booker McConnell plc v Plascow*. In *VDU Installations Ltd v Integrated Computer Systems and Cybernetics Ltd* [1989] FSR 378 Knox J held that a negligent failure by an applicant's solicitor to explain the order accurately constituted a contempt of court. Presumably the same would apply to a supervising solicitor.

6(e)(iv) RIGHT OF THE DEFENDANT TO TAKE LEGAL ADVICE

14.66 The standard order contains a provision that before complying with the order the defendant may obtain legal advice, provided this is done at once and provided nothing is disturbed or moved in the interim and meanwhile the supervising solicitor is permitted to enter (but not start the search). This is an important safeguard in view of the fact that the defendant will not have been present at the hearing of the application and the jeopardy for the defendant who does not comply properly with the order. Search orders are long and complicated such that many defendants may not fully understand the details of the order even as explained by the supervising solicitor.

6(e)(v) REQUIREMENTS REGARDING THE PERSONS SERVING THE ORDER

14.67 The order will permit a fixed number of persons authorised by the claimant and a fixed number of staff of the claimant's solicitors to enter on specified premises (preferably business premises) between fixed hours of the day (presumptively – see PD 25 paragraph 7.4(6) – during office hours on working days). The standard form order requires service between 9.30 am and 5.30 pm on a weekday, unless the court orders otherwise. (However, once the search is started, it continues until the search is complete: see paragraph 1(2) of standard order). The significance of this requirement was demonstrated by *Universal Thermosensors* in which the order was served by a man at 7.15 am on the defendant's wife when she was at home with only her children. At that time she could not obtain legal advice. A woman should not be subjected to the alarm of being confronted, without warning, by a solitary man, with no recognisable means of identification and claiming an entitlement to enter her home and telling her that she was not allowed to get in touch with anyone (except a lawyer) about what was happening. Where the supervising solicitor is male and the order is likely to be served on an unaccompanied woman, at least one person named in the order must be a woman and must accompany the supervising solicitor (PD 25 paragraph 7.4(5)).

6(e)(vi) GENERAL SAFEGUARDS REGARDING MANNER OF EXECUTION OF THE SEARCH ORDER

14.68 It is vital that the search order is served precisely in accordance with its terms. Failure to comply with the provisions may result in the order being set aside and the cross-undertaking as to damages being enforced against the claimant. Non-compliance with the terms regarding service may amount to contempt of court on the part of the claimant's solicitors and/or the claimant. *Columbia Picture Industries Inc v Robinson* [1987] Ch 38 was a case of serious abuse in the service of a search order. Scott J held that the claimants and their solicitors had acted oppressively and in abuse of their powers in executing the order by seizing items not covered by the order, retaining items not covered by the order, and in losing some of the items taken, and also that their conduct was improper in that they had obtained the order with a view to putting the defendants out of business. Scott J also made it clear (at page 77) that if in the course of execution further documents came to light which were not covered by the order, they could not be taken unless the defendant's solicitors were present to confirm and ensure that the consent given was a free and informed one: see also *VDU Installations Ltd v Integrated Computer Systems and Cybernetics Ltd* [1989] FSR 378. A police search should not be carried out simultaneously with the execution of a search order: *IT Film Distributors Ltd v Video Exchange Ltd (No 2)* (1982) 126 Sol Jo 672 (CA), now embodied in the standard orders.

6(e)(vii) LIST OF ITEMS REMOVED

14.69 A list of all material removed must be made by the supervising solicitor and a copy supplied to the respondent. Nothing may be removed until the respondent has had a reasonably opportunity to check the list.

6(e)(viii) SHORT DURATION OF 'GAGGING ORDERS'

14.70 Any order restraining the persons served from informing others of the existence of the order should be for a very limited period – certainly not for as long as a week: *Universal Thermosensors*. See standard form paragraph 5(1).

6(e)(ix) BUSINESS PREMISES: SERVICE IN THE PRESENCE OF OFFICER/RESPONSIBLE REPRESENTATIVE

14.71 The order provides that premises may not be searched unless the respondent or a person appearing to be a responsible employee in control of the premises, is present: see standard form paragraph 2(2).

6(e)(x) CLAIMANT NOT TO SEARCH RIVAL'S CONFIDENTIAL DOCUMENTS

14.72 Arrangements should be made so that personnel of the person who has obtained the order do not search through the documents of a competitor company: *Universal Thermosensors*. In *Lock v Beswick*, because the judge who originally granted the search order was conscious that he was allowing the claimant to see confidential information of a competitor, he extracted a written undertaking from each officer of the employee not to use the information for purposes other than the prosecution of claimant's action. Hoffmann J was of the view (page 386 d) that in such circumstances it would have been sufficient to allow the claimant's solicitors to remove and make copies for their own retention pending an application by the claimant inter partes for leave to inspect them: cf *Centri-Spray Corporation v CERA International Ltd* [1979] FSR 175. The standard form contains an undertaking not without leave of the court to use information or documents obtained as a result of the order nor to inform anyone else of the proceedings except for the purposes of those proceedings (including adding further respondents) or commencing civil proceedings in relation to the same on related subject matter to those proceedings, until after the return date.

6(e)(xi) DUTY AS TO ITEMS FOUND

14.73 Once documents had been seized, they should be copied and the originals returned, and a detailed record must be kept of all items seized: PD 25 and the standard form annexed thereto. Further, where the ownership of property is disputed, the standard form order requires that the articles of property be delivered to the respondent's solicitors within two working days of receiving from them a written undertaking to retain the articles in safe keeping and produce them to the court when required. Normally the search order will be drafted so as not to require the return of originals which are the property of the claimant or which contain confidential information, or are documents which infringe the copyright of the claimant.

6(e)(xii) CROSS-UNDERTAKING AS TO DAMAGES

14.74 The standard order contains the usual cross-undertaking by the claimant as to damages in case the court should later find that the injunction ought not to have been granted. Damages awarded on the cross-undertaking can in search order cases be very high indeed. It is for the claimant's solicitor to explain carefully to the claimant the risks involved. The claimant should produce evidence of his ability to pay under the cross-undertaking: *Vapormatic Co Ltd v Sparex Ltd* [1976] 1 WLR 939.

6(e)(xiii) UNDERTAKING TO ISSUE CLAIM FORM

14.75 If the claim form is not already issued at the time of the application, the order will include directions requiring a claim to be commenced pursuant to CPR r 25.2(3) and PD25 paragraph 5.1(5). These directions are included in the standard form order.

6(e)(xiv)   Right of the defendant to apply to vary or discharge the order

14.76   The standard order contains express liberty to each defendant to apply on notice to vary or discharge the order.

6(e)(xv)   Privilege against self-incrimination

14.77   This is the common law privilege which enables a defendant in civil proceedings to refuse to answer any question or produce any document or thing if to do so would tend to expose him to criminal proceedings: see Section 14 of the Civil Evidence Act 1968. ('Criminal proceedings' include for this purpose proceedings for contempt of court: *Bhimji v Chatwani (No 2)* [1992] 1 WLR 1158). This privilege was considered by the House of Lords in *Istel Ltd v Tully* [1992] 1 QB 315. Where assurances are obtained from prosecuting authorities that no prosecution will take place, the privilege may be lost (*Istel*). However, there must be actual notice to and assurances from the authorities, not merely an order that information disclosed not be revealed to the authorities: *United Norwest Co-operatives v Johnstone* [1994] TLR 104 (CA). It is not adequate protection for a defendant to hand documents in respect of which privilege is claimed to the supervising solicitor: *Den Norske Bank ASA v Antonatos* [1998] 3 WLR 711 (CA).

14.78   Parliament has in piecemeal fashion whittled away the privilege against self-incrimination most significantly (in the intellectual property field) by Section 72 of the Supreme Court Act 1981 which provides:

'(1)   In any proceedings to which this subsection applies a person shall not be excused, by reason that to do so would tend to expose that person, or his or her spouse, to proceedings for a related offence for the recovery of a related penalty:
(a)   from answering any question put to that person in the first-mentioned proceedings; or
(b)   from complying with any order made in those proceedings.
(2)   Subsection (1) applies to the following civil proceedings in the High Court, namely:
(a)   proceedings for infringement of rights pertaining to any intellectual property or for passing off;
(b)   proceedings brought to obtain disclosure of information relating to any infringement of such rights or to any passing off; and
(c)   proceedings brought to prevent any apprehended infringement of such rights or any apprehended passing off ...
(3)   Subject to subsection (4) no statement or admission made by a person:
(a)   in answering a question put to him in any proceedings to which subsection (1) applies; or
(b)   in complying with any order made in any such proceedings,
shall, in proceedings for any related offence or for the recovery of any related penalty, be admissible in evidence against that person or (unless they married after the making of the statement or admission) against the spouse of that person.
(4)   Nothing in subsection (3) shall render any statement or admission made by a person as there mentioned inadmissible in evidence against that person in proceedings for perjury or contempt of court.
(5)   ... in this section 'intellectual property' means any patent, trade mark, copyright, registered design, technical or commercial information or other intellectual property ...'

14.79 Another exception is to be found in Section 31 of the Theft Act 1968 which states:

'(1) A person shall not be excused, by reason that to do so may incriminate that person or the wife or husband of that person of an offence under this Act:
(a) from answering any question put to that person in proceedings for the recovery or administration of any property, for the execution of any trust or for an account of any property or any dealings with property; or
(b) from complying with any order made in any such proceedings;

but no statement or admission made by a person in answering a question put or complying with an order made as aforesaid shall, in proceedings for an offence under this Act, be admissible in evidence against that person or (unless they married after the making of the statement or admission) against the wife or husband of that person.'

14.80 The scheme under these statutory provisions is accordingly that in cases covered by these Acts the defendant is deprived of the privilege against incrimination but is compensated by the fact that any statement made by him which he is thus obliged to make may not be used against him in criminal proceedings.

14.81 However, there are many cases which fall outside these statutory exceptions. Indeed, in cases of fraudulent conspiracies (where the need to obtain the information is greatest) the defendant may be able to invoke the privilege because:

● The case may not concern 'intellectual property' or passing off; and/or
● There is a danger of conspiracy charges falling outside the Theft Act.

14.82 Furthermore, defendants and those advising them have become alive to the possibility of pleading the privilege against self-incrimination not only in relation to parts of the search order which require (by way of interrogatories) the disclosure of information (for example, the whereabouts of funds or names and addresses of suppliers) but to the main parts of the search order requiring the disclosure of documents (other than documents belonging to the claimant in respect of which the privilege cannot successfully be raised: *Istel Ltd v Tully* [1992] 1 QB 315, 325F and 328F). In *Tate Access Floors Inc v Boswell* [1990] 3 All ER 303 (see also *Sonangol v Lundqvist* [1990] 3 All ER 283) Browne-Wilkinson VC in setting aside a search order said:

'Anton Piller orders are only made where there is a strong prima facie case of dishonest conduct by the defendants which indicated that they are likely to destroy the evidence of their fraud. In such circumstances it is almost inevitable that the judge asked to make the order will consider that there is a real risk of prosecution for a criminal offence. If it is possible to say that the prosecution will be of a kind covered by section 31 of the Theft Act 1968 or section 72 of the Supreme Court Act 1981, that will cause no trouble. But if there is a real risk of a conspiracy charge, the judge will not be able to make an Anton Piller order at all and in consequence vital evidence will be destroyed. As it seems to me, apart from cases falling within section 72 (proceedings relating to intellectual property and passing off) in the future it will normally only be proper for the court to make an ex parte order for the recovery of property belonging to the claimants without any related discovery as to documents. To a large extent, the [search order] jurisdiction will become incapable of being exercised. It is for this reason that, for myself, I would welcome early consideration of the problem by Parliament.'

Further, in *Cobra Golf v Rata* [1997] 2 WLR 629, 644G-645C, Rimer J considered that a search order should not be made if there were provisions in it which were 'foreseeably likely to require the defendant to incriminate himself'.

14.83 In the light of this state of affairs there were calls for urgent reform in *Sonangol* and *Tate Access Floors* by the House of Lords in *Istel Ltd v Tully*. However, the position may not be so bleak:

• In a trade secrets case the question will arise whether confidential information amounts to 'intellectual property' within the meaning of Section 72 of the Supreme Court Act 1981. In *Istel v Tully* Lord Lowry (at page 360 H) said that 'commercial information' must be information of the same type ('ejusdem generis') as the other examples of intellectual property listed in subsection (5), which refers to patent, trade mark, copyright, registered design, technical or commercial information or other intellectual property – and therefore the House of Lords rejected the claimant's submission that the information sought as to the defendant's dealings with moneys (to enable the claimant to trace funds) amounted to commercial information within the meaning of section 72(5). However, in our view trade secrets or confidential information can sensibly be (and often are) referred to as 'intellectual property' and the broad phrase 'technical or other commercial information' is apt to describe respectively technical and business secrets. Indeed it is difficult to assign to them any other meaning in view of the other types of information specifically listed in the preceding words.

• For the privilege to be successfully invoked there must be a real risk, or increased risk, of prosecution or on the ground, in respect of any piece of information on evidence, that the prosecuting authority might wish to rely on it as establishing guilt or in determining whether to prosecute: *Den Norske Bank ASA v Antonatos* [1998] 3 WLR 711. In many cases involving claims of breach of confidence against ex-employees the risk of criminal proceedings may be remote. It might be thought to be a delicate line to tread for the claimant to persuade the court that the behaviour of the defendant is serious enough to warrant the grant of a search order but the defendant is not seriously at risk of prosecution outside the Theft Act. However, in practice (outside the realm of large-scale frauds) the court may well regard the behaviour of the defendant as warranting the grant of a search order but not being significant enough to attract conspiracy charges.

• In civil litigation the invocation by a defendant of the privilege against self incrimination may bear with it a price – the court may draw negative inferences against the defendant: *Rank Film Distributors Ltd v Video Information Centre* [1980] 2 All ER 273, 292 a–b (CA). However, if the court refuses to grant a search order on the basis that the defendant may invoke the privilege, the defendant may get the best of both worlds, that is, the protection of the privilege without having to bear the negative consequences of having taken it. The 'solution' offered by the standard form of order ('Respondent's Entitlements' paragraphs (4) and (7)) is that before permitting entry to the premises by anyone other than the supervising solicitor, the respondent may gather and hand over to the supervising solicitor documents which he believes to be privileged for the supervising solicitor to assess whether they are incriminatory or privileged as claimed. If the supervising solicitor concludes that any of the documents may be incriminating or privileged or if there is any doubt as to their status the supervising solicitor must exclude them from the search and return the documents of doubtful status in his possession pending further order of the court. While this is being done, the respondent may refuse entry to the premises by anyone else, and may refuse to allow the search to begin, for a short time (not exceeding two hours, unless the supervising solicitors agree to a longer period). If the respondent wishes to take legal advice and gather documents as permitted, he must inform the supervising solicitor and keep him informed of the steps being taken, but see the misgivings of the Court of Appeal expressed in *Den Norske Bank ASA v Antonatos* [1998] 2 WLR 711, 723F–724B, 728B–C regarding the expedient of ordering a respondent to place incriminating documents in the hands of a supervising solicitor. The standard order also provides for the supervising solicitor to explain to the respondent that he may be entitled to avail himself of the privilege against self-incrimination (or legal professional privilege): *IBM v Prima Data International* [1994] 1 WLR 719.

6(e)(xvi) RESTRICTIONS ON USE OF INFORMATION OBTAINED PURSUANT TO SEARCH ORDER

14.84 There is authority to the effect that documents obtained as a result of the execution of a search order should only be used for the purposes of the proceedings in which the order had been obtained: *Hallmark Cards Inc v Image Arts Ltd* [1977] FSR 150, 154 (CA); *General Nutrition Ltd v Pattni* [1984] FSR 403; *Commissioners of Customs and Excise v Hamlin (A E) &Co* [1984] 1 WLR 509; *EMI Records Ltd v Spillane* [1986] 1 WLR 967. On the other hand, in *Piver SARL v S & J Perfume Co Ltd* [1987] FSR 159 Walton J held that information disclosed by a private investigator while executing a search order could be passed by him to another of his clients whom he concluded was also being defrauded by the defendant. In *Twentieth Century Fox Film Corporation v Tryrare Ltd* [1991] FSR 58 Harman J held that the general rule that information disclosed on disclosure may only be used for the purposes of the action in which it was disclosed, save with leave of the court, had nothing to do with information obtained under a search order. These orders have always been intended to enable proceedings to be taken against third parties.

14.85 The true position would appear to be as stated by Knox J in *VDU Installations Ltd v Integrated Computer Systems and Cybernetics Ltd* [1989] FSR 378, 395, that is, the use to which the information is put should be within the ambit of the purpose for which the court is making the order. One of the purposes of the grant of a search order is to obtain information against other defendants against whom the claimant could pursue his claims: *Sony Corporation v Anand* [1981] FSR 398 (Browne-Wilkinson J); another is to recover property: *VDU Installations*; but not to let a mutual customer know that the defendant had been guilty of an irregularity (*VDU Installations*). If these broader purposes are included within the meaning of 'purposes of the action' there can be no quarrel with the concession of counsel in *Bhimji v Chatwani (No 2)* [1992] 1 WLR 1158, referred to by Knox J at page 1163 E, that documents revealed pursuant to search orders should only be used for the purpose of the action. These broader purposes appear to have gained acceptance and in accordance with the standard form of order, search orders will now ordinarily contain an undertaking by the applicant not, without leave, to use information or documents obtained other than for:

- The current proceedings; or
- Commencing civil proceedings 'in relation to the same or related subject matter' to the current proceedings;

until after the return date. At the return date the judge will be able to consider any application by the respondent requiring that the information be used only in the current proceedings. Note, however, that the fact that discoveries are made may be relayed to, for example, prosecuting authorities: *Process Development Ltd v Hogg* [1996] FSR 45.

14.86   Where a search order is subsequently discharged, the judge has a discretion whether or not to exclude evidence obtained as a result of the order: *Guess? Inc v Lee Seck Mon* [1987] FSR 125. In this case the Court of Appeal of Hong Kong held that irrespective of whether the order had been discharged for innocent or other reasons, if there had been serious and substantial non-disclosure the court should not allow the claimant to use the information obtained, unless there were good and compelling reasons.

6(f) Can a defendant refuse to comply?

14.87   A defendant is treading on thin ice when refusing to comply with a search order. If he does refuse to comply and subsequently fails to persuade the court to discharge the order then he will be in contempt of court. If the defendant uses the time during which the application to discharge is being considered to frustrate the order, for example, by destroying records, the consequences will be grave: *WEA Records Ltd v Vision's Channel 4 Ltd* [1983] 1 WLR 721. If the defendant does obtain a discharge of the order, he is probably still in contempt although the contempt would probably be seen as technical and not meriting any penalty. In *Hallmark Cards Inc v Image Arts Ltd* [1977] FSR 150 (CA) Buckley LJ said that while the search order stands, the party who refuses access to his premises is in default of the order:

> 'But if the party against whom the order is made were to succeed in getting the order discharged, I cannot conceive that that party would be liable to any penalties for any breach ...' (page 153).

See also *WEA Records Ltd v Vision's Channel 4 Ltd* at page 407.

14.88   A somewhat tougher line was suggested in *Wardle Fabrics Ltd v G Myristis Ltd* [1984] FSR 263 in which Goulding J held that the only defence to non-compliance is that the order was void ab initio. Goulding J stated (at page 275):

> 'The fact that [the order] is subsequently discharged is no automatic answer to proceedings for contempt, although the circumstances are appropriate to be considered when the court has to decide on penalties.'

14.89 In *Columbia Picture Industries Inc v Robinson* [1986] 3 All ER 338 Scott J referring to the *Wardle* case stated:

> 'The judge's reasoning is, if I may respectfully say so, difficult to fault. Moreover, if respondents to Anton Piller orders were to be allowed to delay their execution while applications to discharge were being made, the purpose of Anton Piller orders and procedure would be largely lost. Ample time would then be available to those disposed to destroy evidence or to secrete away master tapes to do so.'

14.90 However, Scott J seemed to soften his approach in *Bhimji and others v Chatwani* [1991] 1 All ER 705 in which (while repeating that a defendant who refuses to comply with a search order while making an application to discharge it does so at his own risk), he held that the breach in question was not contumacious and imposed no penalty since:

- It was as a result of alleged legal advice that it was permissible for entry to be postponed pending the application (this advice, if given, was wrong);
- At an early stage the defendant offered to provide reasonable protection of the documents;
- There was no evidence to suggest that the making of the application was merely a device to postpone the search;
- There was no evidence of impropriety by the defendant in respect of the documents in the period of delay;
- The order was oppressive by nature and there was prima facie injustice done to the defendant in being subjected to it.

14.91 The standard form of order provides that a respondent is entitled to apply for variation or discharge, provided

- This is done 'at once';
- The respondent does not disturb or move anything in the interim; and
- The Supervising Solicitor is permitted to enter (but not to start to search).

In the meantime, the respondent can delay commencement of the search for a short time, not to exceed two hours, unless the supervising solicitor agrees to a longer period.

6(g) Applications to discharge

14.92 An application to discharge a search order should be made in accordance with CPR Part 23 (and in particular see r 23.10). In theory, in a case of sufficient urgency an order made without notice can be set aside on an application similarly without notice: *London City Agency (JCD) Ltd v Lee* [1970] 1 Ch 597, and see CPR Part 23. However, the court will rarely suspend a search order on a without notice application without affidavit evidence in support: *Hallmark Cards Inc v Image Arts Ltd* [1977] FSR 150.

14.93 A fully executed search order could be discharged with retrospective effect if it should never have been made: *Booker McConnell plc and another v Plascow* [1985] RPC 425. In this case the Court of Appeal said that an application to set aside an executed search order was not normally a matter of urgency. If the sole reason for applying to discharge was to enforce the cross-undertaking as to damages, that should normally wait until trial. In any event the defendants should wait until the return date in the Chancery Division or a few days in the Queen's Bench Division to make their application unless the matter was one of extreme urgency.

14.94 In *Dormeuil Frères SA v Nicolian International (Textiles) Ltd* [1988] 3 All ER 197 where an application was made to set aside a search order on the basis of material non-disclosure Sir Nicholas Browne-Wilkinson VC said that the appropriate time for such application to be heard was at trial.

14.95 However, in *Tate Access Floors Inc v Boswell* [1990] 3 All ER 303, 316 the Vice Chancellor modified his view, having regard to the decision in *Behbehani v Salem* [1989] 1 WLR 723 (CA) (reported after *Dormeuil*). *Behbehani* showed that although the court has power to grant interim relief, notwithstanding a failure to make proper disclosure at the ex parte stage, in deciding whether to grant such further relief the court has to consider all the circumstances of the failure to make proper disclosure. It should consider whether such failure was innocent or deliberate and weigh the public interest in maintaining the golden rule that the party seeking relief without notice to the respondent should make full and frank disclosure as against the requirements of justice in granting the claimant relief to which he would otherwise be entitled in an application on notice. The Vice Chancellor therefore considered that he had been in error in *Dormeuil* in thinking that normally the question of whether there had been a failure to disclose was not appropriate to be dealt with at the interim stage. While welcoming guidance from the Court of Appeal the Vice Chancellor thought that the reconciliation between the public interest in upholding the golden rule and the public interest in ensuring that the courts are not clogged with long interim hearings is that the investigation of the circumstances in which the ex parte order was obtained should take place at the interim stage only where it is clear that there has been a failure to make a material disclosure, or where the nature of the alleged failure is so serious as to demand immediate investigation.

6(h) Cross-examination of defendant on his affidavit

14.96 Where a claimant believes that disclosure resulting from the search order is inadequate he can apply to the court to cross-examine the defendant as to his compliance with the order. CPR r 34.8 states:

(1) A party may apply for an order for a person to be examined before the hearing takes place.

(3) An order under this rule shall be for a deponent to be examined on oath before:

- A judge;
- An examiner of the court; or
- Such other person as the court appoints.

14.97 Peter Gibson J in the decision of *RAC Ltd v Allsop* (RCJ 3 October 1984, unreported) (referred to and applied in *CBS United Kingdom Ltd v Perry* [1985] FSR 421) said:

'The object of the application must, I apprehend, truly be to obtain further information which it is believed is in the possession of the person the subject of the order but which that person has failed to disclose notwithstanding the earlier order. The object of the application must not be to enable contempt proceedings to be brought so as to punish the person served with the order. Further, it must not be to obtain information which is to be used for the purpose of the action when that action comes to trial.'

14.98 Further, cross-examination is not to be used as a fishing expedition: the claimant should produce evidence that the defendants have further information which they have not revealed. See *Den Norske Bank ASA v Antonatos* [1998] 3 WLR 711 where the 'policing' function of such examination was referred to (page 731F) and the difficult inter-relationship between such examination and the privilege against self-incrimination was discussed.

14.99 However, in *Bayer AG v Winter (No 2)* [1986] 1 WLR 497 Scott J adopted a very negative stance towards cross-examination at the interim stage. He said:

'For my part I find it very difficult to envisage any circumstances in which, as a matter of discretion, it would be right to make such an order as is sought in the present case and as was made by consent in *House of Spring Gardens Ltd v Waite* [1985] FSR 173 (CA). The proper function of a judge in civil litigation is to decide issues between parties. It is not, in my opinion, to preside over an interrogation.'

14.100 In this case, there had been a strong case on behalf of the claimant to show that the first defendant had been selling counterfeit copies of the claimant's product. Scott J suggested that the claimant should seek either an order for specific disclosure or apply for the defendant's committal.

6(i) Foreign defendants

14.101 The courts are reluctant to grant a search order against a foreign defendant in respect of foreign premises, but may do so, if the defendant is served within this jurisdiction. In *Cook Industries Inc v Galliher* [1979] Ch 439 (where the foreign defendant had been properly served within the jurisdiction and filed a notice of intention to defend) the court ordered that the Paris flat of a foreign defendant could be searched and an inventory of its contents be made.

14.102 However, in *Altertext Inc v Advanced Data Communications Ltd* [1985] 1 All ER 395 (where the defendant could not be served within the jurisdiction) Scott J held that a search order should not be made against a party over whom the court does not have jurisdiction. Even if the case is one where leave under RSC Order 11 ought to be given to serve the defendant outside the jurisdiction, a search order ought not to be executed until the defendant has had a chance of applying to set aside the service of the claim form. In this case the claimant (understandably) declined the offer by the judge to grant an order, to be suspended for a short period to enable the defendant to apply to set aside the order granting leave to serve outside the jurisdiction. The whole purpose of a search order was to surprise the defendant. Scott J refused the claimant's application as a matter of his discretion, stating that search orders in respect of foreign premises ought not to be granted except against defendants over whom the courts of England and Wales have unquestionable jurisdiction. It should be noted that Section 7 of the Civil Procedure Act 1997 is limited to premises in England and Wales.

Chapter 15

Final remedies

Introduction

15.1 It is unusual for disputes involving breaches of restrictive covenants or confidence to proceed to trial, the decision of the court at the interim stage often being treated by the parties for practical purposes as determinative of the issues between them. However, whereas formerly the question of liability for legal costs would be negotiated between the parties as part of the overall settlement, under the new summary assessments of costs provisions, legal costs will often have been dealt with by the court at the interim stage (see Ch 13).

15.2 Equally, the parties may proceed to trial without seeking interim relief. This may happen, for example, where the (ex-)employer has reacted too slowly to the perceived breaches by the (ex-)employee so as to disentitle himself from obtaining interim relief. Another example is where the (ex-)employer forms the view that he may not succeed in obtaining interim relief, for example, where he is not good for damages on the cross-undertaking (see para 13.24), or for some other reason the balance of convenience does not favour him. On occasion an (ex-)employer may even decide that the final remedy of an account is a sufficiently effective deterrent to an (ex-)employee, because the remedy of an account may require him to disgorge all his profits to the ex-employer.

15.3 The means of proof at trial are far more cumbersome than at the interim stage (despite the relaxation on the use of hearsay evidence brought about by the Civil Evidence Act 1995). Witness statement or affidavit evidence is the rule at the interim stage (without the need for attendance and examination of witnesses) and hearsay evidence is accepted more readily than at trial.

15.4 We refer below to six forms of final relief:

- Damages for breach of restrictive covenant or for breach of confidence;
- An account of profits;
- Permanent injunctions;
- Delivery up or destruction;
- Declarations; and
- The appointment of a receiver.

1. Damages for breach of restrictive covenants

15.5   Damages are the usual remedy for breach of contract whether by the (ex-)employee or (ex-)employer, and whether for breach during employment, or after the termination of employment, and for breach of post-termination covenants or of confidence or knowing inducement of such breaches .

15.6   Claims b y the (ex-)employer will normally be for loss of profits on contracts or opportunities diverted by the (ex-)employee (see paras 3.52 to 3.64).

15.7   The (ex-)employer is entitled to be placed in the position he would have been but for the breach of covenant. This involves proof that the contract in question would have been placed with the (ex-)employer. Usually, it is not possible to show that the contract in question would definitely have been placed with the (ex-)employer and the loss is more likely to be seen as the loss of a chance. Accordingly, the court will evaluate the chance of which the (ex-)employer has been deprived. This is normally expressed in the form of a fixed percentage chance of making a profit of £x. There may be a considerable problem if evidence is given (perhaps by the solicited customers themselves) that they would not in any event have placed the business in question with the (ex-)employer. In *Industrial Development Consultants Ltd v Cooley* [1972] 1 WLR 443, where the managing director of IDC unlawfully diverted a potential contract to himself, there was clear evidence that the customer did not wish to place a contract with IDC but only with Cooley in his private capacity. Roskill J said that nonetheless the opportunity was there and could not be taken since IDC was not aware of it because of Cooley's conduct. He would accordingly have awarded damages representing a 10% chance of IDC obtaining the contract in question (but, more favourably to IDC, granted to them an account of profits: see paras 15.21 to 15.23 below). In *Sanders v Parry* [1967] 2 All ER 803, where Parry in breach of his duty of fidelity entered into a contract with a client of Sanders (a solicitor), Havers J awarded damages representing the lost chance of retaining the client's work. In the nature of things damages of this kind are extremely difficult to assess:

> 'But the fact that damages cannot be assessed with certainty does not relieve the wrongdoer of the necessity of paying damages for his breach of contract.' (per Vaughan Williams LJ in *Chaplin v Hicks* [1911] 2 KB 786, 792).

15.8   Accordingly, in *Sanders,* Sanders was awarded 12 months' net profit on the basis that, despite evidence of some animosity on the part of the client towards Sanders, it was still possible that he might have remained as a client. Havers J 'picked' a period of 12 months and arrived at a net figure after the deduction of office expenses. In *Robb v Green* [1895] 2 QB 315 Hawkins J referred to the difficulty in assessing damages in cases of this sort, emphasising that he could not grant an indemnity against the whole diminution of his trade, there being other possible causes.

15.9   As in other breach of contract cases the claimant must be seen to have made reasonable efforts to mitigate his loss.

15.10   In *Johnson v Agnew* [1979] 1 All ER 883 (HL) Lord Wilberforce said that damages for breach of contract were normally assessed at the date of the breach but that if to follow that rule would give rise to injustice, the court has power to fix such other date as may be appropriate in the circumstances.

2. Damages for breach of confidence

15.11 The authorities on the measure of damages for breach of confidence are not always easy to follow. However, where damages for breach of confidence arises in the context of a contract, such as the contract of employment, the position is simpler. There is no reason why they should not be assessed in the usual manner for breach of contract, that is, *Hadley v Baxendale* (1894) 9 Exch 341 principles. There ought to be no need to refer to other bases of liability (whether in equity or otherwise) where there is a contract: *Vokes Ltd v Heather* (1945) 62 RPC 135,141 (CA) cited in *Faccenda Chicken v Fowler* [1987] Ch 117, 135 (CA)

> 'Where the parties are, or have been, linked by a contract of employment, the obligations of the employee are to be determined by the contract between him and his employer.'

15.12 Outside the contractual context the measure is the tortious measure of damages. The claimant is entitled to that sum which will put him in the position in which he would have been if he had not sustained the wrong: *Dowson & Mason Ltd v Potter* [1986] 1 WLR 1419 (CA) and *Indata Equipment Supplies Ltd v ACL Ltd* [1998] FSR 248. In *Dowson & Mason* it was held that the particular position of the claimant must be considered:

- If the claimant would have sold or licensed the information, the claimant is entitled to the value of the information either on the basis of the market value of the information or on the basis of a capitalised royalty;
- If the claimant would not have sold the information but used it, for example in the manufacture of his own goods, he will be entitled to damages on the basis of his loss of profits.

Since the claimant in *Dowson* had no intention of selling or licensing the information in question, he was entitled to damages on the basis of his loss of profits. On this basis the Court of Appeal distinguished its decision in *Seager v Copydex Ltd (No 2)* [1969] 1 WLR 809 where the claimant had intended to sell or license the information. In *Seager* the Court of Appeal held that damages were to be assessed at the market value of the information misused by the defendants. Lord Denning MR said (page 813):

> 'Now a question has arisen as to the principles on which damages are to be assessed. They are to be assessed, as we have said, at the value of the information which the defendant took. If I may use an analogy, it is like damages for conversion. Damages for conversion are the value of the goods. Once the damages are paid, the goods become the property of the defendant. A satisfied judgment in trover transfers the property of the goods. So here, once the damages are assessed and paid, the confidential information belongs to the defendants ... The value of the information depends on the nature of it. If there was nothing very special about [the information], that is, if it involved no particular inventive step, but was the sort of information which could be obtained by employing any competent consultant, then the value of it was the fee which a consultant would charge for it: because in that case the defendants, by taking the information, would only have saved themselves the time and trouble of employing a consultant. But, on the other hand, if the information was something special, for instance, it involved an inventive step or something so unusual that it could not be obtained by just going to a consultant, then the value

must be much higher. It is not merely a consultant's fee, but the price which a willing buyer – desirous of obtaining it – would pay for it ... If ... the confidential information was very special indeed, then it may well be right for the value to be assessed on the footing that in the usual way it would be remunerated by a royalty. The court, of course, cannot give a royalty by way of damages. But it could give an equivalent by a calculation based on a capitalisation of a royalty. Thus it could arrive at a lump sum.'

15.13 Accordingly *Seager v Copydex Ltd (No 2)* is only useful authority for the position where the claimant would have sold or licensed the information. It follows of course that if damages are assessed on a loss of profits basis there is no reason to consider the information as having been 'transferred' to the defendant upon payment of damages. However, where damages are assessed on the basis of its value it is logical to treat the property as having been transferred.

15.14 In a claim for loss of profits in respect of specific business the claimant must of course establish:

- That the business in question was obtained as a result of the misuse of the claimant's confidential information;
- That, but for the defendant obtaining the business in question, the claimant would have done so, in whole or in part: see *Universal Thermosensors Ltd v Hibben* [1992] WLR 840, 851.

15.15 The claimant may alternatively seek to establish a general loss of profit by diminution of his trade. The difficulty of so doing or of proving damage to the claimant's goodwill (where loss of specific business cannot be shown) is illustrated by *Universal Thermosensors* (at page 852).

15.16 In the Queen's Bench Division damages will normally be assessed at trial. In the Chancery Division it is usual for damages to be dealt with separately from the hearing as to liability by an enquiry as to damages: as in *Saltman Engineering Co Ltd v Campbell Engineering Co Ltd* [1963] 3 All ER 413.

15.17 On the enquiry for damages the claimant may raise further breaches (not proved at trial) in respect of other items of confidential information: *National Broach & Machine Co v Churchill Gear Machines Ltd* [1965] 2 All ER 961.

15.18 Damages will normally be assessed at the time of the breach unless this will cause injustice (for example, in a case where damages are calculated by reference to the value of the information, if the value of the information has increased considerably by the date of trial): cf *Johnson v Agnew* [1979] 1 All ER 883 (HL).

15.19 In trade secrets cases it is not uncommon for the claimant to claim exemplary damages. These are punitive in nature and are appropriate when the defendant has cynically calculated that his breaches are likely to bring him more profit than is likely to be awarded to the claimant: *Cassell & Co Ltd v Broome* [1972] AC 1027.

15.20 Finally, it should be noted that damages for breach of confidence may be claimed in addition to, or in substitution for, an injunction under Section 50 of the Supreme Court Act 1981 (the successor to Lord Cairn's Act) (although there is authority to the effect that there is no claim in equity for non-contractual damages which are not in lieu of an injunction: *Malone v Metropolitan Police Commissioner* [1979] Ch 344, 366 but see Lord Goff in *Attorney General v Guardian Newspapers Ltd* (no 2) [1990] AC 107, 186 (HL) to the contrary). It should also be noted that the Court may decline to award damages for breach of confidence against a third party who was an innocent purchaser of the information or even where he was the innocent recipient of the information without giving value for it: see *Valeo Vision SA v Flexible Lamps* [1995] FSR 205.

3. Account of profits

15.21 An account of profits is an equitable remedy. It is based on the principle that the defendant who has improperly received or retained profits acquired from the use of the claimant's property (including confidential information) should be made to disgorge such profits. It may be available against a defendant who has committed a breach of fiduciary duty or confidence: *Attorney General v Guardian Newspapers Ltd (No 2)* [1988] 3 WLR 77(HL). This remedy looks to the profit of the defendant while damages look to the loss of the claimant. It is an important part of the armoury of the employer who has suffered (or against whom there is threatened) diversion of contracts or other losses through breaches of fiduciary duty or confidence by an (ex-)director or employee. While the (ex-)employer will normally wish to obtain an interim injunction to restrain further breaches, there may be occasions when it is thought advisable not to do so and, instead, to claim an account of profits made by the (ex-)director/employee arising from such breaches. The idea of carrying on business for the ultimate benefit of the (ex-)employer can constitute as much of a deterrent to the (ex-)employee as an interim injunction. Where a new employee is obtaining the benefit of the breaches of contract of the (ex-)employer, it is necessary to add the new employer as a defendant to obtain an account of profits against him.

15.22 In *Industrial Development Consultants Ltd v Cooley* [1972] 1 WLR 443 referred to in paragraph 15.7, Roskill J held that Cooley had acted in breach of fiduciary duty in failing to pass to IDC all relevant information received in the course of his negotiations with the Gas Board and in guarding it for his own personal purposes and profit. Instead he had embarked on a deliberate course of conduct which had put his personal interests as a potential contracting party with the Gas Board in direct conflict with his pre-existing duty as managing director. He was therefore held liable to account to IDC for all the benefit he had received and would receive under the contract with the Gas Board. The question of whether the benefit of the contract would have been obtained for IDC but for *Cooley's* breach of duty was irrelevant. It was therefore irrelevant that as a result of the order for an account IDC would receive a benefit which it would not otherwise have received.

3(a) When is an account of profits available?

15.23 This is an equitable remedy available only in the case of breach of (the equitable duty of) confidence and breach of fiduciary duty and not (without more) for mere breaches of contract. (See however the considered remarks of the Court of Appeal made *obiter* in *A G v Blake* [1998] 2 WLR 805 816D to

919E to the effect that while damages for breaches of contract are compensatory, restitutionary damages may be available in exceptional cases. The two exceptional cases identified were both cases where profits are occasioned directly by a breach of contract and compensatory damages would be inadequate, namely where the defendant fails to provide the full extent of the services he contracted to provide and for which he has charged the claimant and where the defendant has obtained his profit by doing the very thing he has contracted not to do). Further, since the account of profits is a discretionary remedy, the court will take into account such matters as delay in bringing the proceedings, or whether the claimant has acquiesced in the defendant's conduct, as well as the conduct of the claimant (ie. whether he comes to court with 'clean hands'). In *Seager v Copydex Ltd* [1967] 1 WLR 923 where the court held that the defendant had not acted dishonestly, damages only were awarded. The defendant's innocence may have been a factor in this regard. The position should be compared with that of an innocent fiduciary having to account for profits arising from the use of information where his interest conflicts with his duty: *Boardman v Phipps* [1967] 2 AC 46. Strictly, it would seem that an account can only be claimed for breach of an equitable duty of confidence – making it necessary even where there is a contractual obligation of confidence to plead also breach of the equitable obligation – although it is doubtful that a court would disallow the remedy if only contractual breach were pleaded.

3(b) To what profits is the claimant entitled?

15.24 Where the profits could not have been made without using the confidential information, the claimant is entitled to the whole of it. For example, the price of the goods made by using the confidential information received less the manufacturing cost, and not merely the additional profit made by use of the confidential information: *Peter Pan Manufacturing Corporation v Corsets Silhouette Ltd* [1963] RPC 45. On the other hand, the court may in certain circumstances invoke the principle of proportionality so as to deny the claimant the discretionary remedy of an account of profits altogether. In *Satnam Investments Ltd v Dunlop Heywood & Co Ltd* [1999] FSR 722 the Court of Appeal declined to hold the third party who had received and used confidential information liable to an account of profits. The information was 'not very confidential' and would have been available on reasonable enquiry. Accordingly, it would be inequitable and contrary to commercial good sense to hold the third party liable on the basis that there was a degree of confidentiality in the information when it was disclosed to the third party.

15.25 The position is much more difficult where the claimant's information contributed only in part to the profit, for example, where manufacture was possible by other means but use of the claimant's confidential information enabled the defendant to make the product more cheaply. This may have been the principal reason why an account was not granted in *Seager v Copydex (No 2)*: see in particular Lord Denning MR at page 931 F-932 B. On the other hand the court may approach a case in a fairly rough and ready manner, when in doubt leaning in favour of the injured party as in *Normalec Ltd v Britton* [1983] FSR 318. See also: *My Kinda Town Ltd v Soll* [1983] RPC 15 (a passing off case) in which Slade J said:

> 'What will be required on the enquiry ... will not be mathematical exactness but only a reasonable approximation.'

15.26   See also *Attorney General v Guardian Newspapers Ltd (No 2)* [1988] 2 WLR 805, 859 to 860 where the order for an account of profits against *The Sunday Times* out of the publication of the book *Spycatcher* (based on the inferential evidence of increased circulation) was not limited to profits made from those parts of the book which the newspaper was not permitted to publish. Scott J held that the behaviour of the newspaper in publishing was such that they were in no position to argue against the equity of an order that it account for the profit made out of the entire publication and this was upheld on appeal ultimately to the House of Lords ([1988] 3 WLR 776). There, Lord Keith pointed out (at page 788F) that the newspaper was not entitled in the taking of the account to deduct the sums paid to the publishers of the confidant (Mr Wright) as consideration for the licence granted by them, since neither Mr Wright nor his publisher were or would in the future be in a position to maintain an action in England to recover such payments.

4. Choice between an account and damages

15.27   An account of profits and damages are alternative remedies. It is usual for the claimant to seek damages and in the alternative (at his option) an account of profits (in addition to an injunction and/or an order for delivery up or destruction of material made or acquired in breach of confidence). The particular advantages of seeking an account are well illustrated by *Cooley*. The claimant is not required to prove loss (which is usually extremely difficult – see para 15.7): nor is the claimant required to mitigate his loss.

15.28   The potential advantages for the claimant and attendant dangers for a defendant are illustrated by the case of *Normalec Ltd v Britton* [1983] FSR 318 where a sales agent used confidential information of the identity of customers and their requirements to entice them away from the claimant, as a result of which Walton J held that *the entirety of the defendant's business* belonged in equity to the claimant – even though the business dealt with a large number of matters with which the claimant did not deal. In *Ocular Sciences Ltd v Aspect Vision Care Ltd* [1997] RPC 289, 413 to 416 Laddie J refused to impose a constructive trust where there had been no diversion of business and contamination of the defendant's business by breaches of confidence was small and technically inconsequential.

15.29   However, the taking of an account may be a cumbersome and protracted procedure and has often been criticised. In cases of breach of confidence it is therefore only where clear benefits will accrue to the claimant that this remedy should be pursued in preference to damages. In particular, where the confidential information contributed only partially to the profit, it would be inadvisable to pursue this remedy. In cases of breach of a director's fiduciary duty such as *Cooley* it is less likely in practice that the problems of partial contribution to profit will arise and the taking of the account may be relatively straightforward and often highly advantageous to the claimant. It is also to be expected that where breach of fiduciary duty by an (ex-)director (or senior employee) is concerned the court would not be astute to find that he or she was liable only for part of the profit made: whereas, where the duty to account arises only by virtue of the receipt of the information itself, there is more reason to limit that duty to the profit arising specifically from the use of only that information. It is for this reason that the decision in *Normalec* can be criticised, although Walton J there referred to the defendant as a fiduciary (cf Shaw LJ in *Schering Chemicals Ltd v Falkman Ltd* [1981] 2 All ER 321, 337h) it would seem from the report of that decision that Britton was not a true 'agent' acting for Normalec as principal, but merely an employee. Accordingly the duty to account arose by virtue of the receipt of the confidential information only.

5. Permanent injunctions

15.30 The remedy of a permanent injunction, being an equitable form of relief, is discretionary. However, it will not readily be refused: *Terrapin Ltd v Builders' Supply Co (Hayes) Ltd* [1960] RPC 128, 135 (interim injunction) in which Lord Evershed MR cited the well-known statement of Smith LJ in *Shelfer v City of London Electric Lighting Co* [1895] 1 Ch 287, 322:

> 'A person by committing a wrongful act ... is not thereby entitled to ask the court to sanction his doing so by purchasing his neighbour's rights, by assessing damages in that behalf.'

15.31 Factors which may, however, cause the court to refuse to grant a (permanent) injunction include:

- That damages are an adequate remedy. This is unlikely to be the case where personal information (for example, regarding the private affairs of individuals) is concerned: *Coco v A N Clark (Engineers) Ltd* [1969] RPC 41, 50 (per MegarryJ); but also in most confidentiality and restrictive covenant cases damages will not be an adequate remedy;
- The extent of use of the confidential information. If the contribution was minor, damages may be appropriate: *Bostitch v McGarry & Cole Ltd* [1964] RPC 173, and see discussion of *Seager v Copydex Ltd (No 2)* (paras 15.12 and 15.13) and *Ocular Sciences Ltd v Aspect Vision Care Ltd* [1997] RPC 289, 401, 404, 406 to 407;
- The extent of publication: however, even fairly wide dissemination may not preclude the grant of an injunction, as long as the injunction will not thereby be rendered useless;
- Good faith and change of position on the part of the defendant: see *Seager v Copydex (No 2)*;
- The public interest (relevant to both restrictive covenant and confidential information cases) *Biogen v Medeva plc* (1992) Times, 1 December;
- The special position of employers and employees (non-enforcement of contracts of service); and
- Other factors which may preclude the grant of equitable relief: for example, delay, acquiescence, lack of 'clean hands': *Ocular Sciences*.

15.32 The injunction sought must be framed with sufficient certainty to enable the defendant to know precisely what he may or may not do: *P A Thomas & Co v Mould* [1968] 2 QB 913. In confidentiality cases it is important to identify and prove the existence of a separate body of objective information amounting to a trade secret or confidential information: *FSS Travel and Leisure v Johnson*

[1998] IRLR 22 (CA) (a restrictive covenant case based on confidential information). Confidential information injunctions will normally be limited in time since nearly all confidential information will have limited shelf-life (see para 5.46). Different kinds of confidentiality injunctions may be obtained, for example, springboard injunctions (referred to in Ch 14) and injunctions preventing professionals from acting against their former clients. In *Prince Jefri Bolkiah v KPMG (a firm)* [1999] 1 All ER 516 the House of Lords enunciated the principle that where a former client established that the defendant firm was in possession of information which had been imparted in confidence, that he had not consented to its disclosure, and that the firm was proposing to act for another client with an interest adverse to his in a matter to which the information was or might be relevant, the court would intervene to restrain the firm from acting for that other client, unless the firm satisfied it, on the basis of clear and convincing evidence, that effective measures had been taken to ensure that no disclosure would occur and that there was no risk of the information coming into the possession of those acting for the other client. For further details, see paragraph 16.9.

15.33 In restrictive covenant cases the question of the grant of a permanent injunction may be academic since the period of the restriction will often have expired by the time of trial. However, given the modern tendency of the courts to order speedy trial in such cases, that will often not be the case.

6. Delivery up/destruction

15.34 In relation to materials which belong to the claimant he is, of course, entitled in law to delivery up of that which belongs to him (cf CPR 25.1). In addition, the court may in its discretion (as part of its inherent jurisdiction in equity) order a defendant to deliver up or destroy on oath any materials in his possession or control which contain confidential information of the claimant even though the physical documents belong to the defendant,

> 'with a view to assisting the claimant and ensuring to the claimant the fruits of success in the action': *Industrial Furnaces Ltd v Reaves* [1970] RPC 605, 626.

These orders are thus intended to ensure that the defendant does not continue the misuse of confidential information. In this case Graham J would ordinarily have ordered destruction on oath of the infringing materials but, because he viewed the defendant as unreliable, he ordered delivery up (even though that material might contain confidential information of the defendant).

15.35 Not only documents (including information stored on computer), but also goods embodying the confidential information, may be ordered to be destroyed: *Peter Pan Manufacturing Corporation v Corsets Silhouette Ltd* [1963] RPC 45 (destruction of brassieres made using the claimant's confidential method and design) and see *Ackroyds (London) Ltd v Islington Plastics Ltd* [1962] RPC 97, 105. The destruction of property in this manner is not lightly ordered: in *Saltman Engineering Co Ltd v Campbell Engineering Co Ltd* [1963] 3 All ER 413, 415, while delivery up of infringing drawings was ordered, the court was reluctant to order the destruction of tools which might serve a useful purpose. Instead an enquiry as to damages both in respect of past and future loss (under Lord Cairn's Act) was ordered. In *Reid & Sigrist Ltd v Moss and Mechanism Ltd* (1932) 49 RPC 461, 482 the defendant was ordered to deliver up all items containing the claimant's confidential information.

7. Declarations

15.36 RSC Order 15 r 16 (preserved under the CPR Schedule 1) states:

> 'No claim or other proceeding shall be open to objection on the ground that a merely declaratory judgment or order is sought thereby, and the court may make binding declarations of right whether or not any consequential relief is or could be claimed.'

The remedy is discretionary. It is not often used in confidentiality or restrictive covenant cases.

15.37 A court will not normally decide academic or hypothetical questions: *Re Barnato* [1949] Ch 258 (CA). However, a declaration was awarded to an employer in *Marion White Ltd v Francis* [1972] 1 WLR 1423 (CA) in relation to Marion White's standard covenant provided by all its employees, although the particular covenant sued on had ceased to be operative. Marion White still had an interest with regard to their other employees as to whether such a covenant was enforceable. The Court of Appeal (somewhat reluctantly) exercised its jurisdiction in favour of Marion White (allowing them to amend their pleadings to seek a declaration) to put right the view which the judge below took of the standard clause by granting a declaration 'which satisfied the employer but binds nobody' (per Stephenson LJ at page 1430 H).

15.38 A novel use of the declaration was made by an employee in *Greer v Sketchley Ltd* [1979] FSR 197 who, on being threatened that he would be acting in breach of a restrictive covenant in his contract of employment if he joined a rival (as he intended to do), before joining the rival issued proceedings claiming a declaration that the clause was invalid. Sketchley counterclaimed for an injunction. Lord Denning MR commended this sensible approach. (The clause was held to be invalid). Another example where an employer sought a declaration was in *Commercial Plastics Ltd v Vincent* [1964] 3 All ER 546 where an injunction was sought to restrain Vincent from entering the employment of a particular rival for the period of the covenant together with a declaration that he was not entitled for the same period to enter the employ of any of Commercial Plastics' competitors in their field of work.

8. Receiver

15.39 A further remedy (rarely used) for the breach of confidence is the equitable remedy of the appointment of a receiver to collect and receive all profits made by means of the use of the confidential information.

9. Rectification

15.40 The remedy of rectification of contracts is considered at paragraphs 11.26 to 11.30.

Chapter 16

Discovering competitive activity: the immediate practical issues

Introduction

16.1 There are three broad categories of competitive activity in which the (ex-) employee may be involved:

* Competition during employment.
* Acts preparatory to competing after employment has ended.
* Competition after employment has ended.

Often the (ex-)employee's conduct involves more than one of these categories, normally the second and third, and in some cases all three, see for example *Balston Ltd v Headline Filters Ltd* [1987] FSR 330.

16.2 Discovering an (ex-)employee has engaged in any of these competitive activities, or is proposing to do so, frequently produces a reaction of outrage by the (ex-)employer. Often the (ex-)employer regards the competitive activity as a form of serious personal attack, irrespective of the real commercial threat, and reacts with a degree of haste and irrationality more commonly seen in matrimonial disputes. For example, a common reaction by an employer, who discovers that an employee is to join a competitor, is to terminate the relationship immediately, to have the employee clear his desk under supervision and then to march him unceremoniously off the premises. While this may make the employer feel better, as a course of action it is neither commercially nor legally sensible. Not only will the employer have deprived himself of any opportunity of retaining the employee, he will also have released the employee from the obligation to give or serve out his notice and, where the conduct amounts to a repudiatory breach of the contract (see paras 8.29 to 8.31) which is accepted by the employee, he will have released the employee from all future obligations under the contract. In short, as a result of his actions the employer will have worsened rather than improved his own position. To avoid pitfalls such as these, it is imperative that the (ex-)employer takes stock of the situation and devises his strategy before reacting.

1. Reacting to the discovery

16.3 In every case the (ex-)employer must take the following three basic steps:

* Gather information;

- Take key decisions; and
- Settle a strategy to reflect the key decisions.

16.4 It is also imperative that the (ex-)employer takes these steps without delay. This is commercially important because the employer needs to react to the competitive activity promptly in order to minimise the damage or potential damage to his business. It is also legally important primarily because delay is likely to prejudice any application the (ex-)employer may subsequently make for an interim injunction.

16.5 The three basic steps are the same for each type of competitive activity referred to in paragraph 16.1. In practice, however, there are differences in the factors that have to be taken into account and the options available to the (ex-)employer, depending on whether he discovers the actual or threatened competitive activity whilst he is still the employer or after the employment has ended. For this reason, we will look first at how the steps should be taken where the discovery is made during employment and then simply highlight the differences where the discovery is made after termination of employment. Before turning to that exercise, it is worth pausing to consider an important preliminary issue which is the instruction of legal advisers.

2. Instructing the legal team

16.6 It is vitally important for the (ex-)employer to seek advice from solicitors at the earliest possible opportunity and in any event before any irrevocable steps are taken. The key reasons for this are threefold. Firstly and often most important, where employment is ongoing, the solicitor can avoid the employer committing a repudiatory breach of contract. Second, in cases of competitive activity court proceedings can become imperative at very short notice. Instructing solicitors and counsel at the last minute can result in valuable time being lost and, in some cases, poor quality instructions being given which result in an unsuccessful court application. Finally, a solicitor, particularly one used to dealing with employee competition, will be able to give valuable and speedy advice on strategic matters and on issues such as the prospects of success of any litigation. As will be seen, deciding whether or not to litigate is one of the key decisions the (ex-)employer has to take and without proper legal advice he will not be able to make an informed decision.

16.7 This Chapter looks at the discovery of competitive activity from the perspective of the (ex-)employer. There is, however, one highly relevant point about instructing a legal team which arises initially from the perspective of the (ex-)employee and any new employer but which can of be of considerable importance to the (ex-)employer. The point arises where there is more than one (ex-)employee involved or where a poaching future employer is involved. In those cases, it is very common for the (ex-)employees, and where relevant the poacher, to ask one solicitor to represent them all. For the solicitor warning bells should start ringing immediately and he should only agree to act for all the potential clients after very careful consideration and a full explanation having been given to the potential clients of the consequences of accepting instructions from all of them. Under the Law Society Rules a solicitor is prohibited from accepting instructions to act for two or more clients where there is a conflict or a significant risk of a conflict between the interests of those clients, (Rule 1, Solicitors Practice Rules 1990 and see *Cordery on Solicitors* (9th edn) paragraphs 124 to 127). Additionally, where a conflict arises between clients, the solicitor cannot continue to act for both. In this context, it is likely that he will have to give up acting for both, on the basis that he has acquired relevant knowledge about the client which would affect the way in which he advised the other. Once seized of that knowledge, the solicitor cannot continue to act for one of the 'original' clients, even with the consent of the other (Rule 1, Solicitors Practice Rules 1990 and see *Cordery on Solicitors* (9th edn) paragraph 128). The substance of the rules that apply to Counsel are the same, see the Code of Conduct of the Bar of England and Wales and in particular paragraph 501.

16.8 From the (ex-)employer's perspective, while there may be commercial advantages in only having to deal with a single representative of the 'opposition', the possibility of a conflict arising within the opposition group gives the (ex-)employer the tactical advantage that he may be able to force the opposition to instruct new and separate lawyers on the grounds of conflict. A successful application along these lines at a crucial moment can have a devastating effect, and has been known to lead to complete capitulation to the (ex-)employer's demands. Because of this potential risk we advise extreme caution should be exercised by solicitors and counsel in accepting 'multiple clients'. The competing (ex-)employees and the poacher should only very rarely be jointly represented because of the potential risk of a conflict arising out of the more onerous obligations owed by directors and fiduciaries. Within teams of (ex-)employees there is a little more flexibility but care should always be taken to distinguish between directors and fiduciaries on the one hand and more junior staff on the other. Both groups should normally be separately represented because of the potential risk of a conflict arising out of the more onerous obligations owed by directors and fiduciaries. Similarly, if there is one member of the team who has committed a material breach of contract, for example, by removing his employer's property or by soliciting clients before his employment ended, and other members of the team have committed no breaches, the wrongdoer should be separately represented. Solicitors and counsel should never be beguiled by the camaraderie of potential clients. Law Society Rules and the Code of Conduct of the Bar of England and Wales apply where there is a significant risk of a conflict. In practice, in the context of competitive activity that risk is realised frequently.

16.9 Solicitors hoping to circumvent this problem of conflict by having clients separately represented by different members of the solicitors firm and relying on the creation of 'Chinese Walls' within the firm are likely to be disappointed following the rejection of the adequacy of such an arrangement in the recent House of Lords decision in *Prince Jefri Bolkiah v KPMG* [1999] 2 WLR 215. While the interpretation of that case by Laddie J in *Young v Robson Rhodes* [1999] 3 All ER 524 offers some hope to those seeking to rely on 'Chinese Walls', in the context of employee competition it is unlikely that the rigorous requirements needed to sustain the 'Chinese Wall' will be commercially feasible and the simplest course will be to have separate representation. For the moment, at least, the problems of conflicts are less acute for the Bar. Different members of the same set of chambers are not legally prevented from representing different parties to the same action (provided there is no other question of conflict of interest), see *Laker Airways Inc v FLS Aerospace Ltd and Burnton*

[1999] 2 Lloyds Law Reports 45 on a related but similar point. However, commercially, the Bar is certainly becoming aware of the need for more formal Chinese Walls to be established within Chambers as evidenced by the fact that the Bar Council has established a working party on Chinese Walls.

16.10 Notwithstanding what we have said above in favour of separate legal representation for a poaching employer and the employee he is poaching, and for the employees within a defecting team, it has to be recognised that there is a potential disadvantage with separate representation. On the current state of the law it is far from clear that communications between the different legal teams, or indeed directly between those represented by the teams, will attract privilege. The only basis on which they could do so, is under what is known as common interest privilege. That is a concept well developed in the United States but still in a fairly embryonic form in the UK. The limited authorities there are on common interest privilege suggest that it could be available in the type of situation outlined above, particularly where there is almost an inevitability that the separately represented parties will ultimately be co-defendants see, for example, *Buttes Gases and Oil Co v Hammer* (No 3) [1981], 1 QB 223 and *The Good Luck* [1992] 2 Lloyds Rep 540 and *The World Era* (No 2) 1993 1 Lloyds Rep 363. However the matter is by no means settled, particularly in circumstances where a conflict of interest may arise between the separately represented parties. Consequently great care should be taken in any communication between the legal teams. This is obviously a problem that does not arise where joint representation is elected.

3. Applying the three basic steps: discovery during employment

3(a) Gathering information

16.11 This exercise is essentially the first stage of a disciplinary investigation. There are four questions to which the employer needs answers:

- What is the nature and scope of the competitive activity?
- Has the competitive activity involved any breaches of the obligations owed by the employee to the employer or is it likely to do so?
- What are the role, importance and terms of employment of the employee?
- What sort of threat does the competitive activity pose to the employer's business?

16.12 Preliminary issue: should the employee be suspended? – Inevitably the information gathering exercise will take a little time even where the employer acts expeditiously. The employer often feels uncomfortable with the employee continuing to perform his duties while the investigation is ongoing; and suspension during this period is a commonly adopted solution. One note of caution. As a general rule, suspension is normally only permissible for the purpose of investigation of suspected misconduct. Consequently, if the competitive activity consists of no more than a stated intention by the employee to join a competitor after the expiry of his contractual notice and that course is not prohibited by the contract then there is no legal basis for suspension.

16.13 The right to suspend an employee while investigations are carried out is often expressly reserved in the contract of employment and some contracts include detailed rules about when suspension is allowed, how the employee is to be notified, how he is to be remunerated during the suspension and the maximum duration of the suspension. Where the employer is relying on an express right to suspend then it is important that he complies strictly with the terms of the contract: *Gorse v Durham County Council* [1971] 2 All ER 666. In addition, the employer may be under an implied obligation to act reasonably in exercising his right to suspend although he is not bound to apply the rules of natural justice in doing so: *McLory v Post Office* [1992] ICR 758. McLory had been suspended on basic pay by the Post Office as a result of being involved in a fight in a pub with other Post Office employees. After certain investigations had been made and McLory had given an assurance that there would be no further violence if he returned to work, he was allowed to do so. McLory subsequently brought a claim in the High Court for loss of overtime payments during the period of suspension. The provision under which McLory had been suspended by the Post Office stated, 'In the event of misconduct or where there is a need for inquiries to be made into alleged misconduct you may be suspended from your employment with or without pay'. McLory's initial argument that he had a right to work and to earn overtime payments failed on the grounds that such a term would directly contradict the express right of the Post Office to suspend without pay and therefore could not be implied. McLory next sought to argue that nonetheless he was entitled to overtime payments since the power to suspend had been exercised in breach of implied terms in his contract that as it was put in the amended statement of claim '(b) any suspension of an employee should be only following full information to the employee by the employer of the reason for the suspension; (c) following a suspension, the employee should within a reasonable time be given an opportunity by the employer to answer any matters put forward by the employer as reasons for suspension; (d) any suspension of the employee by the employer should be for such period as was reasonable in all the circumstances; (e) in exercising any contractual right to suspend the [claimants] or any of them the defendant would observe the rules of natural justice and act fairly in the circumstances.' The court held that the rules of natural justice are not imported into a contract of employment and therefore McLory's suggested terms (b), (c) and (e) (in part) failed. However, the court did imply a limited obligation of reasonableness on the Post Office in that it held that the Post Office could only suspend if they had reasonable grounds to do so and could only continue the suspension for so long as those reasonable grounds continue. In the event, however, these implied terms did not assist McLory since the court found that the Post Office had complied with them. The case is, however, a useful indication of the extent to which a general requirement of reasonableness will be implied into an express right to suspend.

16.14 If there is no express power to suspend in the contract the employer's rights are not entirely clear. Such authorities as there are on suspension consider only the question of suspension as a disciplinary sanction. However, in our opinion even where an employee has a right to work it would be reasonably safe for an employer to suspend for a reasonable period to investigate suspected misconduct subject to certain conditions. First, and most important, the suspension must be on full pay and benefits. It is well established that to suspend without pay is a breach of contract unless the employer has an express right to do so: *Hanley v Pease & Partners Ltd* [1915] 1 KB 698. Second, the employer must have genuine grounds to warrant an investigation and, third, he should conduct his investigations expeditiously.

16.15 One difficult question that arises is, what amounts to full pay for an employee paid partly by results? For example, the employee receives a base salary plus a commission for each contract concluded with a customer. Unless the parties have addressed this problem in the contract or there is an agreement covering roughly comparable circumstances, for example a fixed commission during holiday or sickness absences, the best advice to the employer is to make a reasonable and sensible suggestion to compensate the employee at the same time as telling him he is suspended. The employer of such an employee does, however, face an increased risk of that employee arguing that the employer's conduct amounts to a repudiatory breach of the contract. (The question of what amounts to repudiatory breach is considered in Ch 8).

16.16 The suspension letter – The suspension of an employee should always be confirmed in writing and, in appropriate cases, should tell the employee why he is being suspended; although to do so is not obligatory: *McLory*. The letter should tell the employee what he is and is not permitted to do while suspended (in the context of competitive activities it should always be made clear that he should not communicate directly or indirectly with customers and suppliers and he should not attend the employer's premises), when it is anticipated the investigation will be complete, and the arrangements for pay and benefits during suspension. It should also remind the employee of the continuing obligations he owes to the employer while suspended, in particular the relevant express terms of his contract and the implied duty of fidelity. It is also advisable for the suspension letter to require the employee to remain in regular contact with the employer (usually by telephone calls to a named individual at appropriate intervals) and to notify the employer of any change in contact details. By including these requirements the employer reduces the risk of being unable to advance matters by, for example, pursuing the disciplinary process or lifting the suspension simply because he cannot contact the employee. For a recent illustration of how an employee's 'disappearance' can create difficulties see: *Hassan v Odeon Cinemas Ltd* [1998] ICR 127 (EAT), where the effect of Odeon's inability to contact Hassan while he was suspended resulted in his employment continuing for several months after Odeon's final attempt to bring it to an end. The facts of Hassan are somewhat unusual in that his 'disappearance' was a result of compliance with a bail condition requiring him to reside outside London. However, it is yet another example of the degree of importance tribunals are now placing on actual communication with employees, hence the importance of the requirement that the employee stay in touch whilst suspended. See, for example, *McMaster v Manchester Airport plc* [1998] IRLR 112 where a letter of dismissal sent to McMaster while on sick leave was held not to be effective until the day he received it. McMaster was not at home the day the letter arrived and only received and read it on his return the following day. Finally, any matter specifically required by an express term enabling the employer to suspend should be covered in the letter.

16.17 Disadvantages to the employer of suspension – The prime disadvantage is that suspension puts the employee outside the employer's physical control. The employer can say that the employee must not contact customers but in practical terms it is virtually impossible to police that requirement. Moreover, the employee who is already intending to leave to set up in competition or to join a competitor often takes the view that he has little to lose by advancing his plans to compete while suspended. Legally he is undoubtedly wrong but the employer has the problem of proving the wrongdoing. In extreme cases suspension can also present a problem where the only realistic commercial solution to the competitive threat is for the employer to retain the services of the employee. Suspension automatically involves the instigation of the internal disciplinary process and, if it is inappropriately applied, that in itself may be enough to dissuade the employee from remaining even if a significant enhancement of salary, benefits and status is offered to him.

3(a)(i) WHAT IS THE NATURE AND SCOPE OF THE COMPETITIVE ACTIVITY?

16.18 Frequently, allegations of competitive activities are based on gossip which has gradually become more and more exaggerated as it passes from one person to the next. What the employer needs is accurate information from reliable sources supported, wherever available, by documentary evidence, including information on word processors and e-mail. Moreover, he needs as much of it as possible in the minimum amount of time.

16.19 The key questions the employer will need answers to are:

- What is the employee doing or intending to do?
- Who else is or will be involved? In particular, are other employees of the employer participating or likely to do so?
- Are customers involved or will they be involved?
- Where is or will the employee be operating from?
- Are the employer's customers/suppliers being targeted or is that intended?

3(a)(ii) HAS THE COMPETITIVE ACTIVITY INVOLVED ANY BREACHES OF THE
OBLIGATIONS OWED BY THE EMPLOYEE TO THE EMPLOYER OR IS IT LIKELY TO DO SO?

16.20 In many cases the answer to this question is probably yes, but the employer has difficulty in proving it. Some employees cover their tracks very carefully, but most leave a few clues behind them and an employer who searches thoroughly enough will usually find some evidence of breach. Answering this question is made easier by dividing it into five sub-questions covering the areas in which breaches most commonly occur. The sub-questions are:

- Have competitive activities been carried out in the employer's time?
- Has confidential information been misused and/or removed?
- Have other employees/independent contractors been enticed to participate in the competitive activities?
- Have customers or suppliers been notified by the employee or has the employee sought to interfere with the dealings between them and the employer?
- Has there been a failure by the employee or other employees/independent contractors to disclose information to the employer?

If the answer to any of these questions is no, the employer needs to know whether there is any likelihood of any of these activities happening in the future.

16.21 Obtaining the answers to the questions posed in paragraph 16.19 can undoubtedly be difficult but an employer should take a positive attitude and think carefully where he might find the information. Apart from direct questioning of the employee, sources the employer should consider are colleagues of the employee who work closely with him, in particular the employee's secretary/ personal assistant, who can be a mine of information; customer/supplier files; the word processing system including internet and e-mail records and information held on the employee's home computer; any log kept of telephone calls and for those employers who tape telephone conversations, those tapes; itemised mobile telephone bills; photocopying records; security videos and any records kept of attendance at the employer's premises whether they are manual (by signing in) or electronic (security passes) which allow access by use of swipe cards; unusual requests for information, for example, repeat runs of customer lists; and any other unusual or unexplained behaviour such as working late or at weekends for no apparent reason, irregular customer contact and sudden lavish entertaining.

In considering the use of the sources of potential information identified in this paragraph the employer will, however, need to take into account possible arguments of breach of the employee's privacy rights particularly once the Human Rights Act 1998 comes into force (currently expected to be October 2000) and the awaited Code of Conduct on employee surveillance from the Data Protection Registrar is produced. For further discussion of these topics: see paragraph 7.22.

16.22 A particularly difficult issue is whether the employer should approach customers or suppliers. In most cases, these groups of people will not want to become involved in the domestic wrangles between employer and employee and the risk the employer takes by contacting them is that he may mar his relationship with them. In each case it will be a matter for the employer to judge whether the risk is worth taking. To minimise the risk, but maximise the chances of obtaining accurate information, the employer should contact those clients with whom there is a good relationship and preferably one where the employee is not the principal point of contact. Occasionally, it will be a customer who first draws the competitive activity to the employer's attention, for example, by forwarding a copy of a fax from the competing employee in which he is pitching for the customer's future business. In such cases as much information as possible should be obtained from the customer immediately, the employer should make a full note of what the customer tells him and, where appropriate, obtain copies of any documents relevant to the competitive activity sent by the employee to the customer. It is also sensible for the client to be asked whether he is willing to provide an affidavit in case subsequent court proceedings become necessary. Although under the Civil Procedure Rules evidence in interim injunction proceedings will normally be by witness statement, obtaining an affidavit from a customer at an early stage is a form of insurance policy for the employer in case it subsequently becomes commercially unacceptable to enlist assistance from the customer or the customer no longer wishes to be involved in the matter.

3(a)(iii) WHAT ARE THE ROLE, IMPORTANCE AND TERMS OF EMPLOYMENT OF THE EMPLOYEE?

16.23 It may seem rather odd to suggest that these are factors that the employer must establish. One might expect that an employer automatically knows them.

In the case of key employees of small organisations the information may well be available, but in the majority of instances the employer's ideas will be hazy and will need to be clarified.

16.24 In looking at the role and importance of the employee, while the job title will be relevant, not too much reliance should be placed on it. Frequently employees are given rather grander titles than their roles merit, a common example being the title 'Director', which is still regularly used even for quite mundane positions, and ones where the holder is certainly not a director within the meaning of the Companies Act 1985. Similarly, in US companies the title Vice President is commonly used even for comparative junior employees. The key points the employer should look out for are whether the employee is a director or shadow director within the meaning of the Companies Act 1985; the amount of revenue the employee produces directly and indirectly; the employee's key contacts amongst customers and suppliers; the business he could take with him if he left, and the employees or relevant independent contractors that might leave with him or as a result of his departure.

16.25 In establishing the current terms of employment basic points such as whether a written contract has been signed by the employee and whether it has been subsequently varied need to be covered. Often the position is that the employer has sent the employee a Service Agreement containing notice periods and restrictive covenants and simply assumes that the employee has signed it, whereas in fact the employee has either actively objected to it or, more commonly, simply failed to return it. Of vital importance is checking the position about any terms recorded in a Staff Handbook. Commonly, these are updated on a regular basis and this can lead to important terms being incorporated into the contract, for example, new and enforceable covenants as the employees found to their cost in *Credit Suisse Asset Management Ltd v Armstrong* [1996] IRLR 450. For a further discussion on the question of variation of contract see paragraphs 12.6 to 12.17 and 12.33 to 12.34.

16.26 Terms of particular importance that the employer should look out for are (a) the employee's general obligations to the employer and any express terms incorporating the implied duty of fidelity; (b) disciplinary rules and procedures and the right to suspend; (c) the employee's hours of work and any rules regarding outside activities during employment; (d) how the contract may be terminated and whether there is the right for the employer to make a payment in lieu of notice; (e) whether the employee can be sent on garden leave and if so for how long; (f) any variation of duties provisions; (g) confidentiality obligations; and (h) any restrictive covenants applying after termination of employment.

3(a)(iv) WHAT SORT OF THREAT DOES THE COMPETITIVE ACTIVITY POSE TO THE EMPLOYER'S BUSINESS?

16.27 With the answers to the first three questions (referred to in para 16.11) the employer will be able to judge whether the competitive activity poses any real commercial threat to his business and consequently the seriousness with which it should be treated. Often what appears at first to be a threat of real gravity is revealed by closer examination to be of only minor significance. Furthermore, occasionally there is the possibility of diverting the employee from a competitive activity to a complementary activity. As a result the employer has the option of capitalising on the opportunity presented by the employee rather than wasting time on defensive action to protect his business.

3(b) Taking key decisions

16.28 There are five key decisions the employer needs to take:

- Is the employee to be retained or dismissed?
- Should legal proceedings be threatened/instituted against the employee?
- Should legal proceedings be threatened/instituted against any third party?
- Are there steps that should be taken to protect/consolidate the employer's position with clients/customers?
- Are there steps that should be taken to reassure and motivate other employees?

3(b)(i) RETENTION V DISMISSAL

16.29 Retention – Retaining the services of the employee is something every employer in this situation should consider. It is an option frequently rejected out of hand by employers but can be one of the most effective ways of eliminating competitive activities. Whether or not it is a practical proposition will depend on two factors: (a) the likelihood of the employee remaining and (b) the commercial desirability to the employer of his doing so.

16.30 The likelihood of the employee remaining – Generally speaking employees engage in competitive activities because of dissatisfaction with their salary and remuneration packages, frustration at their lack of career progress within the employer's organisation, or sheer boredom. If the root cause of the employee's action can be remedied, and the employer is prepared to remedy it either immediately or in the foreseeable future, then there is often a good chance of retaining the employee.

16.31 Commercial desirability to the employer – This will depend on matters such as the threat the competitive activity poses to the employer's business; the likely cost of retaining the employee in terms of improved salary and benefit package and/or enhanced status; whether there is a critical time factor involved, such as the imminent launch of a new product or the renewal of important contracts for which the employee is vital; and how retention would affect other key employees.

16.32 Steps to retain the employee – Precisely how the employer goes about retaining the employee will depend on the type of competitive activity the employee has engaged in. Where the employee has resigned to join a competitor or is preparing to set up in competition, it will be a matter of persuading the employee that his interests are better served by remaining with the employer. The employer must act quickly, his arguments must be well prepared and he must be willing to waive his rights in respect of breaches of duty arising out of the competitive activity. The employer must address the employee's current dissatisfactions. In practice, the necessary 'carrots' are usually an improved salary and benefit package and/or enhanced status and/or greater security in terms of notice that must be given to him and/or more important/high profile responsibilities. One danger area to look out for, particularly where the employee has already resigned, is that retaining the employee might amount to inducing him to breach his contract with his new employer. It is rare for the new employer to resort to legal proceedings for this sort of breach of contract but if the damages sustained are significant, the fact that the inducer is a competitor may be a sufficient reason for doing so. The key point for the employer is that he should be aware of the risk. Additionally, a well represented employee may well be looking for an indemnity against legal fees, and possibly damages (in respect of the risk of a breach of contract claim he incurs by not joining the competitor) as part of the 'price' of remaining. Indemnities are considered in Ch 11.

16.33 Where the employee has merely been 'moonlighting' for a competitor to earn extra wages, as in *Hivac Ltd v Park Royal Scientific Instruments Ltd* [1946] 2 All ER 350 CA, retention should be a good deal easier. The employee will usually be grateful to have kept his job. The employer can and should impose a severe disciplinary sanction. A final warning is normally appropriate even arguably where a contractual disciplinary procedure prohibits such a warning, for example, because the moonlighting is the employee's first act of misconduct and the procedure does not allow a final warning for a 'first offence'. The reason for this is that the employer can argue that the misconduct merited dismissal but he is simply being lenient in imposing a lesser sanction. The employer need not remedy the reason for the employee's moonlighting at this stage but he should certainly keep it in mind if he needs to retain the employee for any length of time. If, for example, the employee simply needs the extra money to live on, then he may well be forced to leave or to 'moonlight' again after only a short period.

16.34 Dismissal – An employer who is considering dismissing an employee for a competitive activity needs to think carefully how the dismissal will be implemented. In choosing his method he must avoid, wherever possible, acting in repudiatory breach of the contract. What amounts to a repudiatory breach of the contract is considered in Ch 8.

16.35 Methods of implementation – The options available to the employer will include:

- Summary dismissal;
- Immediate dismissal with a lump sum payment in lieu of notice;
- Dismissal with notice where the employee works during the whole of the notice period;
- Dismissal with notice with a payment in lieu of part of the notice period;
- Dismissal with notice where a garden leave provision is utilised;
- Dismissal with notice where a variation of duties clause is utilised.

16.36 The relevance of disciplinary procedures – The procedure adopted by the employer in reaching his decision to dismiss will always be important. Any disciplinary procedure which is part of the contract of employment, that is, which has contractual force, must be followed. If it is not, the employer runs the risk of an argument of repudiatory breach as well as a procedural unfair dismissal. Where, as is common nowadays, the disciplinary procedure is expressly stated to be non-contractual the employer is still well advised to follow it as closely as commercially possible. In any event, the employer should always adopt a procedure which incorporates the majority of the essential features of Disciplinary Procedures as set out in paragraph 10 of the ACAS Code of Practice on 'Disciplinary Praise and Procedures in Employment', the latest version of which came into effect on 5 February 1998. An employer who has no procedure, contractual or non-contractual, should also follow this ACAS Code.

16.37 Why follow a disciplinary procedure? – First, so that the employer is certain of his facts before dismissing the employee and as a result is making an informed commercial decision. Initial evidence may appear very damning against the employee but a proper investigation may reveal a comparatively innocuous breach, or none at all. The employer who acts hastily may lose the services of the employee unnecessarily. Second, to avoid successful claims of unfair dismissal, a point which will be given greater significance when Section 34(4) in the Employment Relations Act 1999, which raises the cap on the compensatory award to £50,000, is implemented. Following the decision of the House of Lords in *Polkey v A E Dayton Services Ltd* [1988] ICR 142, to satisfy the reasonableness test in Section 98(4) Employment Rights Act 1996 the employer must either show that he adopted a fair procedure prior to dismissal or, in the words of Lord Bridge at Page 163 B,

> '... that he acted reasonably in taking the view that, in the exceptional circumstances of the particular case, the procedural steps normally appropriate would have been futile, could not have altered the decision to dismiss and therefore could be dispensed with.'

Whether the employer acted reasonably in disregarding procedural safeguards is judged objectively: *Duffy v Yeoman & Partners Ltd* [1994] IRLR 642 (CA).

16.38 A detailed consideration of the application of the *Polkey* principles is beyond the scope of this book. However, because unfair dismissals are likely to assume much greater financial significance in the near future the following general points are worthy of note. *Polkey* does not render dismissals in breach of procedural safeguards automatically unfair. In each case the impact of and reason for the breach has to be considered by the tribunal in the context of determining whether the employer acted reasonably in treating the reason for dismissal as sufficient. So in *Westminster City Council v Cabaj* [1996] IRLR 960, where the panel which rejected Mr Cabaj's appeal against dismissal consisted of two, rather than three, councillors the Court of Appeal remitted the case to the Tribunal with an indication that the Tribunal would be bound to consider (a) whether the defect in the composition of the appeal panel impeded Mr Cabaj in demonstrating that the real reason for dismissal was not sufficient and (b) the Council's reasons (if any) for disregarding its rules on the composition of the appeal panel. Examples of cases where the employer has successfully come within the *Polkey* exception are unsurprisingly comparatively few but see: *Macleod v Murray Quality Foods Ltd* EAT 290/90 (unreported) and *Ellis v Hammond & Hammond t/a Hammond & Sons* EAT 1257/95 (unreported).

16.39 Thirdly, where the disciplinary procedure is part of the contract, to avoid being in repudiatory breach with the attendant consequences and uncertainty about the date of termination. In both *Gunton v Richmond-upon-Thames London Borough Council* [1980] ICR 755 and *Dietman v Brent London Borough Council* [1987] ICR 737 the failure to follow contractual disciplinary procedures was found to amount to a repudiation of the contract which the employee was entitled to accept as determining the contract. Largely because of the *Gunton* and *Dietman* cases it is now common practice for employers to expressly provide that disciplinary procedures do not form part of the contract of employment. What amounts to a repudiatory breach, and when a contract terminates as a result of acceptance of a repudiatory breach, are considered in Ch 8.

3(b)(ii) SHOULD LEGAL PROCEEDINGS BE THREATENED/INSTITUTED AGAINST THE EMPLOYEE?

16.40 This is not the same question as whether there are good grounds for threatening/instituting proceedings or whether any such proceedings have any likelihood of success, although it does encompass them. This is an overall tactical decision for the employer to make. Usually, where the competitive activity is a single employee 'moonlighting' in his spare time, the threat or issue of proceedings will not be necessary. However, the employer should still consciously make this decision rather than just ignoring the option.

16.41 In the majority of cases the employer will have far greater financial resources than the employee. Consequently, often just the threat of legal proceedings with the cost and uncertainty which that will involve for the employee may be enough to eliminate the competitive activity completely or to reduce it to an extent acceptable to the employer. The questions the employer needs to answer to reach a decision are:

- Will the competitive activity have any significant impact on the employer's business?
- Are there grounds for threatening/instituting proceedings?
- Have those grounds any real prospect of succeeding at an interim hearing and/or full trial?
- What is the potential cost involved?
- What is the likely reaction of the employee?
- What is the likely reaction of other employees?
- What sort of solution would be acceptable to the employer?

The weight that an employer should give to any particular point in reaching his decision will depend on the facts of each case. However, the following comments are of general application.

16.42 Impact of the competitive activity – If this is minimal, on its own it will not normally justify the cost of threatening/instituting proceedings. There may, however, be other reasons why the employer should take action, for example to dissuade other employees from engaging in similar activities that may be much more harmful.

16.43 Grounds for proceedings – In many cases there will be some grounds on which to base proceedings. Provided that it does not lead to any significant delay that would prejudice an application for an interim injunction the employer should endeavour to complete his enquiries before he takes any steps to threaten/ institute proceedings. The stronger the case the employer can present the greater the chance of a successful outcome.

16.44 Merits of proceedings – Assessing the merits of any proceedings is a difficult process. In practice, cases concerning competitive activities are normally disposed of at the interim stage and therefore it is the merits for the purposes of interim proceedings on which attention must be focused. In addition, the employer should not overestimate the strength of the employee's case. Where the employee has breached his duties, for every breach the employer discovers, there are often two or three more of which he is unaware but which have to be taken into account by the employee's adviser.

16.45 Expense – The expense involved depends on whether proceedings are simply threatened or actually issued. Where they are merely threatened, the employer will only have his own legal fees and the cost of management time spent on the matter. Once proceedings have been issued, the potential expense increases significantly. It may include the employee's legal fees, which the employer can, in certain circumstances, be ordered to pay immediately (see paras 13.63 to 13.65) and, in some cases, an award of damages under the cross-undertaking in damages. The question of expense should be carefully addressed at the outset and reviewed regularly. In addition it is vital that the employer appreciates that once proceedings are issued, it may not be possible to put a stop to them without incurring significant expense. This is particularly important where the grounds of claim are weak.

16.46 Employee's reaction – How an employee reacts will normally depend on three factors: (a) the resources they have to fight the employer – third parties such as a new employer/partner may be providing financial backing through indemnities for legal fees and, sometimes, damages; (b) the actual extent of their breaches of duty; and (c) how confident they are either that the employer will give up or be unable to succeed in any proceedings.

16.47 Other employees' reactions – Other employees, and nowadays relevant independent contractors, working alongside the employee will watch carefully to see how the employer responds to the competitive activity. They have two interests in doing so, first to ascertain the likely reaction of the employer if they were to do something similar, and second, to gauge their future prospects with the employer. Other employees/independent contractors may see the departure of the employee as an opportunity for promotion or alternatively a sign that they too should leave to preserve their careers. The employer needs to pay particular attention to the employee's colleagues who work closely with him.

16.48 Acceptable solutions – As early as possible the employer must decide on what solutions would be acceptable to him. Obviously if there are none that can be achieved by the threat or issue of proceedings, that is an argument against such a course of action. For example, if the employer's only acceptable solution is to enforce a covenant prohibiting the employee from joining a competitor, but he has repudiated the contract and that has been accepted by the employee (and there are no other breaches upon which the employer can rely) there is obviously no prospect of success: *General Billposting Co Ltd v Atkinson* [1909] AC 118 (HL).

16.49 In each case it will be a matter for the employer to weigh up all the various factors, for and against, and reach an informed decision.

3(b)(iii) SHOULD LEGAL PROCEEDINGS BE THREATENED/ISSUED AGAINST ANY THIRD PARTY?

16.50 Potential targets for this course of action fall into two broad categories:

(a) third parties who have sought to induce, or conspired with, the employee to breach his contract, for example, a future employer who requires the employee to start before the expiry of the notice he has given to the employer or requires him to breach his duty of fidelity by soliciting business from his employer's customers while still employed by that employer or fellow employees seeking to compete as a team with the employer; and (b) third parties who are the recipients of the employer's confidential information. These types of action are considered in detail in paragraphs 5.47 to 5.50 and 13.25 to 13.27.

16.51 There are two primary reasons for pursuing third parties: to stop/limit the effect of the competitive activity (normally the employer will be pursuing the employee simultaneously), and/or as a means of ensuring that there is a defendant who has the means to meet a damages claim.

16.52 To decide if a third party should be pursued the employer must address the same basic questions that he asked in reaching his decision as to whether or not to pursue the employee. He must consider the likely reaction of the third party and the likely consequences of suing the third party. Often this is the stumbling block with the employer. While he will be relatively relaxed about pursuing an employee, which he regards as essentially domestic litigation, he will often be reluctant to proceed against third parties who are not his employees. There are four basic reasons for this: (a) the third parties' financial resources are likely to be greater than the employee's; (b) where there is a link between the employee and the third party, it increases the chances of the third party providing financial backing for the employee; (c) the potential liability under the cross-undertaking for damages given to a third party such as a competitor will usually be far greater; and (d) the enhanced risk of litigation in the future, for example where the third party is a competitor and the employer subsequently poaches one of his staff.

3(b)(iv) ARE THERE STEPS THAT SHOULD BE TAKEN TO PROTECT/CONSOLIDATE THE EMPLOYER'S POSITION WITH CUSTOMERS/CLIENTS?

16.53 When should steps be taken? – It is not always necessary for any steps to be taken. For example, where the employee resigns, but is then persuaded to withdraw that resignation and customers are unaware of these events, no useful purpose is served by informing them. If, however, the employer (a) knows or suspects that the employee has approached customers directly or (b) knows or suspects that customers are generally aware of the competitive activity or (c) has decided to dismiss the employee, some action will usually be necessary.

16.54 What steps should be taken? – This often depends very much on the particular facts, and needs to be tailored to the individual customer. For some customers the best tack may be to give the competitive activity as low a profile as possible. For others, the only course may be to tackle the issue 'head on'. Whichever approach is adopted, under no circumstances except of course where the employer does not want the customer's business, should the employer leave the customer feeling that they are unimportant. It may seem blindingly obvious but customers are people and if they feel they are not being given appropriate priority (which usually means top priority!), they are more likely to take their business elsewhere, particularly where there is a price incentive. Where the employee is going to leave, the employer must re-allocate responsibility for each customer to another employee. Usually if this is done the best person to consolidate the relationship with the customer will be a senior employee who is known to the customer. For an interim period it may be necessary for that senior employee to look after the customer more or less exclusively but the employer can gradually introduce more junior employees to take on day-to-day responsibility particularly for the more mundane tasks needed by the customer.

16.55 In extreme cases an urgent communication with customers who are aware of the competitive activity, or who the employee has sought to solicit, may be justified. The content and tone of the communication needs to be correct and however annoyed the employer is by the employee's conduct it must not contain any defamatory statements. The communication must inform the customer of what is happening, where appropriate put him on notice of the implications of the employee's conduct and, most important, set out how and by whom the customer will be looked after in the future. Wherever possible the employer should avoid any sort of statement that seeks to tell the customer what he can and cannot do. Such statements are universally disliked by customers and as a result are either ignored or, worse still, actually encourage the customer to take his business elsewhere, usually to the departing employee. The employer should never underestimate the strength of the relationships between an employee and the customers with whom he regularly works. Often the customer identifies only with the employee, not the business that employee represents, and consequently feels that his loyalty is owed to that employee.

16.56   In some high profile cases of employee competition it may also be necessary for the employer to consider making a press announcement or at least having a prepared statement should enquiries be made by the press. Such announcements/statements are often best prepared by the employer's PR company or internal marketing department. They should, however, always be cleared with the employers' solicitors not least because an ill worded statement could in itself amount to a repudiatory breach by the employer and may also be defamatory.

16.57 Where the employee is to remain, generally no specific action is needed, although it is generally sensible for the employer and employee to agree a statement to be used as the basis for responses to questions from customers. In addition, the employer should ensure that in future the customer is not totally dependent on the employee but deals with other employees who can take over if needs be.

3(b)(v) ARE THERE STEPS THAT SHOULD BE TAKEN TO REASSURE AND MOTIVATE
OTHER EMPLOYEES?

16.58 The discovery that an employee is involved in a competitive activity may engender a great deal of gossip among fellow employees and can be very unsettling. It is only natural for the employer to want to address that unease immediately but, as a general rule, it is better to resist temptation until the key decisions have been made and the employer can announce his plans for the future. At that stage the employer will be in a position to tell each employee affected by the matter what the future holds in terms of how the business will be conducted and that employee's future role.

3(c) Settling a strategy to reflect the key decisions

16.59 The first point an employer needs to appreciate is that his strategy must be flexible. Like all strategies it will be based on a number of assumptions and it needs to be capable of being adapted where those assumptions prove to be wrong. Second, in deciding how to implement its strategy wherever manpower permits we strongly recommend that if legal action is to be threatened, responsibility for the strategy is shared by two individuals. The first should focus on the legal aspects including instructing solicitors and counsel and providing witness statements and documents. The second individual should manage the commercial aspects of the strategy including consolidating relationships with customers and taking appropriate steps with existing employees and, where appropriate, recruiting new ones. Some employers feel uncomfortable with this demarcation but in practice it is usually the only sensible way to proceed. Interim injunctions are labour intensive and need to be done at short notice. The time commitment required from senior management of a company is high and generally it is simply not humanly possible for a managing director to give proper attention to court proceedings as well as reassuring customers who will want to be certain that the employer has the right people and commitment to look after their business. Consolidating the commercial position will be as important, if not more so, than the legal proceedings. It may be perceived as less glamorous than the legal side but it will almost always be central to the success of the overall strategy and provided the two individuals communicate effectively with each other the division of responsibilities will facilitate that success.

16.60 In Appendix 1, using the facts and covenants in the Case Study of Excel Copiers Ltd and Brian Thomas (Ch 11, Case study 1) and adding additional facts concerning the competitive activities discovered we have shown how Excel Copiers Ltd might make their key decisions and settle their strategy.

4. Applying the three basic steps: discovery after employment has ended

4(a) Gathering information

16.61 The four questions identified in paragraph 16.11 are the appropriate ones to ask. In addition, in obtaining the information to answer Questions 1 and 2, the ex-employer should still go to the same sources, including their own records and other employees who worked with the employee. The mere fact that the employment has ended does not mean that those sources will not reveal any useful information. They may provide useful evidence of breaches during employment. In addition, they may even disclose helpful facts about the ex-employee's post-termination activities. For example, often the ex-employee remains in touch with old colleagues and it is not at all unusual for an ex-employee to boast to his former colleagues of the business he has taken with him.

16.62 Different considerations may apply on the question of approaching customers. Sometimes the customer may have made it clear that he intends to transfer his business to, for example, the ex-employee's new employer, in which case the employer needs to consider the wisdom of approaching him, since he may be in the class of third parties whom the employer will consider threatening with proceedings or possibly suing. Alternatively, the customer's loyalty may be unknown in which case the employer again needs to tread carefully.

16.63 With regard to ascertaining the terms of employment, the ones the ex-employer will need to concentrate on are the express obligations during and after employment, in particular confidentiality covenants and other post-termination restrictive covenants, if any. That is not to say, however, that the termination provisions are irrelevant. The additional question the employer will have to answer is whether the employment was terminated in accordance with its terms. If there is any question that termination followed a repudiatory breach by the ex-employer, then obviously that would have a significant impact on the key decisions the ex-employer has to take.

4(b) Taking key decisions

16.64 With the exception of the first decision (retention or dismissal) the key decisions are the same. However, because the possibility of eliminating the competitive activity by retaining the employee is not an option, the other possibilities assume a greater importance. In very rare cases, it is possible for the ex-employer to persuade the ex-employee to return but often the only reason the ex-employee will want to do this is because his new venture/employment is going badly. Consequently the ex-employer should think very carefully before taking this step. He should also bear in mind the possibility of a recurrence of the ex-employee's behaviour, perhaps when the employee regards the economic climate as more favourable.

16.65 The threat/issue of proceedings against the ex-employee and third parties is likely to be a more important option to the employer than in the case of breaches by an existing employee. Depending on how long it takes to discover the breach it may also be a more difficult option to pursue. For example, where the ex-employee is settled in to his new position with a competitor and has made contacts with their customers as well as his ex-employer's, the new employer may be more willing to 'protect' the ex-employee and indeed his own position than he would have done had the competition been discovered earlier.

16.66 Again depending on the timing, steps to consolidate the employer's position with his customers, primarily through the allocation of other employees to those customers, may have been taken. If they have not, then obviously it should be done immediately. The same basic considerations apply to other communications with customers.

4(c) Settling a strategy to reflect the key decisions

16.67 In Appendix 2, using the facts and covenants in the Case Study of Smith & Jones HR Services Ltd and Ian Simpson (Ch 11 Case Study 2) and adding additional facts concerning the competitive activities discovered, we have shown how Smith & Jones HR Services Ltd might make their key decisions and settle their strategy. We have also included as Appendix 3 documentation for proceedings by Smith & Jones HR Services Ltd against Ian Simpson. Obviously these documents are intended to apply only to the particular case study and should be used with great care when applied to other facts.

Strategy (1)

Case study 1: Excel Copiers Ltd and Brian Thomas

16.68 Brian Thomas has now been with Excel for three years as Regional Director (South East Region). His employment has been performed in the way anticipated in the facts given in the case study in Ch 11. He has been given the responsibility of liaison with Easy Copy Inc and the negotiation of any changes in the exclusive distribution agreement. The terms of his contract, including the restrictive covenants, are as set out in the case study in Ch 11.

1. Initial discovery

16.69 On 28 July 1999 John Williams, senior sales representative (South East Region) of Excel Copiers Ltd requests a private interview with the Managing Director. Williams says that the previous day Thomas invited him to join a new business which Thomas is setting up, to sell and service photocopiers. Williams says that Thomas showed him briefly a business plan for a company called Copy All Sales and Servicing Ltd, which Thomas described as 'his company'. In a section headed 'projected turnover' a number of Excel's most lucrative customers are named and figures given for annual turnover which correspond to the turnover they are currently producing for Excel. The plan identifies some of the named customers as having confirmed they will transfer their business to Copy All Sales and Servicing Ltd and others as prospects. Williams' recollection was that the majority of customers were ones with service contracts for Easy Copy Inc machinery. Williams presumes that Copy All Sales and Servicing Ltd will also be selling Easy Copy Inc machinery but that point was not specifically referred to by Thomas. Thomas apparently told Williams that he would be inviting other employees of Excel to join his new company (he didn't identify which ones) and would be discussing salaries and so on, once he had some initial reactions. Thomas asked Williams to keep their discussion confidential.

16.70 The Managing Director regards Williams as an honest individual. However, he is the most likely candidate to succeed Thomas as Regional Director if Thomas were to leave. The Managing Director asks Williams to say nothing to anyone about the matter. Having telephoned his solicitor, the Managing Director informs the Finance Director of what he has learnt and together they carry out the information-gathering exercise.

2. Gathering information

16.71 Excel's investigations reveal the following:

- A check at Companies House shows that three months before a shelf company was acquired by Thomas and his wife and its name changed to Copy All Sales & Servicing Ltd. Mr and Mrs Thomas and Mr Thomas' uncle (the Chief Executive of Easy Copy Inc) are the directors and shareholders of Copy All Sales and Servicing Ltd.
- A search of Thomas' desk late the same day produces a copy of the business plan for Copy All Sales and Servicing Ltd which confirms Williams' account of its contents. The business plan also refers to a staffing complement of four salesmen and four engineers, and there are initials with question marks against them which correspond to the initials of some of Excel's sales and servicing staff, including Williams.
- Oral enquiries made of X Ltd, a long-standing customer of Excel who renewed his service contract for Easy Copy Inc machinery last week, reveals that it was approached by Thomas. Approximately three weeks ago the Managing Director received a letter from Thomas telling him about the new company and the services it will provide. The letter invited the customer to consider placing his business with Copy All Sales and Servicing Ltd. The Managing Director, being satisfied with the service from Excel, put the letter in the bin.
- The book kept by Thomas' secretary showing the reference numbers of the jobs she has typed for him reveals that three weeks ago she typed letters to all the customers named in the business plan and several more, including X Ltd. Because of their age, the jobs have been automatically deleted from the word-processing system. However, there are no copies of those letters on the relevant customer files nor on Excel's central copy letter file which should contain copies of all letters sent out each day. Unfortunately Thomas' secretary is on holiday and not due to return to the office for another two weeks.
- Records kept by Excel's weekend security contractors show that Thomas has been a regular visitor to the office on Sundays over the last three months. Thomas does not normally work at weekends and the last three months have been a quiet spell for both Excel and Office Supplies & Sales Ltd.
- Excel decide not to approach Easy Copy Inc at this stage because of the connection between Thomas and Easy Copy Inc's Chief Executive. They also decide not to approach any other customers or the members of staff whose initials seem to appear in the business plan.

2(a) Taking key decisions

2(a)(i) RETENTION V DISMISSAL

16.72 Excel condude that for commercial reasons it is essential that they try and retain Thomas. If he goes it is likely that they will lose the Easy Copy Inc exclusive distribution agreement and a large majority of the servicing contracts, since in practice customers prefer the distributors to also be the servicers of their machinery. Excel realise that they have allowed themselves to become over-dependent on the turnover generated by Easy Copy Inc machinery. They need to retain Thomas while they expand the range of photocopiers they sell and service.

16.73 Excel believe that it will be possible to retain Thomas. They consider that Thomas has sought to compete because of the lack of career path he sees for himself at Excel. Thomas has repeatedly asked whether he is likely to be promoted and to be given a seat on the Board of Directors. Excel are willing to offer him a newly created position of National Sales Director with a seat on the Board and a salary increase of £10,000 per annum. A condition of retaining Thomas is that Copy All Sales & Servicing Ltd is wound up.

16.74 Excel appreciate that they have only a short time in which to achieve their goal of retaining Thomas. If retention proves impossible they plan to hold a disciplinary hearing and, subject to there being any change in the facts, dismiss him summarily. They have rejected the possibility of sending Thomas on garden leave. They regard that option as too expensive and too risky, bearing in mind that they would not be able to police Thomas' activities.

2(a)(ii) THREAT/ISSUE OF LEGAL PROCEEDINGS V THOMAS?

16.75 Since Excel's preferred option is to retain Thomas, they consider that to threaten legal proceedings at the outset would destroy that possibility. The threat of proceedings may, however, be used if Thomas is wavering over whether to leave or stay. If it becomes clear that he is definitely going to persist with his plans, then they will issue proceedings seeking an interim injunction. Their reasons for doing so are:

- Thomas' activities pose a real threat to Excel's business.
- There are good grounds to issue proceedings.
- They believe, rightly, that they have a good chance of obtaining an interim injunction.
- The potential cost is reasonable bearing in mind what is at stake.
- Thomas is likely to be rattled by the issue of proceedings. He is not a wealthy man and it is unlikely that he will receive any financial backing in any proceedings.
- Excel's sales and servicing staff are likely to watch Excel's reaction closely. Each has a non-dealing/non-solicitation covenant in their contract. Pursuing Thomas is likely to encourage others he has approached to stay.
- The most acceptable solution to Excel, after retaining Thomas, would be undertakings to the court in the terms of his restrictive covenants.

2(a)(iii) THREAT/ISSUE OF PROCEEDINGS AGAINST THIRD PARTIES?

16.76 As a matter of principle Excel does not want to sue any third party. They consider it would be commercially unacceptable to be seen to be doing so. They appreciate, however, that there may be merit in notifying some of the customers named in the business plan of the legal position in an attempt to 'warn them off'.

16.77 Excel consider it pointless to write to Easy Copy Inc threatening proceedings. However, if Thomas stays a joint approach will be made by the Managing Director and Thomas to Easy Copy Inc to inform them of the position and to cement the relationship. Excel also do not want to threaten/issue proceedings against any other employee.

2(a)(iv) STEPS TO CONSOLIDATE EXCEL'S POSITION WITH CUSTOMERS?

16.78 The steps will differ depending on whether Thomas stays or leaves. If he stays, a joint approach by Thomas and Excel's managing director will be made to each customer who was aware of Thomas' plans. In addition a review of the arrangements for each of those customers will be carried out.

16.79 If Thomas leaves, Excel will either appoint a replacement from their existing staff or make an interim appointment pending the recruitment of a new employee. An announcement of the appointment will be sent to all South East Region customers of Excel. Some of the customers named in the business plan may also be notified of the legal position.

16.80 A review of the arrangements for each customer in the South East region will also be carried out.

2(a)(v) Steps to reassure/motivate other employees?

16.81 Again these will depend on whether Thomas stays or leaves. If he stays, then action will be limited to announcing his promotion and filling his position. Excel consider it would exacerbate the position to make any reference to the events preceding the promotion.

16.82 If Thomas leaves, those employees who are apparently named in the business plan will be seen immediately and it made clear to them that the company wants to retain their services. The Company is likely to intimate that Thomas' position will be filled from Excel staff.

16.83 By taking the Key Decisions Excel has formulated a rough strategy. The attached flow chart shows how that strategy will work in practice.

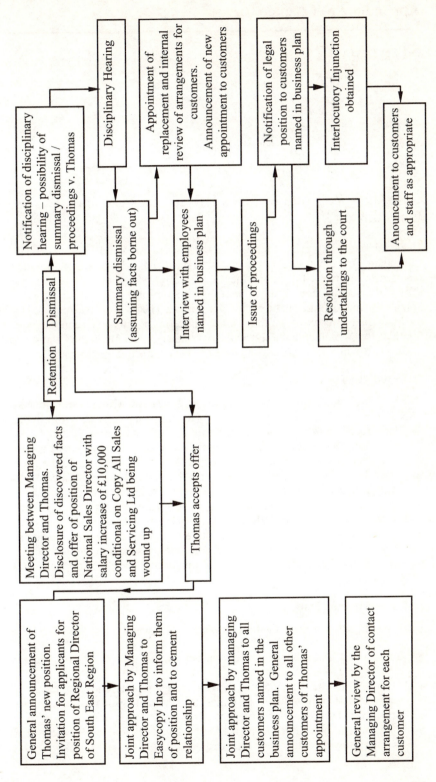

Strategy (2)

Case study 2: Smith & Jones HR Services Ltd and Ian Simpson

16.84 Ian Simpson worked for Smith & Jones for two and a half years as an HR Consultant. Four months ago Ian Simpson resigned giving the three months notice required to terminate his employment on 31 July 1999. He worked until the expiry of his notice period. When he resigned Simpson was asked what he was going to do in the future but he declined to answer. The point was not pursued by the Managing Director of Smith & Jones. The terms of Simpson's contract with Smith & Jones, including the restrictive covenants, are set out in the Case study in Ch 11. No area covenant was included in the contract of employment.

1. Initial discovery

16.85 Fludd Ltd, a customer of Smith & Jones for whom Simpson was responsible while an employee, sent the Managing Director a copy of a letter they have received from Simpson. The letter is on the notepaper of People 'R' Us Ltd, a competitor of Smith & Jones. In the letter Simpson says that he is now employed as a Senior Consultant with People 'R' Us Ltd. He refers to the good working relationship he had with Fludd Ltd in the past and suggests a meeting to discuss how he could assist them with their human resource work in the future. Simpson indicates that as an incentive People 'R' Us are offering a 10% discount on any new annual contracts. In fact, since Simpson's departure Fludd have been looked after by another consultant of Smith & Jones, Ellen Moores. Fludd are satisfied with Ellen Moores as a replacement for Simpson and in their covering fax confirm that they have no intention of transferring their business to People 'R' Us Ltd.

2. Gathering information

16.86 Smith & Jones' investigations reveal the following:

- Some of the files of the customers for whom Simpson was responsible are missing.
- There are important documents, such as strategy reports, and reorganisation reports, missing from files of customers for whom Simpson was responsible.
- The card index which Simpson kept of his customers is missing.
- Simpson's diary in which he marked important dates for his customers such as salary review dates, performance bonus dates and, where relevant, the

date their annual agreements with Smith & Jones expire, is missing.
- Simpson's former secretary, Miss Holt, is interviewed. She tells Smith & Jones that:
  - She overheard a number of conversations between Simpson and Neil, another of Smith & Jones HR Consultants, in which Simpson was trying to persuade Neil to resign with him and go to the same new employer. (Neil has resigned and left the company. By ringing the switchboard of People 'R' Us, Smith & Jones establish that Neil is working there as a consultant. Neil has no post-termination restrictive covenants);
  - A few days before he left, Simpson asked her to print off a client list. He then marked a number of names on the list and asked the secretary to print off a data sheet for each of the marked customers. Miss Holt recalls the majority of names he marked were customers with whom he dealt. The data sheets are Smith & Jones' data base of information about each customer. The type of information they contain includes details of the customer's business, where they have premises, the contact name, numbers and grades of staff, important dates for the customer such as salary review dates, performance review dates, key future events, for example planned redundancies and reorganisations, the date, if any, the annual agreement with Smith & Jones expires and how the customer is being invoiced.
- Smith & Jones see all their other HR Consultants. Two say that they have had offers, through Simpson, to join People 'R' Us Ltd. The others deny having been approached. Of the two offers one was to Hetherington and was written (Hetherington has declined the offer and provides copies of the offer letter and his reply), the other was to Lewis and was oral. Lewis says he has not responded but does not intend to accept.
- Smith & Jones contact two other customers who Simpson looked after but who have very recently sought assistance from Smith & Jones. Both confirm that they received a similar letter to that received by Fludd Ltd.

3. Taking key decisions

3(a) ENTICING SIMPSON AND/OR NEIL BACK?

Smith & Jones do not want either employee back.

3(b) THREAT/ISSUE OF LEGAL PROCEEDINGS V SIMPSON?

16.87 Smith & Jones conclude that proceedings must be issued without delay for the following reasons:

- Simpson's activities pose a real threat to Smith & Jones' business. They have not yet lost any key customers but there is a real risk they will do so. Two are being very slow in renewing their annual agreement and another two have indicated that they are considering using alternative services.
- There have been clear breaches of Simpson's obligations regarding Smith & Jones' confidential information, the non-dealing/non-solicitation covenant and the non-poaching covenant.
- Smith & Jones have a good chance of obtaining an interim injunction.
- The cost of proceedings is justified by the likelihood of success.
- The other HR Consultants will be watching Smith & Jones' reaction carefully. Proceedings are necessary to discourage similar activities by them. All of

them have similar restrictive covenants to Simpson.

- The only acceptable solutions to Smith & Jones would be either undertakings to the court in the terms of the covenants and the return of the property he has taken or a tripartite agreement with Simpson and People 'R' Us Ltd under which Simpson is released from the covenants, except the confidentiality covenant, but in so far as any customer that would have been caught by the covenant places business with People 'R' Us Ltd, a commission of 20% of the sums invoiced for work done in the next 12 months is paid to Smith & Jones Ltd. Again the property taken would have to be returned.

Smith & Jones believe that People 'R' Us Ltd may pay Simpson's legal fees. They do not think People 'R' Us Ltd will terminate Simpson's employment or that of Neil.

3(c) THREAT/ISSUE OF LEGAL PROCEEDINGS AGAINST THIRD PARTIES?

16.88 Smith & Jones do not want to take any steps against any customer or Neil. At this stage they would prefer not to sue People 'R' Us Ltd although they will notify People 'R' Us Ltd of the legal position, drawing their attention to the restrictive covenants and threatening legal proceedings unless Simpson agrees to abide by the covenants.

3(d) STEPS TO CONSOLIDATE SMITH & JONES' POSITION WITH CUSTOMERS?

16.89 Each customer for whom Simpson had responsibility has already been allocated a new HR Consultant and the necessary introductions made. Smith & Jones would prefer not to make any comment linking Simpson's name to a competitor but will keep that under review. Smith & Jones' pricing policy will be reviewed in the light of the 'first year discount' being offered by People 'R' Us Ltd.

3(e) STEPS TO REASSURE/MOTIVATE OTHER EMPLOYEES?

16.90 Smith & Jones' strategy is to present the proceedings as a means of protecting the jobs of the other HR Consultants. By showing that they are taking immediate action they believe that it will motivate the HR Consultants into doing everything they can to keep 'Simpson's Clients' and reassure the HR Consultants that the company will not permit their job security and rewards (commission) to be adversely affected by a defecting employee. The basic plan is to circulate an immediate note to all HR Consultants informing them of the action being taken, with a follow-up note to be sent once the matter is resolved. The possibility of financial incentives to retain Simpson's clients are to be considered as a possibility, although those would not be practical if the possible tripartite agreement materialises.

16.91 The following flow chart shows in diagrammatic form how the strategy will work.

In addition in Appendix 3 we set out draft documentation for court proceedings brought by Smith & Jones HR Consultants Ltd against Simpson.

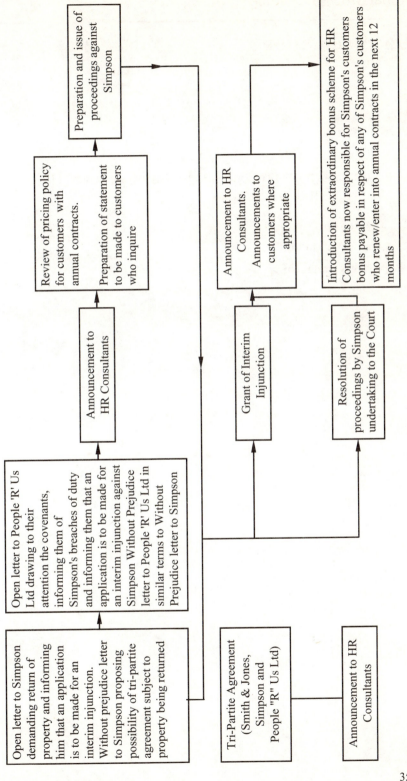

Documentation

Documentation on proceedings by Smith & Jones HR Services Ltd and Ian Simpson

(1)   Claim form

(2)   Application notice

(3)   Witness statement

(4)   Order

Claim Form

In the High Court

Claim No HC12345

Seal

Claimant

Smith & Jones HR Services Ltd

Defendant(s)

Ian Simpson

Brief details of claim

See attached sheet

Value

£

Defendant's name and address	
Ian Simpson 35 Poacher's Way Fastbuck FB1 0XS	Amount Claimed Court fee Solicitor's costs Total amount Issue date

The court office at The Royal Courts of Justice, Strand, London WC2A 2LL is open between 10 am and 4.30 pm Monday to Friday. When corresponding with the court, please address forms or letters to the Court Manager and quote the claim number.

Claim No

Particulars of Claim (attached) (to follow)

Please see attached sheet

Statement of Truth

- (I believe)(The Claimant believes) that the facts stated in these particulars of claim are true.
- I am duly authorised by the claimant to sign this statement

Full name   Becky Sharp

Name of claimant's solicitor's firm   STEPHENSON HARWOOD

signed

Position or office held (if signing on behalf of a firm or company)

- (Claimant)(Litigation friend)(Claimant's solicitor)
- delete as appropriate

Claimant's or claimant's solicitor's address to which documents or payments should be sent if different from overleaf including (if appropriate) details of DX, fax or e-mail.

Stephenson Harwood
One, St Paul's Churchyard
London EC4M 8SH
Tel: 0171 326 4422
Fax: 0171 606 0822
Ref:

Details of claim:

The Claimant's claim is for:

1.   An injunction to restrain the Defendant whether by himself, his servants or agents or otherwise howsoever:

(1) until 31 July 2000, from directly or indirectly (whether on his own account or on behalf of or in conjunction with any person, firm, company, or other entity) providing or canvassing or soliciting or by any other means seeking to provide services of a type provided by the Claimant, which the Defendant shall at any time during the twelve months immediately preceding 31 July 1999 ('the Period') have been employed by the Claimant to provide, to any customer of the Claimant to whom the Defendant has provided services on behalf of the Claimant in the Period;

(2) until 31 July 2000 from directly or indirectly inducing or seeking to induce to leave the Claimant any employee employed by the Claimant as an HR Consultant and with whom the Defendant had during the last twelve months of his employment material contact in the course of that employment with the Claimant;

(3) from using or disclosing any confidential information acquired by the Defendant during the course of his employment by the Claimant, namely:
   (a) the identity of the Claimant's customers;
   (b) the contact names of the Claimant's customers;
   (c) details of the customer's requirements;
   (d) confidential information provided by the Claimant's customers to the Claimant;
   (e) pricing information of the Claimant (including details of special arrangements) and marketing strategy in particular the Claimant's plans to open new offices;

(4) until 31 July 2000 from directly or indirectly (whether on his own behalf or in conjunction with any person, firm, company, or other entity, providing or canvassing or soliciting or by any other means seeking to provide services of a type provided by the Claimant to any customer whom the Defendant has contacted, canvassed or solicited [while he was in possession of] [using any of the information contained in] any of the documents referred to in paragraphs 2(a) to (e) inclusive [or fulfilling any contract entered into with any such customer].

2.   An order that the Defendant do deliver up all documents the property of the Claimant and all copies thereof, and in particular (but without limitation):

(a) customer files of the Claimant;
(b) strategy and reorganisation reports of the Claimant relating to the Claimant's customers;
(c) the card index used by the Defendant containing details of customers;
(d) client lists and data print-out sheets of customer details;
(e) the diary belonging to the Claimant used by the Defendant in the course of his employment with the Claimant.

3.   An order that the Defendant do make and serve on the Claimant's solicitor within seven days after the delivery up in accordance with paragraph 2 an affidavit

or witness statement verifying that the Defendant has fully complied with the terms of paragraph 2 and no longer has in his possession any such documents or copy documents referred to in paragraph 2.

4.   Damages for breach of an agreement in writing dated [   ] a copy of which is served herewith.

5.   Interest pursuant to Section 35A of the Supreme Court Act 1981.

Dated the [ ] day of [   ] 19[ ]

[Note: The 'springboard' injunction is included in the unlikely event that the covenant on which the injunction in paragraph 1(1) is based is struck down. As regards the options in square brackets see paragraph 14.32.]

Application Notice

* You must complete Parts A and B, and Part C if applicable
* Send any relevant fee and the completed application to the court with any draft order, witness statement or other evidence; and sufficient copies of these for service on each respondent

You should provide this information for listing the application

1. Do you wish to have your application dealt with at a hearing?

   Yes ☐ No ☐ If Yes, please complete 2

2. Time estimate .... (hours) .... (mins)

   Is this agreed by all parties   Yes ☐   No ☐

   Level of judge ....

3. Parties to be served.............................

In the High Court

Claim no   HC12345

Warrant no (if applicable)

Claimant (including ref)

Smith & Jones HR Services Ltd

Defendant(s) (including ref)   Ian Simpson

Date

Part A

I (we)[1] Stephenson Harwood (on behalf of) (the claimant)~~(the defendant)~~

intend to apply for an order (a draft of which is attached) that[2] because[3]

for the reasons set out in the witness statement of Christopher Smith

Part B

I(we) wish to rely on: *tick one box*
attached (witness statement)~~(affidavit)~~ [x] my statement of case ☐

evidence in Part C in support of my application ☐

Signed | Becky Sharp | **Position or office held** | Solicitor |

(Applicant)('s Solicitor)('s litigation friend)

Address to which documents about this claim should be sent (including reference if appropriate)[4]

Stephenson Harwood
One St. Paul's Churchyard
London EC4M 8SH
Tel. No. 0207 329 4422

Fax no
Dx no
e-mail

Notes
(1) Enter your full name, or name of solicitor
(2) State clearly what order you are seeking and if possible attach a draft
(3) Briefly set out why you are seeking the order. Include the material facts on which you rely, identifying any rule or statutory provision
(4) If you are not already a party to the proceedings, you must provide an address for service of documents.

Part C   **Claim No**

I(We) wish to rely on the following evidence in support of this application:

Please see attached

Statement of Truth

(I believe) * (The applicant believes) that the facts stated in this application are true
* delete as appropriate

Signed | Becky Sharp | Position or office held | Solicitor |

(if signing on behalf of
Applicant)('s Solicitor)   firm or company)
('s litigation friend)

Date

Witness statement

HC12345

IN THE HIGH COURT OF JUSTICE
QUEEN'S BENCH DIVISION
BETWEEN:

SMITH & JONES HR SERVICES LTD
Claimant

and

IAN SIMPSON
Defendant

WITNESS STATEMENT

I, Christopher Smith of [address] STATE as follows:

Introduction

1.   I am the Managing Director of the Claimant company and am authorised to make this witness statement on its behalf. Except where otherwise appears, the facts and matters set out in this witness statement are within my knowledge. Where I have relied on information from third parties named in this witness statement I believe that information to be true.

2.   I make this witness statement in support of the Claimant's application for the relief set out in the application notice served herewith.

Claimant's business

3.   At all times relevant to this matter the Claimant was and continues to be a company in the business of providing advice on all human resource issues including the recruitment of staff, career development, disciplinary matters, the termination of employment including redundancy programmes and Trade Union/collective issues.

Employment of the Defendant

4.   The Defendant commenced employment with the Claimant on [date] as a Human Resources Consultant ('HR Consultant'). The Defendant's duties were to provide advice on the whole range of human resource issues to the customers of the Claimant.

5.   I refer to attachment ['CS1'], a copy of the contract of employment [dated] entered into between the Claimant and the Defendant. I refer to:

(a) clause 1.1 which states:
'The [Defendant] shall not so as to compete with [the Claimant] during the period of twelve months after the termination of his employment directly or indirectly on his own account or on behalf of or in conjunction with any person, firm, company or other entity provide or canvass or solicit or by any other means seek to provide services of a type provided by the [Claimant], which [the Defendant] shall at any time during the twelve months immediately preceding

363

the termination of his employment have been employed by [the Claimant] to provide, to any customer of [the Claimant] to whom [the Defendant] provided services on behalf of [the Claimant] in the twelve months immediately preceding the termination of his employment.'

(b) clause 1.2 which states:
'The [Defendant] shall not during the period of twelve months after the termination of his employment directly or indirectly induce or seek to induce to leave [the Claimant] any employee employed by the Claimant as an HR Consultant with whom [the Defendant] had during the last twelve months of his employment material contact in the course of his employment with the Claimant and who was an employee of [the Claimant] at the date of termination of the [Defendant's] employment.'

6.   Other provisions of the contract of employment include a confidentiality covenant (Clause 5), the payment to the Defendant of a salary of £35,000 per annum; a commission arrangement whereby the Defendant could earn up to a further £35,000 per annum; use by the Defendant of a company car and provision for private health insurance for the Defendant.

7.   At the time the contract of employment was entered into it was anticipated that the Defendant would be required to travel to and work at customers' premises throughout England and Wales. These customers contracted for the services of the Claimant by way of annual renewal or on a sporadic basis. Further it was anticipated that the Defendant would work with one or more other HR consultants of the Claimant.

8.   (a) During the time he was employed by the Claimant, the Defendant had a considerable amount of personal contact with customers of the Claimant. Customers were allocated to him by me. The Defendant provided advice to these customers on the whole range of human resource issues. Some received advice on an occasional basis, as and when required, while others had annual contracts with the Claimant under which the minimum service was a monthly review – which was carried out by the Defendant. The majority of the customers of the Claimant used only the Claimant for their human resource advice (except in relation to legal advice, which they obtained from their solicitors). In relation to the customers so allocated to him, the Defendant was the only employee of the Claimant dealing with them on a regular basis and therefore he had ample opportunity to gain influence over them. The process whereby a Human Resources Consultant gets to understand the different facets of a client's business and their particular problems and gains the confidence of the client is a gradual one. I believe that the minimum period required to start a new consultant from scratch with a customer and for him to gain the confidence of that customer is twelve months.

(b) The Defendant also had throughout his employment ample contact with other HR consultants of the Claimant, both at team meetings and by way of informal discussions concerning the business of the Claimant in which confidential information of the Claimant referred to in paragraph 12 below would be discussed.

Resignation

9.   On 30 April 1999, the Defendant resigned giving 3 months notice as required by the contract of employment referred to above. He worked until the expiry of the notice period on 31 July 1999. I asked the Defendant what future plans he had, but he declined to answer.

Initial evidence of solicitation of customers

10.   On [date] (within the period of restraint referred to in paragraph 5) I received a letter from Fludd Ltd a customer of the Claimant. Enclosed was a copy of a letter that Fludd Ltd had received from the Defendant. I refer to attachment ['CS2'], a true copy of this letter. The letterhead used for this letter is that of People 'R' Us Ltd, a competitor of the Claimant. As can be seen from the letter, the Defendant offered Fludd Ltd his services in relation to human resources work indicating that he would offer a 10% discount on any new annual contract that Fludd Ltd entered into. I am informed by [name] and verily believe that Fludd Ltd have no intention of transferring their custom from the Claimant.

11.   As a result of the letter referred to in paragraph 10, I initiated an internal investigation to ascertain the extent of the Defendant's activities.

Access to confidential information

12.   During his employment the Defendant had access to the following information which the Claimant regards as confidential: the identity of customers; the contact name for those customers; details of the customers' requirements; confidential information provided by customers to the Claimant; pricing information (including details of special arrangements with customers) and marketing strategy, in particular the Claimant's plans to open new offices. This information was contained, inter alia, on the customer file records, the customer card index, client lists and customer database. The Defendant was well aware of the confidentiality of the information and indeed specific reference is made to each of these categories of information in Clause 5 of his contract of employment ('CS1'). Often at meetings at which the Defendant and other consultants were present I emphasised the confidentiality of this type of information.

Removal of documents and confidential information

13.   I am informed by [name] that as a result of the investigation referred to in Paragraph 11 it was discovered that there are several items belonging to the Claimant that are missing from the Claimant's premises. These items include: files of customers for whom the Defendant was responsible; strategy and reorganisation reports that were within those files; a card index that the Defendant kept containing customer information and the Defendant's diary which contained the details of his customers, salary reviews and performance bonus dates and where relevant the date of the customers' annual agreements with the Claimant.

14.   Further, I am informed by the Defendant's former secretary Miss Holt that on [date] the Defendant requested and obtained from her a computer print-out of a client list. The Defendant then marked certain names on the list and then requested and obtained from Miss Holt a print-out of a data sheet for the customers that he marked. Miss Holt recalls that the majority of the data sheets that the

Defendant requested were customers with whom the Defendant had dealings whilst in the employ of the Claimant.

15.   The data sheets requested contain details of the Claimant's customers including details of the customer's business, addresses, contact names, the numbers and grades of staff, salary and performance review dates, key future dates such as for example planned redundancies and reorganisations, the date, if relevant, of the expiry of the annual agreement with the Claimant and details of customer invoicing.

16.   I am informed by Miss Holt that the Defendant took the above mentioned client list and data sheets with him from the premises of the Claimant.

Further solicitation by the Defendant of the Claimant's customers

17.   On [date] I contacted two further customers namely [name] and [name] with whom the Defendant dealt within the last twelve months of his employment by the Claimant and asked them whether the Defendant or People 'R' Us Ltd had contacted them by means of a letter offering their services in competition to the Claimant. I was informed by [name] of [ ] and [name] of [ ] that they did receive a letter in the same form as the letter to Fludd Ltd referred to in Paragraph 10.

18.   At present there are 2 customers of the Claimant [names] with whom the Defendant dealt whilst in the employ of the Claimant whose annual agreements with the Claimant are coming up for renewal but who are being slow in effecting renewal. Further, another two customers with whom the Defendant dealt in the last twelve months of his employment have indicated that they are considering using an alternative service to that of the Claimant.

19.   I believe that the Defendant will continue to attempt to entice the Claimant's customers away from the Claimant. There is a real threat that the Claimant will lose customers as a result of the Defendant's continued acts of solicitation. Further, I believe that the Defendant has used and is continuing to use the confidential information and documents referred to above in order to solicit the Claimant's customers and that unless he is restrained by virtue of a court order, he will continue to do so.

Enticement of employees of the Claimant by the Defendant

20.   As part of the investigation into the Defendant's conduct I interviewed all the other HR Consultants employed by the Claimant. I refer to attachment ['CS3'], a copy of a letter from the Defendant to Hetherington (an HR Consultant) offering Hetherington an opportunity to join People 'R' Us Ltd. Further, I am informed by [name] Lewis (an HR Consultant) that on [date] the Defendant approached Lewis orally with a similar offer. Both of these Consultants were employees of the Claimant with whom the Defendant worked regularly during the last twelve months of his employment. Both have indicated to me that they will not accept the offer of employment with People 'R' Us Ltd.

21.   I am informed by Miss Holt that she overheard a number of conversations between the Defendant and Neil (an HR Consultant) in which the Defendant was attempting to persuade Neil to resign and join him at People 'R' Us Ltd.

22.   Neil has since left the Claimant and I have learned by ringing the switchboard at People 'R' Us Ltd that Neil is now working for them.

23.   I believe there is a real risk that the Defendant will continue to attempt to entice employees of the Claimant to join him at People 'R' Us Ltd.

Relief sought

24.   I accordingly believe that the Defendant is in breach of his duty of confidence and the non-dealing/solicitation and non-enticement covenants referred to in paragraph 5. I also believe that the Defendant will, unless restrained, commit further breaches of his contract of employment and duty of confidence.

Damages not an adequate remedy

25.   Unless an injunction is granted I believe that the Claimant will suffer considerable loss. I believe that the Defendant will be unable to compensate the Claimant for such loss. As far as I know the Defendant does not have any independent resources save for the salary he now presumably receives from People 'R' Us Ltd. Further, I believe that damages would be extremely difficult to quantify. In relation to loss arising from loss of customers it is extremely difficult to ascertain how long a customer contracting on an annual repeat order will remain with the Claimant. Damage arising out of loss of customers ordering on a sporadic basis would be particularly difficult to quantify. In relation to the loss of employees, it would be very difficult to place a figure on the loss of an employee who has had extensive experience in the field of human resources.

26.   I am instructed by the Claimant to offer the Court a cross-undertaking as to damages. I refer to attachment ['CS4'], the latest audited accounts of the Claimant from which it will appear that the Claimant will be good for damages on its cross-undertaking. The quantum of the Defendant's loss as a result of the imposition of the proposed order would be relatively simple to assess. The Claimant does not seek to prevent the Defendant from earning a living as a Human Resources Consultant, but merely that he should not for a limited period solicit or deal with the Claimant's customers or entice the Claimant's employees. I believe the only loss the Defendant could suffer would be the loss of some or all of any performance-related element of his remuneration package from People 'R' Us Ltd.

27.   In the circumstances, I respectfully request that this Honourable Court make an Order in the terms set out in the Application Notice served herewith.

Statement of Truth

(I believe)* (The applicant believes) that the facts stated in this witness statement are true

*delete as appropriate

Signed   **Position or office held**

                                              Date

Order   **HC12345**

IN THE HIGH COURT OF JUSTICE
QUEEN'S BENCH DIVISION
THE HONOURABLE MR JUSTICE
BETWEEN:

SMITH & JONES HR SERVICES LTD
Claimant

and

IAN SIMPSON
Defendant

IMPORTANT

Notice to the Defendant

You should read the terms of the Order carefully. You are advised to consult a Solicitor as soon as possible.

This Order prohibits you, the Defendant, from doing certain acts and requires you to do certain other acts set out in the Order. You have a right to ask the Court to vary or discharge this Order.

If you disobey this Order you may be found guilty of Contempt of Court and may be sent to prison or fined.

ORDER

An application was made on [date] by [Counsel] for the Applicant to Mr Justice [   ] and w as attended by counsel for the Defendant. The Judge read the witness statements listed in Schedule A and accepted the undertakings set out in Schedule B at the end of this Order. As a result of the application **IT IS ORDERED**

1.   the Defendant must not until after the trial of this action or until further order:

(1) or until 31 July 2000 (whichever date shall be the earliest), directly or indirectly provide or canvass or solicit or by any other means seeking to provide services of a type provided by the Claimant, which the Defendant shall at any time during the twelve months immediately preceding 31 July 1999 (the 'Period') have been employed by the Claimant to provide, to any customer of the Claimant to whom the Defendant provided services on behalf of the Claimant in the Period;

(2) or until 31 July 2000 (whichever date shall be the earliest), directly or indirectly induce or seek to induce to leave the Claimant any employee

employed by the Claimant as an HR Consultant and with whom the Defendant during the last twelve months of his employment had material contact in the course of that employment with the Claimant;

(3) use or disclose any confidential information acquired by the Defendant during the course of his employment by the Claimant, namely:

    (a) the identity of the Claimant's customers;

    (b) the contact names of the Claimant's customers;

    (c) details of the customers' requirements;

    (d) confidential information provided by the Claimant's customers to the Claimant;

    (e) pricing information of the Claimant (including details of special arrangements) and marketing strategy in particular the Claimant's plans to open new offices;

2.   that the Defendant must deliver up all documents the property of the Claimant and all copies thereof, and in particular (but without limitation):

    (a) customer files of the Claimant;

    (b) strategy and reorganisation reports of the Claimant relating to their customers;

    (c) the card index used by the Defendant containing details of customers;

    (d) client lists and data print-out sheets of customer details;

    (e) the diary belonging to the Claimant used by the Defendant in the course of his employment with the Claimant;

3.   that the Defendant must make and serve on the Claimant's solicitor within 7 days after the delivery up in accordance with paragraph 2 an affidavit or witness statement verifying that the Defendant has fully complied with the terms of paragraph 2 and no longer has in his possession any such documents or copy documents referred to in paragraph 2;

4.   that the costs of this application be paid by the Defendant to the Claimant.

Variation or discharge of this Order

The Defendant may apply to the court at any time to vary or discharge this Order but must first inform the Claimant's legal representatives.

Schedule A

Witness Statements

The Claimant relied on the following witness statements:

[*name*]   [*number of affidavit*] [*date sworn*]   [*filed on behalf of*]

(1)   Witness statement of Chris Smith dated [ ]

Schedule B

Undertakings given to the Court by the Claimant

If the Court later finds that this Order has caused loss to the Defendant, and decides that the Defendant should be compensated for that loss, the Claimant will comply with any Order the Court may make.

Index